THE LURE
OF COLOURED ROCKS
AND GEMSTONE JEWELLERY
ISSUE II

D1342994

Issue 2

www.colouredrocks.com

All enquiries should be directed to:

Coloured Rocks Limited
Ivy House
Henley Road
Outhill
Studley
Warwickshire
B80 7DU

ISBN: 978-0-9559972-1-1

Published by Coloured Rocks Limited
First Edition printed in the UK

Designed by Will Nash

4

THE LURE
OF COLOURED ROCKS
AND GEMSTONE JEWELLERY
ISSUE II

By Steve Bennett
and the Coloured Rocks Team

Coloured Rocks Limited
Warwickshire, England

INTRODUCTION TO ISSUE II

Welcome to this second edition of "The Lure of Coloured Rocks and Gemstone Jewellery".

Over the past year so much has happened both at Coloured Rocks and in the jewellery industry, I thought it worthy to bring you an update. In this edition these events have found their way into the book: 35 additional gemstones reviewed and pictured, 11 more fascinating gem cuts explained and illustrated; the Assay Office announcing the hallmarking of Palladium; the discovery of a 11th century Scribbling Ring; the Blue Wittelsbach Diamond becoming the most expensive gem in history, sold at auction at Christie's in December 2008; lots and lots of feedback from our customers.

Plus, in our quest to offer the most diverse range of fine jewellery on the planet, we have acquired two exciting new businesses and are showcasing some of their collections in this volume.

While reading this book, if you find yourself becoming a little addicted to Mother Nature's world of coloured treasures, you should consider turning your new found passion into an income stream and become a Rocks Advisor (see page 389).

HOW TO USE THIS A TO Z BOOK

"The Lure of Coloured Rocks and Gemstone Jewellery" has been written in an A to Z encyclopaedic format, so that you can dip in and out at your leisure. Whenever you come across a new gemstone or hear someone mention a jewellery term that you have not heard before, you can easily use the book's A to Z format to quickly find out more. There is also a quick guide section on pages 370 to 385, which will help in visually identifying many gems, settings and gem cuts.

In keeping with the encylopaedic format, we have not always explained a term every time it is used (otherwise this book would run into thousands of pages). Instead, we have kept repetition to a minimum in the knowledge that you will be able to cross-reference other sections of this book if you encounter any unfamiliar terms.

Let's use an example to make this clear. When reading about 'adamantine lustre' (page 24), you may find it useful to cross-reference 'refractive index' (page 380), if you have not come across that term before.

THANKS

First of all, I did not write this second issue alone. As with everything we do at The Colourful Company Group Ltd, it was a true team effort.

Tony Poole our resident gem expert helped with writing many pieces on gemstones.

Our chief jewellery designer, my wife, worked many hours guiding my research on the history of jewellery. Then, as my English skills are pretty appalling at the best of times, Sian Salmon spent countless hours correcting all of my mistakes (she also wrote the majority of the section on watches).

A big thank you must go to my eldest daughter Hannah: many of her illustrations, in particular her drawings of the Crown Jewels are amazingly accurate.

Thank you to our whole team in Jaipur, India. Especially to Manuj, your help in providing me with a deeper understanding of gem cutting has been invaluable in putting this second issue together. To my brother for working many hours with our fashion photographers Matt, Melissa and Emily in order to produce over 1,850 images for this second issue.

A massive thank you to Will who heads up our small graphic design team, your understanding and interpretation of my sometimes woolly and incomprehensive design briefs is incredible!

A huge thank you to our design centre in the UK.

I must not forget a mention to my six children, Hannah, Matt, Jack, Jessica, Tom and Lili, who all haven't seen too much of their dad recently.

Also I would like to thank the many people who have introduced me to so many new and exciting coloured gemstones and who have helped intensify my passion for the world of coloured rocks; Rayaz, Manit, Shawn, Neeraj, Naveen, Zeeshan, Sompon, Tony, Jim, Naveen, and Mukesh.

Finally, a massive thanks to the whole team for making it a really enjoyable project. I hope you will get as much pleasure from reading it as we did from writing and designing it.

A big thank you to our GemCollector team in Jaipur, India.

Preface by the Author Steve Bennett.

It cannot be denied that our world is dramatically changing. Global warming is happening at an alarming rate of knots: although we do not know how much of this is part of a natural cycle, we can be sure that our generation is certainly contributing to and accelerating this most worrying of events.

Already it is believed that my great grandchildren and possibly even my grandchildren (assuming of course at least one of our six children will want to start a family), will not be able to enjoy a holiday on a colourful Maldivian island - where my wife and I spent our honeymoon, making it a particularly special place for us. The colours of the Turquoise sea gently drifting on to the Citrine shore, edged by lush Emerald plantation is something they simply will not be able to discover.

Living on the Gold Coast in Australia, my sister talks of how beautiful the Great Barrier Reef once was. Prior to the tragic bleaching of 2002, the Barrier Reef was filled with abundant Coral and marine life. However, this disastrous occurrence has not only negatively affected the Barrier Reef, but was said to have had an impact on 54% of the entire world's Coral! Previously, by simply putting on a snorkel and flippers and wading to waist height you could enjoy a kaleidoscope of colour; a visual cocktail only paralleled by the "play of colour" seen in Opals.

It is unlikely that scientists will invent an instant cure for global warming, so unless all of us in the modern world start taking it extremely seriously - thereby slowing this harmful event - who knows what limited spectrum of colours our ancestors will see on our changing coastlines? Will our green fields in the British Isles be as lush as they are today, or will it become barren and desert-like? Will our colourful autumns that beautifully echo the many shades that we find in Sapphire be the same, or will they be replaced by bland, bleached scenes? Will my grandchildren ever see a white Christmas where sunlight dances off icicles like a candlelight flickering in a brilliantly cut Zircon? On a summer's evening, will they be able to stroll along a beach and watch the sunset over the horizon in a glow of Padparadscha colours, or will it be too hot to sit outside? Worse still, will the sea have risen so much they no longer have beaches as we know them today?

You may feel these are very sombre thoughts and perhaps not the best way to introduce you to the fascinating world of coloured gemstones. However, we all need to be aware of our actions and the effect it will have on future generations: to a certain extent that is why I have started at this point. Another reason is that many of the small gemstone mining villages that we deal with (both directly and indirectly) in our search to discover and acquire beautiful gemstones are amongst the first people to feel the negative effects of global warming, as their environments are already precariously balanced. Furthermore, what makes this seem most unfair is the fact that the majority of these mining communities – who remain fairly primitive in comparison to the Western World - have had the least negative effect of all on our planet!

Enough reality for now: the mere fact you have picked up this book means you are at one with nature. If you weren't, then you would

only ever buy costume jewellery from the high street and would not have the faintest interest in discovering more about the fascinating world of Mother Nature's coloured treasures. This leads me nicely to my next point, which is to make a clear and important distinction between the two. First, before I go upsetting nearly every female in the modern world, including many of my closest friends (and my eldest daughter), there is nothing wrong with costume jewellery. Second, I don't see much wrong in treating yourself to a collection of nice shoes, several handbags and a wardrobe full of beautiful clothes.

But here lies the difference: these items are all for one purpose - self-adornment. Their purpose is to make you feel good, now, immediately. I am a firm believer in that you become what you think about; a believer in the power of positive thinking and self-affirmation. Therefore, I truly believe that if your clothes, shoes and jewellery look beautiful, you start to feel beautiful and ultimately become beautiful. However, in several generations' time, will your descendents want to wear your passed down shoe collection, your once trendy clothes or your costume jewellery made of base metal with glass, plastic or crystal beads? The answer is, of course, a heavily resounding 'No', as these are merely consumable items for us to enjoy right now!

Coloured gemstone jewellery set in precious metals, however, is entirely different. The Diamond ring that you have or aspire to own came into existence some 90 million years ago, and if you are fortunate enough to own a piece of Tanzanite or Zircon, these virtually date back to the creation of Earth itself. A genuine gemstone that you acquire may only have been discovered by a fortunate gem miner or someone panning a river bed a short time ago, but it has shone for many years already and will continue to shine for thousands of years to come. Take a Ruby, Sapphire, Topaz, Amethyst, Emerald or any one of Nature's colourful mineral creations, set it into hardwearing 9k gold, 18k gold, Sterling Silver, platinum or titanium and, with reasonable care, it will look just as stunning in a thousand years from now as it does today. How do we know this? Well, as you read through this book, you will find many examples of gems set in jewellery today being discovered in archaeological sites, in bracelets and necklaces dating back over 5,000 years. Throughout this period, they have been surrounded in folklore, myth and legend.

Very interesting, 'but why are they not so frequently seen in everyday life right now?' I hear you ask. The answer is actually quite simple. Running concurrently with global warming is another monumental event which has been developing over the last one hundred years: we have all been brainwashed by very clever marketing executives in huge corporations. Until the early part of the 20th Century, coloured gemstones were far more popular than the Diamond. Coloured gemstones had not been seriously marketed or advertised; the knowledge of their mystical powers and understanding of the association with kings and queens was simply passed on from generation to generation. Plus, no single company dominated the supply of a single gemstone; if you were to heavily advertise Ruby as a brand, then you would not only increase your sales, but the sales of every other company selling Ruby too. What's more, the supply of nearly all coloured gemstones has been fairly sporadic over the centuries, discouraging companies from spending money advertising a coloured gemstone, when it was not certain it would be available to sell six months later.

However, shortly after discovering Diamonds in South Africa in 1867, one company came to dominate the world supply of this sparkling gemstone. In the 1940's the "Diamonds are a girl's best friend" and "Diamonds are forever" marketing campaign hit the streets of America. Hollywood became infatuated with this fairly new gemstone (until it was discovered in South Africa, it was one of the rarest gems on the planet) and over night, it went from virtual obscurity to the number one selling gemstone in the world by a landslide. It was seen as the only gem worthy of being set in an engagement ring. The combination of its sometimes controversial control of supply and undeniable beauty ensures

Jessica Lili

CELL 1
PHOTO REEL 1A
Jessica Lili
Jessica Lili
CELL 2
PHOTO REEL 2A
POP!
Viorelli
CELL 3
PHOTO REEL 3A
Viorelli

that the Diamond has remained the number one selling gemstone until this day.

Luckily, however, over the past decade the coloured gemstone is back with a vengeance. In this informational age, where there is an ever-increasing thirst for knowledge, people are spending more time researching on the internet and reading books about the world we live in. As you read this book and learn more about the fascinating world of coloured rocks, you will start to see the names of gemstones appear in almost everything you read. If you feel this is an exaggeration I challenge you to read a chapter of any reference book over 100 years old without coming across a reference to a gemstone. Have you ever had the experience when a friend shows you a picture of a car they are going to purchase, which you have never even seen before, and then during the following weeks you see lots of them on the motorway? Or you get introduced to a band you have never heard of and then every time you turn on the radio their song seems to be playing? By the time you finish this book, the same is going to happen again. Somebody is going to say "it's jet black", "it's ruby red", "tears of pearls" and you will smile knowing the true origin and meaning of the saying.

It's not just a thirst for knowledge that is seeing the coloured gemstone rising back to popularity: it has a lot to do with the trend towards individuality. Throughout much of the 60's, 70's, 80's and early 90's, there was a move towards conformism. People watched the same TV programmes, wore the same clothes and were easily identifiable in groups. Whether they were real or not, all teenagers wanted to own a Boss T-shirt or a Benetton jumper. It was the time of the super brands. Mass advertising made us believe everyone wanted the same possessions and experiences.

However, in recent years the trend has started to change. Many people no longer want to go on holiday to the same place year in year out, but want to try new experiences, like trekking in Scotland, or visiting the pyramids or the Great

Wall of China. These experiences are no longer conformist, but individual and unique. Similarly, people are now becoming more aware about the environment and are concerned about the working conditions in which their purchases are made. "Fairtrade", "eco friendly", "organic", "bio-organic", "free range" are all phrases we did not know ten years ago, but today, these descriptions are a crucial deciding factor in many people's purchasing decisions. Furthermore, those who buy these goods are often more than happy to discuss their personal opinions with others.

Most of all, we all love to talk to our friends about new things that we have learnt. The beautiful thing about coloured gemstones, with their history dating back thousands of years, is that there is always something new to learn! There is nothing wrong with Diamonds (after all they are a gemstone and therefore we love them too) but once you start collecting coloured gems, you cannot help but feel connected with Mother Nature and begin to experience a mystical, almost magical sensation every time you stop and look at your jewellery. And when someone pays you a compliment as they see the flash of coloured light illuminating your finger, or from a stunning pendant or earrings, you will find yourself automatically launching into a conversation about your particular gemstone. You will find yourself sharing its myths and legends, where it originated from, how it was mined, what the cut is, what the carat weight is and the joy it brings you.

One last thought before we get into the book: if global warming does happen as quickly as some experts predict, and my children and grandchildren do start to lose sight of glorious colours and shades such as those seen in the Maldivian sea, then they will at least have a small compromise, a compromise that their mother and father enjoyed collecting for them. For we have endeavoured to immortalise these colours in our coloured rocks. From the calming and sea-faring blue of my wife's Aquamarine pendant, to the glowing warmth and almost internal inferno of Sarah's Mozambique Garnet ring, to my Maldivian Blue Topaz cufflinks. And the

best thing of all, even if they don't appreciate the designs of our time, they can have the gems removed from the jewellery, have the gold work melted down and turned into cash, or have it used to reset the gem in a more contemporary design.

So as you read through our guide to the lure of coloured gemstones and trace back the history of how they have been set in to jewellery for over 5,000 years, why not turn off the light bulbs, light up a candle and enjoy the mysteries and legends of these wonderful gems, in a surrounding more akin to the way they have been appreciated for thousands of years.

Contents by Gemstone

CONTENTS

General Contents

CONTENTS

CONTENTS

ABALONE

A 2" striking Abalone pendant, set in Sterling Silver by Annabella.

Considered a delicacy by many throughout the world, the Abalone, or Ear Shell, is a Gastropod: a member of the Mollusc family of sea creatures. The creature has a univalve shell, similar to the Limpet and attaches itself to rocks or structures under the sea by suction.

The shell of the Abalone is used in jewellery, and the exceptional and mesmerising colours of the shell are a by-product from farming the shellfish for its meat, making the crafting of jewellery from the Gastropod very eco-friendly. From one side the shell looks rather dull and unexciting and is quite often covered by other sea crustaceans; but from the other side it shines with an array of stunning colours and beautiful iridescence, displaying vivid blues, greens and pinks, all combined in a spectacular modern art styled pattern.

Each shell displays a unique display of colour
and markings, almost like the human fingerprint,
therefore no two pieces are exactly the same. The
gem is ideal for use in large pendants and big,
dangly earrings. In addition to jewellery, you
may have seen this gem inlayed into acoustic
guitars.

ADAMANTINE

When light is reflected off the surface of a
gemstone it is referred to as "lustre" (also spelt
luster). Different gemstones have different types
of lustre and in gemmology there are several
universally accepted terms to describe these
appearances.

Several transparent gemstones with a high
refractive index are said to possess an adamantine
lustre. The word is derived from "Adamas", the
Ancient Greek word for Diamond; a gemstone
which displays a dazzling adamantine lustre.
Other gemstones that feature this captivating
lustre include Zircon and Demantoid Garnet.
In addition to being used to describe an optical
effect, Adamantine is also the name of a gemstone
which belongs to the Corundum family.

Gemstones with a high refractive index, but not
quite that of the Diamond, Zircon or Demantoid,
are said to have a subadamantine lustre. These
include some members of the Garnet family and
fine examples of Sapphire.

ADULARESCENCE

Adularescence is a vibrant, natural
optical effect similar to the shimmering
appearance of the moon on a cloudless evening.
It is caused by the physical crystal structure in
certain gemstones. Its name is derived from
"adularia", a mineralogist term for Moonstone
(a variety of Orthoclase), a gem which has the
ability to demonstrate this stunning visual effect
to the highest level.

When a gem displays an attractive light, which

appears to float below its surface, it is known as an adularescent effect. It can be seen on the surface of several gems where a ghost-like reflection with a bluish-whitish colour is visible. To maximise this glorious visual effect, these gems are often cabochon cut.

This shimmering effect is created in certain gemstones that have a layered type structure. These layers alternate in thickness; the thinner ones are so small that the eye cannot detect the visible wavelengths, scattering the light in multiple directions.

AGATE

Colour	Many different colours
Family	Quartz
Hardness	6.5 – 7
Specific Gravity	2.56 – 2.64
Refractive Index	1.530 – 1.550
Crystal Group	Trigonal
Optical Properties	Vitreous to waxy lustre
Common Treatments	None
Cleaning Advice	Ultrasonic: Usually safe but best with warm soapy water
Care	No special care recommended
Chemical Composition	SiO_2 (Silicon Dioxide)

Agate gemstones have been prized since antiquity and are a variety of Chalcedony, which in turn is a member of the Quartz family. It was given its name by Theophrastus, a Greek philosopher who is believed to have discovered the gem on the banks of the river Achates in the 4th century BC. The gemstone was later mentioned in the Bible as one of the "stones of fire".

Made from silicon dioxide, it has a glassy (vitreous) lustre, and registers 7 in hardness on the Mohs scale. Being such a hard stone, Agate is often used to make brooches and pins. Additionally, as it can also resist acids (unlike a lot of other gemstones) it has also been used to make mortars and pestles to press and combine chemicals.

Many Agates originate in cavities of molten rock, where gas bubbles trapped in solidifying lava are replaced with alkali and silica bearing solutions. Formed as a banded round nodule (similar to the rings of a tree trunk) the gem boasts an exquisite assortment of shapes and colours of bands, which may be seen clearly if a Lapidarist cuts the sections at a right angle to the layers; this is sometimes referred to as Riband Agate.

Other types of Agate include Onyx (Onyx is almost always a dyed Agate), Sardonyx, Ring Agate (encompassing bands of different colours), Moss Agate (with green banding), Blue Agate and Fire Agate.

A big, bold White Agate ring, set in Vermeil. Part of the Sarah Bennett Collection.

Myths and legends suggest that when a person wears Agate, they become more pleasant and agreeable. It is believed to quench thirst, protect against viruses (including fever) and to cure insomnia. Some traditions also believe that Agate can even cure the stings of scorpions and bites from poisonous snakes!

Muslims often have the gem set into a ring and wear it on their right hand and have the name of Allah, Ali (or one of the names of the other eleven Imams) inscribed on the ring.

The gem can be found all over the world, but the main sources of gem-quality material come from the United States - in particular the west; Montana and Idaho - Australia, Brazil, Italy and Madagascar.

A chunky Agate and Carnelian bracelet from the Jessica Lili Collection.

AFGHANISTAN

Positioned at the crossroads of ancient Indian, Persian, European and Asian civilizations, Afghanistan has been at the heart of gem trading routes and expeditions for thousands of years, which have included such eminent figures as Alexander the Great, Marco Polo and the Moguls.

Unfortunately, today Afghanistan is a country known more for its conflicts. But below ground, gemstone mining is still happening and a kaleidoscope of gemstones can be discovered. Ruby from Murgab; Spinel from Kuh-i-Lal mine; Turquoise from Eastern Tajikistan, plus Emerald, Red Jasper, Tourmaline, Amazonite, Kyanite and Garnets: all these add up to make Afghanistan one of the most prolific countries in the world for gemmologists.

It is said that the famous "Black Prince's Ruby" in the Crown Jewels, which is really a Spinel, originated from the Kuh-i-Lal mine in Afghanistan. Writings by Marco Polo suggested that the mine was said to be the oldest gem mine in the world still in operation and records trace its operations back to 101AD. This mine yields not only Spinel, but also Rubies and Garnets. As all three can be similar in colour it is understandable that in years gone by the three

Some of the world's finest Emeralds are discovered in Afghanistan.

A square cut Peridot from the Panjshir Valley.

The city of Kabul where many gem adventures commence.

gems would often be mistaken by gem explorers, who did not have the scientific tools available to us today. The mine is a maze of over 400 tunnels and miners today occasionally come across ancient bones of miners who were trapped in collapsed mine shafts.

If the fact that Spinel mining took place in 101AD impresses you, then how about the fact that Afghans have been mining for Lapis Lazuli for over 6500 years in the Badakhshan province and Panjshir valley. It is said by many gemmologists that Afghanistan has both the largest and best supply of this gemstone in the world.

Most Emerald mining in Afghanistan today is run by small family businesses in the Panjshir Valley. These tiny mining operations are located some 3,000 to 4,000 metres above sea level and are extremely difficult to reach. Afghan Emeralds are often more transparent and somewhat brighter than those found in the likes of Colombia and Siberia.

ALEXANDRITE

Alexandrite is a very valuable and rare Chrysoberyl. It is highly regarded by gem experts, enthusiasts and connoisseurs alike. The gem's uniqueness and value is not often apparent at first sight, but finely faceted, one carat pieces or more rank amongst the most expensive gems in the world – far rarer than fine Diamonds, Rubies, Emeralds and Sapphires.

It is said that the gemstone was discovered near the Tokovaya River in the Ural Mountains of Russia, on the same day as Alexander II (1818-1881) came of age. Hence the gemstone was named after the 16 year old future Tsar. This was deemed appropriate not just because it was discovered on Russian soil, but also because its extraordinary ability to change colour from red to green echoed the colours of the Russian flag at that time.

The first person to raise its awareness in public, Count Lev Alekseevich Perovskii (1792-1856), believed the stone to be a variety of Emerald, but noting it had a strange mineral content, passed it

Colour	Green, bluish green, bottle green in daylight, turning to greenish red, greenish purple
Family	Chrysoberyl
Hardness	8.5
Specific Gravity	3.71 – 3.74
Refractive Index	1.746 – 1.755
Crystal Group	Orthorhombic
Optical Properties	Colour change, strong pleochroic
Cleaning Advice	Ultrasonic, Steam Cleaner or warm soapy water
Common Treatments	Normally not treated
Care	No special care recommended
Chemical Composition	$BeAl_2O_4$

for a second opinion to the Finnish mineralogist Nils Gustaf Nordenskiold.

When initially studying the gem, Nordenskiold was also of the opinion that it was a type of Emerald, but as he was confused by its higher hardness he continued to review it. One evening when working by candle light, he was surprised to see the gem was no longer green but had turned a raspberry red. He then declared the gemstone a new form of Chrysoberyl, which would later be given its own distinct name. Today we know that Alexandrite is in fact a colour change variety of Chrysoberyl.

Alexandrite viewed in daylight.

But now for some bad news! It is a misconception that gemstones that are named "colour change" gemstones, physically change colour. The reality is that when viewed under different lighting conditions, the gem only appears to change colour. When you buy a "colour change" gemstone, to view the strongest change you need to view the gem under candescent lighting (direct sunlight) and then immediately view it under incandescent lighting (for example a light bulb). This procedure is most effective because daylight contains high proportions of blue and green light, while incandescent lighting contains a higher balance of red light. Therefore, when you view Alexandrite in daylight (balanced light) the gem appears green, but when the light source is reddish (incandescent), the gem shows hues of purple or red. Effectively you are looking at an optical illusion! Most changes are incredibly subtle and the saying that Alexandrite looks Emerald by day and Ruby by night, is a little bit of an exaggeration. That said, Alexandrite is a real treasure: so incredibly rare that few jewellers have ever held a piece!

Alexandrite viewed in artificial light.

Not only does Alexandrite have the ability to change colour, it is also a pleochroic gemstone; this means different colours can be seen when the gem is viewed from different angles. The gem is also very durable, measuring 8.5 on the Mohs scale, making it ideal for setting into all types of precious jewellery. Furthermore, it is one of three birthstones for the month of June (Pearl and Moonstone being the other two). In times of upset Alexandrite is believed to strengthen the

A very rare 2.7ct Alexandrite set in a timeless Lorique design.

wearer's intuition, and thus helps find new ways forward where logic and practical thinking will not provide an answer; it is also known to aid creativity and inspire one's imagination.

Although Alexandrite was originally discovered in Russia, other mines of this treasured gem have since been discovered in Brazil and Zimbabwe. More importantly, finds in Sri Lanka and India are providing great interest for those in the gem industry, as they are believed to be part of the same vein running down vertically from the original source in the Ural mountains.

A cluster of vividly coloured Alexandrite in a ring designed by Thomas Rae.

ALLOCHROMATIC

The array of beautiful colours we see in natural gemstones can be created by one of three events:

Firstly, it can be due to the inherent chemical makeup of the crystal; these gems are known as idiochromatic. Peridot for example is idiochromatic.

Morganite is an allochromatic gemstone.

Secondly, a gem's colour can be caused by the optical properties of the gem and its reflection from or just under its surface.

Thirdly, and most common, gems coloured by the presence of impurities are known as allochromatic. All allochromatic gemstones would in fact be colourless without the presence of impurities. The main elements that add colour to gemstones are titanium, chromium, manganese, iron, cobalt, nickel, and copper. The presence of these elements in gems such as Sapphire, Beryl, Spinel and Quartz are the sources of such a vibrant array of beautiful colours.

A kaleidoscope of allochromatic Sapphires.

Take Corundum as an example. In its purest form it is colourless (White Sapphire). When traces of iron are present we see a gorgeous Yellow Sapphire, add a small amount of titanium alongside the iron and you have the famous Blue Sapphire and when chromium is added to Corundum it becomes a rich red Ruby.

Without the presence of impurities, transparent allochromatic gems are colourless and opaque gems are white. In the case of Quartz and Beryl, the colourless varieties are more common, thus actually making them less valuable than those with impurities. For example, compare the price of a colourless 2 carat Beryl (known as Goshenite), to an equivalent carat weight of light blue Beryl (Aquamarine), and the price increases substantially. Then take the colourless Beryl, add a trace of chromium or vanadium and the price explodes exponentially as the gem now becomes an Emerald. However, other gems such as Tourmaline and Jade are rarely found colourless making them more valuable than their coloured equivalents. The allochromatic gemstone Spinel, available in almost every colour imaginable, has yet to be discovered colourless.

ALLOTROPIC

As it is rarely discussed in the gem world, allotropic is a word that you really won't need to remember; however, we have included it so as to highlight how fascinating and monumental the event is which creates gemstones.

First let's start by explaining what the word means. Allotropic chemical elements are those that can take on different forms. The word allotropy is derived from the Greek "allos", meaning "other", and "tropos", meaning "manner".

Now for the fascinating part. Compare for one moment the soft graphite in a pencil to the incredibly hard - in fact the hardest mineral on the planet - Diamond. Both are in fact made of the same material, carbon. But if they are the same, how is it that one is super soft, while the other is incredibly hard?

The Diamonds in this spectacular 2ct Eternity Ring by Tomas Rae are created by allotropic elements.

Graphite is formed at low temperatures and under little pressure very near to the Earth's surface. As it forms, its layers are not bonded together very well, making it soft and ideal for use in pencils and lubricants. Diamonds on the other hand are believed to be created some 93 miles below the Earth's surface, in extreme heat and under immense pressure. This tough environment compresses the carbon atoms into a compact and extremely strong crystal structure.

All these forces are applied for millions of years, and combine to create beautiful, hard wearing Diamonds.

So, next time someone says you're a real Diamond; you might want to reply with, "I'm not that old, I'm not under that much pressure and I've never been that hot!" Having said that, although Diamonds are created under immense heat, they are the best conductors of heat yet discovered, making them extremely cool when touched, so maybe you are a real Diamond after all...

Also, you might want to correct those that tell you that your cremated body may one day be turned into a valuable Diamond. Unless they can create temperatures of around 2,192 degrees Fahrenheit, replicate the pressure of 93 miles of earth bearing down on you and wait until the next two or three ice ages have passed, it might be better looking for an alternative use.

ALLOYS

An alloy is a metal that has been made from two or more different metals. In jewellery terms, most gold and silver pieces are not 100% pure and are deliberately made into an alloy to improve their strength.

Gold for example is such a soft metal that if you were to bite it, you would leave a large imprint of your teeth. Therefore without being merged with stronger metals (the technical word being anneal), gold would be pretty useless in jewellery for everyday wear. The percentage of gold in the alloyed metal is known as its fineness and in the UK the hallmark applied by the Assay office details how much gold is present in the final blend.

Not only by creating alloys can we make Gold and Silver stronger, we can actually change their colour. For example by adding Silver and other white metals to Gold (pure Gold is always yellow in colour), we are able to produce White Gold. By adding a percentage of copper to gold when creating an alloy, Rose Gold can be created.

These illusion set Diamonds in this 2ct spectacular ring by Tomas Rae are created by allotropic elements.

As Gold is a very soft metal, it is normally made into an alloy for use in jewellery.

Locals panning for gems in Ilakaka, Madagascar.

Entrepreneurial Sapphire miner in Sri Lanka searching an alluvial deposit just below the ground.

Me searching for Morganite in Madagascar. The deposit is some 30 metres down this shaft.

ALLUVIAL DEPOSITS

Derived from the Latin word "alluere", "to wash against", alluvial deposits are often a combination of soils, sediments, stones and minerals that have come to rest in historic river beds.

The amount of solid matter carried by a large river can be enormous: the Amazon River is reported to relocate over 700 million tonnes of sediment and rocks to the sea every year!

When exposed rocks at the surface of the earth weather over a period of time, gems may be released. Some of these rocks will dissolve completely, while others will be broken down into smaller pieces. The smaller, loose rocks that survive the erosion process are often washed into rivers or streams and as gems are heavier than most other materials they can easily be trapped in depressions in stream or river beds; this is how concentrations of gems are found.

Over millions of years these rivers dry up and alluvial deposits can be found many hundreds of miles from the nearest river or sea. Gems that are mined from alluvial deposits tend to be rounded, due to the fact they have been rolling along river or sea beds.

Over millions of years, as landscapes continue to change, many alluvial deposits end up being buried deep under ground. What I find most interesting about alluvial deposit mining, is that of the dozens of mines of this type I have visited around the world, no two have used the same method to search and extract the rough material. Whilst small independent artisanal miners may dig deep shafts and then have their neighbouring miner lower them down their hole, big corporate companies will use heavy plant machinery.

When an alluvial deposit is mined, it can often yield a wide variety of different gemstones. Madagascar, which currently has many alluvial mining activities, boasts one of the widest arrays of beautiful coloured gemstones in the world.

MATTOM

Aquamarine Chronograph Watch £89
Citrine and Diamond Cufflinks £59
Aquamarine Ring £40

Colour	Red to brown
Family	Garnet
Hardness	6.5 – 7.5
Specific Gravity	4.3
Refractive Index	1.83
Crystal Group	Isometric
Optical Properties	Various
Common Treatments	Cannot be heat treated
Cleaning Advice	Ultrasonic or warm soapy water
Care	No special care needed
Chemical Composition	Various

ALMANDINE GARNET

One of the oldest Garnets recorded by man, this beautiful gem was featured in writings by the Roman historian Pliny the Elder. In appearance Almandine Garnet varies in colour from a red to reddish orange through to a purplish red and is typically dark in tone.

For thousands of years, Almandine Garnet has been mined in several locations around the world and is often given a different name based on where it is found.

In Sri Lanka it has been called Ceylon Ruby and in days gone by it was often referred to in Australia as Australian Ruby. Another popular member of the Garnet family, Mozambique Garnet, is in fact a mixture of Pyrope and Almandine Garnet.

Of the Garnet family, Almandine is one of the more frequently discovered members and today the gem is mined in Norway, Pakistan, and India. Smaller activities also take place in several states in America.

Colour	Yellowish green to bluish green
Family	Feldspar
Hardness	6 to 6.5
Specific Gravity	2.56 – 2.57
Refractive Index	1.52 - 1.53
Crystal Group	Triclinic
Cleaning Advice	Warm soapy water
Chemical Composition	$KAlSi_3O_8$ (potassium aluminium silicate)

AMAZONITE

This gem is named after the Amazon River; however, although it is mined in Brazil it has never been discovered near the river and we have been unable to find a reliable source that can explain how the gem's name was derived.

Amazonite is a bluish green variety of microcline Feldspar and its appearance always resembles a piece of mottled modern art. This irregular colour distribution varies from green to yellowish green to bluish green, with some specimens featuring white streaks. In the past, finer green Amazonite specimens have been mistaken for Jade.

Amazonite has been said to help calm one's emotions and soothe nerves. It is also believed to enhance creativity and the ability to express oneself, but its strongest of all powers is to make married life happier!

Amazonite is mined in various locations: the most important deposits are in Colorado, while other locations include Brazil, India, Kenya, Madagascar, Namibia, Russia and Zimbabwe.

AMBER

Amber is one of the few gems that is organic and is created from fossilised resin from ancient trees. Over a period of millions of years and exposure to high temperature and pressure, the compressed resin eventually becomes Amber. Because it floats on salt water, if you take a stroll along the beaches on the East Coast of the UK, there is a small chance that you may discover your own piece of the precious stone washed up on the shore! Interestingly enough, until the mid 19th century this was how most Amber was found, and back then it was appropriately named 'Seastone'.

Amber's resin traps all kind of materials, and it is these inclusions which make every piece of Amber unique. The range of inclusions varies from frogs to bugs to leaves; it is not unusual to find a completely preserved fly or insect hidden inside the gem. The wealth of tiny insects trapped inside is due to the fact that when the resin leaked from the tree, it was incredibly sticky as its job was to stop insects from boring into the bark. 'Jurassic Park' may have given us an insight into how the world was a long time ago, but for Zoologists and Geologists, Amber is a lot more resourceful and to-date they have identified over one thousand different species of extinct insects purely by studying the gemstone! It really is a most unique gem, providing a visual snapshot of what life was like around 50 million years ago.

The Baltic States of Estonia, Latvia and Lithuania provide much of the Amber set in jewellery today, as well as the popular Caribbean holiday destination Dominican Republic. Although predominately a rich orange colour, Amber can also be found in yellow, honey, brown and green (Green Amber is formed when plantation is trapped within the resin).

The gem can be warm to touch and can create

Colour	Mainly orange, but occasionally found in green, brown, red, and bluish green
Family	Amber
Hardness	2 – 3
Specific Gravity	1.05 – 1.10
Refractive Index	1.54
Crystal Group	Amorphous
Optical Properties	Resinous lustre
Common Treatments	Heat treated to improve colour
Care	Keep away from extreme heat and boiling water
Cleaning Advice	Warm soapy water
Chemical Composition	Carbon, hydrogen, oxygen

Three shades of Amber in this stylish ring by Annabella.

Colour	Colourless to light yellow, light pink, green or blue.
Family	None
Hardness	5.5 - 6
Specific Gravity	3.02
Refractive Index	1.61 - 1.63
Crystal Group	Triclinic
Optical Properties	Transparent
Common Treatments	Not normally treated
Care	Don't expose to extreme heat
Cleaning Advice	Warm soapy water

static electricity when rubbed. As you can imagine, in years gone by its ability to create static was believed by many to be a magical power. In fact the word "electricity" originates from the Greek word for Amber, "electron". Many people believe that Amber brings good luck and can help people feel better when suffering from diseases.

AMBLYGONITE

Although many believe this gem was first discovered in the UK, Amblygonite was in fact initially discovered in the early 1800's in Germany, by Johann Breithaupt, a mineralogist who was credited with the discovery and identification of 47 different minerals!

Its name is derived from the Greek words for 'blunt' (amblus) and 'angle' (gouia), probably due to unusual angles of the gem's cleavage. It is sometimes referred to as the 'Prophet Stone'. Amblygonite is most often found in white and pastel shades of green, lilac, pink, and yellow, but rarely is of a transparent gem-quality material.

As the gem is rich in lithium, it is often discovered in the same location as Tourmaline and Apatite.

The two largest gem-quality finds of Amblygonite have been in California and France. The current collection on sale at Coloured Rocks was discovered in East Brazil where the Lavra mine, situated at Rio Jequitinhonha (half way between Minas Gerais and the coast), is famous for one of the largest Alexandrite finds in the world. On discovering possibly the most gorgeous Amblygonite ever unearthed, the mine owners partied hard for many days, saying that it was as an important occasion as the time when Alexandrite was found. However, their initial excitement did not last long, as very little of the gem has yet been recovered.

Unfortunately, Amblygonite is very difficult to find. It is also a complete nightmare to cut! With four different directions of cleavage, even the very best Lapidarists find the gem a real challenge to facet! When the clarity of the gem is of a high standard and when it is discovered

A huge 6.3ct Amblygonite discovered at Lavra mine in Brazil.

with delicate tones it is a real treasure. As it is relatively soft, it is best kept as a collectable or mounted in a pendant or earrings.

A rare, green 2.1ct Amblygonite from France.

AMERICAN INFLUENCES

Firstly let's start by saying that Americans spell the word used to describe items worn for personal adornment differently. What is known as jewellery in England is spelt "jewelry" in the USA.

Prior to the First World War, clothing and jewellery trends in the UK were created on home soil, with only a little influence from European neighbours. However, by the 1940's American culture was very dominant in Europe. The influence of Hollywood movies and the prominence of film stars set the fashion in jewellery, make-up, hair and clothes. It was widely believed that Hollywood glamour would rub off on you if you had similar clothes and jewellery, so many in Europe wanted look-a-like copies of outfits and jewellery worn by their screen idols.

The Second World War in Europe halted production of fine jewellery when metals were rationed. Fine precious metal and gem jewellery was simply not available. Quality costume jewellery, which was flourishing in America, became much more acceptable in Europe.

Citrine is today hugely popular in America.

AMETHYST

Throughout history, Amethyst has been one of the most popular and mystical of all gemstones. Its use in very rudimentary jewellery can be traced back as far as the Neolithic period (approximately 4000BC) and samples of it set into gold rings have been uncovered in burial sites from around 2400BC.

Amethyst is the name given to purple Quartz and some believe that its name derives from the Greek word "Amethustos", "A" meaning "not" and "methustos" meaning "to intoxicate". In ancient times, wealthy lords who wanted to stay

Colour	Purple or green
Family	Quartz
Hardness	7
Specific Gravity	2.65
Refractive Index	1.532-1.554
Crystal Group	Trigonal
Optical Properties	Normally good clarity
Common Treatments	Heat treated to improve colour
Care	Can fade slightly with prolonged exposure to sun
Chemical Composition	SiO_2 (Silicon Dioxide)

A vivid African Amethyst in a bold design featured in the Sarah Bennett Collection.

Amethyst is just one of the gems available for use in the Mattom interchangeable cufflinks.

sober were said to have had drinking glasses or goblets made from Amethyst. While pouring wine for their guests they could serve themselves water, as the dark purple hue of the gem would disguise the colour of the drink, thus allowing the lord appear to be partaking in a tipple! Following the same theme, it was thought in ancient times if you wished to save a drunkard from delirium you could mix crushed Amethyst into a person's drink.

One legend from Greek mythology tells the tale of how Dionysus, the god of intoxication, took his fury out on a young beautiful maiden named Amethyst while on her way to pray to the goddess Diana. He let loose fierce tigers, but before they reached Amethyst, Diana turned her into a statue of pure Crystalline Quartz to protect her from the advancing tigers. When Dionysus realised what he had almost done to Amethyst, he wept tears of wine. Legend says his tears turned the colourless Quartz purple, thus creating Amethyst.

Amethyst is mentioned in the Old Testament as one of the twelve stones representing the twelve tribes of Israel and was also one of the twelve gemstones adorning the breastplate of the high priest Aaron (Exodus 39). With its association with piety and celibacy, Amethyst has been set into rings and worn by Cardinals, Bishops and Priests of the Catholic Church since the Middle Ages. Over the years, along with its use by the Church, the gem has also been cherished by royalty and several pieces can be found in the British Crown Jewels. Amethyst was also known as a personal favourite of Catherine the Great.

A bracelet worn by Queen Charlotte of England in the early 1700's was valued at £200 at that time! With inflation that would make it more expensive than the Diamond Skull recently created by Damien Hirst! However, shortly after this period a new discovery of Amethyst deposits were made in Brazil, which dramatically reduced the value of the queen's bracelet.

This provides a good example of how the value of genuine gemstones (just like the stock market) can go up and down based on supply and demand. When mines are eventually exhausted prices tend to increase; as new deposits are found, gemstone prices generally decrease.

Amethyst occurs in many shades, from a light, slightly lavender pinkish to a deep purple similar to that of the Cabernet Sauvignon grape. Amethyst is also pleochroic, which means that when light hits the gem, shades of different colours such as reds and blues can be seen from different angles.

As there is no single dominant organisation or ruling body relating to gemstones, there are often different approaches to how a gem is graded or named. Many organisations within the jewellery industry for instance refer to Green Quartz as Green Amethyst, while others refer to Green Quartz as Prasiolite, Amegreen or Vermarine! This is a really hot topic in the gem world: some believing that the name Amethyst can only be applied to purple Quartz, others saying if a Quartz's green colour is derived from heat treated Amethyst then it should be named Green Amethyst and others saying it should be known as Green Quartz or Prasiolite. Most Green Amethyst has been available since the mid 1950's, has come from Brazil and is heat treated to produce an electrifying transparent olive-coloured green gemstone. That said, Green Amethyst (or what ever you want to call it!) has been known to appear naturally in a small mine in Silesia, Poland, and claims of natural Green Amethyst discoveries have also been made in Namibia, Nevada USA, Zambia and Tanzania.

Different tones of Amethyst have different prefixes; "Siberian Amethyst" refers to darker Amethyst regardless of whether they are from Siberia or not; and Amethyst with a more pinkish tone is named "Rose De France". Amethyst is a hard and durable gemstone measuring 7 on the Mohs scale. In its rough state, the gem often forms in long prismatic crystals, making it ideal for cutting. Because its colour can often appear banded, it is usually cut into round brilliant shapes which helps the gem display a more uniformed colour when viewed through the table or crown facets.

Amethyst is considered a symbol of peace of

This Amethyst ring features in the Jewels of Valais Collection.

A vibrant African Amethyst, featured in a piece by Jewels of Valais.

A Cushion Cut 2ct Amethyst in a stylish ring from Annabella.

Colour	Purple to yellow
Family	Quartz
Hardness	7
Specific Gravity	2.65
Refractive Index	1.54-1.55
Crystal Group	Trigonal
Optical Properties	Bi-coloured gemstone
Common Treatments	Heat treated to improve colour
Care	Can in rare cases fade with prolonged exposure to sun
Cleaning Advice	Ultrasonic or warm soapy water.
Chemical Composition	SiO_2 (Silicon Dioxide)

mind, modesty and piety. Some believe that Amethyst holds powers to change anger to tranquillity and is used by crystal healers to revert negative energy into positive energy. It is popular for its healing and meditative powers, and purifies the mind, body and spirit, helping to realign the chakras. It is also considered an ideal gemstone for those struggling or recovering from alcoholism as it protects against drunkenness.

Amethyst is the birthstone of February. It is also associated with the zodiac signs of Pisces, Aries, Aquarius and Sagittarius. The gem is mined in several countries including the USA, Brazil, Madagascar and Kenya. One of the largest Amethyst mines in the world is in Maissau in Austria and is unusual in that it is open to the public. If you want to travel further, then the Amethyst mines in Brazil are considered to be the best in the world and as long as you don't mind roughing it a little, you're sure to have a great adventure visiting the local artisan miners.

AMETRINE

Ametrine is possibly one of the most interesting and beautiful gemstones to become available on the global gem market during recent years. Currently only found at the Anahi Mine in Eastern Bolivia, it is a fusion of the gorgeous regal purple of Amethyst and the warm sunshine hue of Citrine, beautifully combined in one stone. In the gem industry, Ametrine also goes by the name of Bolivianite, due the location of its source.

Ametrine's bi-coloured effect is uniquely created due to differing temperatures across the gem during its crystal formation. The area with highest temperature forms golden Citrine yellows and the cooler zone forms lilac Amethyst colours. However, this one-off occurrence was a tough trick for Mother Nature to perform, because if too much heat had been applied the entire gem would have become a Citrine.

Many gemstone dealers have tried to emulate this balancing act by heating one end of an Amethyst. However they are all said to have failed as the heat travels too fast through the

gem, making it all turn to Citrine. Cutting the rough of Ametrine is such an important task because it can make or break the beauty of the gem. Usually the Lapidarist (a person who cuts and facets gemstones) will cut the gem into longer shapes so as to draw the eye's attention to its unique bi-colours. The gem looks gorgeous in baguette, emerald and octagon cuts.

Many crystal healers believe that Ametrine holds the same metaphysical properties as both Amethyst and Citrine. It will help guide you through meditation, relieves the stress and strain of everyday life and helps to remove negative emotions and prejudices.

The photograph to the right is an 8ct Ametrine. Many gem experts would value it quite poorly as it is not 50% Amethyst and 50% Citrine. However, this is one of the great things about gemstones, I didn't purchase this piece for its conformity, but simply because I fell in love with it. I knew it was not a text book gem, but something caught my eye and I had to have it. Plus, as others found it a less than perfect gem, I didn't have to pay a fortune for it.

A Jacque Christie 8ct Bolivian Ametrine Set in 9ct Gold.

AMMOLITE

Do you remember back at school when we were taught about fossils? One of the most easily recalled shapes is that of the spiral shelled Ammonite. This small sea creature existed some 70 million years ago and fossilised specimens of two types of Ammonite, the Placenticeras and the Intercalare, when cut can produce the most incredibly kaleidoscopic gemstones, known as Ammolite. Its opaque appearance is similar to that of a Boulder Opal and the gem is often crushed and reconstituted into thin cuts.

Although Ammolite fossils can be discovered all over the world, to-date only those found in Alberta, Canada are of gem-quality. First discovered in 1908, commercial mining took 70 years to become viable and in 1981, Ammolite became officially recognised as a gemstone by CIBJO (The International Commission of Coloured Gemstones). Sources at the current mine claim that they are finding it harder and

Colour	Multicoloured
Family	Organic
Hardness	Variable
Specific Gravity	Approx 2.7
Refractive Index	1.52 - 1.68
Crystal Group	N/A
Optical Properties	Very Iridescent
Common Treatments	Lacquer coating
Care	None
Cleaning Advice	Ultrasonic or warm soapy water.
Chemical Composition	N/A

harder to find and suggest that the gem might be extinct within the next 15 years.

ANDALUSITE

Colour	Brown to Yellow
Family	N/A
Hardness	77.5
Specific Gravity	3.17
Refractive Index	1.63 - 1.64
Crystal Group	Orthorhombic
Optical Properties	Very Pleochroic
Common Treatments	Heat Treating
Care	None
Cleaning Advice	Ultrasonic or warm soapy water.
Chemical Composition	Al2SiO5

Discovered in blue, green and brown colours, Andalusite is a transparent to translucent gem that derives its name from Andalusia in Spain where it was first discovered. The gem is actually a polymorph of two gem varieties: Sillimanite and the hugely popular Kyanite.

There is little folklore and legend surrounding Andalusite, as it was often mistaken for Smokey Quartz, Chrysoberyl or Tourmaline. However, the gemstone benefits from a very distinct and attractive pleochroism, which Lapidarists try and highlight when faceting the gem and which is often used by gemmologists in identifying it.

Andalusite registers 7.5 on the Mohs scale, and in addition to Spain has been discovered in Switzerland, Sri Lanka, Kenya, Mozambique and the USA.

ANDESINE

Colour	Red, Green
Family	Feldspar
Hardness	6 - 6.5
Specific Gravity	2.68
Refractive Index	1.54 - 1.56
Crystal Group	Triclinic
Optical Properties	Possible Colour Change
Common Treatments	Not normally treated
Care	None
Cleaning Advice	Warm soapy water
Chemical Composition	(Ca, Na)(Al,Si)4O8

What an interesting world we live in! I have always explained to my jewellery team that you should never state anything about gemstones as an absolute fact and instead should use phrases such as 'currently one of the rarest gemstones on the planet' or 'sources inform us that the gem will no longer be mined within the next 10 years'. Remember they used to say Garnet comes in every single colour apart from blue, but then what did they discover in Madagsascar in 1998? You guessed it!

It's so easy to get carried away in an industry where people state things as fact, but in reality this industry should by now, after trading coloured gemstones for over 5,000 years, have begun to realise that Mother Nature is never predictable and often seems to do things that makes even the world's best gem experts occasionally look a little silly.

In 2002 at the world famous Tucson Gem Show in Arizona, when a stunning new gemstone called Andesine exploded on to the scene (well,

GEM COLLECTOR

it wasn't brand new, but we will come to that in a moment), there were many stories and myths surrounding its original location and what in fact the gemstone was.

The gemstone is so stunning that the miners of this new source kept its location a real secret and many in the industry incorrectly said that it came from either India or the Democratic Republic of Congo. With so much demand for top quality Andesine, many in the industry were selling very similar pieces and claiming it was from the same source as the very finest material, and as nobody knew exactly where the new source was, nobody could dispute the dealers' claims of origin. Whilst many were uncertain of the location of this new magnificent gemstone, it was certainly being mined somewhere in the Himalayas, a far cry from where it was originally discovered in 1840's in the Andes Mountains in Bolivia, from where its name is derived.

A 1.2ct Andesine solitaire set in 18k white Gold by Tomas Rae.

But what is this gemstone and what is its real name?! Unfortunately, this is still a matter for debate. Firstly a fact: the gemstone is a top quality red gemstone and is a member of the Feldspar family. The finest examples are right up there with Paraiba Tourmaline and Alexandrite. In fact, Andesine shares similarities with both in that there is also a green colour change version of the gemstone which appears very similar to Alexandrite and like Paraiba, part of its magical brilliance is due to the presence of Copper.

There is a real debate at present between what the difference is between Red Labradorite and Red Andesine. What some gemmologists are suggesting is that the difference between the two depends on the percentage of Sodium and Calcium within the gem: if it's high in Sodium then it's Andesine; if it's high in Calcium then it's Red Labradorite. Don't worry if this is getting a little confusing, as it's also confusing the industry!

1.8ct Andesine set in 18k white Gold by Tomas Rae.

Let's side track a little. It is now known that some of the finest Andesine in the world is coming from a mine located some 70km south of the city Xigaze in Southern Tibet. The mine is at 4,000m above sea level where the air is difficult

A vibrant pair of Andesine earrings set in 18k white Gold by Tomas Rae.

to breath and most of the year, because of thick snow, mining is impossible to hazardous at best. The gemstone is rich in Copper, which gives the gemstone an internal fiery glow, which is like no other gemstone yet discovered and which is responsible for its amazingly unique colours. Several gem laboratories have confirmed that the material from this region gets its incredible colours naturally from Mother Nature, whereas many of the specimens on the market, especially those from Inner Mongolia are heat-treated with diffusion.

Therefore what we have decided at Coloured Rocks, is that if we are confident that the gem originates from Tibet, where the mineral is rich in Sodium and where the colour is natural, then we will call it Andesine. Sources say that the mines are already starting to deplete and unless a new vein is discovered they may stop mining within two more seasons. When we source red Feldspar from other regions, for now we will call it Red Labradorite. Don't get us wrong, Red Labradorite is equally beautiful, but for now we want to be able to differentiate between the two, whilst the powers that be make their definitive conclusions.

When it comes to Green Andesine and Colour Change Andesine, these are incredibly rare and beautiful gems also. In fact the colour change variety has some of the best colour change we have ever seen in a gemstone, having the ability to go from a stunning bottle green colour under florescent lighting, to a glorious almost Amethyst purple colour under a strong torch light.

I received a letter from a lovely customer who had taken her jewellery in to be valued and on return was delighted that it had come back at £5000. She was told that the gem was not a Green Andesine but actually an Alexandrite! When I examined the piece it was in fact Andesine and the jeweller had made a basic mistake. Firstly, the two gems look visually different and their refractive indexes are also miles apart! What I always suggest is that when you purchase a rare gemstone, if you want to have it properly valued, you will need to go to an expert in coloured gemstones!

An 18k yellow Gold cluster ring by Tomas Rae.

Colour change Andesine is almost impossible to obtain.

jessica lily

Shiva Eye Pendant
£17

Colour	Yellow, Green, Brown or Black
Family	Andradite
Hardness	6.5 - 7
Specific Gravity	3.84
Refractive Index	1.88
Crystal Group	Cubic
Optical Properties	Vitreous Luster
Common Treatments	None
Care	None
Cleaning Advice	Ultrasonic or warm soapy water
Chemical Composition	Ca3fe2(SiO4)3

ANDRADITE GARNET

You will see from the gem table that Andradite has quite a complex chemical composition. The gem receives its wide variety of colours due to the fact that its complex composition can be a cocktail of manganese, aluminium, titanium or chromium.

There are three main members of the Andradite family of Garnets:

Melanite is the black variety of the gem and is not that often seen in jewellery. Its main ingredient is titanium and it is often discovered near volcanoes and in particular old lava deposits.

Topazolite is normally yellow in colour and receives its name for its similarity in appearance to Imperial Topaz. The gem has been discovered in Italy and the Swiss canton of Valais (the same location that yields the world's finest Marcasite), however it is incredibly rare and very hard these days to find.

Demantoid, the green member of Andradite, is a gemstone that is regarded by many as one of the most collectable of all. What makes the Demantoid variety so keenly sought after is that it has a dispersion greater than that of Diamond. Similar to other green gems, it is the presence of chromium that provides it with such a wonderful, lively green colour. A colour that caught the attention of the Russian jeweller Carl Fabergé who used it in many of his designs. The Demantoid used in his pieces were sourced from the Ural Mountains of Russia, however unfortunately these deposits have become exhausted, not only for Demantoid, but also for equally famous colour change Alexandrite.

The gem group was named after the Brazilian mineralogist José Bonifácio de Andrade e Silva, who in the 1830's discovered and documented four new minerals.

Andradite can also be found in Italy, Switzerland, Norway, Mexico and America.

A very rare 1.1ct Demantoid Garnet.

A .95ct Topazolite from Switzerland.

ANGELITE

Colour	White, Blue
Family	Anhydrite
Hardness	3.5
Specific Gravity	2.87
Refractive Index	1.56 - 1.61
Crystal Group	Orthorhombic
Optical Properties	Vitrous lustre
Common Treatments	Not normally treated
Care	Careful not to scratch
Cleaning Advice	Warm soapy water
Chemical Composition	$CaSO_4$

In February I received a very excited phone call from a good friend of mine who was in Peru! 'What are you doing in Peru?' I asked him. I thought he must be on holiday as there is very little gem mining in the country. It turned out one of his friends had just discovered a small deposit of gemstones and had called him in for his opinion. What had been discovered was a gemstone known as Angelite which is a delicious lilac, pale blue gem variety of Anhydrite, so named for its angelic appearance.

The gem is believed to be related to the fifth (throat) chakra, which helps with communication. Angelite is said to provide the wearer with a heightened awareness and to help one focus on kindness and brotherhood. I have also read that Angelite is very useful for weight control and although my wife (who is very slim) has yet to wear the gem, in her previous career as a pop singer her stage name was coincidently Angelle!

The pastel blue shade of Angelite.

ANNABELLA

The essence of elegance.

For stylish looks in Sterling Silver, be sure to see the Annabella Collection of fashionable jewellery. Every piece is handcrafted to the finest detail and features genuine gemstones set in beautiful flowing designs.

The collection has already proven popular with fashion conscious celebrities and has featured on television and in magazines. Cosmopolitan, Woman and Now have all raved about Annabella pieces and the brand is ideally suited for those who love wearing subtle, feminine and beautiful jewellery.

Colours play a crucial role for Annabella, matching complementing dyed Pearls and coloured gemstones in gorgeous necklaces and bracelets. Look out also for the colourful Annabella watch collection which is due to launch in the Autumn of 2009.

An elegant floral Mother of Pearl ring by Annabella.

ANNA BELLA

ANNIVERSARY GEMSTONES

Anniversaries are traditionally celebrated with the giving of gifts relating to the year of the wedding, civil partnerships or indeed any memorable event.

Around the turn of the 19th century it was popular to give gifts of paper, cotton or leather for the first few years of marriage. However, in more recent times and due to the increasing popularity of fine, rare gemstones, it is more popular to give jewellery to the one you love.

Although there are several variations for a few of the anniversaries, the table on the right details those we believe to be the most universally adopted.

One of the loveliest emails I ever received from a gentleman (stay with me on this one!), was from someone who had found our website while searching on Google to find an anniversary present for his wife. He admitted to have known nothing about gemstones prior to finding our site, but on seeing that Amethyst was the suggest gift for the 6th Wedding Anniversary, he decided to purchase a ring for his wife. His wife was delighted with the gift and commented on how much thought and research he must have put in to find the most appropriate of gifts and on how much he must have spent! He finished his email by saying that the best thing of all, was that the ring cost less than the bunch of flowers he gave her the year before and that he would be back in 12 months' time to buy Onyx!

Year	Gemstone
1	Any gem set in gold
2	Garnet
3	Pearl
4	Blue Topaz
5	Sapphire
6	Amethyst
7	Onyx
8	Tourmaline
9	Lapis Lazuli
10	Diamond
11	Turquoise
12	Jade
13	Citrine
14	Opal
15	Ruby
16	Imperial Topaz and Peridot
17	Amethyst
18	Garnet
19	Aquamarine
20	Emerald
21	Iolite
22	Spinel
23	Imperial Topaz
24	Tanzanite
25	Any gem set in silver
30	Pearl
35	Coral and Emerald
40	Ruby
45	Alexandrite and Sapphire
50	Gold
55	Alexandrite and Emerald
60	Diamond
65	Spinel
70	Sapphire

A cushion cut 2ct Topaz Sterling Silver ring by Annabella.

Colour	Swimming pool blues through to lively light greens
Family	Apatite
Hardness	5
Specific Gravity	3.1 – 3.2
Refractive Index	1.63 – 1.65
Crystal Group	Hexagonal
Optical Properties	Strong pleochroism
Common Treatments	Not normally treated
Care	Be careful not to scratch with metal
Cleaning Advice	Warm soapy water
Chemical Composition	$Ca_5(PO_4)_3(F,CI,OH)$

A wonderful Apatite bangle masterfully designed by Jacque Christie.

ANTIQUE CUSHION CUT

Also known as an "Antique Cut" or "Pillow Cut", the antique cushion cut in appearance is similar to the "Old Mine Cut", which was popular in the late 19th century, and the more modern "Oval Cut".

The antique cushion cut is occasionally used for Diamonds. Although the cut does not have the same ability to display dispersion as the brilliant cut, it is however very romantic in appearance as it is reminiscent of cuts applied to Diamonds worn by previous generations. The cut is often applied to coloured gemstones and can dramatically increase the flashes of lustre seen from the crown of the gem.

APATITE

Although Apatite is really a family of gemstones, as the individual members have very long and difficult-to-pronounce names, the jewellery industry tends to use Apatite as the generic name. Historically, because the gem was often confused with other gemstones, its name is derived from the Greek meaning "to deceive".

The more common colours for Apatite are similar to Paraiba Tourmaline, with swimming pool blues through to lively light greens. That said, other colours occasionally occur: colourless to white, brownish-yellow, greyish-green and one known as the "Asparagus stone" due to its resemblance to the vegetable.

Apatite has been associated with many healing properties and is a gemstone often combined with other gems to further its healing powers. It is also thought to be an aid to seeing the truth about oneself.

When you combine Rose Quartz with Apatite it is meant to draw and give unconditional love; if you pair it with colourless Quartz it can help you see the changes that need to occur in your life; and when combined with Aquamarine it is believed to help you make those changes.

For such a beautiful gemstone, with almost a neon glow, it is difficult to comprehend how many Apatites are created from fossilised dinosaur bones! At just 5 on the Mohs scale, Apatite is one of the softest gems to be set in jewellery, but treated respectably its alluring and luscious glow will keep its owner entranced for many years.

Deposits have been found in several locations including Cornwall in England, Canada, Norway, Russia and Sweden.

AQUAMARINE

Aquamarine is one of the world's most popular and well-known gemstones. Often found with great clarity in a light yet energetic blue, Aquamarine is a real favourite of many gem collectors and in a world that's becoming more and more polluted, Aquamarine offers us all a breath of fresh air.

A member of the Beryl family, Aquamarine's characteristic pale blue colour is created by the presence of iron. Likewise, all members of the Beryl family obtain their colours by the presence of metallic elements, without which pure Beryl remains colourless. Gemstones that are coloured by nature in this way are known as allochromatic. Aquamarine's younger sister Morganite is coloured by manganese, and its older and more complicated sister Emerald receives her personality from the presence of chromium, iron and vanadium.

Its name is derived from the Latin "aqua" for "water" and "mare" for "sea", and many superstitions and legends regarding the sea have been attached to the gemstone over the years. Believed to be the treasure of mermaids, the gem is said to be especially strong when submersed in water. When its powers seemed to be dwindling, to recharge and cleanse the gem many would place the gem in water on the night of a full moon.

In times gone by, as a very last resort, sailors caught in a storm were believed to throw their

Colour	Light blue
Family	Beryl
Hardness	7.5 – 8
Specific Gravity	2.68 – 2.79
Refractive Index	1.567 – 1.590
Crystal Group	Hexagonal
Optical Properties	Normally has good clarity
Common Treatments	Heat treated to enhance colour
Care	No special care needed
Cleaning Advice	Ultrasonic, Steam Cleaner or Warm soapy water
Chemical Composition	$Be_3Al_2Si_6O_{18}$ (beryllium, aluminium)

A rare 5.7ct Aquamarine from Brazil.

A Tomas Rae 1.7ct Aquamarine 18k Gold masterpiece.

A heavyweight gold and Aquamarine pendant by Jacque Christie.

Aquamarines overboard to calm the gods. Sailors were also said to have taken Aquamarine to sea as a lucky charm to protect against shipwreck, and many people today still wear Aquamarine to prevent travel sickness.

Back on shore, Aquamarine is believed to both sooth and prolong relationships, and for this reason is often given as an anniversary gift way before its official listing for one's 19th anniversary. For those frightened of spiders or flying, wearing Aquamarine is said to suppress one's phobias.

Out of the ground, many Aquamarines have a slight green tint and are often heat-treated to turn the gem into a more pure blue. However, over recent years, the lighter, natural colour has become very popular amongst gemstone collectors. In either shade, this birthstone for March is highly sought after for its clarity, transparency and undeniable calmness.

Similar to Amethyst where different shades are given different prefixes, Santa Maria Aquamarine describes those with a deeper shade of blue than normal. The name is derived from the Santa Maria de Itabria gem mines of Brazil, where deep and vibrant Aquamarines have been found - not, as some people believe, from the name of the ship that Christopher Columbus made his first cross Atlantic voyage, or indeed from Santa Maria city in California.

The largest source of the gem is found in the state of Minas Gerais in south-east Brazil, but today Africa is becoming a strong rival, with mining activities in countries such as Madagascar, Mozambique, Nigeria and Tanzania.

ARAGONITE

Mined in just a handful of places around the world, Aragonite is named after the Molina de Aragon mine in Guadalajara, Spain where it was discovered in 1788 (the mine is situated close to the town of Aragon).

Aragonite is a unique mineral gemstone, as it has the same chemical composition also found in organic Mollusks. The crystal structure of Aragonite is also very unusual in that it is often found in needle-like, six-sided prisms. In addition to its initial discovery in Spain, three large Aragonite caves have also been discovered in Slovakia, Mexico and Argentina.

The cave in Slovakia is buried deep in the Slovak Metalliferous Mountains between Jelsava and Stitnik. Known as the Chtinska Aragonite Cave, it was discovered in 1954 and in 1972 it was opened to the public. Unlike most public caves full of stalactites or stalagmites, the unusual crystal structure of Aragonite resembles small shrubs and bushes. One of the main attractions at the mine is the Milky Way Hall, where Aragonites high in the ceiling shine like the stars in the Milky Way. In gemstone terms, the Aragonite in the mine is fairly young; dating back just 13,000 to 100,000 years.

Similar to Quartz, only a tiny percentage of Aragonite is of gem-quality material. Crystal healers believe that Golden Aragonite is important to the 3rd Chakra and White Aragonite is of benefit to the 7th. I also recently read that in some circles, Aragonite is recommended as a healer for painful knees and should be attached with a bandage for an hour each day.

Colour	White, Grey, Yellow or Brown
Family	Aragonite
Hardness	3.5 - 4
Specific Gravity	2.94
Refractive Index	1.53 - 1.68
Crystal Group	Orthorhombic
Optical Properties	Vitreous Lustre
Common Treatments	None
Care	Careful not to scratch
Cleaning Advice	Warm soapy water
Composition	CaCO3

Various different hues of Aragonite.

Art Deco (1910 - 1939)

It was the age of jazz, prohibition and the Charleston. Queen Victoria was no longer on the throne, but countless ideals and influences from her age still remained. It was the 1920's, and the world was about to see a profound new style that would change history forever. The style would be known as Art Deco. It was bold, lavish and elegant and was to radically change the art world, leaving a lasting impression that can still be seen today.

After the Universal Exposition of 1900, a group of French artists created a formal collective which was known as 'La Societe des Artistes Decorateurs' (The Society of the Decorator Artists) of Paris.

A Jewels of Valais piece inspired by designs of the Art Deco period.

A huge Lemon Quartz cocktail ring from the Sarah Bennett 2008 collection.

18k Gold and Sterling Silver combined with a large Citrine in an Art Deco style.

Jessica Lili bracelet echoing the bold colours used in Art Deco designs.

Not entirely of their making, the Art Deco 'movement' began more as an amalgamation of numerous different styles and movements of the early 1900's. Art Deco affected architecture, painting, film, both interior and industrial design, and, most importantly, fashion. Jewellery that came out of the Art Deco movement was forward thinking and extremely bold. Its "in your face" style represented the fast modernization of the world around it.

Art Deco made vast use of triangular, angular and geometric shapes, employing symmetry and repetition. The movement attempted to combine mass production with high-quality art and design. Tiaras, cameos and lavalieres from the Victorian era were now unpopular, and gave way to fashionable cocktail rings, long pendants and bangle bracelets.

Accessories became popular again; elaborately detailed cigarette cases and ladies compacts were all ornately jewelled and became just as important as earrings, necklaces and bangles. Inexpensive stones such as Coral and crystal were used with platinum and gold. It has been suggested that this opulent and lavish style was a reaction to the hard times and rationing of WW1.

The fundamental difference that made the Art Deco period so extraordinary was that the same design ideas put into jewellery were also being engineered in buildings, ships and even household appliances.

Diamonds began to be cut in new and exciting shapes never seen before. Many of these, such as pear cut, emerald cut and marquise cut were extremely similar to the cuts we see today. These new-found gem cuts blended in with the symmetrical and geometrical nature of the jewellery itself.

Colour played an important role in the Art Deco movement: everything became bold, vibrant and vivid. The way colour was applied was often dramatic, reacting to the light, neutral colours used during the previous Art Nouveau period. Gemstones such as Ruby, Emerald, Sapphire, and Coral became popular for this reason.

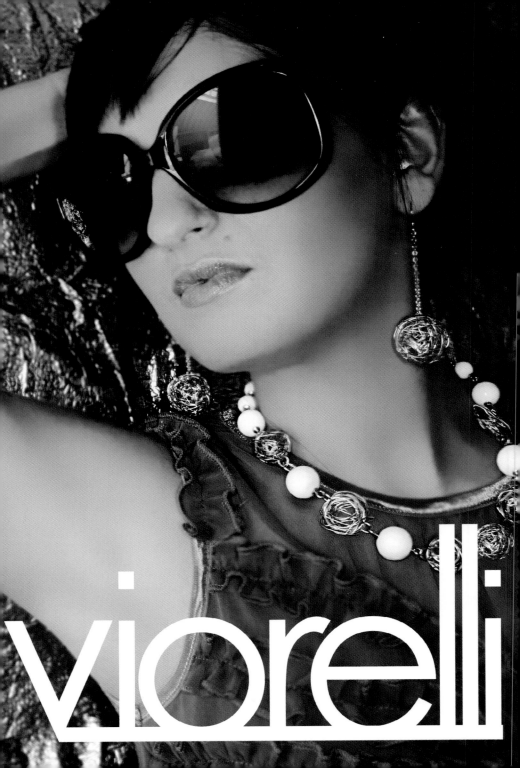

ART NOUVEAU (1880 - 1914)

Art Nouveau was a rich, decorative and poignant era. Its object was not to imitate, but to evoke. Beginning in the latter years of Queen Victoria's rule, and carrying on well into the 20th century, the Art Nouveau movement is one that has gone on to influence and inspire artists and designers for years.

The name of the movement 'Art Nouveau' comes from 'Maison de l'Art Nouveau', a shop in Paris that displayed art of this design. The words 'Art Nouveau' are French and simply mean 'New Art'.

Although the movement as a whole lasted about 35 years, the period in which jewellery was created in this style was much shorter lived; only lasting about fifteen years. However, its influence is not to be underestimated as it has gone on to inspire many styles for years after its original popularity decreased.

Art Nouveau was groundbreaking. It marked a time where designers would start looking at the world around them, taking stimuli from the natural world, rather than looking into history for inspiration. The style, although short-lived in comparison to other eras, was a reaction to mass produced jewellery, popular towards the end of the Victorian period. The jewellery was bold, expressive, exotic and exuberant.

When the first few examples of 'Art Nouveau' were showcased in Paris, there was outrage. It represented a radical change, and was different to anything most people had ever seen. Viewers either loved it or despised it. The 'rebellion' was said to have freed a creative energy that had been suppressed for so long.

Art Nouveau incorporated highly stylised designs with flowing, sinuous, elongated, curving lines. Inspiration came from a wide spectrum, often from nature: ferns, roots, buds, seed pods, sunflowers, spiders and dragonflies. Snakes became an unlikely popular symbol of life,

An Art Nouveau-inspired piece from the Sarah Bennett collection.

A Jessica Lili tumbled gemstone necklace echoing the vibrant colours of Art Nouveau.

A Jacque Christie pendant with flowing lines reminiscent of Art Nouveau.

sexuality and eternity. Unusual designs based on flowers and plants that had not been used before in jewellery were experimented with. Such plants as orchids, mimosa, dandelions, lilies, poppies and mistletoe became popular and widely used. Peacocks, and particularly their feathers, became fashionable and were featured in all types of jewellery. The elegant shape of swans and swallows proved a natural inspiration for the flowing, curvaceous lines of Art Nouveau.

Art Nouveau also used the female form in all its glory, proudly displaying it on necklaces and earrings. The women would have long flowing hair, celebrating the natural woman and her new place in society.

One of the defining techniques of the Art Nouveau period was enamelling. It was used to create patterns or pictures on the desired object, by fusing powdered glass to the surface. There were many different types of enamelling employed at the time, but the most popular, known as Plique a'jour gave an effect that has been likened to stained glass. Plique a'jour gave the jewellery a distinct, almost three-dimensional effect, which was unique to the time. It was notoriously hard to do, and was a sign of the artist's skill. Other types of enamelling were 'basse-taille' and 'guilloche.'

18k Gold and Sterling Silver combined to create an Art Nouveau appearance.

Marcasite and Topaz set in an Art Nouveau style from the Jewels of Valais collection.

ASSAY

Many countries have laws that govern how precious metals are sold and often, to protect the consumer, insist that a hallmark is applied. Assay is the name of the test that is carried out, before the relevant hallmark is applied.

In the UK, it is a legal requirement for all gold jewellery over 1gram and all silver jewellery over 7.78gram to be officially hallmarked by the British Assay Office.

There are four main offices in the UK; all of whom have their own hallmark. All items assayed in Birmingham have an anchor stamped into them; Sheffield a Rose; Edinburgh a castle; and London a leopard.

Even our Silver watches are hallmarked.

All Gold pieces over 1gram are hallmarked.

A 1.3ct Asscher Cut Diamond.

The hallmark includes the purity of the metal: 375 being 9k gold; 750 being 18k gold; and 925 being Sterling Silver. It is also a legal requirement for the hallmark to carry the sponsor's mark; this is normally the initials of the jewellery importer or the manufacturer. In the UK there is also an option for the hallmark to carry a year symbol, which is intended to help further generations trace jewellery back to the date it was hallmarked.

ASSCHER CUT

Introduced by the Asscher Brothers of Holland in 1902, the Asscher cut is also referred to as a square emerald cut.

Just like regular emerald cuts, the Asscher cut has cropped corners and stepped facets running parallel to the girdle, up to the table and down to the culet. Its main difference to an emerald cut is that the table is smaller and there are often more steps leading up to it. This cut was very popular in the 1920's but had gone out of fashion until recent years. Interestingly, this cut has been featured in 'Sex and the City' and has been used for many celebrity engagement rings.

ASSCHER, JOSEPH AND ABRAHAM

The Asscher brothers were famous Diamond cutters in Holland; they were the founders of the Royal Asscher Diamond Company in 1854. The brothers were both entrusted to cut the famous Cullinan Diamond by King Edward VII in 1907.

It is reported that the Asscher brothers studied the Diamond for three months before any work was carried out. Eventually Joseph Asscher, who was under extreme pressure due to being tasked with shaping the biggest Diamond in the world, took his cleaving knife and hammer to the rough Diamond: to his horror his first strike completely broke the cleaving knife, but luckily the Diamond remained undamaged! At the second attempt, the Diamond split perfectly; however, due to the immense pressure he was under, Joseph is alleged to have fainted.

ASTERISM

An optical phenomenon displayed mainly in certain translucent to opaque Sapphires and Rubies, whereby a four or six ray star seems to appear beneath the surface of the gem, which will normally float across the surface of the gem as the light source moves. To observe the effect it is best to view it under a single light source and slowly rock the gem backwards and forwards. The star is caused by "tube like" fibrous inclusions in the gem, which are all arranged parallel to one another. Prior to shining a light source on the gem, it looks quite normal; simply a regular coloured translucent to opaque gem. But as soon as the light is applied, it reflects off the tips of the inclusions and the star is revealed.

A 5ct Sri Lankan Star Sapphire showing six rays.

To maximise the star, the Lapidarist will cabochon cut the gem. Prior to making their first cut, they will study the gem to predict where the asterism will take place, trying to ensure that it appears as close to the top of the dome as possible.

Possibly the most famous of all Star Sapphires is the Star of India. Weighing a huge 563 carats, it is a stunning gemstone and on a recent visit to the Natural History Museum in New York, I was amazed at how long I had to queue just to walk past this star attraction. The gem was donated to the museum in 1900 by the banker J P Morgan. In 1964 the gem was stolen from the museum by an infamous high profiled burglar known as "Murph the Surf" (his real name was Jack Murphy). Luckily for the museum, who were highly embarrassed by their breach of security, the $400,000 gem was later recovered in Miami.

A pair of Burmese Star Rubies.

AUSTRALIA

Although a recently new country in terms of inhabitants, some of the oldest rocks on the planet have been discovered in Australia. This includes a Zircon discovered at Jackson Hills in Western Australia, which has been scientifically dated to have formed 4.4 billion years ago, right near the time the Earth itself was being formed.

Mookite: exclusively Australian.

In July 1994, the Opal was declared as Australia's National Gemstone. Not surprising when you realise that the country supplies more than 90% of the world's gem-quality Opals. Mining for Opals isn't restricted to one area either, but takes place virtually all over the country.

It is believed that Opals were first discovered in Australia in the 1840's by a German gemmologist named Professor Johannes Menge, approximately 50 miles north of the then capital of South Australia, Adelaide. In the 1870's, while samples of the gem had been sent to the UK for evaluation, the first registered mining leases were being signed in the town of Quilpie (later famous for the 'Pride of the Hills' Opal mine).

Around 1900 Black Opals were discovered by children playing outdoors at Lightning Ridge (thank goodness they didn't have computer games in those days, or we may never have found this fantastic gemstone). Mining in the region at the famous "Shallow Nobby's Mine" started in 1903 after a miner by the name of Charlie Nettleton walked 400 miles to set up his operation. The mine is still in operation today.

In 1915, teenager Willie Hutchinson discovered an Opal in South Australia, which led to the establishment of the world's largest Opal mine named "Coober Pedy" - which, believe it or not, originates from aboriginal dialect meaning "white man in a hole". Today it's a lot more than just a 'white man in a hole', as the town with its 45 different nationalities is based both above and below ground. Underground in its Opal mines can be found: a museum, houses, gift shops and even a hotel. As far as mines go, Coober Pedy really is a rare place!

Sapphires and Diamonds are also mined in commercial quantities and Australia is the only country where Mookite is found. Emerald, Agate, Jade, Zircon and Chrysoprase are also found in smaller quantities.

Whilst Opal mining always used to be the main gem topic in any Australian Bar, today talk of the Argyle Diamond Mine in north-west Australia

In 1994 Opal was declared as the national gemstone of Australia.

Coober Pedy is one of the strangest gemstone mining towns on the planet!

Coober Pedy, not much to see above ground.

is rife. This Diamond mine in the region of Kimberley is said to now be the biggest single producer of Diamonds in the world.

When the mine first opened in 1985, most of the workforce was flown to the mine on a weekly basis from Perth. Over time, as the mine became established, the local towns have become more populated and now most workers have relocated.

As well as being the world's largest Diamond mine, locals claim that it is also responsible for around 90% of the world's supply of natural Pink Diamonds. What is also quite unusual about Argyle, is that it is one of the few Diamond deposits that is not hosted in kimberlite.

Australia is becoming famous for its beautiful Pink Sapphire.

AVENTURINE

Aventurine is a member of the Chalcedony Quartz family and is easily identified by its translucent yet sparkling appearance, an appearance that is so striking that its name is also used as a gemstone adjective when describing other gems with a similar sparkling optical effect; "Aventurescence".

Aventurine gets its name from the Italian word "per avventura" - which means "by chance". It is believed that in the 18th century Venetian glass makers accidentally mixed in copper filings while producing their work and the result was a glass that sparkled.

Although green is the predominate colour for this gem, it can also be found in blue, yellow, reddish brown, greenish brown, orange and a most striking pale silvery colour.

Green Aventurine is associated with luck, chance and opportunity and is also believed to increase perception and develop creative insight. Some highly superstitious people never buy a lottery ticket without their lucky Aventurine in their left pocket (the left pocket is chosen because both luck and left start with "L"). Aventurine is also said to increase your libido and with Tourmaline is the anniversary

Colour	Normally green, but occasionally blue, yellow, reddish brown, greenish brown, orange
Family	Quartz
Hardness	6.5
Specific Gravity	2.65 – 2.69
Refractive Index	1.55
Crystal Group	Trigonal
Optical Properties	Its inclusions can make it sparkle
Common Treatments	Sometimes irradiated to change improve colour
Care	Has been reported to fade when left in sunlight for too long
Cleaning Advice	Warm Soapy water
Chemical Composition	SiO_2

A 6ct Aventurine from Brazil.

gemstone for the 8th year of marriage.

Blue Aventurine is said to be a powerful healer that increases positivity and builds inner strength and self discipline. Several people have written that they have felt powerful and assured when wearing blue Aventurine. If you're a non-believer in myths and legends, Aventurine remains a truly beautiful coloured gem, whose lively sparkling mica flecks will have you spellbound.

Aventurine has been set in jewellery for many centuries and as it is typically found in larger sizes than many other gems, has also been used to create vases, bowls and even smoking pipes. Aventurine can be found in Brazil, India, China, Japan, the Ural Mountains in Russia, Tanzania, and the USA.

AVENTURESCENCE

If a gem's surface appearance looks metallic or as if it is painted with glitter, it is said to display aventurescence. This optical effect happens within certain gems which feature a large amount of small disk or plate like inclusions of a mineral with a highly reflective surface (usually haematite, pyrite or goethite). These inclusions act like tiny mirrors and produce one of nature's most fascinating optical affects.

In the mid-18th century, an Italian glass blower was said to have accidentally knocked a jar of copper filings into the molten glass he was using to create vases, and to his surprise the result was a beautiful glass featuring a metallic sparkle. The technique became widely adopted across Europe where it was used to make both jewellery and ornaments.

The glass became known as "ventura", which was derived from the Italian word meaning "by chance". During the following century, a Green Quartz was discovered in Brazil which naturally produced a similar appearance to the Italian glass and was therefore named Aventurine. This is one of the few occasions in gemmology where a gemstone has been named after a man-made item.

In addition to Aventurine, only a handful of other

Even when Sunstone is dyed it still retains its wonderful aventurescence.

gems have been discovered that demonstrate this stunning lively effect. These include three members of the Feldspars family: Moonstone, Sunstone and Labradorite.

AXINITE

'Rare', 'stunningly beautiful' and 'a real collector's gemstone', are the first things that pop into my head when I am asked about Axinite. I first saw a piece of Axinite in the Spring of 2006 and was amazed by its colour, but its incredible rarity meant that it took until April 2009 until I came across it again.

I have just acquired two parcels (April 2009): these are from mines in the Baltistan Valley in Northern Pakistan and are very near to K2 (the second largest mountain in the world). Due to the difficult weather and terrain in the region, it is only possible to operate these Axinite mines for a couple of months every year. The first parcel is from a well established mine that has been producing Axinte for around 15 years. Its colour is a breathtaking dark brown with areas of lilac when viewed from different angles: this material does have inclusions, but this allows the gem to change colour to an almost deep reddish, purple colour. The second parcel is from a fairly new mine: it is a slightly lighter brown with amazing transparency. This parcel was very difficult to get hold of as it is mined in the tribal areas along the undefined border between Afghanistan and Pakistan and my friend Shawn went to great lengths and faced real dangers in order to obtain it for me.

Discovered at the end of the 1700's, Axinite receives its name from the fact that its unusual spatula-shaped crystals are often shaped like an axe! Although it is triclinic (meaning that it does not have an axis of rotation), it benefits from a centre of symmetry (basically meaning that the crystal structure will have a similar face on one side to the other, but it is inverted both left to right and up and down).

A small amount of gem-quality Axinte has also been found in Mexico, the USA, France and Switzerland.

Colour	Yellow to Brown
Family	Axinite
Hardness	6.5 - 7
Specific Gravity	3.29
Refractive Index	1.67 - 1.68
Crystal Group	Triclinic
Optical Properties	Strongly Pleochroic
Common Treatments	None
Care	None
Cleaning Advice	Warm soapy water
Chemical Composition	Complex

A 3.4 Axinite from the original mine near K2.

A very rare Axinite discovered between Afghanistan and Pakistan.

AZTECS

On arriving in America in the late 1400's, Spanish adventurers found two well-developed civilisations in the mid to southern regions of the country; the Incas in Peru and the often dangerous Aztec warriors of Mexico.

The reason we mention this in a gem and jewellery book, is that they were both deeply religious cultures and many of the beliefs and stories relating to the healing properties of gems originate from these civilisations.

Another reason for discussing the Aztecs, is that their influence over jewellery design can still be seen in many pieces today. So fanatical were they with jewellery and gemstones, that many neighbouring countries constantly worried about the threat of attack from Aztecs in search of new minerals. Not only did they craft jewellery for personal adornment and as display of authority, many would make an offering of their jewellery to their gods.

AZURITE

Colour	Blue
Family	Azurite
Hardness	3.5 – 4
Specific Gravity	3.77
Refractive Index	1.7 - 1.8
Crystal Group	Monoclonic
Optical Properties	Often features colourful banding
Common Treatments	None
Care	Very sensitive to heat
Cleaning Advice	Cool soapy water
Chemical Composition	$Cu_3(CO_3)$

Azurite is an intensely deep-blue copper mineral, which is produced by weathered copper ore deposits. It is also known as Chessylite after the name of the mine in which it was found in Lyon, France. Historically, the gem has been set into jewellery as well as being used by the Japanese as a blue pigment in paintings. It was also mentioned by its previous name "Kuanos" by Pliny the Elder (author and philosopher AD23 – 79). However, the gem's vivid blue colour tends to diminish over time, especially when exposed to heat and light, and therefore is rarely used in jewellery today.

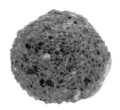

One of the most famous specimens of Azurite is known as the "Newmont Azurite". Originally discovered in Nambia in 1952, the gem was unusual for this variety in that it was over eight inches long. The miner who discovered it allegedly smuggled the gem out of the mine and sold it to pay off his tab at his local tavern.

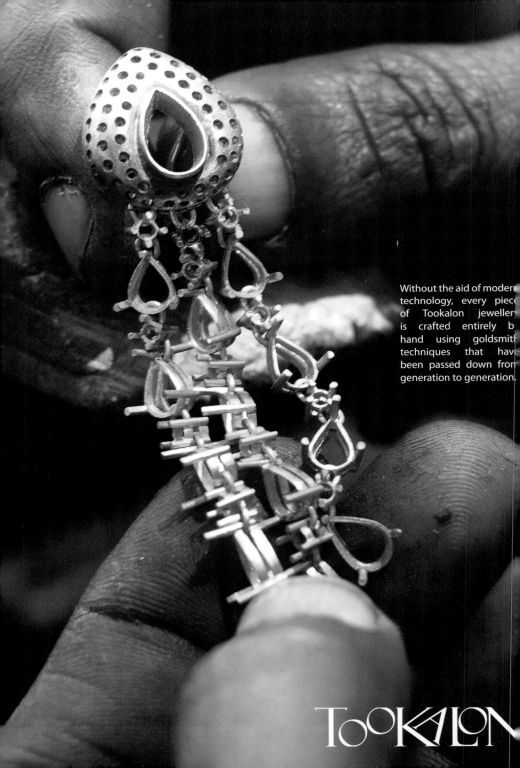

Without the aid of modern technology, every piece of Tookalon jewellery is crafted entirely by hand using goldsmith techniques that have been passed down from generation to generation.

TOOKALON

A Baguette Cut Black Onyx ring set in Sterling Silver.

BAGUETTE CUT

Any gem that is cut into a shape that is thin and long, with parallel facets is regarded as a baguette (or rectangle) cut. Normally a baguette cut would be a step cut and not a brilliant cut gem. The word comes from the French word for stick or rod; this is why French bread is known as a baguette.

The cut is often used on gems where their crystal structure is naturally oblong. When set at right angles to the band of gold in a solitaire ring it can help elongate the look of the finger. The cut is increasing in popularity for channel set Diamond rings, where baguette cut gems are tightly set parallel to each other.

Baguette cuts, as they do not have lots of facets, do not return much brilliance or fire. The cut looks extremely modern and is wonderful at highlighting clarity and depth of colour.

BANGLE

Bangles are solid bracelets worn on the wrist. Normally they feature either a hinge or are able to slip over the wrist - however, some bangles are bent out of shape to get them over the wrist and then bent back into shape to re-secure them.

Bangles are not a new item of jewellery and archaeologists have uncovered bangles made from bones and stones worn by Egyptians over 7000 years ago! Today, with the introduction of techniques for making Palladium and Titanium jewellery, expect to see these strong metals becoming popular in Bangles.

A stunning Pink Sapphire bangle by Jacque Christie.

BARION CUT

First of all the Barion Cut is really more of a family of cuts than an individual cut. Imagine a brilliant cut gemstone constructed with triangular and kite shaped facets and then add facets directly below the crown that look like shape of a quarter moon.

The Barion cut can be applied to rounds, trilliants, ovals, in fact almost any shape where you could create a brilliant cut and to-date over 90 Barion Cuts have been documented.

The Barion cut was invented in 1970 in Johannesburg, South Africa by a Lapidarist named Basil Watermeyer and he named the cut by merging the start of his Christian name with the end of his wife's Marion. Luckily, Watermeyer never registered the Barion as a trademark and openly encourages Lapidaries to use the cut. The cut is very difficult to perform. If you don't get it absolutely symmetrical, the moon-shaped facets can end up looking like a choppy sea! When done properly, the gem's colour will often be increased and the yield (retained carat weight) will normally be higher than a gem of the same size which has been styled in a more traditional cut.

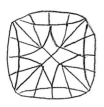

Although the cut is incredibly beautiful, be careful if you are buying a Barion cut loose gemstone with the intention of having it set in jewellery. I would suggest that you may want to speak to your jeweller first as they will normally have to make alterations to the setting to compensate for the non-regular pavilion.

BAR SETTING

Bar setting is similar to channel setting, whereby a single gem or several gems are placed in the channel with supporting metal bars on either side of the stone. It is used when the designer wants to create a look as if the gem is floating.

It differs from tension setting in that the gems are held in a groove and do not rely totally on pressure. As the gems closely butt up to each other at the girdle, there is no metal between the gems. Hence bar setting or channel setting maximises the amount of dispersion and brilliance seen.

Bar set Iolites with Diamond accents.

BAROQUE

The word originates from Portuguese and is usually used to describe Pearls with an irregular shape. However, Pearls don't have exclusive rights on the word: it is also used in music to describe pieces that are elaborate.

Most Freshwater Pearls are Baroque and perfectly rounded ones are extrememely rare. However, Freshwater cultured Pearls tend to be more spherical, as the foreign body injected into the shell (which is used as the catalyst for the Pearl growing process) is normally a perfectly rounded tiny sphere.

BASTNASITE

My close friend Shawn, who is an amazing gem hunter, was born in Pakistan and earlier this year travelled to his home country in search of gem rough. His quest took him into the remote Zagi Mountains where he came across miners hunting a gem known as Bastnäsite.

Baroque Peals by Annabella.

This brown gemstone, which looks similar in appearance to a translucent Smokey Quartz, was first unearthed in Sweden in the early 1800's and was named after the Bastnäs Mine where it was discovered.

Although not a rare mineral (Bastnäsite can be found in many places including America, Africa, China and Mongolia), 'gem quality' material is virtually unheard of. So far we have only acquired several pieces, however Shawn is planning another trip soon and we hope to be able to discover more pieces in the future.

This piece is possibly the rarest Bastnasite on the planet weighing 10.4 cts!

BEADS

When mining for gems, it is common to find a mixture of qualities. While the very best gems are set into rings, pendants and earrings, others that are not to the same exacting standards are often faceted into the shape of a bead, and then drilled to make bracelets and necklaces.

Other types of beads often used in costume jewellery can include glass, plastic, stones, ceramics and wood. Although discoveries in burial sites have shown that beads were used in jewellery thousands of years ago ago, we are unsure whether this primitive form of jewellery was for personal adornment or simply used as a talisman, to protect the wearer.

2 Tiger's Eye beaded bracelets by Jessica Lili.

BEAUTY

For any mineral to be regarded as a gem, anyone in the gem industry will tell you that it must be durable, rare and, above all, beautiful. As "beauty is in the eye of the beholder" and as we all have a different perception of what is beautiful, it is certainly the most difficult of the three requirements to define. In a Diamond, beauty is often measured by its clearness: the clearer it is, the more valuable it is. Coloured gemstones on the other hand, primarily have their beauty judged by the vividness of their colour.

When we see beauty it awakens our feel-good

Just a few of the glorious colours given to us by Mother Nature.

senses. Beauty can be observed in many things including culture, nature, the opposite sex, clothes, jewellery and, of course, gemstones. What makes gemstones more glamorous than almost any other item on earth is the rareness of their beauty. Only when a multitude of necessary chemical elements, the right environment, the correct pressure and the right temperature are combined together - and all for the required period - is Mother Nature able to create such beautifully colourful, natural and rare treasures.

When we think of an object as beautiful it normally means that we are attracted to its colour, shape, style and design. But beauty in gemstones often goes deeper. The beauty derived from knowing the mystery, magic, folklore, legends and history surrounding coloured gemstones is unrivalled by any other purchasable item.

One final thought: the beauty experienced in a place, person or object often makes us feel happiness and warmth, and this feeling is amplified by our memories and past experiences. Let me give you two examples. Firstly, I find my personal gem collection grows more and more beautiful as I gain a stronger and stronger understanding about the gems. The more I research them, the better I know the myths and legends surrounding them, the more beautiful they somehow appear to me. Secondly, I believe that pieces of jewellery that have been received as a gift on special occasions and anniversaries, plus those that have been passed on from previous generations, have an additional inherent beauty.

BENITOITE

When a friend called me up and told me he had been offered a gemstone bearing my name, I thought I had better check it out. As it turned out there was good news and bad news. Unfortunately, like me, my friend is a lousy speller and the gem's name is actually "Benitoite" and not "Bennettoite" (in fairness it is pronounced "ben-ee-toe-ite")! But the good news was that this was to be an introduction to one of the most fascinating and one of the rearest gems that I have ever had the pleasure of adding to my collection.

Colour	Blue
Family	Benitoite
Hardness	6 - 6.5
Specific Gravity	3.68
Refractive Index	1.75 - 1.8
Crystal Group	Hexagonal
Optical Properties	Strongly Pleochroic
Common Treatments	None
Cleaning Advice	Warm soapy water
Care	No special care needed
Chemical Composition	$BaTiSi_3O_9$

Imagine a colour of a light blue Sapphire, combined with the fire of a Diamond and the rarity of winning the lottery 10 times in a row! That's Benitoite! Most pieces faceted around the globe to-date weigh less than 0.5ct and are Swiss blue in appearance and have a slightly cloudy clarity. However, just recently I managed to acquire one piece, which has incredible clarity and a colour similar to that of the finest Kashmir Sapphire. It also weighs a very impressive 0.75ct. I have shown this piece to several of my friends in the trade and every one of them has commented that it is probably the finest piece ever faceted!

One of the rarest gemstones on the planet, this museum worthy Benitoite weighs 0.74ct

First discovered by a gentleman named James Couch in 1907 near the San Benito River in California (hence its name), the gem was originally thought to be a Sapphire. However, shortly after the initial discovery, several tiny pieces were sent to the university of California and a mineralogist named Dr George Louderback identified the specimen as a brand new mineral. In 1985, as 'gem-quality' Benitoite had still only ever been discovered in California, the then Governor George Deukmejian passed a bill formally designating the gem as the official gemstone of California.

For 102 years this gem has been highly prized by gem collectors and mineralogists alike and yet only a handful of top quality pieces have ever been faceted. If you ever visit Coloured Rocks, be sure to ask to see my piece of Benitoite.

BERYL

The Beryl family boasts some of the finest and most historical of gems available. When green, it is referred to as Emerald; when red, Bixbite; when blue, Aquamarine; when colourless, Goshenite; and when yellow it is known as Heliodor, Yellow or Golden Beryl.

The name is derived from the Greek "beryllos", which was used when referring to gems with a precious blue-green colour. In its pure form the gem is colourless, and it is due to different impurities that provide Beryl with its varied offspring.

Colour	Pure Beryl is colourless
Family	Beryl
Hardness	7 – 8
Specific Gravity	2.63 – 2.9
Refractive Index	1.57 – 1.9
Crystal Group	Hexagonal
Optical Properties	Vitreous lustre
Common Treatments	Heating
Care	No special care needed
Cleaning Advice	Warm soapy water
Chemical Composition	$Be_3Al_2(SiO_3)_6$

Pure Beryl is known as Goshenite.

Worn in jewellery for centuries, historical references of this gem can be found in the Bible (Ezekiel 1:16), "the wheels of God's throne are described as having the appearance of gleaming beryl".

The latest addition to the Beryl family is pink Beryl, which was discovered by G.F Kunz in 1911. He named it Morganite after the famous banker J.P Morgan, who was both an avid gem collector and one of Tiffany's (for whom Kunz worked) largest customers.

Members of the Beryl family are mined in several locations: Afghanistan, Brazil, Madagascar, Pakistan, Russia, South Africa and Zambia.

BEZEL SETTING

Often used in gents' jewellery, and for softer or more fragile gemstones, the bezel set holds the gemstone by surrounding it with a band of metal, slightly shaped over the top of the girdle, thus securing the gem. Historically the word "bezel" was used as an alternative name for the crown of a gem (the facets leading from the girdle to the table) and hence the name of the setting.

A bezel set, marquise cut Amethyst.

Bezel settings have been used to hold gemstones in rings since circa 1100AD and are sometimes referred to as a collet settings.

A variant of the bezel setting is the semi-bezel which is where the bezel does not continue all the way around the gem. A semi-bezel setting can emphasise the style of certain designs and also allows more light to enter the gemstone than a full bezel setting.

BIREFRINGENCE

Also referred to as double refraction, birefringence is the splitting of a single ray of light into two rays.

A Red Zircon perfectly demonstrating birefringence.

Double refraction is often beautiful to observe and is best witnessed in Zircon. As the light splits in a faceted gemstone, it hits the inside of the pavilion facets and bounces around like an image in a hall of mirrors. The effect seen when studying a gem that has birefringence through its table and crown facets is incredibly beautiful. In addition to Zircon, the effect can also be seen in Calcite and Moissanite (a man-made gemstone that is sold as a replacement to Diamond).

All birefringent gemstones have two different refractive indices; this makes the optical phenomena very useful for gem dealers to correctly identify certain man-made fakes from real gemstones. In order to measure birefringence, a gem is placed in a refractometer and two readings are taken.

Here, I am learning to use a refractometer in an African gem lab.

BIRTHSTONES

The origin of birthstones is believed to be linked to the breastplate of Aaron. The 1st century historian Josephus (also known as Yosef Ben Matityahu) and St Jerome in the 5th century both wrote about the connection between the breastplate of Aaron and the twelve months of the year. That said, it was not until the sixteenth century in Poland that the wearing of birthstones for the particular month in which you were born became recognised. Prior to this period it is believed that many people acquired twelve different gems and wore them one by one, changing them on the first day of every month.

Over the centuries different countries and different religions have made various alterations to the list. George Kunz in his book "The Curious Lore of Precious Stones" collated various birthstone charts and as it the most comprehensive list we've found, we have included it at the top of the adjacent page.

In 1912, the American National Jewelers' Association compiled a new birthstone list, replacing many of the historical gemstone names with their current names, and in 1938 The American Gem Society made several further amendments. In 1952, the Jewelry Industry Council of America sponsored the birthstone list which remains until this today (with the exception of Tanzanite, which was only discovered in 1967 and was added to the official birthstone list on the 30th of October 2002).

Month	Romans	Isidore Bishop of Seville	Arabians	Poles	Russians	Italians
January	Garnet	Hyacinth	Garnet	Garnet	Garnet Hyacinth	Jacinth Garnet
February	Amethyst	Amethyst	Amethyst	Amethyst	Amethyst	Amethyst
March	Jasper	Bloodstone	Jasper	Bloodstone	Bloodstone	Jasper
April	Sapphire	Sapphire	Sapphire	Sapphire	Diamond	Sapphire
May	Chalcedony Carnelian Agate	Agate	Agate	Emerald	Emerald	Emerald
June	Emerald	Emerald	Emerald	Agate Chalcedony Pearl	Agate Chalcedony	Agate Chalcedony
July	Onyx	Onyx	Onyx	Carnelian	Ruby	Ruby Sardonyx
August	Carnelian	Carnelian	Carnelian	Sardonyx	Sardonyx	Alexandrite
September	Chrysolite	Sardonyx	Chrysolite	Chrysolite	Sardonyx	Chrysolite
October	Aquamarine	Aquamarine	Aquamarine	Aquamarine	Aquamarine	Beryl
November	Topaz	Topaz	Topaz	Topaz	Topaz	Topaz
December	Ruby	Ruby	Ruby	Ruby	Turquoise	Turquoise Chrysoprase

Month	Associated Gemstone
January	Garnet
February	Amethyst
March	Aquamarine or Bloodstone
April	Diamond
May	Emerald
June	Pearl, Moonstone or Alexandrite
July	Ruby
August	Peridot
September	Sapphire
October	Opal or Tourmaline
November	Topaz or Citrine
December	Turquoise, Zircon or Tanzanite

Nowadays there is no excuse not to invest in birthstones. Historically some of the gemstones were often unavailable in many countries and others were not suitable for setting. Today, even though Alexandrite, Spinel and Tanzanite can sometimes be difficult to find, most months now have more than one gem associated with them, leaving us little excuse for not having at least a few pieces of our birthstone in our jewellery box. .

Even with the many changes over the centuries, millions of people still believe in the positive power of wearing your correct birthstone as a talisman. Nobody can deny the positive effects felt when wearing the correct birthstone, even if it is purely because of a placebo.

If those who wear birthstones as amulets and talisman feel strong enough about their beliefs, can the results really be questioned?

Tomas Rae.

4ct Swiss Blue Topaz Pendant
Featuring 30 Diamonds
£76

Colour	Orangey red, red, purple red
Family	Beryl
Hardness	7.5 – 8.0
Specific Gravity	2.66 – 2.70
Refractive Index	1.567 – 1.580
Crystal Group	Hexagonal
Optical Properties	None
Common Treatments	Colourless oil and resin
Care	No special care needed
Cleaning Advice	Warm soapy water
Chemical Composition	$Be_3(AlMn)_2Si_6O_{18}$

Colour	Black
Family	Diamond
Hardness	10
Specific Gravity	3.5
Refractive Index	2.41
Crystal Group	Cubic
Optical Properties	Strong lustre
Common Treatments	Often irradiated
Care	No special care needed
Cleaning Advice	Ultrasonic, steam cleaning or warm soapy water
Chemical Composition	C (Carbon)

BIXBITE

Also known as Red Emerald and Scarlet Emerald, Bixbite is regarded by many as the rarest member of the Beryl family of gemstones. The gem is named in honour of the legendary mineralogist Maynard Bixby (1853 – 1935) of Utah, America, who was believed to have first discovered the gem in 1904.

Many gems marketed as Bixbite are in fact a different gem known as Pezzottaite. The confusion arises as both their chemical construction and appearance are almost identical. Bixbite, however, is currently only mined in two locations on the planet: the Wah Wah Mountains in Utah, America and also in the Catron and Sierra Counties within New Mexico. Pezzottaite, on the other hand, was first discovered in Madagascar in 2002, although the mines are now said to be depleted; luckily there has been a recent discovery in Afghanistan.

The gem's stunning red appearance is due to the presence of manganese, and even though the gem is normally heavily included and at best translucent, many collectors regard the gem as a greater acquisition than Ruby.

BLACK DIAMOND

Black Diamonds are a stunning and very fashionable variety of Diamond. Although it lacks dispersion and the internal brilliance of its colourless sister, a quality Black Diamond has the ability to display an intense surface lustre, with an almost metallic shimmer.

Natural Black Diamonds are extremely hard and beautiful, and are found predominantly in Africa. As with all Diamonds, they were formed in the earth many millions of years ago and have been pushed to the Earth's surface by volcanic eruptions.

Black Diamonds have become increasingly popular in recent years. Although not strictly black, they contain numerous dark inclusions that give this Diamond its characteristic black look. Many Black Diamonds undergo treatment to intensify the blackness of their colour.

BLACK GEMS AND ASSOCIATIONS

Black is the ultimate dark colour that conveys elegance, although strictly speaking it is not truly a colour at all. Black gems, as with any object that is black, do not reflect any visible light. Coloured gemstones obtain their colour by the way their atoms absorb and reflect different colours of the spectrum. A red gem, such as a Ruby, absorbs all of the green and blue colours of the spectrum and reflects only the red rays, while colourless gemstones such as Diamonds and Zircon reflect all colours of the spectrum. Black gems on the other hand, absorb all colours and therefore none are reflected back to the eye.

In ancient times, when men wore black they were said to have good sense and fortitude, while single women wearing the colour were said to be fickle and foolish (don't shoot the messenger! I'm just quoting ancient history: when women wear black today they are not foolish at all, quite the opposite). When married women wore the colour however, it stood for perseverance and constant love. The colour was also associated with Saturdays and the planet Saturn.

Black is also the colour of rebellion, which could be true in the gem world as there are so few gems that are naturally black; indeed, these could be deemed as nature's rebellions. Only a handful of gems found on Earth are naturally true black: Jet and Haematite. Black Onyx is actually a Chalcedony, which has been dyed using a technique that is over 2000 years old. The black gem Tektite was created millions of years ago when a meteorite fell to earth and morphed with Earth's rock to create one of the few out-of-space gems. Black Diamonds are rarely strictly black, as they nearly always feature dark inclusions which create an appearance similar to that of a black raven feather with a shimmering black lustre.

Black Diamonds displaying an intense surface lustre.

Black Onyx is dyed using ancient dyeing techniques.

The metallic sheen of Haematite.

viorelli

www.viorelli.com

BLOODSTONE

Treasured in ancient times, Bloodstone (also known as Heliotrope) served as the birthstone for March, until it was replaced in 1912 by Aquamarine. Once referred to as the martyr's stone, medieval Christians often carved Bloodstone into scenes of the crucifixion. According to legend, the origin of this gemstone formed when Christ's blood fell to the foot of the cross, staining Jasper below. A fine example of carved Bloodstone can be found in the Louvre featuring a seal of the German Emperor Rudolf II.

The virtues ascribed to this gem are that it is good for circulation of both energy and blood in the body. It is said to aid in the removal of energy blocks, and placing several pieces of this gemstone in the home is suggested to enhance the flow of life energy.

Bloodstone is a member of the Chalcedony group of gems, who in turn belong to the cryptocrystalline family of Quartz. The gem is mined in the USA, Brazil, China, India and Australia.

Colour	Red, green, bluish green, all with red spots
Family	Cryptocrystalline Quartz
Hardness	6.5
Specific Gravity	2.59 – 2.60
Refractive Index	1.535 - 1.539
Crystal Group	Trigonal
Optical Properties	Features colourful spots
Common Treatments	None
Care	No special care needed
Cleaning Advice	Ultrasonic or warm soapy water
Chemical Composition	SiO_2

Bloodstone.

BLUE DIAMOND

Natural fancy-coloured Diamonds are amongst the most expensive and valuable of all gemstones. Coloured Diamonds, especially Blue Diamonds, are becoming increasingly popular with collectors and celebrities.

Nothing quite matches a Blue Diamond in colour: being comparable to a crossbreed of the deepest London Blue Topaz and darkest Santa Maria Aquamarine, it really does have a uniqueness all of its own. Highly prized, Blue Diamonds are exceptionally rare and historically could cost up to 20 times more than white Diamonds of the same clarity and carat weight. Today, some colourless Diamonds have the ability to be turned blue through treatments.

The most famous Blue Diamond of all time is the Hope Diamond.

A striking Blue and Black 1ct Diamond Ring.

A rare AAA vivid Blue Tanzanite.

The vibrant blues of Swiss Blue Topaz.

BLUE GEMS AND ASSOCIATIONS

Reputedly the most popular male colour, blue promotes calmness and tranquillity and is aesthetically perceived as a cool colour. It lowers the heart rate and breathing, and is also believed to suppress appetite.

When a man wears blue he is said to be wise and thoughtful; a lady in blue is said to be polite and vigilant. The colour is associated with Friday and the planet Venus.

When it comes to blue gems there are several to choose from, the most famous being Sapphire. Although today Sapphires have been discovered in many different colours and hues, historically it was believed that the only colour Sapphires could be found in was blue. Since its discovery in 1967, Tanzanite has now become possibly the most sought after of all blue gemstones.

If you are looking for a light blue gem with great clarity, then March's birthstone Aquamarine might be your preferred choice. Topaz is another gem that is available in blue and is given different prefixes, dependent on its shade. Sky Blue Topaz is the name given to the lighter of the Topaz shades, Swiss Blue refers to medium shades and dark blue is known as London Blue Topaz.

The ultimate collectable of all blue gemstones has to be Benitoite. This gemstone is incredibly rare and has an appearance similar to Tanzanite, but is so rare that it is approximately a million times rarer than Diamond.

Other blue gems include Iolite and Kyanite; sometimes Zircon, Diamond and Spinel can be found in blue. For many years Garnet was said to come in every colour except blue; however, everything changed recently when there was such a discovery in Madagascar.

Not all blue gems however are transparent: Turquoise, Sodalite, and Amazonite are all attractive opaque blue stones. Probably the most collectable opaque blue gem at the moment is known as Larimar.

Natural blues of Turquoise.

Make
Everyday
A Glamour
day

Jacque Christie

BLUE MOONSTONE QUARTZ

One of the most intriguing discoveries in Brazil over the past 10 years is the small deposit of Blue Moonstone Quartz in one of the oldest gemstone mines in South Brazil. Some 30 feet underground in a small area known as "The Urugaena", a thin seam of slightly grey Quartz was discovered. At first it didn't look that exciting underground says the mine owner; 'under mining lighting it appeared a greyish material with white bands and slightly smoky zoning, however when it was brought to the surface it had the appearance like that of a cross between Moonstone and Blue Fire Opal, it's truly a real treasure and a heavenly gemstone.'

My good friends who facet the gemstone tell me that to get the very best out of the gemstone and to maximise its milky look that appears to mix Moonstone with Fire Opal, you have to be very patient when studying the rough, being sure to view it from every single angle before making the first cut. Get it right and the gemstone is truly beautiful, get it wrong and it just doesn't have the same gorgeous almost magical appearance.

Blue Moonstone Quartz has so far only been discovered in Brazil and locals believe that the gemstone instils and nurtures love and also puts you at peace with nature.

Colour	Blue
Family	Quartz
Hardness	7
Specific Gravity	2.66
Refractive Index	1.5 - 1.55
Crystal Group	Hexagonal
Common Treatments	Heat
Care	None
Cleaning Advice	Ultrasonic or warm soapy water
Chemical Composition	SiO_2

BLUE GARNET

Garnet was said to be available in "all colours except blue". That is, until its discovery in 1998 in the Bekily mines located in south Madagascar. What is even more exceptional about this gem is that it is a colour change gemstone - similar to Alexandrite - but in this instance the change is from a blue to a stunning purplish pink.

Similar to Malaia Garnet, the gem is a blend between Pyrope and Spessartine Garnets. The colour change is more pronounced than that of Alexandrite and is caused by the presence of vanadium.

Colour	Pale blue to mauve
Family	Garnet is a family in its own right
Hardness	6.5 – 7.5
Specific Gravity	3.4 – 4.3
Refractive Index	1.7 – 1.89
Crystal Group	Some Garnets are Isometric & some cubic
Optical Properties	Various
Common Treatments	Cannot be heat treated
Care	No special care needed

Colour	Pale blue to deep rich midnight blue
Family	Corundum
Hardness	9
Specific Gravity	3.9 – 4.1
Refractive Index	1.76 – 1.77
Crystal Group	Trigonal
Optical Properties	Strong pleochroism
Common Treatments	Normally heat treated
Cleaning Advice	Ultrasonic, Steam Cleaning or Warm soapy Water
Care	No special care needed
Chemical Composition	Al_2O_3

Colour	Pale sky blue to deep rich blue
Family	Topaz
Hardness	8
Specific Gravity	3.5 – 3.6
Refractive Index	1.6 – 1.63
Crystal Group	Orthorhombic
Optical Properties	Strong pleochroism
Common Treatments	Normally heat treated
Care	No special care needed
Cleaning Advice	Warm soapy water
Chemical Composition	$Al_2SiO_4(OH,F)_2$

BLUE SAPPHIRE

Blues are still amongst the most popular and sought after type of Sapphire and have been the prized possessions of emperors, kings, queens and collectors for thousands of years. Of all the coloured gemstones it is possibly the most renowned and demanded. Royalty have been known to give Sapphires over Diamonds as engagement rings because they are known to be far rarer than the latter. The most notable producer of fine Blue Sapphires is Sri Lanka and it is often referred to by its previous name Ceylon Sapphire.

As Sapphire is renowned for being blue, when the word is used without a colour prefix, it is assumed that one is talking about Blue Sapphire. All other colours are regarded as "fancy Sapphires" and should be prefixed with their colour. Just as in the wine world it is improper to say Chardonnay Chablis, it would be equally wrong to say Blue Sapphire when describing the Blue variety: being politically correct you simply say Sapphire.

BLUE TOPAZ

Blue was once amongst the rarest colour to be seen in Topaz. Today, however, gem experts are able to turn the colourless variety into an array of glorious blues through treatments. The technique they use is similar to that which naturally occurs in several areas of Brazil, where Blue Topaz has been discovered naturally. There are three stunning Blue Topaz colours: Sky Blue; London Blue and Swiss Blue:

London Blue Topaz

London Blue Topaz is generally the darkest shade of the Blue Topaz and is incredibly striking, with a colour reminiscent to the deeper areas of the Mediterranean Sea.

Swiss Blue

This name is give to Blue Topaz which are lighter than London Blue Topaz but darker in colour than Sky Blue Topaz.

Sky Blue Topaz

This is the lightest variety of Blue Topaz and when they have great clarity can look similar to Aquamarine.

BLUE TOURMALINE

Although Tourmaline is available in a wider spectrum of colours than almost any other gem variety, not all are so frequently found. Pure Blue Tourmalines are incredibly rare and more often than not tend to be a greenish blue. In some gem circles the dark blue variety is renamed Indicolite. Don't expect to see these in high street shop windows, as they really are only discovered as one-off pieces!

A rare, vividly coloured 1.8ct Indicolite.

BOLIVIA

Currently the only source of Ametrine in the world is found at the Anahi Mine located in the province of Santa Cruz in Eastern Bolivia. Just like the mines in neighbouring Brazil, Bolivia also provides naturally occurring Citrines and dark, vivid Amethyst.

A very rare, bi-coloured Amethyst from Bolivia.

Ametrine, which is half Citrine and half Amethyst, first appeared set in jewellery in the 1970's. But soon after its discovery, some gem experts claimed that the gem's unusual bi-colour effect was artificially created in laboratories and as a result the gem lost popularity. Once it was proven that this was not the case and the bi-colour was in fact due to a natural phenomenon occurring only in this one region of the world, demand for this unusual gem started to increase.

As the gem is mined in just one location, from time to time the owners of the Anahi mine seem to deliberately cut back on excavation so as to ensure there is less supply for the gem than there is demand. If you think that's a bit naughty, it's nothing in comparison to what has happened with Diamonds over the years!

A rare, bi-coloured Citrine from Bolivia.

A hand-made Mother of Pearl bracelet from Tookalon.

BRACELET

A bracelet is an item of jewellery that is worn around the wrist and can be made out of various materials, including silver, gold, plastic and metal. The name bracelet comes from the Latin word "brachile" which means "of the arm."

Egypt is believed to be the country which invented the original bracelet, but not as we know it today. Egyptians would use bones, stones and wood, strung together with animal hair. The earliest bracelets are believed to date back as far as 2500BC; when women wore bracelets in this period it was primarily to show how wealthy their husbands were. It wasn't until approximately 200BC that bracelets were first believed to have being worn purely for personal adornment.

There are different types of bracelets that are known and worn today, one of which is the charm bracelet, which archaeological discoveries have found were worn by the Pharaohs. Charms were believed to bring good luck, and men would use any materials they could beg, borrow or steal, with the belief that once made into a charm they would ward off any evil spirits.

Bracelets will always be a part of our culture and as fashion changes so do the different styles of bracelets. For example, the Romans and Greeks wore short sleeved shirts, making the wearing of bracelets on the upper and lower arm popular. In Victorian times, Marcasite bracelets set with big gems such as Jasper and Jet were highly fashionable. Today, gents Titanium bracelets are fashionable and ladies charm bracelets are back in fashion and hotter than ever before

BRAZIL

The fourth largest country in the world, Brazil is not only the number one source of Emerald, but also home to possibly the widest array of coloured gemstones seen in one area. Tourmaline, Chrysoberyl, Alexandrite, Topaz, Quartz, Amethyst and Citrine, and a host of other glorious gemstones, are currently mined in the country.

The state of Minas Gerais (which translates to General Mines) is probably the best known of the 26 Brazilian states with regards to gems. Located on the West Coast, it is believed that millions of years ago this area was connected to Africa. Given the similarity of gems found in these two now distant continents, it would be difficult to argue otherwise.

While panning for gold in 1714, Diamonds were discovered in the region for the first time. When news of the find reached the Portuguese government, they announced that the mines were a property of the crown and made the area a no-go zone for miners, insisting that all gems and gold found would belong to the royals. In 1720, Portuguese Colonists created the Minas Gerais state, and the first official gold mine was opened one year prior when the Passagem Gold Mine was established. Shortly after Topaz was discovered in the region, Amethyst, Aquamarine, Citrine, Chrysoberyl, Diamond, Emerald, Kunzite, Morganite, and Tourmaline were discovered.

Christ the Redeemer, Rio de Janeiro, Brazil.

The gem-bearing pegmatites (a course grained rock in which gems are often discovered) in Minas Gerais are considered amongst the most important in the world. The hilly landscape in the region, caused by the erosion of softer materials, has left many pegmatites for gemmologists and miners to explore.

Today, most of the mining in Minas Gerais, similar to that in Afghanistan and Madagascar, is done by small-scale artisanal miners (informal mining). These entrepreneurial individuals or small teams work in alluvial gravel deposits and in stream beds, with very little technology and often still pan for gems in the way you will have seen in Western movies with people panning for gold. Their lifestyle is considered better than that of subsistence farming; there is always the belief and potential that a substantial reward will be discovered tomorrow!

Brazil is one of the largest exporters of cut Emeralds in the world and is also famous for its neon green and swimming pool blue Tourmalines, known as Paraiba Tourmalines.

Brazil: a gemstone treasure chest.

Paraiba Tourmaline was originally discovered in the Paraiba state of Brazil.

Although Citrine is normally created by heating Amethyst, Brazil (along with the Isle of Arran in Scotland) is one of the few places in the world where the gem can be discovered in its natural yellow colour.

Whilst being one of the most important sources of rough gemstones, the country hasn't been associated with quality gem cutting. Today, however we are seeing much more investment in training in gem cutting.

BREASTPLATE OF AARON

It is believed that the tradition of birthstones arose from the Breastplate of Aaron, a ceremonial religious garment that was set with twelve gemstones that represented the twelve tribes of Israel and which also corresponded with the twelve signs of the zodiac and the twelve months of the year. It is referred to in the book of Exodus in the Old Testament of the Bible and was made for Moses' brother Aaron and his sons to be worn as a garment so they could serve as priests.

Taken from Exodus:

"It is to be square – a span long and a span wide and folded double. Then mount four rows of precious stones on it".

"In the first row there shall be a Ruby, a Topaz and a Beryl; in the second row a Turquoise, a Sapphire and an Emerald; in the third row a Jacinth, an Agate and an Amethyst; in the fourth row a Chrystolite, an Onyx and a Jasper".

The Breastplate of Aaron is of interest to gem lovers as it is an early account of the use of gemstones as both decoration and symbolism. The breastplate is described in the Bible as the "Breastplate of Judgement" or the "Breastplate of Decision". As they used ancient biblical descriptions for the gems, unfortunately it is difficult for translators to determine several of those used with exact certainty. Therefore, the list of gems varies slightly depending on which translation is used.

An artist's impression of the Breastplate of Aaron.

BRILLIANCE

There are three main terms used to describe the way light interacts with a gemstone: 'lustre', the surface reflection of light; 'dispersion', when light inside certain gemstones is split into the colours of the rainbow; and 'brilliance', the return of light to the eye from within the gemstone (hence why it is also known as 'internal lustre').

Everyone who collects gemstones will have their own views about what attracts them to certain coloured stones and not to others; I for one can't always put my finger on why I love certain gems in my collection more than others. However, an interwoven mixture of a gem's colour, clarity and cut are normally the main reasons, even if the conscious mind does not necessarily realise it. These three elements also play a major role in the amount of brilliance seen in a gemstone.

When the colour of a gemstone is more vivid, its brilliance will normally not be as high. For example, you will see more brilliance in a Sky Blue Topaz than in a London Blue Topaz. The better the clarity, the fewer obstructions light has to negotiate in order to enter and exit the gem. Most important of all is the cut of the gem: if the angles of the facets are poorly applied, the gem will not come to life!

Whilst a Diamond is cut to display a mixture of brilliance, dispersion and scintillation at their best, the key priority when shaping a coloured gemstone is how to best display the gem's colour; and in the case of transparent gems how to also maximise the gem's brilliance. The most important factor in the cut is the angle of the pavilion facets; in simple terms, the facets on the underside of the gem act like mirrors on which light is reflected. However, don't expect all gemstones to have the same proportions and angles of that familiar picture of a Diamond, as different gemstones have different optimal angles for the return of light (known as a gemstone's 'critical angle').

The best way to see brilliance is to hold the gem

A Blue Topaz ring from the Sarah Bennett Collection demonstrating brilliance.

A Pink Tourmaline ring by Tomas Rae showing gorgeous brilliance.

Brilliance in abundance in Tsavorite.

so that your light source is hitting the facets on the crown and then slowly move it from side to side in a rocking motion. What you should see is patches of light within the gem; these will reflect the gem's true hues and show the saturation of the colour. If you can't see any brilliance, then the gem is opaque (not transparent), heavily included, too dark in tone or poorly cut.

BRILLIANT CUT

The "Brilliant Cut" or round cut is the most popular cut for Diamonds and is often used for transparent coloured gemstones as it is an ideal shape for maximising the light returned through the top of a gem.

The brilliant cut we know today has been developed throughout recent history by a number of cutters. It was first introduced in the middle of the 17th Century and at that stage featured 17 facets on the crown. A Venetian polisher called Vincent Peruzzi increased the number of facets to 33 and by the end of the 17th century, the Lisbon cut and Brazilian cut featured 58 facets, giving rise to a dramatic increase in the gem's beauty through greater dispersion and higher brilliance.

In 1919, Marcel Tolkowsky studied the round brilliant cut and detailed geometric calculations to further improve the cut. He specified the exact angles of the facets and the percentage of the gem that should be above and below the girdle in order to maximise the brilliance and fire seen in a Diamond. Even today, almost 90 years later, Tolkowsky's calculations are still adhered to by most Lapidarists when cutting round brilliant cut Diamonds.

The modern round brilliant cut consists of 57 facets (sometimes 58 if at the point where the pavilions meet, a small facet is added running parallel to the crown). There are 33 cut on the crown and 25 on the pavilion. Please note that the brilliant cut is not exclusively used on round gemstones and if you see an oval, trilliant etc, where the facets appear to be a mix of triangles and kite shapes, then that is a brilliant cut.

Scintillation on the crown facets perfectly showing their kite shape.

A brilliant cut Diamond set in an engagement ring by Lorique.

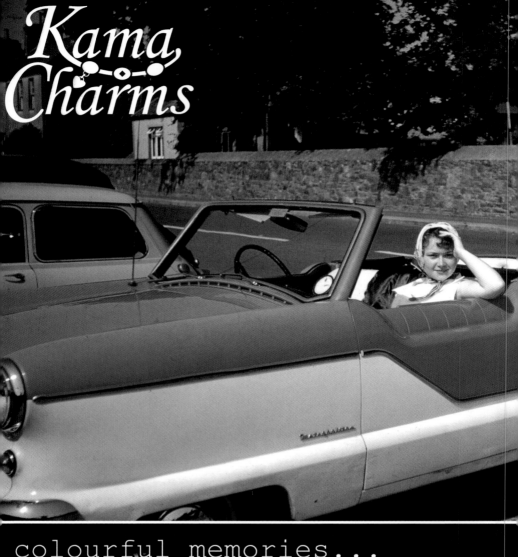

Kama, Charms

colourful memories...

A briolette Lemon Quartz lobster claw charm.

A bronze bracelet believed to date back to the Bronze Age.

BRIOLETTE CUT

The briolette cut is used for gemstones that are hung rather than set and therefore normally do not have a table facet. The cut is sometimes referred to as a drop cut and the facets are normally triangular.

There is no crown or pavilion with this cut and it is primarily designed to allow the stone's facets to show a high amount of lustre.

Briolette cut gems are often partially drilled and then glue is used to secure a metal pin within the gem. This type of hanging setting is often seen in earrings and necklaces. Some beaded bracelets and necklaces also utilise the briolette cut, but in these instances a hole is drilled through the gem which is then strung on a wire.

BRONZE AGE JEWELLERY

The Bronze Age can be split into three periods; Early Bronze Age (3500-2000 BC), Middle Bronze Age (2000-1600 BC), and Late Bronze Age (1600-1100 BC).

Metalsmiths in the Bronze Age developed an astonishingly high level of skill in bronze and gold working and used twisting and forging methods to make wrist and neck torques.

Towards the final stages of the Early Bronze Age and the start of the Middle Bronze Age, a new type of jewellery appeared in the Budapest region. This new jewellery included rings which were not complete bands as they are today, but instead had twisted ends. Other types of jewellery included spiral necklaces, and corkscrew and half-moon styled earrings.

The spread of jewellery along the Danube area helps confirm the formation of the trade route of the Early Bronze Age. From this jewellery, mostly found in Bronze Age graves, it has been possible to reconstruct what was fashionable in the Middle Bronze Age.

BRUTING

When a harder mineral is used to grind a softer mineral into a different shape, such as faceting a gemstone, the action is called bruting. Fossilised evidence shows us that the first animals to walk upright were on the earth 2 to 3 million years ago, and hominids (early humans) are known to have first made basic tools around 1 million years ago. With this understanding it is believed that man's ability of bruting rocks, and possibly even drilling them, could date back 1 million years. Our primitive relatives realised that some rocks were harder than others and learned that other rocks could fracture in a controlled manner. Therefore it is logical to assume that the very first gem to be shaped using the bruting method probably dates back up to a million years ago!

Early gems were bashed into shape!

BUFF TOP CUT

This is a cut that combines two classic styles. The top is domed with a cabochon cut, while below the girdle, the gem has facets on its pavilion. The cabochon cut on the top allows for a smooth surface that allows a high amount of lustre and brilliance to show through from the facets below; it also gives the illusion of depth as the eye is drawn into the centre. This cut is very popular in gents' jewellery.

Some in the gem trade use the term buff cut to describe cabochon cut gems that are shallow in depth.

A buff cut 4.6ct Moonstone set in Sterling Silver.

BURMA

Due to Burma's recent political instability and trade embargoes placed on the country, some of the world's finest Sapphires, Rubies and Spinels are not available in some countries such as America.

Although some gems have funded conflict (especially Jade which has been mined under military rule and therefore Burmese Jade should be totally avoided), many of the gems being smuggled out of the country along its border with

Burmese Rubies are some of the finest in the world.

A Butterfly made of Burmese Rubies set in an 18k White Gold pendant.

Thailand are by small artisanal miners, who are selling the gems to support their families during the country's instability. If you can be sure of how the gems were mined and can trust your sources, then there is no reason why you should still not purchase them. After all, the world's finest Rubies come from Burma and with all the country's recent traumas, with military rule and cyclones, if you can be sure some of your cash ends up directly in the pocket of those that need it most, then it surely adds even more beauty to the gems you acquire.

Although there are several areas in Burma where gems are unearthed, the most famous gem region in the country and possibly in the entire world is the Mogok Valley. Known by many in the trade as the "Valley of Rubies", it is without doubt the most important supplier of Rubies in the world.

Similar to most gem mining communities, there is very little technology or mechanisation involved in the industry with most of the mining taking place in alluvial deposits, using buckets, spades and sieves.

In addition to Ruby, local entrepreneurial miners also unearth Sapphire, Garnet, Moonstone, Chrysoberyl and Peridot.

BURMITE

Although Amber is most commonly found in the Baltics, it has also been discovered in several other locations around the globe. In keeping with other naming conventions for Amber, where Rumanite is named after its origin of Romania, Simetite which is Sicilian in origin, Burmite is the name given to Amber which is found in Burma.

Although popular with local people, Burmite is often cloudy and therefore hides many of its hidden treasures locked within the gem. Therefore it is normally less expensive than those specimens found in Poland and the Baltics. That said, as many people who collect gemstones and jewellery often like to collect these items based on their origin, at Coloured Rocks we try and source gems from a wide variety of countries.

Burmite is the name given to Amber from Burma.

SARAH BENNETT

GEMSTONE
JEWELLERY

CABOCHON CUT

Used mainly for gemstones that are translucent to opaque, the cabochon cut is a dome shape with no facets other than its flat bottom.

Normally the dome is highly polished to increase its lustre, and when viewed from above the outline of the cut is typically an oval. That said, round cut cabochons have become increasingly popular over past four or five years.

Cutting "en cabochon" is also applied to gemstones which demonstrate optical phenomena such as Asterism and Chatoyancy.

The Cabochon cut has been popular for over 2000 years. One word of caution though, don't be tempted to polish the flat surface underneath a cabochon cut gem; it is intentionally left unpolished as it returns more light into the gem. If polished, you may find your gem is not as vivid in colour as before.

A cabochon cut Labradorite in a design by Annabella.

CAMBODIA

There are two main provinces in Cambodia that mine gemstones. Paillin in the west of Cambodia is located very near to the Thai border and for many years has been the source of quality Sapphires. However, similar to its neighbours, yields over recent years have continued to fall and most mining in the region today is undertaken by small mining organisations.

A 1.3ct Cambodian Zircon in a design by Tomas Rae.

In the north-east of the country, near its borders with Vietnam, lies Ratanakiri. This historic location without any major roads is virtually inaccessible (especially in the rainy season) by the outside world. The region is one of the most beautiful and undeveloped areas in Cambodia, where electricity and running water are almost non-existent. It is also one of the few places on Earth where traditional tribes still exist, cut off from the outside world.

Although their numbers are decreasing, it is estimated that some 60,000 tribespeople still reside in its tree-topped hills. Other than subsistence farming, gemstone mining is one of the few commercial activities to take place in the region.

A 1.4ct Zircon from Ratanakiri.

Ratanakiri actually derives its name from combining two Cambodian words for "gems" and "mountains". The main gem mined in Ratanakiri is Zircon and many agree that some of the best quality in the world comes from this tribal area. Other mines produce limited quantities of Amethyst and Peridot.

CAMEO

Sculptures or coins which use raised images are known as "cameos". One of the main materials used to create a cameo is Agate. Several Agates are naturally discovered where the stone is made up of several distinct coloured layers. To imagine this, think of a white slice of bread sitting on top of a brown slice. The artist carves away at the white piece of bread and leaves a design where the raised image is white on a brown background, thus creating a cameo.

Some of the most impressive examples of cameos date as far back as the 6th century BC, found in amazing sculptures in Greece. Designs are normally portraits of famous people, biblical scenes or religious figures. While Agates are the most common gemstone used to make Cameos, shells and imitation gems are now also frequently used.

CAMPBELL R BRIDGES

In 1967, Scottish gemmologist Campbell R Bridges discovered a beautiful green gemstone hidden in a potato shaped rock in Tanzania.

After performing gemmological tests, he found it to be Grossularite, an extremely rare member of the Garnet family. Unfortunately, very shortly after discovering the gem, the Tanzanian Government nationalised all mines and Campbell was forced to leave the country.

Not a man known to give up - and having already received interest from Tiffany & Co. in the gem - Campbell traced the vein in which it was originally found back to Kenya.

In 1971, after searching for the gem for over a year, he rediscovered it in the Tsavo National Park; an area of intense natural beauty where the film 'Out of Africa' was filmed and the park on which 'The Lion King' was based. Campbell was finally able to officially register the deposit and obtained permission to mine.

At the beginning of his expedition, Campbell lived in a tree house so as to avoid being eaten by local predators, and to avoid the gems that he mined from being stolen, he put them in a hole full of pythons.

In 1974, Campbell agreed with the then President of Tiffany & Co., Henry Platt, that the gem should be named after the park in which it was found, and in keeping with the normal gemmological naming process to end its name with "ite", the name Tsavorite was agreed.

A 0.8ct Tsavorite in a classic design by Tomas Rae.

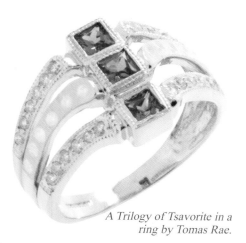

A Trilogy of Tsavorite in a ring by Tomas Rae.

CANADA

What connects the Labrador dog and the gemstone Labradorite? They are both named after the Labrador peninsular in eastern Canada where they both originated.

Ammonite is found at the Milk River in Alberta; Emerald and Aquamarines are found in Yukon; and Amethyst mines can be found in Ontario. The country's other mining activities are very diverse. The largest export by carat weight is Nephrite Jade, mined in northern British Columbia, along with the blues of Sapphire and Iolite. Opal is also an important export, though to a smaller degree. Recently, Canada has become a fairly substantial source for Diamonds.

Labradorite is named after the Labrador peninsula in Canada.

CANARY DIAMOND

Canary Diamonds have an incredibly deep, intense yellow colour. Unlike Citrine, which often has orange tones, a Canary Diamond is similar in colour to a petal of a blooming sunflower.

The Tiffany Diamond is a spectacular Canary Diamond, weighing in at a massive 128.54 carats. Interestingly, 30 of the 100 largest Diamonds in the world are yellow.

Canary Diamonds accenting a Moldavite in an 18k Gold Ring.

CARAT

Carat is a measurement of weight and should only be applied to genuine gemstones.

There are 5 carats to a gram and this measurement is now recognised around the world (even in the U.S. where the metric system isn't used). Carats can be further broken down into points, where 100 points equals 1 carat. As different gems have different densities, carat weights only have a loose bearing on the size of the gem.

The word originated from the Carob seed, which was once regarded as one of the most uniformed, naturally occurring items to be found on earth, with each seed being similar in weight.

A Carob seed pod from Majorca.

The term carat should not be confused with the term karat, which is a measure of gold purity (in some countries the problem is made worse as the word to describe the purity of gold is also spelt carat). To simplify matters, in the jewellery trade when we describe a gem as nine carats in weight we write 9ct and gold purity is written as 9k, 14k, 18k etc.

CARBUNCLE

This is not a word you are going to come across too often in the modern gem world, but a short explanation may help when reading older literature, where it is frequently used.

Throughout the past five thousand years, names of gemstones have continually evolved, as better identification has led to a far wider array of different species. It is believed that the initial use of the word Carbuncle was to describe any gemstone that was red.

Over time, the word was further restricted to cabochon cut red gems and later in history it was adopted as the initial name for Ruby. At this time other civilisations were naming Ruby "ratnari", which is Sanskrit for "king of gems".

Carbuncles are mentioned in the Bible in Exodus 28:17 and 39:10; Ezekiel 28:13 (which refers to the Carbuncle's presence in the Garden of Eden) and Isaiah 54:12: "And I will make thy windows of agates, and thy gates of carbuncles, and all thy borders of pleasant stones ."

It is quite fortunate that the name is no longer used as it is also the name of a bacterial infection and an abscess!

CARDINAL'S RING

The Cardinal's Ring is a gold ring which is given by the pope to cardinals and bishops on their consecration. The rings normally have a gemstone set into them, often a Sapphire, and are engraved with the coat of arms of the pope. Although they are unlikely inspire to today's jewellery designers, I felt they were of significance to be featured in this book.

CARNELIAN

Carnelian (sometimes spelt Cornelian) is a member of the Chalcedony group of gems, who in turn belong to the cryptocrystalline family of Quartz. This gem has been treasured throughout history and for centuries has been engraved and cut into signet rings.

Derived from the Latin word meaning "fleshy," because of its orange to reddish orange colour, it is also referred to as Red Chalcedony or Red Agate, due to the stunning red tints created from the presence of iron oxides.

Romans believed that the different colours of the stone represent the sexes; dark symbolises man, and light symbolises woman. When Carnelian grades into brown it is referred to as Sard. When it is a stronger white colour it is referred to as Sardonyx, and if the gem is extremely dark it can be called Jasper.

Carnelian is surrounded in myth and legend. It was believed by some that it stops bleeding and heals wounds. Egyptians thought that the gem had strong powers in the afterlife and would help to make people feel calm about death: in an excavation site uncovering the tomb of a Sumerian Queen from the third millennium BC, a robe has been discovered encrusted with the gem; presumably for this reason. They also believed that amulets of Carnelian could help the soul's journey into the next life.

Although the gem has been discovered in Cornwall, England, as well as in France, the main sources of Carnelian are Japan, Brazil and Uruguay. India has some very old Carnelian mines still in operation, which tend to produce gems with a strong reddish brown colour.

Colour	Reddish orange to a flesh colour
Family	Chalcedony Quartz
Hardness	6.5
Specific Gravity	2.6
Refractive Index	1.54
Crystal Group	Trigonal
Optical Properties	Vitreous to waxy lustre
Common Treatments	Occasionally heat treated
Care	No special care required
Cleaning Advice	Ultrasonic, Steam Cleaning or Warm soapy water
Chemical Composition	SiO_2

CARTIER

Cartier, the world famous French jeweller, first started trading in 1847 by Louis Francois-Cartier. Louis' son Alfred continued the family tradition and after taking the reins of the company from his father, elevated it to a different level.

A Jessica Lili Carnelian Bracelet.

The following generation saw three Cartier brothers: Louis, Pierre and Jacques. Pierre and Jacques initially left the company business to travel the world and later returned to the company to establish the London and New York stores. Each brother then developed the brand in different countries.

Louis was responsible for creating some of the company's most famous and much loved designs. These included the Art Deco designs and the Mystery Watches - not to mention the 'Tutti Fruity' range of colourful jewellery.

Cartier soon became an extremely popular brand and was worn by royalty and celebrities alike. In 1902, the Prince of Wales said that Cartier were the kings of jewellery and jewellery for kings.

The Tutti Fruity bracelet (first seen in 1925) is still fashionable today. The cuff style bracelet, which has various stunning gemstones, wouldn't look out of place on the runways of various international fashion shows. The long, engraved Emerald and Diamond necklaces, as well as the Pearl necklaces with engraved Rubies are designs that have stood the test of time.

In 1936, the 'Hindu' necklaces were introduced, and contained Emeralds, Diamonds, Rubies and Sapphires. The gemstones were engraved in traditional Indian designs. In 1941, the Emerald Kingfisher brooch was extremely popular. A stunning yellow gold necklace with Turquoise and Amethysts was personally designed for the Duchess of Windsor in 1947.

Today, Cartier still uses similar designs such as setting different coloured Sapphires in white gold. Cartier cleverly mixes a selection of gemstones such as Moonstone, Chalcedonies, Tourmaline and Aquamarine to create thrilling necklaces. Indeed, Cartier is possibly the world's largest luxury jeweller.

I often ask jewellery designers where they take their inspiration from and after you have listened to endless stories of how nature provides them ideas, if you can assure them that it's only natural to evaluate competitors styles and concepts, then often the word Cartier will be mentioned.

CASTING

A process used to make multiple copies of the same piece of jewellery whereby an original master piece is made and then duplicated. The most common method used today is wax replacement casting.

Once the original piece has been made by a craftsman, it is inserted into a rubber mould to create an impression of the design; the result is a Master Rubber Mould. Hot wax is then injected into the rubber mould and left to solidify.

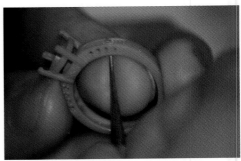

Perfecting a wax model.

The wax model is then removed from the Master Rubber Mould and the process is repeated until the required numbers of pieces are made. The models are then attached to a wax pole (known as a wax tree) and the completed tree is then placed inside a cylinder, and cast is poured around the tree and allowed to set. Next, the cast is put into a hot oven and all the wax turns back into a liquid and is drained from the cast. Next the gold or silver in heated into a liquid and poured into the cast. Once the cast cools the metal is then set.

The cast is then broken and where there was once a wax tree, there is now a metal tree. The craftsmen remove the individual pieces of jewellery and finish the surface of the metal with files and normally end by polishing the piece.

With the exception of "one of a kind" pieces, all rings, pendants and earrings are made this way today. Whilst the casting method is very efficient and flexible, it can obviously only cast one type of metal at a time. Therefore, when two metals are combined to make the same design, they are cast separately and then bonded together by the jeweller.

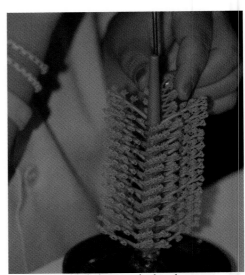

Wax moulds being attached to the wax tree.

CATHEDRAL SETTING

A modern design used for rings, where the designer wants to show off the cutting of the gemstone. When viewed from the side, the shoulders of this ring split into two levels

A simple yet elegant engagement ring by Tomas Rae featuring a cathedral setting.

imitating the arches of a cathedral. The setting is often used for engagement rings and in more recent times, for displaying solitaire Tanzanites and Sapphires.

CEYLON (SRI LANKA)

Previously known as Ceylon, the island of Sri Lanka, located south of India, has rightly earned its name as the 'Gem Island' (Ratna Dweepa). In addition to mining world-class Corundum (the family name for Rubies and Sapphires), the island is also home to Alexandrite, Garnet, Moonstone, Peridot, Spinel, Topaz, Tourmaline and Zircon.

This island has been known for its splendid array of colourful Sapphires and deep red Rubies for over 2000 years. When it comes to Sapphire, Sri Lanka is best known for its Blue Sapphire (known as Ceylon Sapphire) and its stunning orangey pinkish Padparadscha Sapphire (named after the lotus flower also found on the island).

Ceylon Sapphire is typically a stunning light-blue gem with amazing clarity and Princess Diana chose a Ceylon Sapphire as the central gem in her engagement ring. The main source for the gem is the mining region of Ratnapura, located 65 miles south-east of Colombo, the capital of Sri Lanka. The town is also the main focal point for trading gems in Sri Lanka and its name in Singhalese means "gem town".

Mining in Sri Lanka is primarily undertaken by artisan miners (informal mining), however the government is working hard at putting more formal procedures in place, apparently for a twofold purpose: to help preserve the landscape and to increase the percentage of profit received for each and every gem found. In order to do this, they aim to increase the skill levels of gemstone cutters and gem treatment companies within the country.

The mines are generally based on alluvial deposits and old river beds. As in Madagascar, to access the layers of gem bearing deposits,

Located to the south of India, Sri Lanka is a gemstone treasure chest!

the miners dig, by hand, small vertical holes 10 to 30 feet into the ground and then create tunnels horizontally. This avoids upsetting the landscape and is often less labour intensive than creating an open pit mine.

Often you will hear stories about the mis-identification of gemstones. Ceylon with its treasure trove of different gemstones, which are mined primarily from small independent miners, who in the main don't have access to gem experts, has played a lead role in many famous misidentifications. Take Tourmaline for example, it was only identified as a separate gem species when a bag of "mixed gems" were sent from Ceylon to Holland in 1703. Then there was a parcel of gems sent to Dublin in the 1940's that was though to be Spinel, one of the pieces turned out to be a new discovery, which we now know as Taaffeite.

An incredibly rare 5.45ct Celyon Sapphire in a ring by Lorique.

CHAIN

Either used to display pendants and charms or as a piece of jewellery in its own right, the chain have been used for many centuries. Although most metal chains (including gold and silver) are made by machine, there are a few jewellers around the globe that still make every link by hand.

Tookalon chains, for example, are made from thin wires of silver, shaped to the required size and then individually soldered together.

There are numerous names for standard styles of chains and these include: bill chain; barrel and link chain; belcher chain; cord chain; curb chain; Diamond trace chain; rope chain; strap chain; trace chain. Many of these chains when on sale in Europe are produced in Italy.

A handmade chain and bracelet by Tookalon.

Be extra careful of buying cheap chains abroad! My assistant Barry once bought a chain on a Spanish beach, after seeing it had an 18k stamp. When he brought it into the office the following week, I explained to him that it was not an official hallmark; indeed, it turned out to be polished brass! When it comes to gold if the price seems too low, it's probably not real!

A machine-made Italian gold chain.

CHAKRAS

The word Chakra describes a ball of energy from within the body. Derived from the Sanskrit word for a wheel, it is visualised as a spinning energy that interacts with other Chakra to give us health, energy and wellbeing. There are many books written about the body's Chakra system, all of which detail philosophical theories and models of wellbeing which were first described in ancient India.

The physical body and consciousness is said to consist of seven Chakras located at major points in our nervous system, starting at the base of the spinal column and moving upward along the backbone to the skull. When they are working in balance and interacting with each other, they evenly distribute energy throughout the body, thus aiding mental wellbeing, decision making and rejuvenation. They almost act as a door to allow life energy to flow from the body into your aura.

Different Chakra interact with different parts and aspects of our body. All senses, perceptions, experiences and conscience can be divided into seven categories: the Crown, Brow, Throat, Heart, Solar Plexus, Sacral and Root.

It is maintained that stress can manifest itself as illness in the human body and is believed to happen when the body holds onto negative energy (through problems with rotation in certain Chakra). Having a finely tuned Chakra system means that negative energy is not trapped, thus allowing it to escape from the body easily.

Chakra can be healed and cleansed by gemstones, colour and sound. Concentrating on certain colours or sounds is believed to aid the overall balance of the Chakras. For example, the Throat Chakra is cleansed by the colour blue and the noise created from the word "eye". Try it yourself – imagine your throat, the colour blue and make the sound of the word "eye". Keep doing this for as long as you can.

Gemstones are believed to be in tune with Chakra

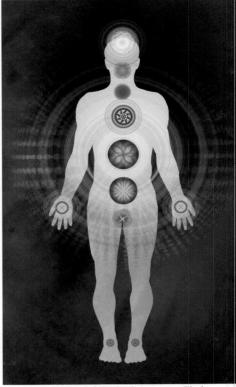

The location of the body's seven Chakras.

Seven gemstones associated with Chakras.

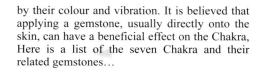

by their colour and vibration. It is believed that applying a gemstone, usually directly onto the skin, can have a beneficial effect on the Chakra, Here is a list of the seven Chakra and their related gemstones…

Root Chakra

Garnet, Black Tourmaline, Haematite, Smokey Quartz, Bloodstone and Ruby.

The Root Chakra is connected with our sense of earth and grounding. It is also beneficial to instinct and survival.

Haematite

Sacral Chakra

Amber, Azurite, Malachite, Clear Quartz, Jade, Ruby, Carnelian and Citrine.

Related to water, emotions and sexuality, it connects with our grace, depth of feeling and ability to accept change.

Malachite

Solar Plexus Chakra

Citrine, Amber, Moonstone, Peridot, Calcite and Topaz.

Related to our willpower, creativity and autonomy, it brings us energy and spontaneity.

Citrine

Heart Chakra

Malachite, Emerald, Green Tourmaline, Rose Quartz, Kunzite and Rhodochrosite.

The middle Chakra of the seven is the Heart Chakra, related to love, persona, mind and body; it helps us love, have peace and feel compassion.

Kunzite

Throat Chakra

Lapis Lazuli, Sapphire, Aquamarine, Turquoise, Kyanite, Blue Topaz and Azurite.

This is located around the throat and therefore is related to communication and also creativeness.

Azurite

Brow Chakra

Turquoise, Watermelon Tourmaline, Labradorite, Amethyst and Moonstone.

Also known as the 'Third Eye' Chakra, it is believed to relate to the act of seeing - both physically and intuitively. When this Chakra is healthy it gives clarity of thought and vision.

Turquoise

Crown Chakra

Amethyst, Opal, Tourmaline, Diamond and Clear Quartz

The Crown Chakra has a direct association with consciousness, to give knowledge and understanding in spiritual connections and bliss. It aids clarity of thought and knowledge to what we know, and also develops wisdom and understanding of the greater world.

Amethyst

CHALCEDONY

It has been suggested that Chalcedony was one of the earliest materials used by man. Not only has the stone been mentioned as one of the twelve gems in the breastplate of Aaron, there is reference to its use in creating the foundation of the city walls of the 'New Jerusalem'.

In the 7th century BC, it was used to make cylindrical seals in the area of Mesopotamia.

Over time, as well as being set in jewellery and carvings, Chalcedony has been shaped into knives and tools. In particular it is used to carve attractive cameos, and is one of the gemstones used in commesso; a technique of fashioning pictures with thin, cut-to-shape pieces of brightly coloured gemstones (extremely popular in the 16th century in Florence, Italy).

The name derives from Chalkedon (an old Greek town) and the generic name 'Chalcedony' is also the name for all fine-grained Quartzes.

Colour	Bluish grey to greyish white
Family	Quartz
Hardness	6.5
Specific Gravity	2.59 – 2.61
Refractive Index	1.544 - 1.553
Crystal Group	Trigonal
Optical Properties	Waxy silky lustre
Common Treatments	Sometimes dyed
Cleaning Advice	Ultrasonic, steam cleaning or warn soapy water
Care	Can fade in extreme heat

A natural purple Chalcedony.

A large marquise cut Chalcedony set in a modern Sterling Silver ring.

Chalcedony comes in an array of colours including hues such as milky blue, creamy white and soft grey. The gem is usually semi-transparent or translucent and its waxy lustre gives it an almost magical look.

This bewitching stone is thought to drive out dread, hysterics, melancholy, mental illness, and to reduce fever and prevent depression. Wearing Chalcedony promotes tranquillity and harmony, and is also said to stimulate creativity.

Chalcedony is still a very popular gem today and even inspirational jewellery brands such as Boodles and Lorique set cabochon cut Chalcedony gems in 18k gold.

The gem is mined in various parts of the world including Brazil, Madagascar and Sri Lanka and is normally located in volcanic and sedimentary rocks.

CHAMPAGNE QUARTZ

Champagne Quartz is a reasonably unknown member of the family: its rich champagne colour sets it apart from the darker Smokey Quartz.

Champagne Quartz has amazing clarity and the fascinating pale brown shade makes this a true collector's piece. Its appearance can often resemble that of a Cognac Diamond and it looks stunning set into white gold rings and pendants.

Champagne Quartz by Sarah Bennett.

CHAMPAGNE TOPAZ

Champagne Topaz is one of the few naturally coloured brown gems on the planet and can be discovered in light to medium shades of brown.

The gem is primarily mined in Mexico, however there have been some very small deposits of naturally coloured Champagne Topaz found in Nigeria, Mozambique and Russia.

Colour	Pale brown to mocha brown
Family	Topaz
Hardness	8
Specific Gravity	3.5 – 3.6
Refractive Index	1.6 – 1.63
Crystal Group	Orthorhombic
Optical Properties	Strong pleochroism
Common Treatments	Sometimes heat treated
Chemical Composition	$Al_2SiO_4(OH,F)_2$

C

CHANNEL SETTING

A setting where the gems (often Diamonds, Rubies or Sapphires) rest in a channel and are only secured by a slight rim which runs the length of the channel. The design is becoming very popular for Eternity rings, and the gemstones are normally round cut, square cut or baguette cut. This style can only be used for gemstones that are faceted to precise dimensions (precision cut), as they all need to be of identical size in order to sit firmly in the channel. Please note, that it is very difficult to re-size a channel set ring.

Pink Sapphires in a channel set ring by Jacque Christie.

CHATOYANCY

From the French words "chat oeil," meaning cat's eye, the word chatoyancy is used to describe the optical effect that certain gemstones have, which resemble the opening and closing of an eye.

The phenomenon is commonly called cat's eye effect, for when the light hits the surface of the polished gemstone, a narrow line of light appears, which looks dramatically similar to that of a cat's eye.

An exremely rare Cat's Eye Fire Opal.

Chatoyancy is an effect caused by tiny fibrous inclusions that are naturally arranged in a parallel configuration.

For a gemstone to show this effect it must be cabochon cut, and its inclusions must run parallel to the base. Examples of gems that can feature chatoyancy are Aquamarine, Moonstone, Quartz, Chrysoberyl and of course, Tiger's Eye.

One word of warning, I spoke to a lady once who told me that her beloved Chrysoberyl had lost its cat's eye look. After asking her for a little bit more detail, she informed me that a few days prior it had been cleaned by a friend. What transpired was that the friend not only cleaned the top of the cabochon cut gem, but also polished the flat surface underneath. The result was that light which was previously locked in the gem, now seeped through the bottom.

A well cut cabochon Chrysoberyl.

CHARMS

The use of charms can be traced all the way back to Ancient Egypt, when Pharaohs would wear charms as an identifier for the next life. In the Roman Empire, Roman Christians used charms as a way of identifying themselves to other Christians. During the Middle Ages knights used charms to represent their family's origin, political standing and profession. Queen Victoria embraced charms as a fashion statement during the Victorian Era. At the end of the Second World War, soldiers leaving islands in the Pacific purchased little handmade trinkets to bring home to their loved ones.

A Milano Charm that clips onto jewellery using a Lobster Claw.

Although there are a wide variety of charms available, they tend to all fall into one of three different types. Firstly, charms can be made with a lobster claw clasp or other fastening device, which allows the charm to be attached to other items of jewellery. Secondly, a charm can be designed with a hole in the middle, making it possible to slide the charm on to existing necklaces or bracelets. Finally, some manufacturers will make jewellery with a selection of charms permanently attached to the jewellery. As it is not often practical to mix thread-able charms with attachable charms, if you are about to start a charm collection, the first decision is to choose which style of charm you are going to collect.

If you're looking to buy someone a gift for a special occasion, like passing a driving test, a 16th or 18th birthday or for winning a sports event, by giving an appropriate charm you will find they have something to treasure for a lifetime which will remind them of the event. I personally started a small collection of charms for my daughters three years ago and intend to keep adding to them on special events. I believe that in addition to photographs and videos, charms are one of the best catalysts for memories.

Two Kama Charms that thread onto a chain or cord.

Today, charms bring to life many different styles, important eras, and civilisations. As with other pieces of jewellery, charms can be passed down through the generations.

Tomas Rae.

17" 3ct diamond necklace set in 18k white gold
£1299

CHECKERBOARD CUT

A style of faceting the table and crown of gemstones that often increases the surface lustre of the gem. The best way to imagine this style of cutting is to visualise a chessboard rotated so one of the corners is resting on a desk, and the individual black and white shapes are no longer square, but Diamond-like in appearance.

The cut is normally applied to large coloured gemstones and is particularly popular on cushion shaped gems. Although the effect usually covers the entire gem above the girdle, it is occasionally only applied to the crown.

The checkerboard is normally applied to opaque and translucent gems, although occasionally it is used for transparent gems that have less than perfect clarity. As mentioned above, the style lends itself to cushion shaped gems; however it can also add an extra dimension to trilliant, oval and heart shapes.

Checkerboard cut Smokey Quartz in an opulent pendant by Sarah Bennett.

CHILE

The Andes Mountains in Chile are in the press a lot at the moment for their award-winning wines; but at an altitude of 11,000 feet, some of the best quality Lapis Lazuli in the world is mined. Even though the country has hundreds of active and dormant volcanoes - which would normally yield dozens of different gemstones, including Diamonds - as yet very few other gems have been found.

Therefore if you want to own a product of Mother Nature from Chile, I would recommend either their Chardonnay or Malbec. If you're not a wine drinker, try skiing or snow boarding in Chile, their slopes are amongst the best in the world. Though their Lapis Lazuli is amongst some of the finest in the world, many people are disappointed with its colour, as it is not as deep as that from Afghanistan. Do keep your eyes on Gemcollector.com, because one of my best gem hunting friends is currently in Chile!

Lapis Lazuli; one of the few gems found in Chile.

CHEMICAL SYMBOLS

As you read through this book, you will have noticed that alongside each gemstone is a little table of attributes. The final entry in most of these tables is labelled "chemical composition". Below are the chemical symbols that you will see used in these tables, however, please note that as I didn't want this book to turn in to some sort of science lesson and prefer to focus more on a gem's beauty than its composition, so where a gem is constructed from a multitude of chemicals I often refer to them simply as having a "complex composition"!

Iron turns Corundum into vibrant Yellow Sapphire.

Aluminum	Al
Beryllium	Be
Bohrium	Bh
Boron	B
Cadmium	Cd
Californium	Cf
Carbon	C
Chlorine	Cl
Chromium	Cr
Cobalt	Co
Copper	Cu
Fluorine	D
Gold	Au
Hydrogen	H
Iron	Fe
Lithium	Li
Magnesium	Mg
Manganese	Mn
Nickel	Ni
Oxygen	O
Palladium	Pd
Platinum	Pt
Potassium	K
Rhodium	Rh
Silicon	Si
Silver	Ag
Tin	Sn
Titanum	Ti
Vanadium	V
Zinc	Zr

When Titanium and Iron are present in Corundum, Blue Sapphire can be created.

Copper is added to Gold to produce Rose Gold.

Freshwater cultured Pearls from China in a pair of Jessica Lili earrings.

A Marcasite choker from the Jewels of Valais collection.

CHINA

Today, one of the biggest effects that China has on the jewellery market is in the provision of Cultured Pearls. Although this technique of assisting nature in producing its natural treasure originated in Japan, the Chinese have recently become a bigger player.

Jade is one of the most worn gems in the country and there are many historic tales of Chinese jewellers taking top grade Diamonds and making them into tools purely to cut their more precious Jade.

When it comes to coloured gemstones, it is difficult to state with any degree of accuracy exactly what size the gemstone export market of China is, or to know for definite all of the areas where gems are being mined. However, the Yunnan Province bordering Burma and Vietnam is known to operate Emerald mines, and the province of Hunan near the Yangtze River produces some fine Peridot.

On the East Coast of China is Shandong; here mines produce large size Sapphires, but in general their colour tends to be very dark.

CHOKER

A style of necklace that sits high around the neck. In Europe, chokers tend to be 14" to 15" in length, where as necklaces are normally 16" to 20" in length. Worn by royalty and the rich and famous, chokers are often seen as an essential piece of jewellery for those attending prestigious events.

Whereas most necklaces are made out of precious metals, chokers often tend to be made out of softer materials. Velvet, lace, leather and ribbons are often used to support gemstones and they are normally connected to the choker with a fastening that can easily be detached.

That said, the design team at Annabella recently developed a collection of Chokers. These are made of a "mesh like" design, so that it becomes stretchable.

CHRISTIAN NAMES AND GEMSTONES

There has been a tradition that dates back many centuries where certain gemstones are associated with Christian names. Possibly the most famous gemmologist of the last two hundred years, George F. Kunz, wrote in his book "The Curious Lore of Precious Stones", "there is established a very pretty custom of assigning to the various masculine and feminine Christian names a particular gem". It is believed by many to be a very strong talisman when the correct Christian name gem is worn and the effect is believed to be even stronger when the gem is set alongside one's birthstone.

Turquoise is perfect for Theresa!

Feminine Names	Gemstone
Alice	Alexandrite
Ann	Amber
Belle	Bloodstone
Caroline	Chalcedony
Catherine	Cat's Eye
Charlotte	Carbuncle
Dorothy	Diaspore
Edith	Eye Agate
Elizabeth	Emerald
Emily	Euclase
Emma	Epidote
Florence	Fluorite
France	Fire Opal
Gertrude	Garnet
Grace	Grossularite Garnet
Hannah	Heliotrope
Helen	Hyacinth
Irene	Iolite
Jane	Jacinth
Jessie	Jasper
Josephine	Jadeite
Julia	Jade
Louise	Lapis – Lazuli
Lucy	Lapidolite
Margaret	Moss Agate
Martha	Malachite
Marie	Moldavite
Mary	Moonstone
Olive	Olivine
Pauline	Pearl
Rose	Ruby
Sarah	Spodumene (Kunzite or Hiddenite)
Susan	Sapphire
Theresa	Turquoise

Masculine Names	Gemstone
Abraham	Aragonite
Adrian	Andalusite
Albert	Agate
Alexander	Alexandrite
Andrew	Aventurine
Arnold	Aquamarine
Arthur	Amethyst
Ben (Benjamin)	Bloodstone
Bernard	Beryl
Charles	Chalcedony
Dennis	Demantoid Garnet
Dorian	Diamond
Edmund	Emerald
Edward	Epidote
Ferdinand	Feldspar
Francis	Fire Opal
Fredrick	Fluorite
George	Garnet
Gregory	Grossularite Garnet
Henry	Heliolite
James	Jade
Jasper	Jasper
John	Jacinth
Lawrence	Lapis – Lazuli
Mark	Malachite
Matthew	Moonstone
Nicholas	Nephrite
Oliver	Onyx
Osmond	Opal
Patrick	Pyrope Garnet
Paul	Pearl
Peter	Porphyry (Feldspar or Quartz)
Philip	Prase
Raymond	Rose Quartz

Masculine Names	Gemstone
Richard	Rutile
Roger	Rhodonite
Roland	Ruby
Stephen	Sapphire
Theodore	Tourmaline
Thomas	Topaz

Pearl is perfect for Pauline!

CHROMIUM

Chromium is a steely grey metal that can be found as a chemical element in the periodic table and although jewellery is rarely made of it, it does have an important role to play in jewellery.

Many gemstones are allochromatic: this means that their colour is derived from small traces of elements or impurities not included in the chemical composition of the gem. Chromium is the main red colouring agent in Corundum and turns the mineral into the precious Ruby. However, in gems such as Tsavorite Garnet and Emerald, its presence is the reason why we get such vibrantly vivid greens. And, as if by magic, its presence in some Chrysoberyl is what provides it with its ability to colour change from green or bluish-green in daylight, to a soft shade of red, purplish-red or raspberry red in artificial light (incandescent light). When this colour change is present in Chrysoberyl, we rename the gemstone Alexandrite.

CHRYSOBERYL

Ruby receives its colour from chronium.

Formed almost 250 million years ago, but only discovered in 1789, Chrysoberyl acquired its name from an amalgam of two Greek words; "chrysos", meaning "golden" and "beryllos", meaning "gem crystal".

Being one of the rarer, lesser-known gemstones, it should not be confused with the mineral "Beryl". Although their names are related, that is where the similarities end.

Due to its high content of iron, Chrysoberyl is formed in various shades of green, yellow and sometimes a reddish brown; in rare cases it has been found in a bluish green. It is an extremely hard gemstone, measuring up to 8.5 on the Mohs scale; making it the third hardest naturally occurring gemstone known to man.

Chrysoberyl was extremely popular in Victorian and Edwardian eras and is thought that supply was much more plentiful in those times than it

Colour	Green, yellow
Family	Does not belong to a family
Hardness	8 – 8.5
Specific Gravity	3.5 – 3.8
Refractive Index	1.746 – 1.755
Crystal Group	Orthorhombic
Optical Properties	Vitreous lustre
Common Treatments	Not normally treated
Care	Very tough
Cleaning Advice	Ultrasonic, steam cleaning and warm soapy water
Chemical Composition	$BeAl_2O_4$ (variable composition)

is today, hence the reason why very little of the stunning gem has been set in jewellery over the last decade.

Folklore suggests that Chrysoberyl aids one in striving for excellence, endowing peace of mind to the bearer. Some even believe that its mystical powers aid the wearer in gaining self-confidence, allowing them to comprehend the fact that they already have all they really need.

Chrysoberyl is also believed to increase the healing properties of other gemstones. In partnership with the correct gem, it is maintained it can treat serious illness.

There are two extremely rare varieties of Chrysoberyl: the highly acclaimed Alexandrite and Cymophane.

Cymophane is commonly known as "Chrysoberyl Cat's Eye" or lesser known as "Oriental Cat's Eye". The reason for this is that Cymophane has an optical property known as chatoyancy, which, due to its structure, simulates the opening and closing of an eye.

Legend suggests that Cymophane would protect the wearer from evil, warding off spirits and demons. It is also believed to help balance emotions, bringing peace and understanding to situations in one's life.

Alexandrite is the ultimate Chrysoberyl and is highly regarded by gem experts, enthusiasts and connoisseurs alike. When you view Alexandrite in daylight (balanced light) the gem is green but when the light source is reddish (incandescent), the gem shows tones of purple or red.

One of three birthstones for the month of June, Alexandrite is believed to strengthen the wearer's intuition, and thus, helps find new ways forward where logic and practical thinking will not provide an answer. It is also known to aid creativity and inspire one's imagination.

Chrysoberyl is found in America, Brazil, Italy, Madagascar, Russia, India, Sri Lanka and Zimbabwe.

A 3ct Chrysoberyl from Madagascar.

Alexandrite is a colour change Chrysoberyl.

How Chrysoberyl arrives at our cutting facility in Jaipur, India.

CHRYSOPRASE

Colour	Leek green through to apple green
Family	Chalcedony Quartz
Hardness	6.5
Specific Gravity	2.59 – 2.64
Refractive Index	1.530 - 1.550
Crystal Group	Trigonal
Optical Properties	Vitreous to waxy lustre
Common Treatments	Not treated
Care	No special care required
Cleaning Advice	Ultrasonic, steam cleaning or warm soapy water
Chemical Composition	SiO_2

Chrysoprase is regarded as one of the most valuable gemstones in the Chalcedony group (the name given to the Cryptocrystalline family of Quartz).

The name is derived from the Greek words "chrysos prason", meaning "gold leek". As you can imagine, the gem is a bright leek green translucent gemstone. Its shades vary from very pale green through to a "Golden Delicious" apple green.

Whereas most other green gems owe their colour to the presence of chromium or vanadium, Chrysoprase derives its colour from traces of nickel. The gemstone is generally opaque but occasionally translucent stones are found.

Similar to the lustre of Apatite, the lustre of Chrysoprase is often resinous. The opaque variety can sometimes have a swirling marble effect running through the gem. This effect is similar to that sometimes seen in Jade; however, in Jade it is regarded as a somewhat negative attribute, but it is seen as a valuable and beautiful quality in a Chrysoprase gemstone.

The gem is said to encourage hope and joy, as well as clarifying problems and restlessness. Crystal healers also believe that it soothes headaches and relieves loneliness. Others believe that Chrysoprase promotes emotional balance and grants inner strength and peace, thereby leading a person to a greater sense of self-confidence.

According to folklore, it may also be used as a shield or protector from negative energy and was once used as a talisman protecting sailors on sea voyages. It is advised to place a piece of Chrysoprase near the front entrance of the home to ward off negative energies.

Deposits have been found in Australia, Brazil, India, Madagascar, Russia (in the Ural Mountains near to where Alexandrite was discovered), Zimbabwe, South Africa, and Tanzania. Even California has a deposit of Chrysoprase.

A cabochon cut Chrysoprase.

Uncut Chrysoprase.

Endless colourful possibility...

ssemble your own uniquely individual piece of jewellery

CITRINE

Stunning, vibrant and glowing yellow, this gemstone has a warm, tantalising tone that seems to have magically captured the last glow of a sunset. Quality Citrine can brighten up even the dreariest of winter days. Though its name suggests a bright yellow - its name is derived from the French word for "lemon" - it is the slightly darker, almost pale orange colours that are most highly prized.

As Citrine is a member of the Quartz family, it is also sometimes referred to as Citrine Quartz. Along with Topaz it forms the birthstone of November and is also recognised as the gemstone to celebrate the 17th wedding anniversary.

History, folklore and legends of Citrine are interwoven with that of Yellow Topaz, as throughout the centuries Citrine was often wrongly identified as Topaz. Technically speaking, the difference between the two is a fluorine aluminium silicate. For those of us who rely on a less scientific differentiation, Yellow Topaz has a higher refractive index, is slightly more dense and is harder than Citrine. However, unlike Topaz, Citrine does not suffer from cleavage problems, making it ideal for cutting into unusual shapes and for use in bespoke jewellery.

In its golden form, the ancients revered the gemstone as a gift of the sun and they considered it a physically powerful antidote to the viper's venom. The gemstone is thought to have the power to disperse depression and manage anger. If a man wears the gemstone he is thought to become more striking and intellectual. For women, it is said to make her fertile, happy and contented.

The benefits of Citrine are multifaceted. Folklore suggests that the gem can have a cooling effect and can alleviate nocturnal fears. It is also believed that the gem can warn the wearer of illnesses and the presence of poisons, thus protecting from sudden death. As well as remove toxins from the body, it is said to be good for healing the heart, kidneys and liver, as

Colour	Yellow to orangeish yellow
Family	Quartz
Hardness	7
Specific Gravity	2.6 – 2.7
Refractive Index	1.532 - 1.554
Crystal Group	Trigonal
Optical Properties	Normally has great clarity
Common Treatments	Heat treated to improve colour
Care	Can fade slightly if exposed to extreme light
Cleaning Advice	Ultrasonic, steam cleaning or warm soapy water
Chemical Composition	SiO_2

An elegant setting for a Blue Topaz with impeccable clarity by Annabella.

well as aiding digestion. Some Crystal Healers also believe that the gem helps to fight diabetes. Other mystical powers include the ability to calm and soothe and to act as the signature of wisdom and peace.

Much of the Citrine set into jewellery today comes out of the ground as either Amethyst or Smokey Quartz and through the globally accepted process of heat treatment (the gem is heated to a temperature in excess of 470 degrees), is turned into vibrant Citrine.

In the past, natural Citrine or Yellow Quartz has been discovered on the Isle of Arran in Scotland, France, and Spain. Nowadays, most of the naturally coloured Citrine on the market is mined in Brazil. If you are trying to find a Citrine whose colour is completely natural, then look for one where the colour is slightly paler and slightly clouded.

With a hardness of 7 on the Mohs scale it is very resistant to scratches and (as mentioned above) as it does not suffer from any cleavage problems, it is an incredible all-round winner for jewellery designers, and is sure to remain at the forefront of contemporary jewellery for many years to come.

CLARITY

Clarity, along with colour, is possibly the most important factor affecting the quality and price of a gemstone. An inclusion free gemstone can command a high price; those that are heavily included can make the gem appear dull and lifeless. Strictly speaking, clarity literally means "clearness" rather than lack of inclusions and refers to the gem's ability to allow light to move freely through it without obstruction. Nonetheless, clarity is often used to refer to the lack of inclusioions.

Some gems are naturally clearer than others. Amethyst, Citrine, Aquamarine and Topaz for example should have good clarity: when they don't their price is substantially reduced. Other gems such as Ruby and Emeralds are rarely clean and nearly always have inclusions. Along with depth of colour, Clarity is the main reason that Ruby, for example, can sell for between £100 and £10,000 per carat!

CLARITY GRADING COLOURED GEMS

Most people are aware of the GIA's (Gemological Institution of America) grading system for Diamonds, however few are aware of their clarity grading for coloured gems.

It is important to explain that Mother Nature's wide array of gemstones are formed by several different natural processes. While some are exposed to immense pressure, others are created at extreme temperatures and are then cooled rapidly, and other gem types develop in soluble liquids.

Due to the different circumstances in which they are created, some gem varieties naturally have better clarity than others. For example, in terms of clarity, a top quality Emerald would only be comparable to a poor clarity Topaz.

For this reason, the GIA have devised a grading system that separates the main gem varieties into the three groups; Type I, Type II and Type III. Type I gem varieties are those that form under conditions that normally result in gemstones that are eye clean. Type II gemstones are those that more often have noticeable inclusions. The final grading, Type III, is reserved for gemstones that have had a very traumatic upbringing, with immense pressure and a violent gemmological home-life: these gems are only in the rarest of occasions eye clean and normally have very visible inclusions.

Put simplistically, knowing if the gem you are looking to buy is a Type I, Type II or Type III will help you in analysing whether its level of clarity is good for that gem type or not. To the right we have tried to simplify the GIA system for grading the clarity of coloured gemstones. Look for the subtle difference in wording between the three different types, in the higher ratings:

Aquamarine is a type I gem in terms of clarity.

Sapphire is a type II gem in terms of clarity.

Rubellite is a type III gem in terms of clarity.

	Type I	Type II	Type III
Gems	Aquamarine, Morganite, Chrysoberyl, Smokey Quartz, Kunzite, Topaz, Green Tourmaline, Blue Zircon, Tanzanite.	Alexandrite, Sapphire, Ruby, Garnet, Iolite, Peridot, Amethyst, Citrine, Spinel, Tourmaline, Zircon.	Emerald, Red Tourmaline (Rubellite), Pink Tourmaline, Watermelon Tourmaline
VVS	Very, Very Slightly Included - Minute inclusions that are difficult to see using 10X, and are not visible at all to the naked eye	Very, Very Slightly Included – Minor inclusions that are somewhat easy to see using 10X, but still not visible to the naked eye	Very, Very Slightly Included – Noticeable inclusions that are easy to see using 10X, but usually not visible to the naked eye
VS	Very Slightly Included – Minor inclusions that are easier to see using 10X, but still not visible to the naked eye	Very Slightly Included - Noticeable inclusions that are easier to see using 10X, and may be slightly visible to the naked eye	Very Slightly Included - Obvious inclusions that are easy to see using 10X, and usually visible to the naked eye.
SI1	Slightly Included 1 – The inclusions are easily seen using 10X, and are noticeable with the naked eye	Slightly Included 1 – The inclusions are easily seen using 10X and are large or numerous, and are noticeable with the naked eye.	Slightly Included 1 – The inclusions are large and numerous using 10X, and prominent with the naked eye.
SI2	Slightly Included 2 – The inclusions are more easily seen using 10X, and are quite visible with the naked eye	Slightly Included 2 – The inclusions are easily seen using 10X and are large or numerous, and are very noticeable with the naked eye	Slightly Included 2 – The inclusions are large and numerous using 10X, and very prominent with the naked eye
I1	Included 1 - The inclusions are very obvious and they have a moderate negative effect on the overall appearance or durability of the gemstone	Included 1 – The inclusions are very obvious and they have a moderate negative effect on the overall appearance or durability of the gemstone	Included 1 – The inclusions are very obvious and they have a moderate negative effect on the overall appearance or durability of the gemstone
I2	Included 2 - The inclusions are very obvious and they have a severe negative effect on the overall appearance or durability of the gemstone	Included 2 – The inclusions are very obvious and they have a severe negative effect on the overall appearance or durability of the gemstone	Included 2 – The inclusions are very obvious and they have a severe negative effect on the overall appearance or durability of the gemstone
I3	Included 3 – The inclusions are very obvious and they have a severe negative effect on both the overall appearance and durability of the gemstone	Included 3 – The inclusions are very obvious and they have a severe negative effect on both the overall appearance and durability of the gemstone	Included 3 – The inclusions are very obvious and they have a severe negative effect on both the overall appearance and durability of the gemstone

CLARITY OF DIAMONDS

Few things in nature are perfect: this includes Diamonds. As with other gemstones, Diamonds have internal features, which are called inclusions and can sometimes have surface imperfections, which are known as blemishes.

The level of these inclusions and blemishes set the Diamond's level of clarity. This level, along with its colour, quality of cut and carat weight, will have a direct impact on both the Diamond's rarity and its price. Though clarity characteristics may have a negative effect on a Diamond's value, they are incredibly useful to separate a Diamond from its fake competitors, whose man-made inclusions, if present, are noticeably different to those of the real thing.

As no two Diamonds have the same inclusions or characteristics, it is possible to identify individual Diamonds from their inclusion fingerprint. Inclusions have also helped scientists identify how Diamonds are formed.

Blemishes do not necessarily have an overall impact on value, as any surface scratches or imperfections can be removed. This is not true of inclusions. If they are close to the surface they can of course be removed by re-cutting the gem; however, this obviously impacts on the overall Diamond weight.

Combined with the other three C's (colour, cut and carat weight), a Diamond's clarity has a direct influence on its value: the cleaner the gem, the rarer it becomes. Flawless is the top grade in the Gemological Institute of America's (GIA) clarity grading system. Diamonds graded Flawless have no visible inclusions or blemishes under 10x magnification. Flawless Diamonds are extremely rare; to put it into context, it is possible to spend a lifetime in the industry without ever seeing one.

Although there are other standards used in the jewellery industry, the most widely used clarity guide is that of the GIA:

Flawless (FL)

A flawless Diamond shows no inclusions or blemishes under 10x magnification.

Internally Flawless (IF)

To classify as an IF, a Diamond must show no inclusions under 10x magnification but can have some minor blemishes such as surface grain lines. Sometimes these blemishes can be removed by a Lapidarist and polished to become a Flawless Diamond.

Very Very Slightly Included (VVS1 and VVS2)

These Diamonds contain extremely tiny inclusions that are difficult to see or identify under 10x magnification. Usually the inclusions appear like pinpoints, tiny feathers, internal graining or tiny cavities.

Very Slightly Included (VS1 and VS2)

These Diamonds contain small or minor inclusions that can be observed under 10 x magnification by experienced jewellers (unless trained in Diamond grading you would be unlikely to spot them under this magnification). Normally VS Diamonds have small included crystals, small clouds or small feathers.

Slightly Included (SI1 and SI2)

Slightly included Diamonds contain inclusions noticeable under 10x magnification to a jeweller. Typically, these inclusions are clouds, included crystals, knots, cavities or feathers.

In addition to the GIA system, many in the trade will talk about an SI3 grade as being somewhere between SI2 and I1. However, even though the European Gemmological Laboratory (EGL) now recognise the grading, to-date the GIA have not added it to their official guide.

Included (I1, I2 and I3)

Included Diamonds are where inclusions

are obvious under 10x magnification, they might contain large feathers, or large included crystals. Usually this kind of inclusion can affect transparency and brilliance.

Beyond I3 there are Diamonds that have inclusions visible to the naked eye: these are referred to as Pique or PK and some in the industry often talk about them as "frozen spit".

As a rule of thumb, if you are buying a Solitaire Diamond Ring you should try and purchase an SI2 or above. If this is out of your budget, then often it is worth buying a smaller carat weight to achieve this quality.

For Trilogy Diamond Rings or Eternity Bands, try and stretch to I1 or better. When it comes to buying a Cluster Diamond Ring or one with accented Diamonds, then choosing I2 or above will often be fine. Of course, that said, different people have different opinions.

If a retailer does not specify what quality the Diamonds are, then either they don't know - in which case it is questionable whether you should buy from them (after all, even the worst car salesman knows what power the engine is) - or, worse still, they don't want you to know!

A modern 2ct illusion set Diamond Ring by Tomas Rae.

CLASPS

A clasp is used at either end of a chain or cord to make the piece into a continuous loop. For bracelets and necklaces there are numerous different styles of clasps used in modern jewellery, and designers decide on which style to use based on the weight and the type of metal being used, while also taking into consideration the overall value of the jewellery.

Although they can at times be a little fiddly to use, Lobster Claw clasps are one of the most widely used locking devices in jewellery today as they are lightweight yet extremely reliable,

Clasp styles commonly used are: Barrel and Torpedo Clasps; Boxed Clasps; Hook Clasps; Magnetic Clasps; Spring Ring Clasps; T Bar Clasps; and Toggle.

A Sterling Silver clasp showing both the official hallmark and our workshop's 925 stamp.

A Trilogy of claw set Rhodolite Garnet.

CLAW SETTING

Claw setting, or 'prong setting' as it is more commonly known, is the easiest method of setting a gemstone and is probably the most popular setting. The claw setting allows the optimum amount of light to pass through the stone, maximising its brilliance.

There are usually four or six "claws" of metal that reach around the gem's girdle to hold it in place. Although the pieces of metal on show can be carved or be made into creative shapes, they are usually rounded to prevent catching.

CLEAVAGE

This describes the tendency certain gemstones have to break in preferred directions, providing a more or less smooth surface. This is particularly important for the Lapidarist, as he or she will need to take this into consideration when deciding on the orientation of the gemstone (where to make the first cut).

Due to its cleavage Kyanite is very difficult to facet.

In the three-dimensional structure of certain crystals, atoms are bound more tightly to each other in some directions and more loosely in others. As a consequence, when strong forces are applied, relatively clean breaks may occur in these "weakest link" directions. Breaks which are so smooth as to appear to have been polished are called 'perfect cleavages'.

Since cleavage, or lack of it, is specific to certain gemstones, it is used by gemmologists as a good identification tool. Gemstones with easy or perfect cleavage, particularly when they are in multiple directions, are difficult to facet and at greatest risk during the cutting stage. Not all gems have a cleavage: examples being Tourmalines, Sapphires and Garnets.

CLEOPATRA'S EMERALDS

For thousands of years, royalty have been renowned for having fabulous collections of gems and jewellery. One of the most famous collections was that of Cleopatra, who was said to be fanatical about Emeralds. Egypt was the earliest known location for Emerald mining, not far from the Red Sea. This mine was claimed by Cleopatra as her own, taking it from the Greeks.

She didn't stop at Emeralds either: she also laid claim to the oldest source of Peridot in the world, which was found on the desert island of Zeberget. This probably explains why a lot of Cleopatra's Emerald collection actually turned out to be Peridot.

As well as using the stones for lavish jewellery, Cleopatra and the ancient Egyptians believed Emeralds could be used to treat eye diseases and that the green colour represented fertility and rebirth. The dead were often buried with Emeralds to symbolise eternal youth. When visiting dignitaries left Egypt, Cleopatra presented them with her likeness carved into large Emeralds.

In 1817, the 'lost' mines of Cleopatra were rediscovered. However, due to heavy mining between 3000 and 1500BC, the supply of Emeralds there has long been exhausted.

CLINOHUMITE

If it wasn't for my friend Shawn, here is another gemstone I would not have been able to acquire. Even though Shawn was born in Pakistan and is pretty much a local, in these current troubled times he faced many dangers when travelling to the remote locations of the Pamir Mountain in Tajikistan, where this extremely rare and valuable gem was discovered.

With an appearance similar to that of a mineral crossbreed of Hessonite Garnet and Sphalerite, Clinohumite is a delightful, bright yellowish orange gemstone.

Clinohumite is a real must-have for gem collectors. It is a member of the Humite family of minerals (named after the English gem collector Sir Abraham Hume) and is closely related to the more common Chondrodite.

Colour	Yellow to Orange
Family	Humite
Hardness	6
Specific Gravity	3.2 - 3.9
Refractive Index	1.63 - 1.66
Crystal Group	Monoclinic
Optical Properties	Pleochroic
Common Treatments	None
Care	None
Cleaning Advice	Warm soapy water
Chemical Composition	Complex

In addition to the glorious yellowish orange gems coming from Tajikistan (which were only first discovered in the 1980s), there has more recently been a small deposit discovered in northern Siberia. However, the gems from this region tend to be a far darker reddish brown and they are slightly softer on the mohs scale.

From our extensive research into this gem, we believe that to-date there has been no more than a couple of thousand carats ever faceted! In addition to the tiny pockets unearthed in Tajikistan and Siberia, there have also been other discoveries of Clinohumite in such countries as Tasmania, Austria, Brazil and Canada, however none of these have yet to yield any gem grade material.

A 1.7ct pear cut Clinohumite

CLOUDY

This is an effect often seen in gems such as Diamonds and Emeralds, which is normally caused by a mass of small inclusions, often of a fibrous nature.

Not only does it diminish the appearance of the gem, but it also reduces its ability to demonstrate brilliance and dispersion (also known as fire). Almost without exception, cloudy gems are less valuable than a clear gemstone of a similar colour, cut and carat weight.

Emerald is a classic cloudy gemstone; the inclusions often being referred to as "Jardin".

CLUSTER RINGS

Nothing catches the eye more than a flash of scintillation off the table or crown facets of a gemstone. Big solitaire rings are great for demonstrating vividly coloured gemstones, while trilogy rings are symbols of love. With their mass of facets scintillating like a Christmas tree, cluster rings are real head turners. I have a saying, 'there is more lustre in a cluster', a term which many of the jewellery presenters I have trained over the years now use as often as 'trilogy rings represent the past, the present and the future'.

The famous Coloured Rocks 'Hedgehog' cluster ring.

Whilst it is true that smaller gemstones normally cost less than larger ones, the extra cost involved in faceting lots of gemstones, then sorting them to find the very best matches in colour and clarity and then having the jeweller set each gem individually in the ring, cannot be underestimated. Some cluster rings produced by Tomas Rae for example, have taken two days just to set the gems in each piece.

Although most cluster rings tend to have the same gemstones set, occasionally using different colours can often result in a stunning piece being created. Because gemstones vary in colour and clarity as well as in their saturation and tone, selecting gems of different types, with different colours is a true art form. Get the combination wrong and the ring can be very unattractive: select the right gems, with the right tones and shades, and a masterpiece is created. Once again this is an area of expertise in which the jewellery gem sorters at Tomas Rae are exceptional.

Another famous Coloured Rocks 'Hedgehog' cluster ring.

COATED GEMS

A gemstone which is covered by an artificially applied transparent material or mineral to enhance its colour and appearance, is known as a coated gemstone. The technique is often used with coloured Topaz to create Mystic Topaz, and colourless Quartz is turned into Mystic Quartz using the same process.

Unlike heat treatment used on gemstones - a technique that dates back several thousand years - gemstone coating is a relatively new process. As opposed to heat-treating, no one is yet completely sure how durable coating is, therefore any coating should be declared by retailers.

Some people argue that if a genuine gem is coated after being cut, it is no more valuable than a synthetic or a fake: this is ludicrous. It's similar to a beautiful lady who wears a permanent colourful coat to enhance her image. The lady is still a real gem who is unique and individual, but is simply dressed up.

Without this new process, we would not enjoy the mesmerising effects of Mystic Topaz, Mystic Quartz and the sensational Fuchsia Pink Topaz.

Two Blue Mystic Topaz rings set in a hand made piece by Tookalon.

SPICE
T O P A Z

Indulge in Brilliance

GENUINE TOPAZ
12 BREATHTAKING COLOURS
FINEST CUTTING
PATENTED TECHNOLOGY
NON RADIATED
PRECISION CALIBRATION
EVERLASTING DURABILITY
NON COATED

Patent Number 6872422
Exclusively distributed in Europe by Coloured Rocks

COCKTAIL RINGS

Big, bold and colourful, the cocktail ring has long been a fabulous accessory for women all over the world.

Most cultures at some point or another have used jewellery for adornment, and in Western cultures extravagant jewellery has been enjoyed for many years. What better way to do this than with a cocktail ring? They really are show stoppers of incredible beauty and usually exquisitely designed.

Traditionally worn on the fourth finger on the right hand, from the Diamond trading slogans 'your left hand says "we" and your right hand says "me"', and 'Your left hand rocks the cradle and your right hand rocks the world', they are also known as right hand rings and Dinner Rings.

Cocktail rings gained popularity in the 1920's at the start of the Art Deco period and produced dazzling jewellery in stark contrast to other periods. The fashion for women was to have short hair, and they wore clothes such as flapper dresses. The jewellery fashion of this period was alluring and luxurious. It was the done thing to listen to jazz and be a free spirit, and the flamboyant jewellery complemented the playful and decadent attitude of the time. In America, where illegal cocktail parties were held during the prohibition period (1920 – 1933), it was thought of as daring and controversial to be seen at the parties wearing these bright dazzling cocktail rings. Women would show their defiance of the law and flaunt their wealth and style at these soirees.

They can be absolutely breathtaking and allow the wearer to step into a world of high-class glamour and delight. They are unquestionably stylish, stunning and sexy; ostentatious yet graceful. A cocktail ring generally has one exciting gemstone that is the main focus of the ring, although it may have other gemstones that will complement it, while not distracting from the focal piece. They can also feature pearls, especially black pearls, as well as cabochon cut

These cocktail rings above and on the next page are from the 2009 Sarah Bennett vermeil collection.

gemstones. A cocktail ring gemstone normally starts at around 3 carats in size. Cocktail rings are an excellent way to spice up any outfit. Today, celebrities are often seen at film premieres and openings wearing cocktail rings. Whether it be Sarah Jessica Parker from "Sex and the City", who wore a huge, knuckle-sized cocktail ring for the final episode party of the show or diva Jennifer Lopez, who was seen wearing a 6.1 carat cocktail ring, the stars of today seem to have the same love affair with these rings as their predecessors, inspiring a whole new generation to start wearing them. From Madonna to royalty, it seems the cocktail ring is enjoyed and celebrated by all.

Boodles, Garrard, Chopard, Lorique and Bulgari are all making exquisite pieces, often in restricted numbers. Mixing old school glamour with witty design is one of the best ways of wearing the cocktail ring. Coco Channel herself, with her renowned avant-garde taste, was often seen wearing cocktail rings

COLOMBIA

Located to the north of South America, Colombia has for many years been the world's premier source of quality Emeralds. These treasures are unearthed in an area known as the 'Emerald Belt', which is a sedimentary basin located near the Andes mountains. There are three main mining areas for Emerald: Coscuez, Muzo, and Chivor; and Colombians have been mining their prized possession since the early 1500's. However, over recent years, these miners have had to dig deeper and deeper, decreasing the number of top quality Emeralds found. With yields continually falling, new mining operations have been set up in La Pita, and some reports suggest as much as 50% of Colombian Emeralds are now found at this location.

One Colombian tale tells of the Spanish conqueror Conquistador, who in the 1850's, prior to the opening of the Muzo mine, attempted to drain the huge Lake Guatavita in Sesquilé by cutting a hole in the lake's rim. He believed that" below the lake, which is said to

A 2.3ct Colombian Emerald

have been created by a huge meteorite hitting the area, lay great treasures. He could not have been more right: at the edge of the lake he discovered both gold and Emeralds.

COLOUR

The world we live in is full of light, which can be broken down into seven different wavelengths, with each wavelength relating to one of the seven colours seen in a rainbow: red, orange, yellow, green, blue, indigo and violet. Each of these wavelengths has different lengths: the bluish colours are the shortest, the greenish colours fall in the middle and the reddish colours are the longest.

When light hits an object, depending on the type of material, some colours are absorbed and some are reflected. The reflected wavelengths are what our eyes perceive as the colour of the object.

The different hues, tones and saturations (the three main elements of colour) seen in gemstones are due to the presence of differing elements and often the same gemstone can naturally be found in a multitude of different colours. Take Garnet, Spinel and Tourmaline: these three gemstone families are available in a wide spectrum of colours, and this is due to differing chemical compositions, different physical structures, and sometimes caused by the presence of inclusions.

The depth of colour in a gem, amongst other things, can greatly affect the value of the stone. Generally speaking, the more vivid the colour, the greater the value. Unfortunately, with some gems such as Emeralds and Bixbites, better depths of colour are normally caused by a greater occurrence of inclusions and imperfections. When it comes to Diamonds, valuations relating to colour are very different compared to almost all other gems. A Diamond's value is usually greater the nearer it is to colourless.

There are many reasons why coloured gemstones have been worn for thousands of years. Folklore, legends, myths, healing benefits, talismans, birthstones and zodiac gems are all exciting topics that relate to gemstones and often act as

The wonderful colours of nature.

Colourful watches by Jessica Lili.

Colour change Garnet from the Tomas Rae collection

A precious colour change Sapphire.

Andesine; the new kid on the block in the world of colour change gemstones.

an inspiration to acquire a certain piece. But for me, the most important motivator for buying any gemstone, is its colour. If it's vivid, if it's beautiful, if it reminds me of other colours seen in nature, then I simply have to have it!

See also hue, tone and saturation.

COLOUR CHANGE GARNET

If you thought that colour change gemstones was a phenomenon exclusively reserved for Alexandrite, then you will be surprised to learn that Colour Change Garnet is equally as alluring and equally as rare.

Its colour change is similar to Alexandrite in that under different lighting conditions, it appears to change from a greenish blue, to a brownish red.

The gem has been primarily discovered in Tanzania and Madagascar, where it is a cross between a Pyrope and Spessatite Garnet, but a small deposit has also been found in Idaho America where the gem is a blend of Pyrope and Almandine Garnet.

COLOUR CHANGE GEMS

Firstly the bad news: it is a misconception that "colour change" gemstones physically change colour. The reality is that when viewed under different lighting conditions, certain gems (including some Chrysoberyl and some Garnets), only appear to change colour.

The change in colour is due to the fact that these vary rare gemstones absorb different colours of the spectrum from different light sources.

When you buy a colour change gemstone, to view the strongest change you need to view the gem under candescent lighting (direct sunlight) and then immediately view it under artificial light (incandescent light). The reason for this is that daylight contains high proportions of blue and green light, while incandescent lighting contains a higher balance of red light.

For example, when you view Alexandrite in daylight (balanced light) the gem is green but when the light source is reddish (incandescent), the gem shows tones of purple or red. Effectively you are looking at an optical illusion!

Most changes are incredibly subtle, and the saying that Alexandrite looks Emerald by day and Ruby by night is a slight exaggeration. That said nobody can deny the inherent beauty of coloured gemstones.

Alexandrite; the most famous colour change gemstone of all.

COLOUR GRADING OF DIAMONDS

Many people are under the assumption that Diamonds are always colourless, but this is in fact untrue. Diamonds actually come in a wide range of colours, such as the famous blue Hope Diamond, or the 128ct canary yellow Tiffany Diamond.

Diamonds that are colourless, light yellow and brown, all fall in the normal colour range that people are used to. Truly colourless Diamonds are extremely rare and therefore command the highest price. Subtle differences in colour can affect the value dramatically.

Because Diamonds are not all the same colour, the Gemological Institute of America (GIA) introduced a Diamond Colour scale. This colour scale is the most widely used and was developed by Richard T. Liddicoat in the 1950's.

The scale is from D to Z: these letters do not represent or describe the actual Colour of the Diamond, but instead represent how colourless the Diamond is. Obviously, the less colour the better it will display its unique fire and brilliance. Whilst the GIA scale is shown to the right, there are several other standards used by organisations such as AGS and CIBJO.

Colour	Grade
D	Colourless
E	Colourless
F	Colourless
G	Near Colourless
H	Near Colourless
I	Near Colourless
J	Near Colourless
K	Faint
L	Faint
M	Faint
N	Very Light
O	Very Light
P	Very Light
Q	Very Light
R	Very Light
S	Light
T	Light
U	Light
V	Light
W	Light
X	Light
Y	Light
Z	Light

COLOURED ROCKS

The Coloured Rocks studios where Rocks TV is broadcast.

Coloured Rocks is a family owned international jewellers that specialises in designing and retailing exquisite gemstone set jewellery. All of our pieces feature genuine gemstones set in wonderful timeless designs, hence our saying "created by nature, designed for your next generation".

Our Design Centre and TV Studios are set in a Victorian Manor House in Historic Warwickshire and our Call Centre and Distribution Facilities are in a modern office environment in nearby Worcestershire. In order to create a team who are passionate about serving our customers, our totally independent and family run business aims to provide the very best working conditions for our team members and to create an atmosphere where people love to come to work.

Whilst most of our distribution and design is done in the UK, the majority of our gemstone work is done in our facility in Jaipur, India. Here we cut, sort and manage our entire gem inventory. By completely controlling this process, often including the complex journey from mines to consumers, we are able to offer the very best prices on the planet. When it comes to crafting our jewellery, in order to produce a wide array of styles and take advantage of different talents and techniques around the world, many of our brands license the final jewellery production to other companies.

Our standard procedure is to provide our manufacturing partners with both the loose gemstones and master designs and to then ensure they craft the jewellery to our high exacting standards. We believe our business model is one of the most cost effective in the jewellery world, offers complete control and benefits from not restricting our creative talents to just one workshop or one country.

The Coloured Rocks website.

In addition to our UK Broadcast and Design Centre and our Jaipur Gem Centre, we also have offices in Bangkok, Switzerland and Australia.

COLOURLESS GEMS

When someone mentions colourless gems to you, I bet the first image to enter your head is a Diamond! Why is this? Well it's probably all to do with the fact that over the past 60 years the Diamond has been marketed so heavily, that it has become the most talked about gemstone on the planet. However, it certainly is not the rarest and with over 60 million carats cut each year, with the exception of Quartz, nearly all other colourless gems are far rarer!

One of the most stunning colourless gems has to be Zircon. Just like Diamonds, Zircon has the beautiful ability to show dispersion and the visual effects caused by its double refraction can leave you speechless. What makes Zircon even more special is that many specimens were created 4.6 billion years ago, right at the time the earth itself was formed!

Goshonite the colourless Beryl is also a very attractive clear gemstone and Danburite from Connecticut, USA, looks so much like a Diamond that in Japan it is known as the Japanese Diamond.

In addition to transparent colourless gems, there are also several opaque white gems. These include White Agate, White Opal, White Aventurine and of course let's not forget the organic Pearl.

Don't think for one moment that I am not a fan of Diamonds, because that is certainly not the case. However, I do like to put Diamonds into perspective and to try and readdress the imbalance in the gem world, an imbalance caused via marketing, by focusing my attention on other lesser hyped gemstones. After all, if you read through ancient history books and the bible, it is not the Diamond that is widely documented, but the likes of gemstones often overlooked today like Beryl and Zircon.

So next time you are looking for a colourless dazzling gemstone, remember it's not only Diamonds that can make you sparkle.

Diamonds display a dazzling adamantine lusture.

Double refraction causes the amazing visual effect in Zircon.

We recognise the natural beauty of White Topaz in its own right.

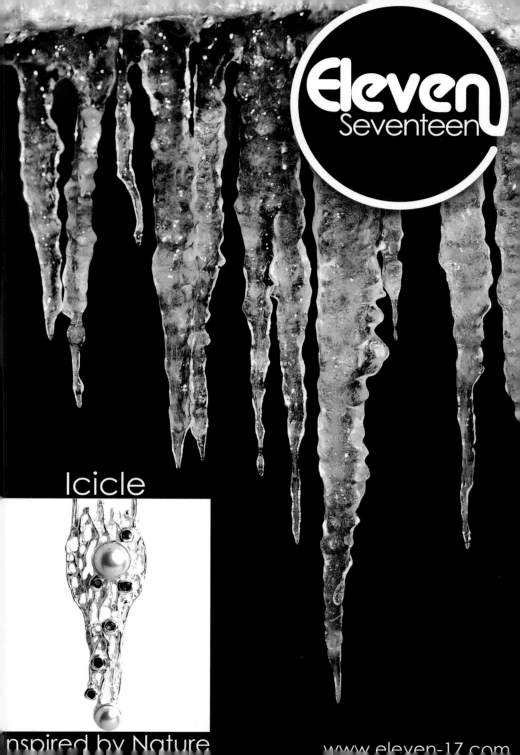

Eleven
Seventeen

Icicle

Inspired by Nature

www.eleven-17.com

MILANO
CHARMS

Jewels of Valais
SWITZERLAND

Tomas Rae

SARAH BENNETT
GEMSTONE
JEWELLERY

LORIQUE

MATTOM

Jacque Christie

TooKALON

14 JEWELLERY
COLLECTIONS
ONE SHOPPING DESTINATION
WWW.COLOUREDROCKS.CO

COLOUR SATURATION

Many people confuse colour saturation with colour tone. When saturation is discussed in relationship to gemstones, it relates to the purity or intensity of the hue, whereas tone relates to the shade of the colour.

The GIA saturation scale ranges from 1 to 6:

The highest grade, 6, is used for hues that are pure and are described as vividly saturated. From grade four onwards, there should be no grey/brown in the hue.

Rating	Green to Blue Coloured Gemstones (Cold)	Red to Yellow Coloured Gemstones (Warm)
1	Greyish	Brownish
2	Slightly greyish	Slightly brownish
3	Very slightly greyish	Very slightly brownish
4	Moderately strong colour	Moderately strong colour
5	Strong colour	Strong colour

Colour	White or colourless
Family	Topaz
Hardness	8
Specific Gravity	3.5 – 3.6
Refractive Index	1.6 – 1.63
Crystal Group	Orthorhombic
Optical Properties	Strong pleochrism
Common Treatments	Normally heat treated
Care	No special care required
Chemical Composition	$Al_2SiO_4(OH,F)_2$

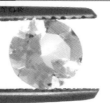

COLOURLESS TOPAZ

White Topaz has an intense fire rivalled in other colourless gemstones only by Diamonds and Zircon and is a perfect alternative to both in jewellery.

White Topaz has an amazing, lively brilliance, but is used infrequently due to its rarity. White Topaz is perfect for jewellery as its good hardness and durability allows it to be set into almost any jewellery design.

Colourless Topaz is also used as the base gemstone for mystic coatings and also for the new colouring technology known as Spice Topaz which is exclusivley available in Europe by Coloured Rocks. Take a look at the Spice Topaz section later in this book and be amazed at the colours we have achieved.

COMPASS CARD CUT

Designed by Merrill O. Murphy, a Lapidarist and gem collector from New Mexico, the compass card cut is normally applied to round shaped gemstones and when viewed from the table facet (as its name suggests) you see a traditional style compass card. For those into sailing or for those looking for direction in life, this cut is a must have.

Although as this edition goes to print we are still unable to bring this cut to you, my team of lapidaries are working hard at trying to perfect it and we are hoping to be able to bring it to you in the near future.

Compass cut viewed from the pavilion..

CONCAVE CUT

The concave cut is becoming increasingly popular for coloured gemstones over two carats in size. Whereas most cuts aim to return as much light back to the wearer as possible, the concave cut aims to lock light within the gem.

The appearance is similar to the experience of driving in a snow storm at night and watching the effect of your headlights on the snow, which appear to create thousands of small parallel beams of light flying towards your windscreen.

The effect is created by applying small concave facets on the pavilion of the gem, and occasionally by adding them to the crown of the stone. Picture a series of waves in an ocean or a tin roof and you are thus imagining how the underside of a concave gem is created.

As this technique cannot be applied by the traditional horizontal Lap, Lapadarists have to use a vertical grinding wheel to add the concave facets to the gem. Most cutters will first apply traditional facets to the pavillion and then slowly add pressure to the gem on the edge of the grinding wheel to add the concave cut. The easiest way to visualise this is to imagine spinning the wheel of a cycle through butter. As adding concave facets requires real skill, often today companies will use computer-aided machinery.

A table view of a concave cut pavilion.

A pavilion view of a concave cut Mystic Topaz.

CONFLICT (FREE) DIAMONDS

Also known as Blood Diamonds or War Diamonds, Conflict Diamonds are those that are mined in regions where there are wars, and are sold to finance rebel activities and conflicts. In 2006, the film "Blood Diamond", starring Leonardo DiCaprio, was based on the Civil War in Sierra Leone in the 1990's. The story is based on the fate of two men as they try to recover a rare pink Diamond that they believe will change their lives.

Most quality jewellers only use reliable suppliers to ensure their Diamonds are conflict free.

All of Coloured Rocks' Diamonds are conflict free.

CORAL

Coral is believed to be the oldest form of gemstone jewellery, with some pieces dating back as far as 23,000BC.

Found in many different colours, throughout history each variant signified different metaphysical properties: for instance, Black Coral is said to guard against misfortune, while Pink Coral is said to bring good health.

The Romans believed that Coral had magical and medicinal properties and many Roman children would wear Coral around their neck to protect them from danger.

Victorian babies born into wealthy families were given Coral teething rings.

Black Coral is the rarest colour, and when polished it shines with such a radiant lustre that you can almost see your own reflection. It is found in the waters off Lahaina, Maui and is carefully collected by hand (this is governed by strict harvesting practices to preserve the reef and to ensure that only fossilised Coral is collected, therefore protecting the living coral).

Pink Coral is a very dense and hard gemstone. Its colour runs through the entire pink spectrum,

Coral designs from Jessica Lili.

from almost white to a deep salmon shade.

Red Coral has a history pre-dating Rome, and has been highly regarded since early civilizations for its colour, lustre and texture. Red Coral and Pink Coral are usually from the coasts of France, Italy, Africa and Japan (which also has White Coral).

Golden Coral is found off the coast of Hawaii, Australia and the West Indies. Other locations for Coral include The Red Sea, Algeria, Tunisia and Malaysia.

A sumptuous Coral and Sterling Silver bracelet.

Essentially, Coral is calcified skeletons of sea creatures that grow in tree-like formations. Most Coral used for the production of jewellery is from the Mediterranean Sea or from the Pacific Ocean near Japan and Taiwan.

CREATED GEMS

Synthetic, lab grown and created gems are all man-made and should therefore not be compared to real gemstones. As they are created by man, they are not rare and as they are not rare they should not even be called gemstones.

One thing that really annoys collectors of gemstones and those who respect the work of Mother Nature, is when people advertise man-made gems such as Cubic Zirconia and Moissanite and measure their weight with carats! This is completely misleading. These are man-made items and should only be measured in grams and ounces. However, these laboratory-made equivalents do often have the same physical, optical and chemical properties as a genuine gemstone. Nevertheless, they are still not the real thing. Plus, as they can be reproduced in any quantity, they can neither be classed as rare nor be considered to have any intrinsic value.

CROWN

In gem terms, the crown refers to the portion of a gemstone above its girdle (its widest part). The crown acts as a lens, focusing the light, which is

Created gems - NOT available at Coloured Rocks!

Crown

*The crown facets sit between the
table and girdle of a gemstone.*

then reflected back by the pavilion (the portion of the gem below the girdle). The crown on a round brilliant cut gem has 32 facets, while the crown on an Emerald cut typically has 24.

CROWN JEWELS

Ever since the crowning of the King of Wessex in the 9th century, jewellery has played a very important and intriguing role in the lives of the royal family. Kings and Queens of England have amassed a huge wealth in crowns, robes and other pieces of ceremonial regalia, but unlike most collections which remain locked away in museums, the Queen of England frequently wears numerous pieces from the collection.

The Crown Jewels, which form part of the Royal Collection, are displayed in The Jewel House at the Tower of London and are world-famously guarded by the Yeomen Warders (better known as 'Beefeaters'). The Jewel House has been used to store the Crown Jewels since the 14th century, when it was felt that the previous storage room at Westminster Abbey was not secure enough. I am always telling my friends abroad that The Crown Jewels on display in the Tower of London are more like a royal jewellery wardrobe, rather than a museum. If you have never seen The Crown Jewels and you are serious about gemstones and jewellery, then you really must at some stage visit the Tower of London. Unlike the chaos caused by six million people a year trying to stand in front of the Mona Lisa in the museum's Salle des États in Paris, viewing the Crown Jewels is an orderly affair. While standing on a slowly moving conveyor belt, you pass within feet of many fascinating pieces including: The Sovereigns Sceptre (which is set with the Cullinan I Diamond); The Crown of Queen Elizabeth The Queen's Mother (which is set with the Koh-i-Noor Diamond); Queen Mary's Crown (set entirely with Diamonds); and The Imperial State Crown (featuring the Black Prince's Ruby). This amazing experience lets you achieve a real sense of the importance that coloured gemstones have played with royalty over the past 1200 years.

H.B

The Imperial State Crown.

As long as the room is not heaving with visitors,

when you hop off the end of the conveyer you can normally walk back to the beginning of it and start again. Be sure to travel along both conveyor belts: one runs behind the wall of glass and the rear of the jewellery is just as impressive as the front! Once you have studied all of the glorious pieces, the huge Emeralds, Diamonds, Sapphires, Spinels and Rubies set into Crowns and Sceptres, then slowly amble along the rest of the corridors taking in the splendid trumpets, swords and maces that have been used in Coronation ceremonies for over 1200 years.

CRYSTAL FORMATION

The study of crystallography can be quite overwhelming and without first obtaining a degree in science, is difficult to grasp. Here we have tried our best to explain how crystals are formed in plain English.

First, it is important to understand that most coloured gems are also minerals (other than those which are organic such as Pearl, Coral, Amber, Jet etc).

Secondly, take it as a fact that most minerals occur as crystals.

Finally, crystals are formed when billions and billions of tiny atoms link together in a precise three-dimensional pattern that is repeated over and over again.

So how do crystals grow? In the beginning, a few atoms start to hang about together, not on street corners, but normally in water-based solutions or molten rock in fissures and cavities. Over time, as their environment around them changes, they start to connect with each other in bigger and bigger clusters. Each new atom that joins the group must join in a precise way, and those that follow must also be identically locked in.

When other groups of crystals start to grow in the same space, they stunt each other's growth and prevent them from forming into beautiful gemstones; the net result being an igneous

All crystals are made with precise atom structures.

Pyrite forms naturally in a cubic crystal structure.

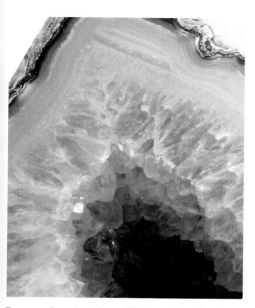

Gems such as Amethyst, Citrine and Chalcedony often form inside geodes.

rock and not a valuable mineral waiting to be discovered by gem hunters.

Those rare groups that manage to keep space around them, who find themselves in the right temperature zone, those that experience just the right amount of pressure and a steady recruitment of new like-minded atoms, joining at just the right rate over a prolonged period of thousands and thousands of years, might just evolve into that one tiny fraction (one hundredth billionth to be exact) of the Earth's crust that you would feel proud to wear on your finger.

However, these odds diminish even further: as the crystal needs to be free of major faults, it needs to be hard enough to withstand the cutting process, yet not too brittle to break. It needs to be large enough to be set into jewellery and above all it needs to be attractive. These additional factors deny the majority of the four thousand plus minerals identified to-date to obtain the "gemstone" title. As you can hopefully now appreciate, gemstones really are rare!

CRYSTAL FORMATION ANOMALIES

Twinning

To understand twinning, think about human twins. If they are born under normal circumstance, both can be identical at birth and grow up independently of one another. Twinned crystals are like Siamese twins, something unusual happened during their early development and they became attached. They then have to grow side by side and share the same living space.

Twinning can occur while certain minerals are forming, where their structure may be reflected, repeated incorrectly or rotated, resulting in the creation of a twin crystal.

A twinned structure will share more than one face, and the shape of the crystal might be dramatically affected or the material properties could be noticeably altered. Twinning is often due to changes in temperature or pressure during

Sphene can often be twinned.

or after formation.

Twinned crystals can often make it difficult to correctly identify a gem species. For example if a Chrysoberyl becomes twinned, its structure looks like it is a hexagonal crystal, however the actual crystal structure of a Chrysoberyl is orthombic.

Much of the Sphene I have recently received from Pakistan is heavily twinned, which only adds to the incredible beauty of this amazing gemstone.

Polycrystalline

Crystals that are composed of many crystal structures that have grown together are called polycrystalline. These gemstones are extremely durable and difficult to break. Jadeite and Agate both have polycrystalline structures.

Cryptocrystalline

Where the crystal structure is too small to be seen by the eye and a microscope is required, the crystals are known as microcrystalline or cryptocrystalline (from the Greek word 'crypto' which means 'hidden').

The biggest gemstone family Quartz is divided into two groups, Crystalline Quartz and Cryptocrystalline Quartz. Crystalline Quartz include Amethyst, Citrine, Rose Quartz and Smokey Quartz, whilst Cryptocrystalline Quartz includes Chalcedony, Jasper, Carnelian, Bloodstone and Onyx.

Phantom crystals

If a crystal stops growing and later starts again, during this dormant period it is possible for other crystals that have grown alongside it to be trapped inside. This effect can often occur with Quartz. These crystals can either be very unattractive (and obviously not suited for use in jewellery) or on the odd occasion form a real masterpiece.

Phantom crystals are hugely popular with Crystal Healers who believe that they help you put past experiences into perspective.

Agate has a polycrystalline Stucture.

Chalcedony is a cryptocrystalline gemstone.

Jasper is a cryptocrystalline gemstone.

PREMIUM economy

MILANO
C H A R M S

CRYSTAL HEALING (LITHOTHERAPY)

Since antiquity, man has believed in the healing abilities of certain gemstones. The study of the use of minerals in medicine is known as lithotherapy, and although there is no scientific proof behind any of the suggested remedies, there are still hundreds of thousands of people who believe in the mystical powers of crystal healing.

My own personal assistant, Barry Wiggins, who has struggled with severe back pains for many years, was once recommended to carry a piece of Snowflake Obsidian and Haematite in his pocket. I must point out that this was long before I met him and therefore is totally independent of any influence I may have had on him - in fact I only found out about his experience several months ago when the topic of crystal healing was being discussed for this book.

Barry has been carrying the gems in his pocket for many years and believes so much in their powers that he even puts them in his shorts when he goes swimming! For eight years now, Barry has been free from back pain. Of course, it could be coincidence or it could be that there are powers that we just don't understand. One further explanation could be that Barry believes in their powers so much that it acts as a placebo.

Eminent writers throughout history, including Aristotle (384 -322BC), Pliny the Elder (23AD – 79AD) and Abbess Hildegard von Bingen (1098 – 1179AD) have documented many beliefs associated with different gemstones. Many believe that gems are linked to planets, suns and moons. Others believe that as most gemstones have taken millions of years to create, they have somehow captured powers from Mother Nature along their journey. Certain healing gems should be regularly exposed to the sun in order to recharge their powers, whereas other gems should be placed on the terrace or window sill two nights before the full moon. Some gems are said to have their powers enhanced if the gem is buried in soil overnight.

Though there is no scientific evidence that links gemstones to medical benefits, we have decided to include the following chart that we have compiled from studying the works of many crystal healers, as we believe that as long as they are not used to replace medicine and are only used in conjunction with proven remedies, then no harm can be done. After all, the power of positive thinking is known to be better for our health than having a negative outlook.

Headaches: - Gems associated with helping prevent and cure headaches, although totally unproven, include: Amethyst, Azurite, Diamond, Lapis Lazuli, Malachite, Moonstone, Emerald and Tiger's Eye

Arthritis: - Gems associated with helping alleviate the pain of arthritis, although totally unproven, include: Apatite, Aquamarine, Amber, Garnet, Pyrite and Tourmaline.

Eyes: - Gems associated with helping prevent and cure problems with sight, although totally unproven, include: Aquamarine, Emerald, Eye Agate, Chalcedony, Onyx and Sapphire.

Sore Throats: - Gems associated with helping prevent and cure sore throats, although totally unproven, include: Opals, Sodalite and Blue Topaz. Silver is also said to help alleviate sore throats.

Heart Ailments: - Gems associated with helping blood circulation, although totally unproven, include: Aventurine, Carnelian, Morganite, Rhodonite Garnet, Rose Quartz, Ruby, Topaz and Turquoise.

Pancreas: - Gems associated with the pancreas, although totally unproven, include: Amethyst, Citrine, Garnet, Moonstone, Obsidian and Green Tourmaline.

Sciatica: - Gems associated with sciatica, although totally unproven, include: Amethyst, Citrine, Diamond, Emerald, Jasper, Carnelian, Pearl, Rose Quartz, Peridot, Ruby and Tiger's Eye.

Testicles: - Gems associated with maintaining healthy testicles, although totally unproven, include: Chalcedony, Diamond, Garnet, Jade, Rubellite, Tiger's Eye and Zircon.

Varicose Veins: - Gems associated with aiding the relief of varicose veins, although totally unproven, include: Aquamarine, Amber, Diamond, Garnet, Pearl, Ruby, Sapphire, Topaz and Zircon.

CRYSTAL SYSTEMS

There are seven different common types of crystal groups (crystal systems) and they are used to describe the "lattice" that makes up a crystal. A Lattice is the three dimensional framework of atoms arranged in a symmetrical pattern and is what provides each individual un-faceted gemstone its characteristic and natural shape.

It all sounds complicated, so I'll recall a true story which might help explain it a little better. The year was 1783; Rene Just Hauy, a forty year old Frenchman, was about to make a big discovery. He had studied botany, but an accident was about to dramatically change his field of interest and place him in the history books of science. One evening, he slipped and dropped a large calcite crystal to the floor. It had been lent to him by a friend and as hurried to pick up all of the shattered pieces, he noticed how all the fragments, no matter how big or small they were, all had an identical shape.

After studying these fragments in great detail, he became the first person to arrive at the conclusion that crystals are constructed by a large number of smaller units, all of which have an identical shape. He named these individual units "integrant molecules".

From the studies initiated by Hauy, we now know that a gemstone's outer shape is generally a reflection of its regimented internal structure. The story does not end here however. Fast forward sixty-seven years to 1850, when another French scientist, Auguste Bravis, discovered that there were only fourteen different orderly

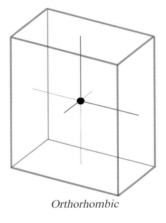

Orthorhombic

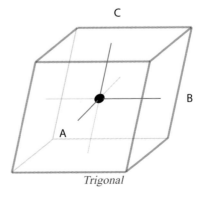

Trigonal

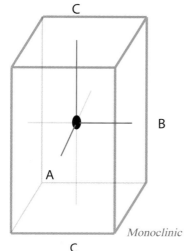

Monoclinic

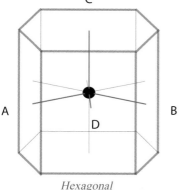

Hexagonal

arrangements of atoms found in crystals. Later studies by Max von Laue (the German Nobel Prize winner for physics in 1914) and then the works of William Bragg demonstrated how X-rays passing through minerals would scatter in distinctive and regular patterns.

Through the work of these three gentlemen (technically it was four because William Bragg's son was also involved in his father's research), today it is universally accepted that there are seven different crystal systems in which nearly all gemstones fall into: cubic; hexagonal; tetragonal; orthorhombic; trigonal; triclinic; and monoclinic.

Rubies and Sapphires, members of the Corundum family, originate from trigonal crystals. Members of the Beryl family such as Aquamarine, Morganite and Emerald are from the hexagonal crystal group. Peridot and Topaz come from the orthorhombic crystal system, and Diamond, Garnet and Spinel are members of the cubic system.

In addition to the seven crystal systems, there are a few gems that have no directional structure; these are known as "amorphous" (most dictionaries describe the word as lacking organisation or unity). Examples of amorphous gems are Amber, Jet, Moldavite and Opal.

CUFFLINKS

Cufflinks predate the sewn-on buttons that are often used today and date back as far as the seventeenth century when wealthy men began wanting to fasten their sleeves with something more precious than ribbons or ties. Cufflinks began with small chains which had gold or silver beads fixed to each end. The chain would be put through the cuff and pulled taut until the bead was flush against the sleeve, hence the name was derived from the "cuff" of the shirt cuff and the "link" of the chain.

Cufflinks were now an important part of a gentleman's apparel; however, it was not until the Industrial Revolution really set in motion that the availability of cufflinks increased

Mattom interchangeable Gem Cufflinks.

beyond those that could afford to have them custom made. Slowly, as the popularity for the cufflink grew, so too did manufacturing techniques. Chains were replaced with rods and easy to open and close clasps. During the early 1900's cufflinks started to be worn by the middle to upper classes, not just for formal occasions, but for every day wear.

As a greater variety of cufflinks were now being manufactured, the designs became more sophisticated and tailored. Shirt makers increased their ranges of shirts and incorporated pre-cuffed shirts and even disposable cufflinks.

During the later part of the 20th Century, the cufflink has at times had varied popularity peaks. Formal events, one of the main reasons for the original rise in the cufflink's popularity, became one of the reasons that they declined during the 1990's. This was because most people attending formal functions hired tuxedos and, more often than not, these were supplied with buttons!

However, in today's media frenzied environment, major male icons including David Beckham, Pierce Brosnan and Lewis Hamilton have all been pictured donning gem set cufflinks. Large companies like Tiffany and Cartier and designer brands like Mattom and Tookalon are now promoting the wearing of cufflinks like never before and they are once again growing into a popular fashion item and, of course, a symbol of a gent's status.

Tookalon handmade cufflinks.

The best cufflink findings in the world are made in Ireland.

CULET

The culet is the bottom facet of a gemstone and should run parallel to the table. However, the term is liberally used in the jewellery industry to describe the bottom point or bottom ridge of a faceted gem.

So as to avoid breakages, sometimes the point is removed at the bottom of the gem and a culet facet is added. This is the reason why some Round Brilliant Cut Diamonds have 57 facets and some have 58. The difference relates to whether the culet has been flattened or not - or more often whether or not the salesman has a clue about what he is talking about!

Culet ➡

The culet can either be a point at the bottom of a gemstone or a flat facet.

On an octagon cut or emerald cut gemstone, the very bottom of the gem is not a point, but resembles the keel on a boat. All of these are commonly referred to as the culet of the gem.

CULLINAN DIAMOND

One of the largest Diamonds mined to-date, the Cullinan Diamond was originally over 3000cts in weight and was discovered by the Premier Diamond Mining Company in Cullinan, South Africa in 1905. The stone was later named after Sir Thomas Cullinan, the owner of the mine.

Since then, the gem has been separated into 105 independent Diamonds, all of which are said to be highly prized. The largest descendant from the Cullinan Diamond is the Star of Africa (also known as Cullinan I), which weighs in at a massive 530ct, and in 1907 King Edward VII had it set into the Royal Sceptre. Until 1985, it remained the largest faceted Diamond in the world and was then surpassed by the Golden Jubilee Diamond which weighs 545cts - and which, incidentally, was discovered in the same mine!

To learn more about this historic Diamond, it's worth buying a copy of "Diamond - A Journey to the Heart of an Obsession", by Matthew Hart.

CULLINAN REPLICA CUT

Obviously it's highly unlikely that we will ever be able to own the Cullinan I or the Cullinan III Diamond, as I can't imagine the Queen having her Lapidarist removing them from the Crown Jewels so that she can sell them on eBay!

The best way I can describe the shape of these cuts is to say that they are pear shape in outline but the narrow end has been rounded off rather than coming to a point. There are two reasons why the original lapidaries would have done this with the Cullinan I and the Cullinan III: firstly

Cullinan I replica

Table View

Side View

Pavilion View

Cullinan II replica

Table View

the techniques they had in the early 1900's were not as sophisticated as they are today, but more importantly, when you have a Diamond that weighs 530ct and another that weighs 94ct, as a Lapidarist you are not going to be too keen on dramatically reducing the gem's weight just to arrive at a perfect point!

So the clever people in the lapidary team at GemCollector.com, have spent many hours studying these famous Diamonds (well pictures of them to be more accurate), in order to replicate them in the very finest detail. That said, as you can see from the diagrams we have deliberately rounded the point a little more than the originals, so as to accentuate the cut.

Side View

Pavillion View

CUSHION CUT

Firstly, cushion 'cut' is slightly incorrect; it should really be referred to as a cushion 'shape', as the name refers to its shape and not its cut. It became popular in the early 1900's when Diamonds were ground down rather than cut. Its name comes from its resemblance in shape to a cushion or pillow (sometimes it is referred to as 'pillow cut').

The cushion cut is like a squashed square to rectangular shape and when applied to Diamonds often has 57 or 58 facets. However, unlike the round brilliant cut, there is not an established set of measurements to be followed when faceting this cut.

There are three main types of cushion cut; the Antique Cushion is similar to that of a pillow; the Square Antique Cushion, as its name suggests, is similar to a square cushion that you may have on your sofa and the Antique Cushion Triangle looks exactly how it is described!

Many cushion shaped gemstones have a checkerboard table and crown, which provide stunning scintillation. The cut does not demonstrate as much dispersion or brilliance as a round brilliant cut or a princess cut, however it is incredibly idyllic, and its classic look makes it very popular for both Diamonds and gemstones.

A cushion cut electric Pink Topaz ring from the Jessica Lili collection.

Kama Charms

popdiamonds

jessica lili

ANNABELLA

MILANO
C H A R M S

viorelli

Jewels of Valais
SWITZERLAND

Tomas Rae.

ARAH BENNETT
GEMSTONE
JEWELLERY

L O R I Q U E

MATTOM

acque Christie

Eleven
Seventeen

TooKALON

14 JEWELLERY COLLECTIONS
ONE SHOPPING DESTINATION
WWW.COLOUREDROCKS.COM

Tomas Rae.

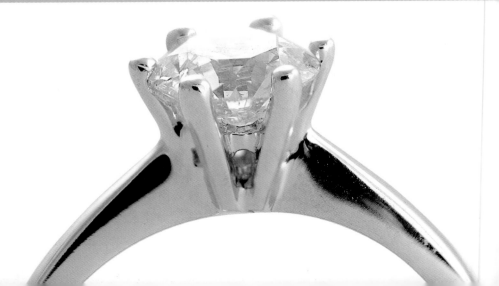

CUPIO CUT

"TOO hot to be round, to cool to be square", that's how this gem cut was first described to me by Jimit Sanghvi the president of K P Sanghvi. His family have been in the Diamond cutting business for three generations and several years ago they set out to develop a revolutionary new cut for quality Diamonds.

Featuring 73 facets, this six-sided hexagon cut really does bring a Diamond to life. When compared to a standard round brilliant cut which has 57 or 58 facets (depending on whether a culet facet is applied) the Cupio's extra array of facets brings out incredible amounts of brilliance and fire within the Diamond. In laboratory "brilliance tests", the cut seriously out performs the standard Princess Cut.

Cupio's name is derived from the Latin word for "desire". As well as trade marking this incredibly brilliant cut, the company has also protected the saying "live inside the circle, think outside the box". The cut has proven to be very popular in the both the USA and in Japan and I am very proud to say that Coloured Rocks is one of the first (if not the very first) to launch this dazzling cut in the UK. The Cupio Cut is available in a fifth of a carat, quarter carat, half carat, three quarter carat and one carat sizes and for those who desire to be different, this cut is ideal.

CUPRITE

Cuprite is a very rare gem that has the colour of a Pyrope Garnet, but a brilliance greater than that of Diamond. Both the gem's colour and its name are derived from the presence of copper ("cuprum" is Latin for Copper).

In addition to its wonderful brilliance, the gem also has an almost metallic appearance, an appearance that for many years caused darker specimens of the gem to be often confused with Haematite. Gem quality Cuprite can be found in several places in Europe; Cornwall (although not over recent years), France, Germany, Austria and Greece.

Colour	Red
Family	Cuprite
Hardness	3.5 - 4
Specific Gravity	6.1
Refractive Index	2.84 - 2.85
Crystal Group	Hexoctahedral
Optical Properties	Adamantine Lustre
Common Treatments	None known
Care	Careful not to scratch
Cleaning Advice	Warm soapy water
Chemical Composition	Cu2O

CUT

The cut of a gemstone is extremely important, and is a key factor in determining its value. For example, a beautiful colour, eye clean clarity and a large carat weight will mean nothing if the stone is poorly cut.

The first step when cutting is to decide if the gem is principally going to sparkle or shine. Opaque gems are often cabochon cut to maximise the surface lustre (shine) and transparent gems are faceted to maximise the refraction of light from within the gem (sparkle). The reason transparent and sometime translucent gemstones are therefore faceted is to let them effectively inhale light from the facets above the girdle, then to encourage the light to bounce of the facets below the girdle and then to exhale sparkles, and in some cases turn the incoming white light into a rainbow of colours.

The responsibility for transforming a rough gem excavated from a mine or an alluvial deposit, to a valuable sparkling or shining gem lies entirely on the skills and expertise of the Lapidarist.

There is a lot of confusion surrounding the meaning of cuts and many people often refer to shapes as cuts, so much so that the industry itself, in an attempt to simplify matters, or in some cases naivety, often refers to certain shapes as a cut. The cut of a gem really should be used to describe either the arrangement and shape of the facets, or the quality of the workmanship. It should not refer to the outline shape of the gem.

There are also certain cuts that are named after the person or the company who initially designed them. The Asscher cut, the Leo cut and the Flanders Brilliant Cut are all examples of famous cuts that were primarily designed as alternative ways for shaping Diamonds.

An oval shape with a concave cut.

A marquise shape brilliant cut.

An octagon shape step cut.

CUTTING

Performed by a Lapidarist, cutting is the art of shaping a gemstone. After Mother Nature has spent millions of years creating the gem, the

Here I am learning the art of Lapidary.

Citrine being cut on a modern Lapidarist's lap using Diamond paste as an abrasive.

A gemstone attached to a traditional 'Dopstick' to secure it while being faceted.

Colour	Green, yellow
Family	Does not belong to a family
Hardness	8 – 8.5
Specific Gravity	3.5 – 3.8
Refractive Index	1.746 – 1.755
Crystal Group	Orthorhombic
Optical Properties	Vitreous lustre
Common Treatments	Not normally treated
Care	Very tough
Cleaning Advice	Ultrasonic, steam Cleaning and Warm soapy water
Chemical Composition	$BeAl_2O_4$ (variable composition)

Lapidarist will spend hours, sometimes days, cutting the gem to ensure that they maximise its brilliance and beauty. The result should be a symmetrical gemstone, regardless of whether it is faceted or cabochon cut.

The style of the cut or fashioning chosen will depend on the optical and physical properties of a particular gem. The Lapidarist should always aim to make the gemstone look as beautiful as possible, maximising its brilliance, its fire, its colour, all the while ensuring that the final shape is symmetric. However, all too often these days, Lapidarists are put under pressure by their customers to maximise the yield of the rough, thus forcing them to focus on producing a final gemstone with the highest possible carat weight, even if it means the gem does not perform at its optimum beauty or, worse still, in some cases a shape that is not symmetrical!

Next time you have a chance to evaluate a loose coloured gemstone, especially one of the rarer ones, study the cut and ask yourself if it has been cut to maximise its beauty or its carat weight. You'll be amazed after a few attempts how easy it is to tell.

In the past, the likes of Amsterdam and Antwerp dominated the Diamond cutting scene; today, as with most coloured gemstones, the majority are cut and faceted in Asia.

CYMOPHANE

A variety of Chrysoberyl, Cymophane differs in its appearance in that it features chatoyancy (cats eye effect).

Unlike cats eye seen in other gem varieties, the effect seen in Cymophane can often be wavy. Just like its sister Alexandrite, Cymophane is a real collector's gemstone and because of its chatoyancy Cymophane is always cabochon cut.

The gem is yellow to green in appearance and at 8 to 8.5 on the Mohs scale, it can be worn every day. Cymophane shares the same folklore and legends as Chrysoberyl. When found with colour change characteristics, it is renamed Alexandrite.

jessica lili

Sponge Coral Bracelet
£19

Colour	Colourless and occasionally yellow or pink
Hardness	7 – 7.5
Specific Gravity	2.98 – 3.02
Refractive Index	1.63 – 1.64
Crystal Group	Orthorhombic
Optical Properties	Displays strong brilliance
Common Treatments	Not normally treated
Cleaning Advice	Warm soapy water
Chemical Composition	$CaB_2(Si_4O)_2$

DANBURITE

First discovered in Danbury, south-east Connecticut, USA in 1839, Danburite is normally white or clear; however, some small deposits have also heralded grey, yellow, pink and even brown Danburite. This precious gemstone is ideal for setting in jewellery, and although the extreme clarity of the colourless variety is highly sought after, it is also very sublime when found in light pink.

When colourless, on a visual inspection this gemstone can easily be mistaken for a Diamond, due to its high refractive index. Its crystal structure is very similar to Topaz, and when found in its rough state generally appears prismatic with a diamond-shaped cross section. As the gem is a relatively recent discovery, there is yet little folklore or legend surrounding it. That said, crystal healers believe that the gem has strong healing capabilities.

Danburite occurs mostly in metamorphic limestone and in addition to Danbury, Connecticut, the gem has also been found in Japan, Burma, Switzerland, Madagascar, and Cornwall in England. The finding of these new deposits is great news for Danburite fanatics, including myself, as the original mines in Danbury are now covered by town houses!

Incredibly rare Chocolate Danburite

DE BEERS

In the mid 1800's, Diamonds were only found in a handful of riverbeds in India and Brazil, and the global quantity of faceted Diamonds would have fitted into a small suitcase. In 1870, a large deposit was discovered in South Africa, dwarfing previous finds. The British financial backers behind the first South African mines went on to form De Beers.

In 1947, De Beers created the marketing slogan, "A Diamond is forever", and today the company is still the largest global advertiser of the gemstone.

In addition to advertising, the company's activities also include mining and exploration. It is said that each year they are, in one sense or another, involved in the sale of around 40% of the world's Diamonds.

It was De Beers who made Diamond the defacto gem for engagement rings.

DEMANTOID GARNET

Rarer than possibly any other Garnet, the green Demantoid is a member of the Andradite family.

It is the most brilliant of Garnets in the sense that it displays the most brilliance and the most dispersion (brilliance being the technical word for the sparkle caused by the return of white light from within the gem, and dispersion being the breaking down of white light into the colours of the spectrum). In a sparkling competition, Demantoid would compete head on with Diamonds and its name derives from Dutch for "Diamond like". Its luminosity is so intense that it is even said to sparkle in the dark!

Colour	Bright green to grass green
Family	Garnet
Hardness	6.5 – 7.5
Specific Gravity	3.4 – 4.3
Refractive Index	1.7 – 1.89
Crystal Group	Isometric
Optical Properties	Various
Common Treatments	Cannot be heat treated
Cleaning Advice	Ultrasonic or warm soapy water
Care	No special care is needed
Chemical Composition	Various

A vivid and rare 0.7ct Demantoid Garnet.

Interestingly, it was first discovered in the Ural Mountains of Russia, some 30 years after the discovery of Alexandrite in the same area.

The Russian jeweller Carl Fabergé was fascinated by the gem, and soon afterwards Tiffany's started setting the gem into jewellery. In the early 1920's, mining for the gem in the Ural Mountains came to a halt and the gem pretty much became extinct until it was rediscovered in Namibia in December 1996.

Now, just as you are starting to get to grips with how gemstones are valued, Demantoid blows a hole in your confidence! The Namibian Demantoids are truly gorgeous and almost inclusion free. However, the original Russian Demantoids often had inclusions caused by the presence of Byssolite fibres. These were known as "horse tail" inclusions and added to the uniqueness of the gem. Therefore, breaking the normal rule of "less inclusions = higher price", the stunning, inclusion-free Namibia Demantoid Garnets, are worth less per carat than the heavily included Russian Demantoid!

Diamond has a density of 3.51

DENSITY

The density of a gemstone, or its specific gravity, is an important concept to comprehend in order to understand why two different gemstones, of the same cut and physical size, can have two very different carat weights (a carat is a measurement of weight and not size).

Take four of the most precious gemstones in the world: Emerald, Sapphire, Ruby and Diamond. Cut them into identical shapes, and the Emerald will be the smallest carat weight, the Diamond will sit in the middle and the Sapphire and Ruby will be the heaviest. It is exactly the same principle as a 10cm cube of lead would weigh far more than a 10cm cube of Balsa Wood.

Every gem has its own unique construction and therefore has its own density. This measurement is known as the gem's Specific Gravity (or SG for short) and is often used to correctly identify gemstones that are similar in visual appearance.

Amber is the lightest of all gemstones and has a density of only 1.05

The chart below should prove useful in helping you understand if you have two gems similar in size, which one will have the bigger carat weight. For example, a well-proportioned, round brilliant cut, one carat Diamond would normally be approximately 6.5mm in width, whereas a 6.5mm Emerald will weigh less than one carat and a Sapphire of the same size will weight approximately 1.2 carats.

Gem	Specific Gravity / Density
Agate	2.65
Alexandrite	3.68 - 3.78
Amethyst	2.65
Amber	1.05
Apatite	3.1 - 3.2
Aquamarine	2.63 - 2.91
Citrine	2.65
Diamond	3.51
Emerald	2.63 - 2.91
Garnet	3.50 - 4.30
Goshenite	2.6 - 2.8
Jade	2.90 - 3.10
Moonstone	2.55 - 2.76
Morganite	2.63 - 2.91
Onyx	2.65
Opal	1.98 - 2.25
Peridot	3.22 - 3.45
Quartz	2.65
Rubellite	3.03 - 3.25
Ruby	3.96 - 4.05
Sapphire	3.96 - 4.05
Spinel	3.58 - 4.06
Sunstone	2.55 - 2.76
Topaz	3.50 - 3.60
Tourmaline	3.03 - 3.25
Zircon	4.60 - 4.70

Quartz based gemstones have a specfic gravity of 2.65 making them one of the lighter gemstones.

The specific gravity of Garnets can vary between 3.5 to 4.3.

Rubies have a higher density than Diamonds.

Colour	Colourless, black, yellow, pink, blue, purple
Family	Diamond
Hardness	10
Specific Gravity	3.5
Refractive Index	2.417
Crystal Group	Cubic
Optical Properties	Strong brilliance and dispersion
Common Treatments	Normally not treated
Cleaning Advice	Ultrasonic, steam clean or warm soapy water
Care	No special care required
Chemical Composition	C (Carbon)

Diamond engagement rings by Tomas Rae.

DIAMOND

Said to be "a girl's best friend", the name derives from the ancient Greek word 'adamas' meaning invincible.

In the gem world, more people are employed in mining and cutting Diamonds, than for any other gemstone. The quality of this gem's colour, clarity and cut are more tightly measured than for any other gemstone, and although there are various standards used across the globe, that of the Gemological Institution of America (GIA) is the most widely used.

Diamond is a gemstone made of pure native crystallised carbon. The value of a similar carat weight of Diamonds can vary dramatically, based on their clarity and colour - and to some extents more importantly - how well the gemstone has been cut.

As the hardest natural mineral known to man and 10 on the Mohs scale, Diamonds can only be cut and faceted by other Diamonds, and although they are extremely hard, they are also quite brittle, making them one of the more difficult gems for Lapidarists to shape.

Its very high refractive index (2.4175–2.4178) is what gives the gem its famous sparkle; its strong lustre is described as an adamantine lustre. One of the main differences to other gemstones is that a lack of colour is highly prized. The closer to colourless a Diamond becomes, the better dispersion (the splitting of light into its constituent colours) it will display.

Until the late 1800's, Diamonds were among the rarest gemstones on the planet, and due to their incredible hardness, coupled with the belief that cutting them would reduce their magical powers, were often not faceted. Unlike biblical gemstones such as Amethyst, Topaz, Ruby, Sapphire, other than records by Pliny the Elder AD 23 – 79, very little was documented about Diamonds until the 14th century. In fact, it was not until this period that the first rudimentary facets were being applied to the gem. As many Diamonds are octahedral in shape (imagine two Egyptian Pyramids being attached to each other at the base), by simply adding a table facet, many early cuts closely resembled the outline shape of today's "Brilliant Cut".

Then, in the late 1800's, everything began to change with the discovery of Diamonds in South Africa. In a very short period of time, gems from this region would account for over 90% of those on sale; through huge marketing campaigns by the owners of these new deposits, the new kid on the gem block went from being fairly unknown, to unquestionably the global leader within half a century!

A Princess Cut Diamond Engagement Ring.

For those interested in studying advertising and marketing, the rise of the Diamond to the status of "the world's most popular gemstone", overtaking many rarer, more colourful gems, gems who have been linked with royalty, religion and powerful leaders for thousands of years, gems who are steeped in folk lore and legend, is a real textbook marketing campaign.

The youngest Diamonds are believed to have been formed over 100 million years ago! They crystallise when carbon is put under immense pressure of between 45 and 60 kilo bars and at a temperature ranging from 900 - 1300 degrees Celsius. For these conditions to occur naturally, it is believed that Diamonds were created some 90 to 120 miles beneath the earth's crust. This means that they actually form while still inside the mantle, an area made up of hot flowing magma. The only other valuable gem on the planet to crystallise under these hostile conditions is Peridot. Once gem hunters understood that Diamonds were transported to the surface of the earth in old volcano pipes, now known as Kimberlite pipes, more discoveries shortly followed.

Illusion set Diamond pendant.

Although Africa is still a major supplier of Diamonds, today it holds less than 50% of the market share, and it cannot control the market as much as it once did. New big players on the

Simple yet elegant Diamond studs.

Channel set baguette cut Diamonds.

A Tomas Rae Blue Sapphire ring inspired by Lady Diana's Engagement ring.

Colour	Colourless, Green or Yellow
Family	Diaspore
Hardness	6.5 - 7
Specific Gravity	3.4
Refractive Index	1.7-1.75
Crystal Group	Orthorhombic
Optical Properties	Colour Change
Common Treatments	None
Cleaning Advice	Ultrasonic or warm soapy water
Composition	AIO(OH)

scene include India, Canada, Russia, Australia and Brazil.

It's taken for granted that the larger the carat weight of a good quality gem, the larger the price, but why is this the case? In simplistic terms, larger gems are rarer than smaller gems and in the case of Diamonds, only one in a million faceted Diamonds are said to weigh over one carat.

DIANA - PRINCESS OF WALES

Although Princess Diana tragically died at a young age, in such a short time she accumulated a beautiful collection of jewellery that is estimated to be worth in excess of fifteen million pounds. Her pieces wonderfully blended traditional jewellery styles with more contemporary pieces.

The engagement ring she received from Charles in 1981 was not the normal Solitaire Diamond ring of the time, but a stunning 18K Ceylon Sapphire surrounded by small accented Diamonds. As a wedding present the Prince of Saudi Arabia gave Diana a set of pendant, bracelet and earrings all set with Sapphires.

On receiving an Emerald necklace from Queen Elizabeth, it is said that Princess Diana had it converted into a gorgeous Tiara. The Queen also gave Diana a Pearl and Diamond Tiara which is known as the Cambridge Love Knot.

DIASPORE

Many readers of this book may be familiar with the gemstone Zultanite, this is a gemstone from Turkey which is in fact simply a brand name used to describe Diaspore mined in the region.

This gemstone demonstrates the "colour change" phenomenon at its very best. Although the gem is normally a lovely pastel green, colourless and yellow specimens have also been discovered. The gem ranges from transparent to translucent and is without doubt one of the most precious gemstones yet discovered on our planet. Unfortunately, samples that are both transparent and have strong colour change can demand over $1000 per carat!

I have recently discovered a very small supplier of Diaspore from the Banska Stiavnica region of Slovakia, and we are currently having this gemstone cut in Bangkok. The gem is simply stunning! It has a very light green colour, similar to that of Green Amethyst (also known as Prasiolite) and when you change your lighting from candescent to incandescent, it has the ability to glow a beautiful orange colour.

Although it was first documented in 1951, don't expect to see any vintage pieces of jewellery set with Diaspore, this is because until the recent introduction of modern lapidary skills, as the gem is extremely difficult to cut (due to its cleavage and shallow crystal habits), on the rare occasion the gem was discovered it was never faceted. In fact it wasn't until the 1980's that anyone dared risk attempting to facet this rare stone, a gem which by many is referred to as "Turkish Alexandrite".

As one of the rarest gemstones on the planet, Diaspore is a must for gem collectors. Its high level of hardness means it is also suitable for setting in jewellery. As well as our find in Slovakia and the well-known mines of Turkey, small deposits of the gem have also been found in Colorado, Massachusetts and North Carolina in the USA, Poland and Russia.

A beautiful and rare 3ct Diaspore discovered in Slovakia.

DIFFUSION

Coloured gemstones have undergone treatment for thousands of years. As long as the treatment is permanent, it is widely accepted that the role of enhancing Mother Nature's treasures is important for maintaining the popularity of genuine gemstones.

To best understand diffusion, first of all let's remind ourselves that most gemstones are "allochromatic" (see page 29), meaning they receive their beautiful colours through the

presence of impurities. For example, Beryl is a colourless gemstone until impurities are present: iron turns the gem into an Aquamarine; chromium and vanadium turn the gem into an Emerald; and the presence of manganese creates Morganite.

One of the oldest treatments of coloured gemstones is heat treatment, whereby rough gem material is heated to extremely high temperatures in order to continue the work of Mother Nature. Virtually all Sapphire and Ruby on the market today is heat-treated.

Diffusion is a technique whereby certain natural elements, those used by nature in colouring allochromatic gems, are placed on the surface of the gem during the heating process and the colour is diffused into the gem. The treatment is permanent, however the colour created through diffusion normally only penetrates a small distance within the gem. Therefore if the gem is chipped or re-cut, the less vivid colour underneath will be visible.

One of the latest developments in diffusion treatment is from a company in India; the company is a partner of Coloured Rocks and shares the same office complex in Jaipur as the team at GemCollector. This new technique uses thin film thermal technology to diffuse the colour deeper into the gemstone, making its beauty more resistant to chips and knocks. The technique has just received a U.S. Patent and is widely used by many of the brands within the Coloured Rock portfolio. This research has also led to some amazing new colours in Topaz and Quartz and these can be recognized by the names "Spice Topaz" and "Spice Quartz".

One of the most common treatments of diffusion is with Star Sapphires and Star Rubies, where the treatment is used to enhance the beautiful asterism effect.

Beryllium treatment and cobalt treatment are other forms of diffusion. And when buying Sapphires and Rubies, unless stated otherwise, it is safe to assume that that the gem has most likely undergone some form of diffusion.

Rubies and Sapphires are often diffused.

Eleven
Seventeen

English Rose

Inspired by Nature

www.eleven-17.com

Colour	Normally green
Family	Does not belong to a family
Hardness	5.5 – 6.5
Specific Gravityv	3.2 – 3.5
Refractive Index	1.65 – 1.72
Crystal Group	Monoclinic
Optical Properties	Strong pleochroism
Common Treatments	Not treated
Care	No special care needed
Cleaning Advice	Warm soapy water
Chemical Composition	$CaMgSi_2O_6$

A vibrant 1ct Russian Diopside ring by Jacque Christie.

Jacque Christie Russian Diopside Earrings

DIOPSIDE

Not a particularly well known gemstone, Diopside was first described in the early 1800's and derives its name from the Greek words "dis and "opse", meaning "two faced", in reference to the two ways of orienting the gem before cutting (Diopside is unusual in that it has perfect cleavage in two directions).

Due to the presence of iron, the colours of the gem vary from yellow to pale green to dark bottle green. Two of the most popular varieties are Black Star Diopside (normally cabochon cut if the gem demonstrates chatoyancy or asterism) and Chrome Diopside which, as the name suggests, gets its vivid green colours from chromium.

Many people believed that this gem would only ever be found in a green colour. However, in Italy it has been found in very small deposits to be blue, where it is also referred to as Violan.

Diopside forms in metamorphic rocks and the crystals are short and columnar, with a square or 8-sided cross section. It has a hardness of 5 – 6 on the Mohs scale; though this is fairly soft when compared to other gems, it is durable once set in jewellery.

The main deposits for Chrome Diopside are in Southern Siberia, Russia and many people in the trade now refer to it as Russian Diopside - after all, chrome is associated with old-fashioned car bumpers! The gem is also mined in Sweden Germany and the USA.

DISPERSION

White light that we see all around us, from either the sun or indoor lighting, is actually made up of different colours, all of which have different wavelengths. Each of these wavelengths as they pass from air into a denser material, such as glass, bend (refract) at different angles. When denser material such as a gemstone (or a glass prism like those used in schools) demonstrates this effect, the light bounces off its inclined surfaces and the split becomes visible to the eye.

Not all gems demonstrate dispersion, and it is dependent on their refractive index and their density, plus of course how well the gem is cut. Zircon and Diamond are two of the most well-known gems that offer beautiful dispersion, but the top of the class is the lesser-known gemstone Sphene.

Other names often used to describe dispersion are fire and scintillation; however, scintillation is also used by some people to describe surface lustre.

Diamonds that show the best dispersion are those that are colourless. The best way to understand this is to imagine how tinted glass acts as a filter, through which very few colours are seen.

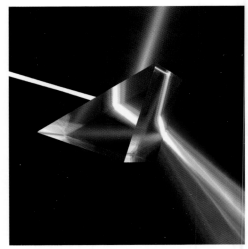

Dispersion as seen through a glass prism.

DOMINICAN REPUBLIC

Known as a holiday destination in the Caribbean, the Dominican Republic is also a large producer of Amber, where most of its mines are near the city of Santiago. Unfortunately, over recent years the amount of gems they are recovering has diminished. Some reports even suggest that over the past 25 years, yields have dropped by as much as 80%. As well as the more traditional orange Amber, Santiago is also currently producing around 2,500 carats of blue Amber per month.

The island also mines a gemstone known as Larimar, which is a blue gemstone that looks similar to Turquoise and has yet to be found in any other country in the world. Although locals have been aware of the gem for centuries, it wasn't until 1974 that it became known to the gem world.

After finding the gem, a gentleman called Miguel Mendez named it by combining his daughter's name Larissa and the Spanish word for sea, "mar". After his initial discovery on the beach he followed a stream inland, where he

An Amber beaded necklace from the Dominican Republic.

Larimar is exclusively found in the Dominican Republic.

A badly constructed doublet Opal. (Not sold by Coloured Rocks)

discovered the gem set in a host rock. Today the Los Chupaderos mines are still the only source of Larimar in the world.

It is quite romantic to think that this holiday destination mines gemstones of just two colours, the Amber of its golden sunsets and the blues of the Caribbean Sea!

DOUBLET

This is a technique used to fuse two materials together. One of its more common uses today is with Opals, where two are fused together to achieve more depth in the gem. While this is widely accepted in the jewellery industry, the seller should always disclose whether the gem is a doublet, as it is far less valuable than a single piece of Opal.

The doublet technique is easily identifiable in a loose gemstone, where when viewed from the side you will often witness bands. It is a lot more difficult to spot in a gem which has already been set into jewellery. If you are offered a cheap Opal ring and the seller tells you that you should not get Opals wet, he is probably referring to the glue that has been used to bond the layers together!

A triplet is produced in the same way as a doublet, but has three layers. Again, when talking of Opals, it is normally the middle layer that is the genuine gem.

Also, some cameos are doublets; however, a genuine cameo is made out of a single piece, where the gemstone has natural bands of different colours.

DRESDEN DIAMOND

Found in the Bagagem mine in Brazil in 1857, this famous Diamond weighed in at 119.5cts before it was cut into a brilliant cut 76.5cts gem (because the current value of 1ct equating to 1/5th of a gram was only introduced in 1907, the weight of 76.5ct, would have been slightly different than today's measurement).

It was named after E.H. Dresden, a London Merchant who bought it in Rio de Janeiro and sold it to an English trader in Bombay (now Mumbai). His estate later sold it to Mulhar Rao, Gaekwar of Baroda. The Gaekwar dynasty ruled the state of Baroda in western India from the mid-eighteenth century until 1947.

Under the same name, but for different reasons, is the world's most famous Green Diamond. It is pear cut and weighs a huge 41 carats. The gem was purchased by Fredrick Augustus in 1743 and is reported to be kept at the Dresden Palace.

DRUSY

Natural Drusy

For many years I avoided selling this gemstone, as I felt that its appearance was so different to other gems and so loud in its outward look, that many customers when seeing it set in jewellery for the first time, would immediately jump to the conclusion that it was fake! However, other than the fact the gem is often treated to provide or improve its colour, the physical appearance of the gem is totally natural.

Drusy is not a facetable gemstone, but has an appearance of broken sugar cubes attached on to the surface of a stone. The gem formed millions of years ago when flowing hot water carrying dissolved silica was forced into gaps between rocks. If the hot chemical cocktail was cooled rapidly then groups of small crystals were occasionally formed. The gem's full name depends on what rocks these small crystals were resting on as they formed. Drusy Quartz is the most well known of all Drusy gems and you can often find it attached to either Amethyst or Citrine. From Brazil we can also find Drusy Agate, Drusy Carnelian (a gorgeous orangish yellowish colour) and Druzy Chalcedony.

There are also many different spellings for the name within the gem industry, if you see Druse, Druzy or Drusies, they all refer to a thin layer of small quartz crystals, attached to another mineral.

Crystal Healers have used the gemstone for centuries believing that it will give you increased

The above two gems, although genuine, have been heavily treated .

energy and lead you to a perfectly balanced life. Others believe that it provides the wearer with extra sensory perception (ESP)!

DURABILITY

Durability is one of the characteristics that allows a stone to be classed as a gem: the higher the durability and resistance to wear, the more highly prized the gemstone often becomes.

A gem must be durable enough to withstand the stresses and forces involved in faceting and setting in jewellery, along with standing up to everyday wear.

There are three aspects of durability: these are hardness, toughness and stability:

Hardness is the ability to resist scratching;

Toughness is the ability to resist breaking or chipping;

Stability is the resistance to changes caused by environmental factors such as temperature, chemicals and light.

DYED GEMS

A dyed gemstone is one that has an artificial stain added to improve its colour. For example, using a technique that was invented some two to three thousand years ago, Black Onyx obtains its jet black colour by dyeing an Agate. Also, some Pearls are dyed to provide jewellery designers with greater flexibility.

Gemstones that have fractures or a porous surface can be dyed. While it is widely accepted that Black Onyx is dyed, as Pearls can naturally be found in several different colours, retailers should disclose if their Pearls are dyed. The terms dyeing and staining are often used interchangeably.

In order to increase the intensity of their colour, Lapis Lazuli is sometimes dyed and take a look later in this book at Quench Crackled Quartz, where dyes are used to create a very unusual effect.

Members of the Quartz family are extremely durable.

Quench Crackled Quartz's appearance is created by dyes.

Make Everyday A Glamour day

Jacque Christie

EARRINGS

Earrings have been worn for thousands of years; however, prior to Victorian times they were primarily used to display coloured gemstones, rather than the jewellery itself being the prized possession. Without doubt, no piece of jewellery better displays the dispersion and brilliance of coloured gemstones than a pair of dangling earrings.

Archaeological discoveries show that earrings are thought to have originated in Asia and the Middle East; the oldest being the hoop and pendant, dating back to about 2000 BC. Pierced earrings date back to ancient Egypt to around 1500 BC. Earrings were always a sign of wealth and prosperity and, as with most jewellery, only affluent women could afford to wear rare gemstones and the precious metals of which earrings were made.

Hook earrings date back to Greek and Roman times and many examples of Garnet earrings have been discovered dating back to Anglo Saxon times.

Classic hanging Pearl earrings by Annabella.

During the Renaissance (14th to 17th century), shorter hair became more fashionable and this led to a surge in the popularity of earrings.

During the Georgian era, a type of earring known as the 'girandole' came into fashion and some say they defined the period. They were of a distinguishable design that had a gem set near to the ear lobe and then three others hanging from it. These earrings were very heavy and often caused the ear lobes to elongate. We can see earrings around today that have used the girandole as inspiration.

Queen Victoria had a huge influence on the design of jewellery as a whole and earrings were no exception. In the 19th century she wore long jewelled earrings and set a new trend for women across Europe.

Designed by Sarah Bennett, these large Honey Quartz earrings have been checkerboard cut.

Today, earrings are favoured among women of all ages as well as young men (although fashion dramatically changes when it comes to men and earrings). There are many different styles and types of earring available including: stud; hoop; hugged hoop; solid hoop; hollow hoop; clusters; and dangling. There are also as many fastenings including: screw back; butterfly back; shepherd's crook; and levered backs.

A great designer will always take into consideration the gem, the metal and size when deciding the best way to secure the earring to the lobe. You will always see screw backs on expensive Diamond earrings as not only are they considered the most secure method for attaching earrings to the ear, they also have an element of class about them, announcing that the wearer is of a certain status to be able to afford to wear genuine Diamonds and not imitations.

With coloured gemstones it's often attractive to match earrings with pendants.

Wherever possible, designers will set gems that are destined to sparkle in drop earrings, allowing the light to catch the gem as the wearer's head moves, thus enabling them to maximise the visual effect of their brilliance or dispersion. So while the gem does all the hard work for you, you're free to relax and enjoy your evening, absorbing the countless compliments you will receive.

Jacque Christie Ruby and Sapphire reversible earrings.

EDWARDIAN ERA (1901 - 1910)

The above rings from Jewels of Valais are inspired by the Edwardian era.

Lasting only nine years, the Edwardian period is often forgotten in a sea of Art Deco and Art Nouveau. Often referred to as the "Gilded Age", the Edwardian period takes it name from the rule of King Edward VII, reigning from 1901 to just 1910.

When Edward VII began his reign, Britain was still very much engrained in the Art Nouveau movement.

The class system was still very evident from Victorian times, but rapid economic changes were taking place in order to push social change. People were becoming interested for the first time in the lives of the poor, women's rights and socialism. Although the country was changing, there was still a big divide between the lower and the 'ruling' classes. It was not until the outbreak of WWI that the previous century's ideas, ethics and ideologies were finally put to rest.

During the Edwardian years, more jewellery was bought than ever before. Like so many other periods, Edwardian style and fashion overlapped with its predecessors. But when WWI broke out, people panicked. Jewellery was locked away in vaults, and much was sold to make money in order for the owner to survive.

Designs gradually started to change from the rich boldness of Nouveau to become more understated. Edward's reign was seen as elegant and sophisticated, and this was reflected in the jewellery of the period. Diamonds, a quintessential part of Edwardian jewellery, were cut into fine and delicate shapes, designed to blend in with the fragility of the lace, silk and feathers worn by Edwardian women. Many believe that Edwardian jewellery is amongst some of the finest ever fashioned. The Edwardian period's innovation is highlighted through the vast progress made in the cutting and shaping of gemstones. Many cuts and shapes created in this era were later developed and used extensively during the Art Deco movement.

Platinum was very popular and was often used to showcase the brilliance, fire and lustre of many gemstones. The metal was often 'scalloped' or had lightly engraved patterns said to resemble lace. Artisans (jewellery makers) experimented and pushed the platinum foundries to see how it could be forged, and the result was extremely thin and light pieces of jewellery.

Another defining feature of the period was a type of setting known as 'milgrain'. It was carried out by creating a thin rim of metal, textured with tiny grains that secured the gemstone in place. This created the effect of an invisible setting, as very little metal was used to hold the gemstone in place.

A white on white colour scheme became popular, as Diamonds and Pearls were set in platinum, creating a refined, elegant look. Elegant, lacy circle brooches, bar pins, stars and crescents became fashionable. A particular favourite was the 'negligee', a pendant that had two drops of unequal length hanging from a chain or stone.

During the Edwardian period, the Princess of Wales, Princess Alexandra and the King's wife all had a fundamental influence upon fashion and the creation of jewellery.

Today, people like to copy the fashions of the rich and famous, and the Edwardian period was no different. When the King and Princess Alexandra travelled to India, the Princess was fascinated by the style and fashions of her Indian counterparts, known as Maharajas. She subsequently bought and adopted some of the styles she was fond of, bringing them back to England. Her influence started fashions for Diamond ornaments, known as 'aigrettes', Pearl necklaces with tassels, known as 'sautoirs', and the most memorable to many; chokers.

Amethyst was a favourite stone of the Princess, and because of her influence, it was common to see it used in jewellery at the time. Violet Amethyst was often used in partnership with Prasiolite (Green Amethyst) or Peridot and Pearl. This combination of stones formed the same colours as the ones used to represent the women's rights, or 'suffragette' movement. The first letter of each colour, G, W and V (Green,

Jewels of Valais

White and Violet) stood for 'Give Women the Vote', and was popular for supporters to wear at the time.

As in any period, not everyone is able to afford the high-end jewellery being worn by kings and queens. The Edwardian period was no different: because of this, less expensive items were also being designed. Half hoop bangles, bar brooches, gypsy rings, snake rings and gold chain bracelets set with pearls became popular amid the working classes. Although most of this jewellery was actually made in the late Victorian period, it is still acknowledged as Edwardian.

Unfortunately, only four years after Edward passed away, World War I broke out. The lavish and proud displays of prosperity that had become such a part of Edwardian society were brought to an untimely end.

EGYPTIAN JEWELLERY

Even as far back as 3000BC, gold was the preferred metal for jewellery making in Egypt. Its rarity made it highly sought after and its softness made it easy for ancient jewellers, with little equipment, to work with. Elegant bracelets, earrings, necklaces, rings, armlets, collars, and head ornaments were all produced in the land of the Pharaohs.

In 1922, excavations led by Howard Carters uncovered Tutankhamen's tomb. Inside lay many gold artefacts, all revealing how delicate and precise the detailed art work of this ancient period was.

Different coloured gems and different coloured jewellery symbolised different things in ancient Egypt: red represented blood, and Cleopatra's favourite colour, green, represented new growth and fertility. Dark blue was seen to represent the protective night sky.

When Lapis Lazuli could not be found, jewellers would resort to using coloured glass. Yes, even four thousand years ago, fake and imitation gemstones were often used in Egypt. Made from

A Tookalon bracelet with an Edwardian colour scheme.

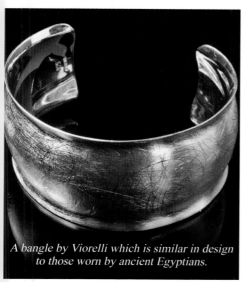

A bangle by Viorelli which is similar in design to those worn by ancient Egyptians.

glass, these items filled the demand for colours that were not always readily available (you have to remember that back then, gems were normally mined fairly locally and you couldn't just order a gem on the internet from halfway around the world!)

One highly valued gemstone the Egyptians used that wasn't readily available in Egypt was Lapis Lazuli. This was imported from neighbouring countries and as far away as Afghanistan to create imitation Scarab beetles (thousands of these almost sacred Egyptian amulets have been found).

The offering of gems to Cleopatra on papyrus.

Cleopatra, co-ruler of Egypt with her father Ptolemy XII Auletes, was an avid Emerald collector. However, many historians now believe that some of Cleopatra's many prized gemstones were not Emerald but were in fact the birthstone for August; Peridot.

Remains of Cleopatra's gemstone mines were discovered circa 1817 and are situated on the Red Sea coast.

Eight Cut

Also known as the "Single Cut", an eight cut is a variation of the brilliant cut and is often used on Diamonds under .05ct. Despite its name, it actually has 17 or 18 facets (depending on if a culet facet has been added).

On the crown, there are 8 facets plus the table, and below the girdle there are a further 8 facets on the pavilion. As with a round brilliant cut, the pavilion is slightly deeper than the crown.

The eight cut, or single cut, is applied to very small gems where it is impossible to apply more facets. Furthermore, when gems are set on solid backgrounds (such as watch faces or certain cufflink designs), if no light is able to enter from the back, then the eight cut is normally applied.

Also, on the odd occasion when translucent or opaque gemstones are faceted into round shapes, they are often eight cut rather than round brilliant cut.

Small eight cut Diamonds.

E

Colour	Green, red to pink, blue, orange, yellow, colourless, multicoloured
Family	Tourmaline
Hardness	7.5
Specific Gravity	2.9 – 3.2
Refractive Index	1.635 - 1.650
Crystal Group	Trigonal
Optical Properties	Strong Pleochroism
Common Treatments	None
Care	No special care required
Chemical Composition	$Na(Li,Al)_3Al_6Si_6O_{18}(BO_3)_3(OH)_4$

ELBAITE

Like many gem families, Tourmalines are split into several sub-species. Most gem quality Tourmalines fall into the Elbaite group. Its name is derived from the small island of Elba, Italy, where the first gem was discovered in 1913.

Chances are that if you own a colourful Tourmaline, then it is a member of the Elbaite subspecies. As it will most likely have been formed from a three or six sided elongated crystal structure, the shape of your gem is more likely to be an elongated baguette or oval rather than a round shape. All Elbaites are strongly pleochroic (different colours can be seen when viewing the gem from different angles) and its members include Rubellite which is Red, Achroite - colourless, Siberite - lilac to violet, Paraiba - neon blue to green and Indicolite - blue.

ELEVEN SEVENTEEN

Inspired by nature, every design in the Eleven Seventeen collection is said to resemble a view of nature's splendours and landscapes. From the very first design modelled on the hedged maze found in the grounds of the company's "Design Centre" to glistening icicles hanging from a rock on a frosty morning, all pieces commence by capturing an image of nature.

Colourful Citrines and Rubies are used to represent the rising and setting of the sun, while Topaz and Sapphire represent the changing shades of the sky. Peridots and Tourmalines create images of nature's green scenery, and Zircon and Quartz simulate a cold winter scene.

Many pieces within the collection perfectly represent the gentleness of nature, by being finished with a uniquely developed technique which diffuses the lustre of the silver and gold. Most pieces in the Eleven Seventeen collection are handcrafted in Chang Mai, Thailand, which itself is surrounded by nature's wonderfully colourful scenery. Eleven Seventeen designers say that its range is "how Nature would most likely design her own jewellery".

A multi-gem bangle from the Eleven Seventeen collection.

Citrine, Topaz and Amethyst set in a very modern Eleven Seventeen design.

viorelli

Colour	Green
Family	Beryl
Hardness	6.5 – 7
Specific Gravity	2.67 – 2.78
Refractive Index	1.560 – 1.605
Crystal Group	Prismatic
Optical Properties	Vitreous lustre
Common Treatments	Oiled and waxed
Care	Occasionally may need to be re-oiled and waxed
Cleaning Advice	Warm soapy water
Chemical Composition	$Be_3Al_2(SiO_3)_6$

Two of our buyers selecting rough Emeralds.

EMERALD

To own an Emerald is to own a piece of history, a piece of nature and a work of art. Each one is truly individual. With its array of inclusions and clouds, the gem is not famed for its crystal clarity, but is steeped in so much history that we automatically ignore the gem's imperfections when we study a piece and accept that these impurities are simply "the fingerprints of Mother Nature".

The gem world is a strange place to reside if you are looking for logic and reason: with so many other green gems available with almost perfect clarity and in some cases greater rarity, it is not at all logical that Emerald is still viewed as the king of the green gems. Its price is often greater than Diamonds of a similar carat weight. So when you own an Emerald, treat it as your own work of art, get to know its lines, its patches, its identity and don't let anyone tell you it is anything other than gorgeous - after all beauty is in the eye of the beholder.

Some Emeralds have an almost velvety appearance, and are one of only a few gems where inclusions are not only tolerated, but considered to be part of the gem's character. As a general rule, a vivid Emerald, full of inclusions, will normally demand a higher price than a flawless one paler in colour.

Its name is derived from the Greek word "smaragdos", a label given to a number of gems with the colour green in common. Representative of the 'colour of spring' Emeralds are said to signify hope, new growth and eternal life.

As with Peridot and Alexandrite, Emerald is only available in one colour: green. This wonderful creation of nature is a variety of the Beryl family (a mineral group that includes Aquamarine, Morganite and Heliodor) and receives its colouring from traces of chromium and vanadium within its crystal structure.

Mined over 4000 years ago in Egypt, during the reign of Pharaoh Sesostris III, this precious stone has been held in high regard since antiquity.

Many virtues are ascribed to this jewel - said to promote constancy of mind, to quicken the intelligence, and drive away evil spirits. Emerald is believed to bring wisdom, true friendship and foresight in to the future.

Pliny the Elder, first century AD author of the great "Natural History", wrote "...no colour is more delightful in appearance. For although we enjoy looking at plants and leaves, we regard Emeralds with all the more pleasure because compared with them there is nothing that is more intensely green". Although not a believer in myths, Pliny did go on to say, "And after straining our eyes by looking at another object, we can restore our vision to normal by gazing at an Emerald". He also correctly identified Emeralds as part of the Beryl family.

The Greeks who were working at the mines of Alexander the Great were said to have yielded their gems to the Egyptian Queen, who was notorious for her love of Emeralds. In 1817, "Cleopatra's mines" - once thought to be myths - were discovered on the coast of the Red Sea.

Shah Jahan, the architect of the Taj Mahal, wore them as talismans inscribed with sacred text. His 'Mongul Emerald' is noted as one of the two most famous Emeralds, dating back to 1695. It is an impressive 10cm tall and weighs 217ct; in September 2001 it sold for $2.2 million dollars at auction to an anonymous bidder. The second most renowned Emerald is the 632ct 'Patricia Emerald' and is on display in the National History museum in New York.

Emerald was revered as a holy gemstone by the Incas and Aztecs and was associated with Venus, goddess of love and beauty by the Romans. Emeralds are associated with the astrological sign of Taurus. It is the birthstone for May and the anniversary gemstone for the 20th, 35th and 55th year of marriage.

Most Emeralds on the market are treated at the time of cutting with wax, oils or resins. Unlike nearly all other gemstones, most treatments applied to Emeralds are not permanent and to maintain the gem's unrivalled beauty, need re-

Three opulant Emerald pieces by Tomas Rae.

applying every 5 to 10 years. Because of their brittle crystal structure and normal mass of inclusions, cutting the gem is a real challenge. Very few gem cutters will even attempt to cut larger Emeralds, and the likes of Tel Aviv in Israel and Jaipur in India have produced many Lapidarists who specialise in applying the Emerald Cut. On a recent visit to one of my licensed workshops in Jaipur, I was fascinated to watch an Emerald cutter slowly shape a 3ct Emerald. Rather than the cutting wheel so often used in Thailand where the craftsman spins the wheel with his feet, Jaipur craftsmen attach a rod-cum-bow to the wheel. It must be four to five feet in length and as they slowly pull it backwards and forwards in a very serene manner, the cutting wheel begins to spin. Then, with a skill passed on from many generations, they delicately cut and grind the Emerald on the hand-driven grinding wheel.

Stones displaying bluish overtones are sourced from Colombia; these are highly coveted and considered by connoisseurs to be some of the world's finest. Unfortunately, as I write this piece, these Emeralds are becoming increasingly rarer as mine owners are having to dig deeper and deeper - and with very little success. Other sources of Emeralds include Brazil, Pakistan, Siberia, Zambia, and Zimbabwe.

An 18k Gold Emerald ring by Tomas Rae.

EMERALD CUT

As the name suggests, this shape and cut was first used on Emeralds, which, due to their brittleness, led to a high occurrence of damaged gems while being cut by Lapidarists.

Any gem that has an outline shape that is either rectangular or square and whose facets are parallel to the girdle are known as a step cut. When the corners are then cut off, trimmed or truncated to create an octagonal outline shape, the cut is then referred to as an emerald cut.

The cut is often applied to gems that are either brittle, or to those where the gem's true beauty lies in its clarity and colour, rather than the amount of brilliance it displays. For example, The round brilliant cut is currently the most

An emerald cut Emerald.

popular cut for Diamonds as its shape and arrangement of facets returns the most brilliance and dispersion, however, some Diamonds that have incredible clarity are emerald cut, so as to best display this feature.

When trying to identify an emerald cut, look for an octagon shape with the facets on the crown running parallel to the girdle and then, when you turn the gemstone over, instead of looking for a culet that is a single point, you are looking for a culet that is more like the keel of a boat.

An emerald cut 1.7ct Pink Sapphire.

Often you will also find that the emerald cut gem has more than one step up to the table and more than one step down to the culet. Again, this makes the gem more robust and also retains a higher yield (more carat weight).

The number of facets on the gem depends entirely on how many steps are applied above and below the girdle. In our opinion, the most common emerald cuts that we see have 50 facets, a table, 24 crown facets and 25 on the pavilion. However, it is also common to see emerald cuts that have small facets applied to the girdle; in these cases the gem is likely to have 58 facets.

ENGAGEMENT RING

It is written that the first appearance of an engagement ring was in 1215 when Pope Innocent III declared it necessary for a waiting period between a marriage proposal and the wedding. To show his intention to marry his loved one, the man gave his wife-to-be a plain metal band.

One style of engagement ring featured the birthstones of the two people getting married and later this was extended to a six stone ring where the birthstones of the parents were added, with the bride's parents' birthstones to the left and those of the groom's family to the right.

Another popular design was the four stone engagement ring, where the birthstone of the bride and groom were in the centre, flanked by

An emerald cut Green Quartz.

Modern Engagement ring by Tomas Rae.

the birthstone relating to the months in which the two sets of parents got married.

In Victorian times, the "Regards" and "Dearest" engagement rings became popular, whereby each of the 7 letters for the word 'Regards' or 'Dearest' were represented by a gemstone starting with that letter. For a Regards ring for example, a Ruby, Emerald, Garnet, Amethyst, Ruby, Diamond and Sapphire were often used.

Possibly the earliest writings of a Diamond Engagement ring was that of the marriage of the Archduke of Austria, Maximilian I, to Mary of Burgundy in 1477. However, it took a further 500 years for the Diamond ring to become the standard gem used in an engagement ring. This was due to the hugely successful De Beers' (the largest Diamond mining and distributor in the world) marketing campaign "Diamonds are Forever" in 1947.

Today there are three main gem varieties that feature as the lead stone in the majority of engagement rings: Diamonds (primarily colourless, but also occasionally black or yellow), Sapphires (blue and pink) and Rubies.

When it comes to the supporting metal band, although 18k gold is regarded by some as the standard for engagement rings, many people still prefer the harder wearing and more durable 9k gold. As the ring is likely to be worn everyday and all other pieces of jewellery are going to need to complement it, the most important decision to make is whether the metal should be yellow or white.

Two profiles of a classic Engagement ring by Tomas Rae.

Colour	Brown
Hardness	5 - 6
Specific Gravity	3.25
Refractive Index	1.66 - 1.67
Crystal Group	Orthorhombic
Common Treatments	None
Care	None
Cleaning Advice	Warm soapy water
Composition	(MgSiO3)

ENSTATITE

Just like Moldavite, Enstatite is a gemstone from out of space! It's possible that this gemstone was once a natural satellite orbiting the planet Mercury.

In 1952, a large Enstatite weighing over 100kg landed in a farmer's field in Canada. From its angle of impact, which created a crater 1.5 metre deep, scientists believe it to have come from the inner solar system.

I have recently managed to purchase a small parcel of extremely special Enstatite. Totalling 126ct (average 3ct per piece), not only is it from out of space, it also demonstrates wonderful chatoyancy!

In appearance Enstatite normally has a look like a brownish Jasper and has been discovered in such countries as India, Canada, South Africa and Sri Lanka.

EPIDOTE

A mineral not often used in jewellery today, but one which has been used sporadically for several hundred years. Its colour is normally a yellowish green, however it can also be found grey, brown or nearly black.

The gem is formed in metamorphic rocks and has high iron content. Although it is widely abundant, gem-quality Epidote is rarely found. When it is discovered, it is similar to Tourmaline in appearance and displays beautiful pleochroism and good transparency.

The gem has been unearthed in New York, Australia, France and Russia.

Colour	Green, brown, black
Family	Epidote
Hardness	6 – 7
Specific Gravity	3.3 – 3.5
Refractive Index	1.736 – 1.770
Crystal Group	Monoclinic
Optical Properties	Strong Pleochroism
Common Treatments	None
Care	No Special care required
Cleaning Advice	Warm soapy water
Chemical Composition	$Ca_2(Al,Fe)_3$ $(SiO_4)_3(OH)$

ETERNITY RING

As the shank of a ring is a full circle, it symbolizes eternal love. The earliest records of an eternity ring dates back some four thousand years. Traditionally it had gemstones (normally Diamonds or a combination of Diamonds, Rubies and Sapphires) in a continuous circle around the ring. However, as the cost of this is often very high, and as it cannot be resized, most eternity rings today have gemstones set in just half of the ring, and are referred to as 'Half Eternity Rings'.

The eternity ring is normally given as a sign of a lasting marriage and some husbands give them to their wife after the birth of their first child.

In the late 1500's (Elizabethan era) the "Alliance Ring" became a popular eternity ring and

1ct of baguette cut Diamonds in this eternity ring by Tomas Rae.

Fire Opal unearthed in Ethiopia.

featured a snake design where the head of the snake chased its own tail around the band.

Today, most eternity rings are slim in design and feature gemstones that are channel set. The most popular gems used are Diamonds, Sapphires, and Rubies. To a lesser extent, the birthstone of the person who is receiving the eternity ring is also used.

ETHIOPIA

Although Ethiopia has the second largest population in Africa, its gem trade focuses around one gemstone: Opal. Current mining activities are unearthing Fire Opal, White Opal, Crystal Opal as well as many other varieties.

EUREKA DIAMOND

The Eureka Diamond (coming from the Greek meaning "I have found it") was one of the first historical Diamonds to be found in South Africa.

The name comes from a great story about a shepherd named Klonkie who found a pebble in 1866 near the Orange River. A couple of months later a neighbour offered to buy it, but his mother didn't want to be paid for it so she simply gave the stone away. The stone was later cut and weighed 21 carats!! Obviously, the mother did not realise the amount of money that stood to be made from this brilliant stone!

It was eventually sold for £1500 to Sir Philip Wodehouse, and was shown in the Paris Exposition in 1886. Soon afterwards it was cut into a brilliant oval, which then weighed 10.73 carats. The stone then disappeared and didn't resurface until 1966 when De Beers consolidated mines bought it.

It is really hard to believe that such a precious stone has been passed through so many hands! On its 100th birthday in 1967 the Eureka was taken to Cape Town's parliament where it is still on display. But why all the fuss for a Diamond that weighs 10ct? Well, it is believed that the Eureka Diamond was in fact the very first Diamond to be discovered in South Africa and that makes it truly special.

EXTENDER CHAIN

An extender chain is used to lengthen necklaces or occasionally bracelets. In Europe the two most common lengths for necklaces are 16" (40.6cm) or 18" (45.7cm). Extender chains can either be added to a piece of jewellery whilst it is being manufactured or can be purchased as a separate item. When purchased separately, they are typically small chains of approximately 6" (15.2cm) in length and feature a small lobster claw at one end. The extender is then attached to the end of the existing necklace to add length. When an extender chain is an integral part of a necklace, it tends to have links that are large enough for the lobster claw to be attached at any point. This allows the wearer to choose the optimum length for the piece and is very useful when layering multiple necklaces. For bracelets, it is more common to use toggle clasps, with three or four identical large hoops attached at one opposing end, allowing the bracelet to be adjusted easily. Lengths in Europe typically range from 6.5" (16.5cm) to 8.5" (21.6cm).

A Necklace with a built in extender chain

EXTINCTION

Have you ever looked at a gem such as a Mozambique Garnet and the outer edge looks darker than the middle of the table? This is due to less light being reflected from this area of the gem. The effect varies from gem to gem, but the biggest factor is the angle of the pavilion facet; the steeper the angle, the greater the extinction.

Heavily included gems tend to display less extinction. The inclusions scatter light in different directions within the gem, often returning brilliance to the outline of the gem. Measuring extinction is a valuable tool in helping gemmologists recognise origins for certain gemstones. For example, a Burmese Ruby normally shows less extinction than a Thai Ruby due to its higher level of fluorescence, which to a certain extent negates the level of extinction seen within the gem.

A Rhodolite Garnet clearly demonstrating extinction.

FABERGÉ

We have included Fabergé in our A to Z, because many people often hear the words "Fabergé Egg" in conversations regarding jewellery and don't understand its origin.

Although the Fabergé family's jewellery history can be traced back to the 1600's in Russia, the story really establishes itself in 1885 when Peter Fabergé was commissioned to make a jewelled egg as an Easter present for the Tsar to give to his wife. He received international acclaim at the great exhibition in Paris in 1900 and was later commissioned by the British Royal family. The House of Fabergé still remains very influential in the jewellery industry today.

The egg was so well received that Fabergé was asked to make several more as special presents for royalty. Over a period spanning 30 years, 69 of these extremely precious, highly decorated golden eggs were commissioned. Each one not only differed on the outside, but internally the egg held different surprises, similar to the chocolate

One of many famous Fabergé eggs.

Easter eggs that children receive today. Instead of chocolate, however, the surprises inside were often large Rubies and other precious gemstones.

Of the 69 jewelled eggs that Fabergé made, the whereabouts of 61 are still known today; the majority of which are on display in museums.

FACETS

The small, flat surfaces on the external faces of a gem are referred to as facets. When you hear someone refer to the cut of the gem, it simply means how well the facets are symmetrically balanced or how close they are to well-known standard profiles. For example; the Tolkowsky round brilliant cut design, calculated by Marcel Tolkowsky in 1919, has 57 facets, where all of their angles are precisely detailed, such as to maximise the brilliance and lustre of a Diamond.

Facets are applied to the table, crown, and pavilion of a gem and sometimes are even cut onto the girdle (the widest part of a gem).

A well faceted Padparadscha coloured Spice Topaz .

FANCY CUT

When a cut of a gem does not fall into one of the main categories such as a brilliant cut, an emerald cut, a cabochon, or princess cut, it is often referred to as a "Fancy Cut". This type of cut is often used to gain a higher yield out of the rough stone. As the skills of Lapidarists increase, along with a greater understanding of how certain cuts reflect and refract light in different ways, fancy cuts are becoming more and more popular. Just like playing music or painting, lapidary is a real artform!

Fancy Cuts are also known as "Freeform Cuts" and the GIA refer to those that have less than six sides when viewed from the top as "Small Freeform" shapes; "Large Freeform" refers to those that have more than six sides. Please note that if you are purchasing loose fancy cut gemstones, they are unlikely to fit into standard jewellery designs and if you want to have them set, you will need to find a jeweller that makes pieces by hand.

Tookalon pieces are often designed around fancy cut gemstones.

FELDSPAR

Colour	Colourless, blue-green, green red
Family	Feldspar
Hardness	6 – 6.5
Specific Gravity	2.54 – 2.59
Refractive Index	1.522 – 1.530
Crystal Group	Triclinic
Optical Properties	Biaxial
Common Treatments	None
Care	No special care required
Cleaning Advice	Warm soapy water
Chemical Composition	Various

There are many members in the Feldspar family: whilst some are used to create bathroom tiles, others are ground and used in cleaning products. Although this doesn't sound particularly glamorous, it is important to appreciate that several gemstones are made of the same elements as common place goods. It is purely the work of Mother Nature - a magical combination of the right amount of time, the correct pressure and temperature, plus the addition of the right colouring agents - that can, in the rarest of cases, produce glorious, valuable gemstones.

As a mineral, Feldspar is very common and forms a large percentage of the Earth's crust. However, on the odd occasion that it develops into gem-quality material, it has the ability to supply gemstones with some of the most ravishing optical effects known to man. In common with members of the Beryl family, all of its descendants receive their colour from impurities within their structure (known as allochromatic gems).

All gems in the Feldspar family also have cleavage in two directions, one of which is perfect. Its name is derived from the German words "feld" meaning "field" and "spar" which is a term used for gems with a perfect cleavage.

It is this perfect cleavage that provides its members with glorious schiller (wonderful iridescence), and in the case of Sunstone its beautiful metallic aventurescence. Other members of the Feldspar family include Orthoclase, Moonstone, Labradorite and Albite.

Orthoclase, a member of the Feldspar family.

Labradorite, a member of the Feldspar family.

FIBROUS

A gem is said to have a fibrous look if, as the name suggests, it has a cloth-like appearance. This is usually created by the gem having a structure where the crystals or the inclusions are parallel to each other. Kyanite and Scapolite are often said to have a fibrous lustre and many gemstones that demonstrate chatoyancy also are fibrous.

Kyanite often has a fibrous lustre.

Colour	Green to Brown
Hardness	6 - 7.5
Specific Gravity	3.25
Refractive Index	1.65 - 1.68
Crystal Group	Orthorhombic
Optical Properties	Chatoyancy
Common Treatments	None
Cleaning Advice	Warm soapy water
Composition	AI2Si05

Filigree detail designed by Sarah Bennett.

FIBROLITE

What is the difference between Fibrolite and Sillimanite? Well in 1802 a Mr Bournon named a mineral with a chemical composition AI2SiO5 as Fibrolite, then as far as I can work out in 1824 for no apparent reason at all, a Mr G. T Bowen decided to change its name to Sillimanite!

So why in this book do we have two headings, one for Sillimanite and one for Fibrolite? Well I debated for a while whether to combine the two, however, as the industry tends to name pieces which show chatoyancy as Fibrolite Cat's Eye and those that don't as Sillimanite, I decided to document them separately.

A small parcel of Fibrolite Cat's Eye that I have recently acquired for GemCollector.com, contains nice translucent brownish yellow cabochon cut gems from Sri Lanka.

FIGURAL JEWELLERY

Although figural jewellery dates back some 3000 years, it became very popular in Victorian and Art Nouveau times. Figural jewellery is designed to look like popular figures or animals such as butterflies, birds and even snakes.

Today, the term is more widely used to describe any jewellery that is shaped into a fun design. From a car pendant to a cat charm, from a snake ring to a peacock brooch, all can be referred to as figural jewellery.

FILIGREE

A word often misused to describe jewellery with lots of detail. Filigree is a process where gold or silver wires are soldered onto the side of a piece of jewellery to create beautiful patterns. For example, the Sarah Bennett Jewellery Collection features silver rings that have intricate gold detail soldered on the shoulders.

Today the phrase is more often used to describe

the crown of a ring where holes have been cut, drilled, punched or indeed styled into a mould. The more accurate name for this style of work is "ajoure".

It is believed that Filigree got its name by combining the Latin words for thread "filum", and "granum" meaning grain.

FINDINGS

In jewellery, findings refers to certain parts of the jewellery that are created separately from the main piece and often have an element of mechanism in them. Cufflink arms, clasps on bracelets and necklaces, and butterfly earring backs are all types of findings.

Butterfly backs are today the most popular findings for securing earrings.

FINENESS

To increase the strength of precious metals such as gold and silver, they are often alloyed with other metals. The percentage of the precious metal in the final alloy is known as its level of fineness.

In most countries it is common to express fineness in parts per thousand. For example 9k gold is 375 parts per thousand (37.5% gold) and is therefore hallmarked 375. The reason why it is then referred to as 9K gold and not 375K is that pure gold in the karats measurement system is 24K and therefore 37.5% of 24k is equal to 9K.

An earring post showing the hallmark 750 which denotes 18k gold and CR which is Coloured Rocks' official Hallmark.

FIRE (DISPERSION)

Fire, or dispersion, is caused when a gemstone splits white light into the seven main colours visible to the naked eye by refraction. The light disperses in the gem and reflects on its inner surfaces.

Refraction in a gemstone is caused by the change in speed as light travels from air into the gemstone. The specific properties of the gemstone slow the white light down until the different wavelengths separate into the seven colours: red, orange, yellow, green, blue, indigo

Sphalerite has three times more fire than Diamond.

Sphene has a greater fire than Diamond.

Colour	Orange - Red
Family	Opal
Hardness	5.5 - 6.5
Specific Gravity	2.15
Refractive Index	1.37 - 1.45
Crystal Group	Amorphous
Common Treatments	Heat Treated
Care	None
Cleaning Advice	Warm soapy water
Chemical Composition	Hydrated Silica

2ct Fire Opal by Jacque Christie.

and violet. However, the human eye can only see three colours; red, blue and green. These are called additive primaries, and it's from a mixture of these three colours that the human brain can create every possible colour.

It's very easy to concentrate on the physics of this phenomenon without looking at the sheer beauty and rarity. Nothing catches your attention more than a flash of colour from a Zircon or a Diamond seen across a crowded room or across the table on the finger of a dinner partner.

FIRE OPAL

Unlike regular Opals, where the body colour is normally white through grey, Fire Opal is a stunning orange to yellowish-orange colour, which has a beautiful warm fiery glow. It really is one of the most unique stones in the gem world. Quality transparent Fire Opal is very rare indeed and therefore very expensive, however if you are on a tight budget and want to add one to your collection then go for a piece that is translucent to opaque, these are still very beautiful and have a cloudy appearance similar to Blue Moon Quartz.

Although Fire Opal can be found in a handful of small deposits around the world, such as Guatemala in the USA, Brazil, Canada and Turkey, the most significant discovery has been in Mexico. High up in the mountain region where extinct volcanoes shape the landscape, there are several mines now producing small quantities of Fire Opal. Most of these mines are open cast; however as the Fire Opal tends to be discovered in crevices and cavities, there are some regions where it is found in long winding narrow passages, where the sides are over 50 metres high.

Throughout history, many religions and cultures around the world believed that Fire Opal was created in the waters of paradise. The Aztecs worshipped the gem and named it "quetzalitzlipyollitli", meaning the "stone of the bird of paradise".

There are many suggested benefits to wearing

this gemstone but, before we even look at what crystal healers believe, let me start by saying that like Citrine or Lemon Quartz, when you wear a piece of Fire Opal, you find it almost impossible to look at it and not smile. Stare at it for more than a few seconds and you feel a complete warmth, a sense of happiness with the world and a feeling of being at one with nature. The gem is believed to bestow courage, to increase willpower and energy. Others believe that it brings the wearer peace and harmony.

FLAW

In gemstone terms, a flaw is an imperfection on the surface or within the gemstone. The most common flaws are cracks and inclusions. In most gemstones the more flaws there are, the lower the value of the gem. A perfect or near perfect gem is known as a flawless gem.

Moldavite's flaws are gasses from out of space.

FLOWER CUT

In 1919, Marcel Tolkowsky detailed what he believed was the perfect round cut for a Diamond, providing all of the relevant angles and proportions of facets to best display the gem's ability to disperse and refract light. To this day the gem cutting industry still follows his findings. When the largest Diamond trading company in the world, "De Beers", wanted to introduce a new gem cut, they naturally turned to the Tolkowsky family. This time, Gabi Tolkowsky developed the "Flower Cut".

When it comes to Diamonds, the cut is very useful for such gems that don't have great colour or clarity, as the extra facets on the crown effectively mask some of the gem's internal appearance. The "Flower Cut" that Tolkowsky introduced was actually a series of different designs; all were based on the same theme. In order for the cut to grow in popularity it was deliberately not patented and over the last twenty years, many people have developed their own style of the cut.

A flower cut Amethyst in a modern and youthful design from Jessica Lili.

Peridot often demonstrates strong fluorescence.

Songea Rubies beautifully demonstrating fluorescence.

Tolkowsky did not design one flower cut, but several. The original designs included: the 63 faceted Dahlia which was based on an oval cut, the 73 faceted Marigold which was based on an octagon cut, the 73 faceted Zinnia based on a round cut and the lesser known Fire Rose and Sunflower designs.

FLUORESCENCE

Throughout history, there have been stories about magical gemstones that somehow had the ability to glow. While in the ark, Noah was said to have provided light by hanging Garnets. One of the early names for Ruby, "Carbuncle", related to its ability to glow. Even the legendary writer of "Natural History", Pliny the Elder (AD23 to AD79) wrote about curious luminous gems. Today we know this mystical ability of certain gems to glow as fluorescence.

Fluorescence produces vivid colours when an ultraviolet light source is directed at a gemstone. As we have discussed under the heading "colour", visible light is broken down into the colours of the rainbow, all of which have wavelengths that are visible to the naked eye. Ultraviolet light however, has a short wavelength (less than 400nm) and is not visible to the naked eye; the ultraviolet light that the sun emits, although not visible, is what causes sunburn. When different gems are exposed to ultraviolet light, they behave differently. Although none get sunburnt, some are affected by the light, and while the source is present, give off a strong glow. Burmese Ruby for example, becomes intensely bright when seen in direct sunlight. Put simplistically, the cause of this effect is due to the fact that ultraviolet light is more energetic than visible light, which boosts the energy of certain electrons, causing them to glow.

In 1852, Professor George Stokes - in a poorly light room - allowed a small amount of sunlight through a small hole in a window blind to fall onto the surface of a colourless Fluorite gem. He noted how the ultraviolet light enhanced the appearance of the mineral. The word fluorescence yet again demonstrates how many words in the English language are derived from the colour and optical properties of gemstones.

The term should not be confused with phosphorescence. Phosphorescent gems are those that retain their luminosity within the gem after the removal of the ultraviolet light. For example, similar to the phosphorescent arms used in some watches, gems such as Kunzite, when taken into the shade after being exposed to ultraviolet light, may continue to glow for several minutes.

Now if we want to get incredibly technical, there are two more events worthy of a mention. Triboluminescence is the emission of light as a result of friction. Certain Feldspars and occasionally Diamonds and Quartz possess this ability. Some minerals have the ability to glow when they are heated, which is known as thermoluminescence. Apatite and fluorite can possess this ability.

It was an experiment with Fluorite that helped Professor George Stokes identify Fluorescence.

FLUORITE

Fluorite is a beautiful gemstone, but as it is softer than many gems, few jewellers attempt to set it into precious metals. That said, those jewellers that have experience working with Fluorite, find the gem fairly easy to prong set into pendants and earrings.

Interestingly, the most famous location for this amazing gem, a gem that often is bi-coloured, is Castleton in Derbyshire, England. This is where the famous Blue John is found and is highly prized as an ornamental stone. The English miners used to call the crystals 'ore flowers' and gem collectors for many years have referred to fluorite as 'the most colourful mineral in the world'.

Its name is derived from the Latin word "fluere", which means "to flow" and refers to the gem's low melting point. As mentioned under fluorescence, the household fluorescent tube owes the "fluorescent" part of its name to this gemstone.

The reason for this is that many pieces of Fluorite fluoresce when placed under ultra-

Colour	Colourless, yellow, green, blue, purple, red, black
Family	Does not belong to a family
Hardness	4
Specific Gravity	3.1 – 3.2
Refractive Index	1.43
Crystal Group	Cubic
Optical Properties	Vitreous lustre
Common Treatments	Often heat treated to improve colour
Cleaning Advice	Warm soapy water
Care	Be careful not to scratch with harder materials

A rare 1.1ct yellow Fluorite.

African Zebra Fluroite.

violet light. Although blue is the most common colour to fluoresce in Fluorite, it is also possible to see red, purple and green glowing within the gem. The colour of the fluorescence varies due to the presence of different impurities and these are often used by gemologists to identify the gem's origin.

As well as being discovered in the UK (where it is of gem-quality), Fluorite is also mined in various states in the USA, including Oklahoma, Kentucky, Colorado, Arizona and even New York. Other countries that mine Fluorite include Germany, Switzerland, Mexico and Canada.

I have recently purchased some gorgeous Fluorite rough from Africa. The gem is banded and is therefore known as "Zebra Fluorite", but rather than the colours being black and white, they are lovely blend of "Rose de France" purple and a teal green. Whilst most Lapidarists would only cabochon cut Fluorite, our team have cut the gemstone into ovals and emerald shapes.

FOIL BACKED

It is said that deception in the jewellery industry is the oldest form of fraud known to man, and one of the oldest tricks is to add coloured foil to the tip of the culet to improve a gem's colour. Although most companies practising this form of deceit today have been closed down, don't be surprised if your great grandmother's bezel set coloured gemstone is set on a foil base.

FOOL'S GOLD - PYRITE

Pyrite is a pretty, shiny, sparkling gemstone that is far underrated within the world of gems. Its "claim to fame", or "Achilles heel" depending on where you stand, is that was it often mistaken for gold. Pyrite occurs in a number of interesting shapes and sizes and has come to be known as "fool's gold". Its similarities to gold are extremely close. However, Pyrite does not mark or dent when bitten, whereas gold famously does. Interestingly though, Pyrite often gets found next to gold deposits, so in years gone by if one had found Pyrite then a little more searching could have yielded the miner a more lucrative find.

Colour	Similar to a dark brassy colour
Family	Does not belong to a family
Hardness	6 – 6.5
Specific Gravity	4.9 – 5.2
Refractive Index	Does not refract light
Crystal Group	Cubic
Optical Properties	Shines like gold
Common Treatments	None
Care	No specific care requirements
Composition	FeS$_2$ (iron)

Pyrite also has the same chemical make up as Marcasite, although the crystal structure is different. The name Marcasite stems from the Arabic word for Pyrite (see Marcasite) and the gem industry uses the term Marcasite when often it is Pyrite. The name Pyrite comes from the Greek word "pyr" meaning "fire" because when the gem is struck it releases sparks. As it is highly reflective, the ancient Aztecs and Incas would polish large slabs of Pyrite and use it as a mirror. In the Stone Ages it would be used to start fires and was a natural way for prehistoric man to survive harsh conditions.

The difficult task of separating Gold from Pyrite.

Pyrite is thought to possess the power of balancing between your left and right side of the brain and throughout the ages it was thought that owning a piece of Pyrite would help you gain great wealth and prosperity. In more modern times Pyrite has been used in the arms industry and also has many industrial uses. In World War II it was mined for its sulphur content, which made sulphuric acid (in high demand at the time).

It can be mined the world over but some of the most well known deposits are in Oruro and Colavi, Bolivia. Larger and more cubic forms of Pyrite can be found in Spain and also on the Island of Elba, off Italy. Very high quality specimens can be found in Freiburg, south-west Germany.

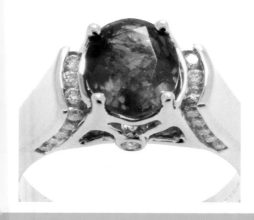

GALLERY

Today, this word is used in jewellery to describe the portion of a ring where a gemstone or gemstones sit. If the design has lots of areas where light can pass through, it is said to be an open gallery and if the top of the ring is solid, it is said to be a closed gallery.

In days gone by, the gallery referred to a strip of metal that circled the gem and was cut into a design resembling the top of a castle wall, where the raised parts were bent over the gem to act as prongs. As gold and silver are very malleable metals, jewellers can often apply very intricate designs to the gallery.

Although the term is primarily used in association with rings, effectively the area where any gemstone sits on, i.e. earrings, bracelets, pendants and necklaces, is in fact a gallery.

GARNET

The Garnet is associated with fire, passion and blood. The associations of this extremely popular gemstone are numerous: it is the birthstone for January; associated with the astrological signs of both Aquarius and Leo; and is also the recommended gift for both the 2nd and 6th wedding anniversaries.

Garnet occurs in a kaleidoscope of natural colours including red, orange, yellow, green, purple, brown, black, pink and colourless. Although there are some 30 different gems in the Garnet family, they all fall into one of six main families/species; Almandine, Andradite, Grossular, Pyrope, Spessartite or Uvarovite.

All Garnets feature the same cubic crystal structure; a wide range of differing chemical compositions and physical structures then provides us with so many wonderful varieties and natural colours. Because members of the Garnet group are unusually linked due to their crystal structure (referred to as isomorphic), their differences in composition mean that their hardness can vary from 6.5 to 7.5 on the Mohs scale. The following gemstones all belong to one of the six Garnet families/species: Mozambique Garnet, Colour Change Garnet, Hessonite, Malaia Garnet, Mandarin Garnet, Rhodolite, Tsavorite, Demantoid and Mali Garnet.

Garnet is steeped in history; it can be dated as far back as 3500BC, as it was discovered in a necklace uncovered in Egypt on the neck of a mummified body. Its name is derived from the Latin word "granatus" as it is similar in shape to the seed of a pomegranate. Incidentally, in Greek mythology this fruit is also regarded as a gift of love, and is said to symbolise eternity.

This jewel supposedly has the ability to illuminate even the darkest of rooms; it is written that Noah used the gem to light the inside of the ark. Another story tells of an old widow who, upon finding an injured crow in her garden, spent months nursing it back to good health. The widow became very attached to the bird and

Colour	An array of colours
Family	Garnet
Hardness	6.5 – 7.5
Specific Gravity	3.4 – 4.3
Refractive Index	1.730 – 1.760
Crystal Group	Some are isometric & some cubic
Optical Properties	Various
Common Treatments	Cannot be heat treated
Cleaning Advice	Ultrasonic or warm soapy water
Care	No special care needed
Chemical Composition	Various

6ct Garnet in a handmade ring by Tookalon.

A breathtaking Rhodolite Garnet bangle.

*Mozambique Garnet set
in the crown of a Mattom watch.*

when the bird was fully recovered, she wept as she reluctantly released it. After several weeks had passed, while in her bed one night, the bird flew into her room and placed a large red Garnet at the side of her bed: the gem was said to have filled her room with light.

There are many other legends that involve Garnet's mystical lighting and brightening capabilities (known technically today as fluorescence). For example, it has been suggested that Eastern Indians rubbed Garnet gemstones on themselves in belief that the gem's glowing qualities would be transmitted into their glowing wellbeing. Several cultures have finely ground Garnet and heated it to act as a medicinal remedy for illness. Some healers continue to use it today as a cure for nightmares.

When studying the myths and legends surrounding Garnet, whether it be stories relating to the Aztecs, Romans, Egyptians, Native Americans or British Royalty, there is one theme common in all civilisations, across all periods of recorded time: Garnet is the ultimate gift of love. Today the gem continues to be a symbol of love, passion, eternity and warmth.

GEM COLLECTOR.COM

Do read this section with caution, as GemCollector is incredibly precious to me and therefore I am going to be very biased when discussing it! GemCollector has been designed from the ground up to offer: the widest range of loose gemstones on the planet; the best value for loose gemstones on earth; the widest range of shapes and cuts available anywhere, the ability to custom-make jewellery by separately choosing the gem and the jewellery setting. I could go on and on, but if you are serious about collecting gemstones, then you simply must check out www.GemCollector.com.

The pricing at Gemcollector is very unique too! Whereas most gem traders will set their prices separately for each variety of gem, we have

*GemCollector.com provides free
presentation boxes to its customers.*

G

approached this from a totally different point of view and have worked on creating a simple pricing model, whereby we add the same minute margin to each piece. What this means for collectors is that the price they pay is always the lowest possible for the quality of gem they are acquiring and that no gem is artificially inflated due to its market perception.

Every loose gemstone is supplied in one of our totally transparent gem pots, which magically appear to suspend the gem in mid air. And with your first purchase you get a storage box to keep all of your pots.

GEM FAMILIES

This heading was a difficult one to decide on, because it could so easily have come under the heading gem groups or gem species. The whole topic of which gem is related to which family or which group or which species, is complicated by the fact that various organisations in the gem world, use different terminology for different connections.

Let me try and make it as simple as possible by looking at the GIA's description found in their publication of the "Gem reference guide" in 1988. Even though it was written 21 years ago, I still feel it is the most comprehensive and accurate guide ever written on the technical aspects of gemstones and with regards to this subject, they are very clear on their views.

Firstly the GIA teach us that there are only two "Groups" of gemstones and these are the Feldspar and Garnet Groups. I personally add a third group to this and treat Organic gemstones as a group name.

All other parents such as Quartz, Tourmalines and Beryls are know by the GIA as "species". However, today it is more common to hear these referred to as "families". So don't get confused if you hear either term, they are simply referring to the same thing.

To the right the species/family names are shown along with their main family members.

Beryl
- Aquamarine
- Bixbite
- Emerald
- Hemidor
- Morganite
- Yellow Beryl

Chrysoberyl
- Alexandrite
- Chrysolite
- Yellow Chrysoberyl

Corundum
- Sapphire
- Padparadscha
- Ruby

Spodumene
- Kunzite
- Hiddenite

Organic
- Pearl
- Jet
- Amber
- Coral

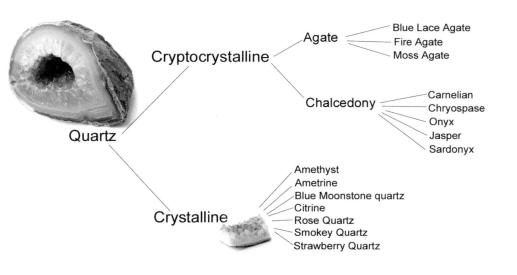

Cryptocrystalline

Agate
- Blue Lace Agate
- Fire Agate
- Moss Agate

Chalcedony
- Carnelian
- Chryospase
- Onyx
- Jasper
- Sardonyx

Quartz

Crystalline
- Amethyst
- Ametrine
- Blue Moonstone quartz
- Citrine
- Rose Quartz
- Smokey Quartz
- Strawberry Quartz

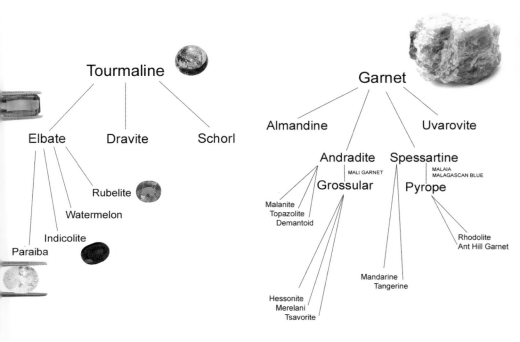

Tourmaline

Elbate   Dravite   Schorl

Rubelite
Watermelon
Indicolite
Paraiba

Garnet

Almandine   Uvarovite

Andradite   Spessartine
MALI GARNET   MALAIA MALAGASCAN BLUE
Grossular   Pyrope

Malanite
Topazolite
Demantoid

Rhodolite
Ant Hill Garnet

Hessonite
Merelani
Tsavorite

Mandarine
Tangerine

So let us look at two examples which will hopefully make it easier to understand: (1) Tsavorite Garnet is the variety name of a rare Green member of the Grossularite Garnet species/family, which is in turn part of the Garnet group. (2) Amethyst and Citrine are varieties of the Quartz species/family.

To slightly complicate this three-tier system, in some families/species, there are separate branches/sub species (these are not industry terms but are the best names Tony Poole and I could come up with). For example the Quartz family/species can then be further divided into Cryptocrystalline (whose crystals are microscopic like in Chalcedony and Agate) and Crystalline sub species, such as Amethyst, Citrine, Smoky Quartz, Strawberry Quartz and Rose Quartz.

But what is it that relates certain gems to others? Well that's unfortunately not quite as straightforward! The reason why some gems are related to others depends on which families you are talking about and most families are grouped for different reasons. All members of the Quartz species/family are related due to their chemical composition being the same (SiO_2). All Beryls also share the same chemical composition $Be_3Al_2Si_6O_{18}$. Tourmalines on the other hand, all share the same crystal structure, but may vary in chemical composition.

Feldspar

- Albite
- Amazonite
- Andesine
- Labradorite
- Moonstone
- Sunstone

Jade

- Jadeite
- Nephrite

Corundum

- Sapphire
- Padparadscha
- Ruby

Zoisite

- Anyolite
- Thulite
- Tanzanite

GEMSTONES

Like blind tasting a good wine, when trying to correctly identify a gemstone, be sure not to jump to conclusion based purely on its visual appearance, or you may come unstuck more often than you think. In identifying different gemstones we look firstly at their colour, hardness, lustre, dispersion and brilliance. If we are still unsure of a gem type, we can accurately measure its refractive index, specific gravity, cleavage, and fracture. Many gemstones display optical characteristics such as asterism, chatoyancy, pleochroism and double refraction, which can also be used to help distinguish one variety from another.

Red Andesine is considered by many to be the most beautiful gem on the planet.

Spalerite is incredibly rare.

Sapphire is extremely durable.

To be classed as a gemstone, a mineral must be beautiful, rare and durable:

Beauty

Beauty is very subjective, but in general the attributes of gems which excite our sense of beauty include colour, transparency, lustre, brilliance, pattern and optical phenomena and, in some cases, distinctive inclusions.

Rarity

There are two types of rarity involved with gemstones: relative and inherent. Relative rarity is when gems occur in many locales and often in large deposits, however, the vast majority of the material is not of gem-quality, therefore this is relative rarity. The mineral Corundum, for example, from which we get precious Rubies and Sapphire, is widespread and abundant, but the amount of gem-quality specimens found are incredibly rare and usually in extremely small pieces. Inherent rarity is when minerals occur in only a few locations or in very small deposits. Alexandrite, Tanzanite and certain Garnets fall into this category.

Durability

A gem must be able to withstand the stresses and forces it undertakes to be cut, polished and set into jewellery. It must also be tough and stable enough to be worn every day.

GEODES

A geode is a hollow rock, often constructed of limestone and normally in a shape resembling a badly shaped rugby ball, and once opened can contain gemstones. Amethyst, Quartz, Citrine and Chalcedony, and - to a lesser extent - Peridot gems are often discovered inside geodes.

GEORGE FREDERICK KUNZ

George Frederick Kunz was born in the Big Apple, New York on the 29th September 1856.

Although he studied science at The Cooper Union, he never completed his course. His interest in mineralogy was self-taught from reading books and field research and by his late teens he had amassed over 4000 mineral specimens.

He made many expeditions looking for different specimens that he would then take to colleges and universities for them to use as material when studying. While working on his expeditions he became friends with many important people in the world of gemmology and at the age of just 23, his incredible knowledge of gemstones and enthusiasm saw him appointed to the board at Tiffany and Co.

It was Kunz who discovered Morganite, which he named after his company's bankers J.P Morgan. Kunzite was also named in respect of this legendary gem hunter who remains, until this very day, one of the most famous and important mineral specialists of all time.

Kunz wrote hundreds of articles on gems and gemmology, and was appointed to the board of many mineralogical societies, including being a research curator for the Museum of Natural History in New York City. Possibly the best gem book ever written, "The Curious Lore of Precious Stones" is written by Fredrick Kunz.

He married Sophia Hanforth in 1879 who sadly died in 1912. It wasn't until 1923 that Kunz married Opal Logan Giberson, but the marriage was unsuccessful and shortly after he decided to annul the marriage. Kunz died on the 29th of June 1932 at the age of 76.

Kunzite is named after George Frederick Kunz.

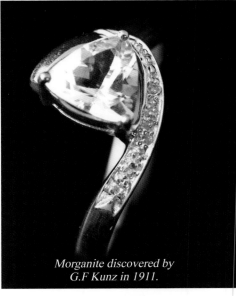

Morganite discovered by G.F Kunz in 1911.

GEORGIAN ERA

In 1714, German-born George of Hanover ascended to the throne to become King of England. Reigning as Monarch for just 13 years, he was quickly followed by George II, III and IV. This era, ended by the death of George IV in 1830, is now known as the Georgian period.

The term 'Georgian', as we know it now, is most often used when referring to architecture,

A Georgian-inspired Aquamarine ring from the Jacque Christie collection.

It was during the Georgian era that the cushion cut was introduced.

the arts and social history. Georgian Jewellery incorporates the majority of the 18th century, and the first few years of the 19th. When old fashions departed and new ones arrived, people would melt down their old jewellery, extract the gemstones, and have them made into a piece in the latest fashion. This is one of the reasons that sadly, like jewellery from so many eras, today there are very few pieces in circulation, making those that have survived the melting pot, incredibly collectable and coveted the world over.

During the Georgian period a revolution took place within architecture and the arts. Varying styles and fashions adorned the period, and jewellery, as always, followed these fashions.

Unlike today, all jewellery in the Georgian period was hand-made. Because of this the gemstones were cut with irregularity, making each piece unique. During the reign of George I, the style was called Rococo and during the reign of the following Georges it moved on to what we now call the 'Gothic Revival' and the 'Neo-classical' period.

For jewellery, the period was an exciting time of discovery, experimentation and innovation. Designs often favoured nature as inspiration, and nearly all pieces featured coloured gemstones. The focus of the piece was usually on the gemstone, with the metal being less important. Diamond cutters experimented with different shapes and cuts, and it was during this time that the now popular 'cushion cut' and 'rose cut' were invented.

Due to increasing demand for gemstones, jewellery makers started to use other substances instead. These alternatives, to the naked eye, resembled the gems so much that they were even worn by Royalty! An alloy was discovered, named 'Pinchbeck', after its inventor Christopher Pinchbeck, which could be used as a cheap substitute for gold. It wasn't used for very long though, as the secret formula died with its creator.

During the 1750's Rubies, Emeralds and

Sapphires became extremely desirable, and other lesser-known gems in the UK such as Amethyst, Garnet and Pearls became increasingly popular. Rock crystal and Marcasite were also being used more frequently.

A common design in Georgian jewellery was the 'crowned heart design', a gemstone cut into a heart shape, with a gold or silver crown placed on top. It symbolised love crowning a rule over life. Silver was often used over gold, as the whiteness of the silver accentuated the lustre of the gems used. Designs made of gold wire tightly wound together known as Cannetille became popular. The design commanded its own jewellery, but was also used as an addition to previous ideas.

Stylised floral designs fell back in favour, and 'Sevigne', or 'floppy' bows also grew in popularity, often being used in brooches.

Mourning jewellery, (jewellery to honour the dead), also came into vogue during the Georgian Era. After a loved one had passed away the jewellery would be worn for a set period. Designs included skulls, skeletons and other symbols and motifs of death. Hair was even used in some designs!

A type of earring known as the 'girandole' came into fashion and some say is defining of the period. This distinguishable design had a gem set near to the ear lobe and then three others hanging from it. These earrings were very heavy and often caused the ear lobes to elongate. We can see earrings around today that have used the girandole as inspiration.

Necklaces, often brooches on ribbons, had rings on both ends, where a ribbon would be threaded through and tied into a bow at the neck. Necklaces referred to as 'Stomachers', large brooches on a ribbon that would hang down to the stomach, were in fashion for a period. Bezel settings, flat gold designs and black and white enamelling are all distinguishing features of Georgian jewellery. To intensify their colour, gemstones were often set onto foil, their backs being hidden away, showing only the face of the gem.

Black jewellery was used for mourning in the Georgian Era.

Eleven
Seventeen

The Maze

Inspired by Nature

www.eleven-17.com

GEMSTONE FORMATION

Gem Formation

In order to understand how gems are formed, it is helpful to understand a little about geology. Our planet, which was created about 4.5 billion years ago, is comprised of several layers: the crust, ranging from 3 – 25 miles deep (only 1% of the Earth's volume), the mantle (which is over 80% of its volume) and the inner part of Earth known as the core. The core has a solid inner and a liquid outer and it is this part of Earth which, for obvious reasons, is the least known and studied.

Most of the mantle consists of magma, and giant segments of Earth's crust - along with the solid upper mantle - float on this fluid liquid and move slowly over it. These big plates, some the size of continents, are known as tectonic plates. It is the movement of these plates that is responsible for many of the huge events that continually shape and reshape the landscape of Earth. These include volcanoes, earthquakes and periods of mountain building where vast ranges including the Alps, Andes and Pyrenees were formed.

Earth's crust is made up of three types of rock: igneous, sedimentary and metamorphic. Igneous rocks are those which have solidified from a molten state. Sedimentary rocks are formed due to compacted sediment layers formed by weathering, pressure and often heat. Metamorphic rocks are formed when tremendous temperature and pressure have changed the formation of either igneous or sedimentary rock or other metamorphic rocks. While all non-organic gemstones begin their existence in one of these three rock structures, their journeys and experiences can be vastly different. There are many different scenarios and environments which lead to the creation of gemstones with differing chemical structures, crystal structures, hardness, colours and optical qualities. It is important to stress that while the creation of some gems will always be due to the same geological event, others can be created in

Magma flowing from volcanoes creates igneous rocks.

Citrine is formed in geodes.

Emerald is often created hydrothermally.

Beryl can be hydrothermally created.

*Peru Spice Topaz may
have been formed in Pegmatites.*

a variety of manners. Below we detail the main monumental natural events that are responsible for the creation of some of the most valuable treasures on Earth.

Gems Created From Water

Believe it or not, rain falling to the Earth's surface millions of years ago is responsible for the creation of several vibrant gemstones that we treasure today. As water passed through cracks in Earth's crust, it sometimes gathered different chemicals, creating a gem-forming 'cocktail'. During this journey, the liquid dissolved different minerals and rocks; eventually it became too saturated, and came to rest in cracks and crevasses. Given time and pressure, these solutions eventually turned into a new solid mineral. It is through this process that Opals, Turquoise and Malachite were formed.

Hydrothermally Created Gems

As the name suggests, hydrothermal gems are created similarly to those formed from water based solutions, but with the addition of heat. Imagine the journeys of two different fluids meeting at the same point. The water based solution filters downwards through cracks and gaps in Earth's crust, while hot magma solutions, often rich in fluorine and beryllium, are rising through veins and crevices. As they meet, the resulting cocktail features many different chemicals and minerals, and percolates at an incredibly high temperature. Over a period of time, as it begins to cool it produces crystals with complex chemical structures. Many Beryls were formed this way, and as you start to understand this incredibly hostile hydrothermal environment, you begin to appreciate the source of inclusions and patterns seen in Emeralds.

Pegmatites

First of all, let's remember that an igneous rock is one which has been formed from solidified magma. Pegmatites are created when magma is forced into crevasses and other cracks and is allowed to solidify over a period of time. In very simplistic terms, gemstones formed in pegmatites are similar to those hydrothermally formed, but the main ingredient in pegmatites is magma rather than water. The magma squeezed into openings is under incredible pressure, and provides an ideal environment for crystals to grow. Some of the world's largest pegmatites are in Minas Gerais, Brazil. These yield a magnificent array of coloured gemstones including Topaz, Aquamarine and Tourmaline. Other gems that form in pegmatites include Kunzite, Fluorite and Hiddenite.

Metamorphic

We discussed earlier that a metamorphic rock is one that has changed its form ('meta' meaning changed and 'morph' meaning shape). Interestingly, although immense pressure and heat is needed to create a metamorphic rock, the original mineral does not actually melt. There are two different types of metamorphism and we need to have a basic understanding of both, as they are homes to different gem types:

Contact Metamorphism occurs when magma (lava) forces its way into cracks and crevices of existing rock formations. Due to the incredible heat of the magma, the rocks which it comes into contact with recrystallise into new minerals. Sri Lanka (formerly Ceylon), one of the best gem treasure chests in the world, is a prime source of gems created through the act of contact metamorphism. It's incredible to think that if this event had not happened, Prince Charles would not have been able to give Princess Diana her electrifying Ceylon Blue Sapphire Engagement ring! Other gems that are created through this process include Garnets, Ruby and Spinel. High in the mountains of Afghanistan, Lapis Lazuli is also created in this way. Burma sits on an area rich in metamorphic rocks and much of its high quality Ruby and Jadeite are formed contact metamorphism.

Regional Metamorphism, as its name suggests, is not confined to cracks and crevices and happens across a wider area. These rocks are often created in environments running along the edges of tectonic plates. As these plates collide with one another, the igneous rocks of each plate

Aquamarines can often be formed in a hostile hydrothermal environment.

Rubies are often formed by contact metamorphism.

morph with one another under colossal pressure. As the rocks near the point of melting, and over a sustained period of millions of years, they can produce some incredibly beautiful crystal structures.

As you can imagine, gems formed from the coming together of two different plates, both of which can feature many different minerals, can lead to combinations that are very specific to one area. This is in fact the reason why Tanzanite has only been found in one place on the planet. The morphing of two tectonic plates underneath one small area in Tanzania produced a specific cocktail that has yet to be discovered anywhere else on this planet.

Mantle Gemstones

So far, we have discussed events that happen in the Earth's crust or along its inner edge. Two gemstones however, are created deep in the Earth's mantle; Peridot and Diamond. As these are formed some 90 miles beneath the earth's surface, and the deepest mine in the world, the East Rand gold mine in South Africa, is only 2.1 miles deep you might wonder how these gems are discovered. Well, they are primarily brought to the surface of the earth or near to its surface in old volcanic pipes. These are known as kimberlite pipes.

Interestingly, as Diamonds can crystallise at incredibly high temperatures in magma beneath Earth's crust, it is believed they may be the most common crystal on the planet, however, other than those embedded in kimberlite pipes, the remainder is just impossible to reach.

Tanzanite is formed by regional metamorphism.

Peridot is formed deep in the Earth's mantle.

GEMSTONE MINING

Mining is one of the oldest industries known to man, and the "Lion Cave" Hematite mine in Swaziland is believed to date back to 4,100 BC. According to records by Marco Polo, the Kuh-i-Lal mine in Afghanistan, which first mined gemstones in 101AD, is the oldest gem mine in the world that is still in use today!

There are many different procedures and techniques used in mining; some as simple as using a pick and a shovel, some using panning techniques similar to gold panning in the Wild West, some using explosives and others using the latest in high-tech equipment. However, regardless of the level of sophistication used, all mining commences with the exploration or 'prospecting' process. Even with an immense amount of research into this field, gem hunting today is still very much a hit and miss process.

Large-scale corporate gemstone mining.

Around the globe, gem mining happens on all levels. From entrepreneurial artisanal miners in Madagascar who often work with buckets and spades, to huge Diamond mines using the biggest machinery you have ever seen. Mining for Lapis Lazuli is done by small tribes in Afghanistan, and in the Peridot mines of the San Carlos Apache Reservation in Arizona, it is done exclusively by Apache Indians. Gemstone mining ranges from the corporate, such as the large sophisticated corporation that owns the Tanzanite One mine, to the more informal "pay to dig" schemes operated in some states in America (similar to "pick your own" strawberries in the UK). In Australia, there is even an underground Opal mining village at Coober Pedy!

As you can see, gemstone mining is anything but standardised, and hundreds of thousands of people globally earn a living from trying to discover and extract the most precious of Mother Nature's creations.

Gemstones are discovered primarily in two different ways: they are either mined directly from the host rock in which they were formed, or in alluvial deposits where the gems have been separated from their host rock. Once a gem has been discovered, mines are then established either above or below ground.

Above ground (surface mining) techniques include: open pit mining, quarrying, strip mining and mountaintop removal. Underground mining techniques include: drift mining, tunnelling, shaft mining, bore hole mining, caving, room and pillar mining and retreat mining.

An entrepreneurial artisan miner searching for Sapphire.

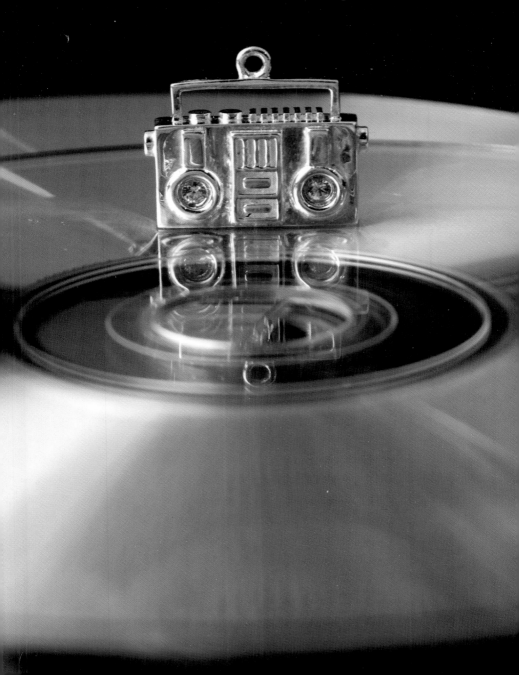

GEM SORTING

One of the most difficult and time-consuming tasks when making a cluster ring or gemstone bracelet is matching the gems. As Mother Nature never creates any two gemstones identically - all varying slightly in hue, tone, saturation and clarity - before gems are set in jewellery, a massive task is undertaken by a Gem Sorter, who is responsible for making a selection of stones that are as similar as possible.

Let's assume we have an Amethyst cluster ring with 20 gems in each and that we are to make 10 pieces. Applying basic maths we will need to sort through 200 gems. However, in jewellery terms this is not the case. To arrive at the end result of 20 rings, all with near as perfectly matched gemstones as possible, the Gem Sorter will have to study and compare the characteristics of possibly 500 to 1000 gems from which to make the selections.

Without doubt, this process is one of the most skillful of all in gemstone jewellery making. I have spent countless hours in sorting departments, questioning why one gem was rejected over another, frequently unable to actually see any noticeable differences without the aid of magnification.

One thing that I wasn't aware of until recently, is that when selecting coloured gemstones for a ring such as a half eternity band, very experienced Gem Sorters will actually differentiate between the gems they select for the centre of the ring to those on the shoulders. The reason for this is due to the fact that the angle at which you view these gems is minutely different depending on where it sits within the band, therefore small adjustments are made in the selection so that to the eye the look is consistent across all gemstones! This is extremely important when matching gemstones with vivid colours.

Unfortunately I will never make a good Gem Selector as my eyesight is not finely tuned and to be quite honest, the task requires the very highest levels of patience!

To make the ring below we may have to search through hundreds of gems to find those that perfectly match.

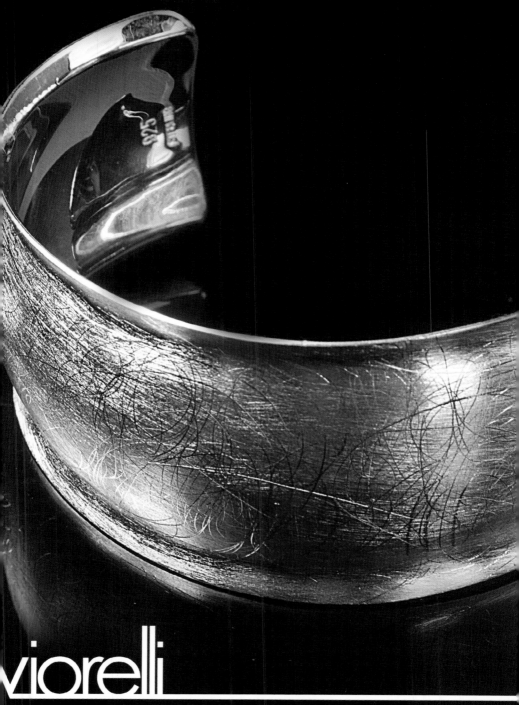

viorelli

very viorelli.

GIRDLE

The girdle of a gemstone refers to its widest point and is where the bottom of the crown meets the top of the pavilion.

Though it is normally a sharp point, on larger gemstones it sometimes has very small vertical facets applied. The term is only applied to faceted gems and is not used in connection with cabochon or tumbled cuts.

Typically, the girdle is the place where a gem is held when set in jewellery. In a channel, tension or bar setting, the girdle is held in a groove between the metal, and in a prong setting the stone is held just above the girdle on the crown. In a bezel setting, the supporting metal is bent over the girdle all the way around the perimeter of the gemstone.

The girdle of this Black Diamond is on show in this setting.

GLYPTOGRAPHY

Some ancient Greeks who believed coloured gemstones derived from the heart of nature are said to have preferred to use Diamonds to carve inscriptions into their coloured gems, rather than setting them in jewellery. The ancient art of engraving messages into gemstones is known as Glyptography.

Shah Jahan, the famous builder of the Taj Mahal, was so fanatical about gemstones and their ability to bring good fortune that he took his favourite Emeralds and had a Glyptographer inscribe them. He wore them as a talisman and the most renowned of his collection, a 78 carat Emerald has the Persian inscription, "he who possesses this charm shall enjoy the special protection of god".

Ancient glyptography applied to an Emerald.

GOLD

Gold is one of the oldest metals used by humans and was originally found in alluvial deposits. Gold mining can be traced back to 2500BC, when Egyptians mined the mineral to

Gold bullion bars, as supplied to jewellery workshops.

Gold nuggets straight out of the ground.

set into jewellery.

Today the largest gold mines in the world are in South Africa, as are the largest Diamond mines.

Around 65 to 70% of processed gold is used in jewellery, with the remainder being used by industry. The most malleable of all metals, just one small gram of gold can be beaten into a sheet of one square metre, measuring just 4 millionths of an inch thick. It can be made so thin it becomes transparent and is often used to tint glass windows. Other uses include electrical circuits and wiring; just one ounce can be stretched up to 40 miles before it breaks.

Gold weight is measured in "Troy" ounces. These weigh more than a normal ounce, with just 12 troy ounces equalling a pound. When you see the price of gold being quoted in a newspaper or on the evening news, it is the current price for one troy ounce of pure gold.

Over the past five years, gold has risen from around $300 per troy ounce to over $950. Obviously jewellery should be purchased primarily because it is beautiful. However, as gold can always be melted and re-sold, all pieces of gold jewellery will always retain an inherent value. Many people feel that gold is a good investment because when economical times are good, they can wear their jewellery and when times are hard, gold prices are normally at their highest.

For jewellery purposes, gold is usually alloyed with other metals to increase its sturdiness (pure gold only registers 2.75 on the mohs scale). To do this it has to be heated to over 1337 degrees Kelvin (2,063 Fahrenheit) and then annealed with harder metals such as copper, silver, platinum or nickel. The minimum purity for Gold in the UK, and by far the most popular in terms of volume, is 9k (37.5% pure). In Germany 8k Gold is the minimum legal standard, whilst in America it is 10k.

In medieval times gold was considered good for your health, following the belief that something so beautiful and rare had to be good for you.

GOSHENITE

Colour	Colourless
Family	Beryl
Hardness	7.5 – 8
Specific Gravity	2.6 – 2.8
Refractive Index	1.57 – 1.6
Crystal Group	Hexagonal
Optical Properties	Good dispersion
Common Treatments	Not treated
Cleaning Advice	Warm soapy water
Care	No special care required
Chemical Composition	$Be_3Al_2Si_6O_{18}$

Due to its seemingly pure appearance, Goshenite (or White Beryl as it is sometimes known) has been named the "mother of gemstones".

As other Beryls received their colour from internal impurities, early gemmologists assumed that the gem must be pure; however, it was later discovered that Goshenite was unique in that it had other chemical impurities that actually suppressed its colour.

Since the first century AD, the excellent qualities of this transparent Beryl have made the perfect alternative for other colourless gemstones, such as Diamond. When it is polished and faceted it makes a fantastic and classy gemstone that sits elegantly in white gold.

In Ancient Greece, the Greeks used Goshenite to make the first ever glasses, as it was perfect for lenses. Maybe this is why it has been said that this gemstone can help with sight.

In addition to aiding poor eyesight, it is also believed to help fight fatigue, lending strength when you become exhausted. It can help you clear your mind, and bring truth and clarity to your psyche. As well as being used for glasses, its transparency has made it ideal for making small crystal balls.

When it is free of inclusions, it really is one of the most beautiful gemstones on the planet and rightly deserves its nickname "mother of gemstones". This clear, colourless gemstone exudes amazing brilliance, scintillation and fire.

The name for this gemstone derives from Goshen Massachusetts, which was one of the first areas to discover the gem. Today it can be found in several countries, but most are mined in Brazil, America and Canada.

Whilst its other family members, Emerald, Red Beryl, Heliodor, Aquamarine and Morganite are all exquisite gemstones, there is something magical about the purity of Goshenite.

A 16.3ct Goshenite discovered in Canada!

A large Goshenite set in a Coloured Rocks design.

Greek key design cufflinks from Mattom.

A vivid cluster of Russian Diopside.

Green Aventurine.

Greek Jewellery (Early)

In ancient Greece, gold beads in the shape of shells, flowers and beetles were very common. In Northern Greece, beautiful necklaces and earrings have been excavated from numerous burial sites.

By 300BC, the Greeks were using gems such as Emeralds, Garnets, Amethysts and Pearls. When it was not possible to acquire real gems, they resorted to using coloured glass, stones and enamelled stones. Carved Agate cameos and gold filigree works were also extremely popular in the period.

Green gems and Associations

The colour green is synonymous with growth and nature, and is known for both its healing and relaxing properties. Most theatres and television studios have "Green Rooms" where actors and actresses relax before performances.

When worn by men, the colour green is said to signify joyousness and transitory hope. In antiquity, when green was worn by women it was believed to represent childish delight and a will to change. The colour is associated with the planet of Mercury and Wednesdays, and in ancient times the graves of young virgins were said to have been covered in green foliage. The colour has long been associated with sight and to that end has been said to help with forward thinking. As far back as 300BC, Theophrastus, a famous Greek philosopher, wrote about the benefits Emeralds would have on one's eyesight.

The most famous of all green gemstones is the Emerald. The gem is normally more heavily included than others, though its vivid shades are said to aid the circulation of energy in the body and help remove energy blocks. For those who like less included

green gemstones, Green Sapphire, Peridot and Green Amethyst (also known as Prasiolite) are very popular.

Colour	An array of colours
Family	Garnet
Hardness	6.5 – 7.0
Specific Gravity	3.4 – 3.7
Refractive Index	1.7 – 1.89
Crystal Group	Isometric
Optical Properties	Various
Common Treatments	Cannot be heat treated
Care	No special care needed
Cleaning Advice	Ultrasonic or warm soapy water
Chemical Composition	$Ca_3Al_2Si_3O_{12}$

A heavenly Hessonite Garnet ring by Lorique

GROSSULAR GARNET

This variety of Garnet gets its name from the botanical name for a gooseberry; "grossularia". However, in its purist form the gem is white and only becomes different colours such as pink, green and brown when found with different chemical compositions. The tones of Grossular Garnets are often light, making them a very popular gem.

What actually groups members of the Grossular (also known as Grossularite) family together is that in the main they are made up of the minerals calcium and aluminum (Ca3Al2(SiO4). However, sometimes, either mineral can be replaced by iron.

Hessonite is a stunning brownish orange Grossular Garnet and unfortunately derived its name from the Greek word meaning "inferior" as it has the least hardness of all Garnets. It is sometimes referred to in the gem trade as the Cinnamon Gem, due to its similarity in colour. In antiquity the Greeks and the Romans set the gem in jewellery, but it was often mistaken for Zircon. Hessonite is said to increase your happiness and to extend your lifespan. Ancient Hindus believed the gem was formed from the fingernails of the demon Vala.

The best known Grossular is the Tsavorite Garnet. Tiffany's in New York gave the gemstone its name after the Tsavo National Park in Kenya where it was discovered by Scottish gemmologist Campbell R Bridges.

In "The Curious Lore of Precious Stones" the famous gemmologist George Kunz wrote, "The use of green stones to relieve disease of the eye was evidently suggested by the beneficial influence exerted by this colour upon the sight. The verdant Emerald represented the beautiful green fields, upon which the tired eye rests so willingly".

GYPSY SETTING

A gypsy setting is very similar to a bezel setting, where the crown of the gem is the only part exposed and the table of the gemstone is almost level with the surrounding gold or silver.

This setting is ideal for softer gems and is often used for gemstones that have not been calibrated, or where the jewellery is made by hand.

Even by applying a little bit of pressure with your fingers, as gold is a very soft, metal prongs can easily be bent out of shape. Therefore, as men generally tend to be a bit heavy handed, you will often see the gypsy setting used to secure gemstones in gents' pieces.

I for one only have gypsy, bezel or channel set rings and do not trust myself to support my gemstones with a prong setting!

A Tookalon handmade ring with a gypsy set Lemon Quartz.

Colour	Cream to Purple
Family	Sodalite
Hardness	5 to 6
Specific Gravity	2.25
Refractive Index	1.48
Crystal Group	Cubic
Optical Properties	Tenebrescence
Common Treatments	None
Cleaning Advice	Warm soapy water
Chemical Composition	Complex

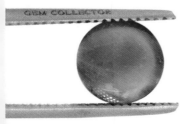

HACKMANITE

If you are looking for a very unique gemstone to add to your gem collection, then take a look at the very rare variety of Sodalite known as Hackmanite. This gem absorbs direct sunlight (ultra-violet light) which turns the gem from a pale creamy colour, to a stunning purplish violet colour. Whilst a highly phosphorescent gemstone like Kunzite will absorb the sun's ultra-violet rays, and then glow in the dark for a short period, Hackmanite's actual body colour will change under the same conditions and this change can last for a very long period. The absorption of light in some gemstones is known as phosphorescence, whereas the phenomena which leads to an actual colour change is known as "tenebrescence".

The gem is translucent to opaque in appearance and at 5.5 – 6 on the Mohs hardness scale is best kept as a collectable or set into a pendant.

As far as I am aware, Hackmanite of this type

has only ever been discovered in Afghanistan and Burma. However, Hackmanite has been found in Canada and the USA which actually changes colour in the opposite direction when exposed to ultra violet light! As this second edition of this book goes to press, I am still trying to source some Hackmanite from Afghanistan.

A Hackmanite necklace by Annabella.

HAEMATITE

Soothing and calming, Haematite is believed to help balance your emotions and mental state of mind. It can also dissolve negativity and encourage the wearer to strive for their hopes, dreams and desires.

Haematite (also spelt Hematite) is a beautiful iron-based gemstone that varies in colour from shiny black to a silvery grey. It is also found in a brown to deep, reddish brown and it is from this variety that it receives its name from the Greek word "haima" for 'blood'. In history, cultures including the Aztecs, Egyptians and prehistoric man all used the stone in crushed form for decorating the body, burial tombs, and painting on walls to produce decorative art.

As Haematite is a relatively heavy gem, it is often used in figurines and cameos. In Victorian times Haematite became very popular in jewellery and was often used as a sign of mourning. During the last 50 years it has gained popularity in North America, whereas its use in European jewellery has subsided.

The gem is opaque and when polished has a metallic lustre. It is normally cabochon cut, although it is occasionally round or square cut.

Today the gem is widely sourced, resulting in many believing it to have lost its gem status and refer to it only as a mineral. Some of the best gem-quality deposits stem from Switzerland and Italy.

In the UK it has been found in Cumbria, the Forest of Dean and Barrow-in-Furness. Large finds of quality Haematite have also

Colour	Black to dark grey and occasionally red
Family	Does not belong to a family
Hardness	5.5 – 6.5
Specific Gravity	5 – 5.3
Refractive Index	2.94 – 3.22
Crystal Group	Trigonal
Optical Properties	Great surface lustre
Common Treatments	Not normally treated
Care	No specific care required
Cleaning Advice	Ultrasonic, stteam cleaning, warm soapy water
Chemical Composition	Fe_2O_3 (iron)

Help balance your emotions with a Haematite necklace from Annabella

been found in Minas Gerais in Brazil.

HALLMARKING - A HISTORY

Hallmarking dates back to the 1300's when Edward I instituted the assaying and marking of precious metals. When the hallmark was introduced, it was the first ever law to protect the consumer. It was not only introduced to protect the public from fraud, but also to protect traders from unfair competition.

Hallmarking is as necessary today as it was then. When precious metals such as gold and silver are used in jewellery, as they are too soft in their pure form, they are alloyed with much cheaper but stronger metals like copper and bronze. The hallmark primarily identifies the purity level of the gold.

The statute of 1300 stated that the wardens of the Company of Goldsmiths in London could go to workshops in the city and assay silver and gold. Initially, silver was the only precious metal that was marked, with the symbol of the leopard head; the mark still used by the London assay office today.

In 1363, the maker's mark was also added to the hallmark, starting out as pictorial stamps; as literacy improved initials replaced the symbols. The wardens of the goldsmiths didn't move to Goldsmiths Hall until 1748. They then started to pay a salaried assayer to test and mark items that were submitted.

In 1773 a date symbol was added to the hallmark and was introduced to make the individual assayers accountable for their work. Every year the date symbol changed and if you have an old piece of jewellery at home, maybe a piece that has been passed down the generations, and would like to know when the piece was first made then have a look at it under a microscope and see if you can find the hallmark. Assuming it hasn't worn away, study the date symbol and then go to www.theassayoffice.co.uk and on their website

The Birmingham Assay office.

The Birmingham Assay office uses the latest in technology for Hallmarking.

you will be able to see all symbols used since 1773.

The Hallmarking Act of 1973 confirmed that all precious metals were to be assayed and also introduced the marking for platinum.

Before 1998 it was compulsory that the hallmark comprised four pieces of information: the sponsor's mark, the metal standard mark, the assay office symbol and a date stamp. Since 1998 the date stamp has been optional.

HALLMARK SYMBOLS

SPONSOR'S MARK

STANDARD MARK

The 'hall' of the word hallmark, is simply the place where the metals are tested. The first 'hall' in Britain was the 'Worshipful Company of Goldsmiths', a place where today a record of every British hallmark is kept. When hallmarks were first founded they were engraved by a mutually trusted party, or a guardian of the craft. Today the marks have to be made by a recognised 'Assay Office'.

There are four assay offices in the UK today, they are: London, Sheffield, Birmingham and Edinburgh, and each has their own identifying symbol. London has the mark of a leopard head, Sheffield has the symbol of a rose, Birmingham has an anchor and Edinburgh's mark is a castle.

Along with the assaying office symbol and the sponsor's symbol, by law the item must be stamped with the "standard mark", which denotes the level of purity of the precious metal being used.

It is a legal requirement to hallmark jewellery containing over 1 gram of gold, over 7.78 grams of silver or over 0.5 grams of platinum; otherwise the piece cannot legally be sold in the UK as gold, silver or platinum.

Today the forging of a hallmark is a punishable offence by up to ten years in prison, but years ago it was considered treason and punishable by death!

ASSAY OFFICE MARK

DATE LETTER

HARLEQUIN RING

Very popular in Victorian times, the Harlequin Ring features different gemstones in either a band or a cluster ring, where the first letters of each gemstone can form a word.

For example, a ring featuring a Ruby, Emerald, Garnet, Amethyst, Ruby and Diamond was known as a 'Regard' ring. Another type of Harlequin ring was the 'Dearest' ring which often featured a Diamond, Emerald, Amethyst, Ruby, Emerald, Spinel and a Topaz.

HEART CUT

The heart cut or heart shape is often based on the round brilliant cut and its outline shape is similar to a pear cut with an additional cleft (or v-shape) cut into the rounded end. As the globally accepted symbol of love, the heart cut is often used for red gemstones such as Ruby, Spinel, Garnet and Rubellite.
When used to shape a Diamond, the heart cut is certainly very romantic, but also enables a lot of brilliance and fire to be exhibited. To display the cut at its best, the gem is normally held in a design with two small prongs on the shoulder and a 'v' shaped prong at its point. Though there are no set measurements for this gem cut, it is normal practice to have a width that is slightly narrower than its height.

A very well crafted heart cut Topaz surrounded by Si Diamonds.

HEART IN HEART CUT

We all know that buying a piece of jewellery for someone close to you is a symbol of ultimate love. To elevate the message often a red coloured gemstone such as a Ruby or Garnet is given, or a piece of jewellery where the actual design is a heart shape. I guess the pinnacle up to now would therefore be a heart shaped piece of jewellery, with a heart shaped red gemstone in the centre. But if all of this is getting too much for you, or you want to try something a little different, something very few people on the planet have, then look out or a gem cut known as

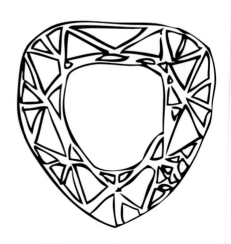

the "Heart in a Heart".

This very special cut is incredibly hard to master but, if done correctly, when viewing the gem from the table you will see an outline shape of a heart and then, by a unique arrangement of facets on the crown, you will see a heart within a heart.

This romantic cut is achieved by only using triangular shaped facets on the crown of the gem by reducing the percentage of the gem that sits above the girdle. Although there are very few Lapidaries in the world that attempt this cut, if you do come across a piece it's really worth adding it to your collection.

HEAT TREATMENT

Many gems today are heat-treated. Virtually all Rubies and Sapphires are heat-treated; without this technique we would not be able to convert the dull brownish-green gem Zoisite into the glamorous Tanzanite.

Without heat treatment there would be no vivid blue Tanzanite.

Within the industry, heating gems to enhance their colour and beauty is a widely accepted practice that dates back two thousand years and is simply seen as the continuation of a process started by nature. Unless stated otherwise, the practice is so common that you should always assume that the gems you are buying have been heat-treated. Some gem families however, such as Spinels and Garnets are not heat-treatable.

HELIODOR

A clear and flawless Heliodor will exude brilliance and sparkle like a Canary Diamond. Because of its rarity, Heliodor is a gemstone highly appreciated by collectors and enthusiasts alike.

Precious Beryl was another name given to this golden yellow variety of Beryl in order to distinguish these beautiful gems from yellow Topaz and Citrine.

Heliodor is from the Greek words for sun, "helios", and gift, "doron", thus Heliodor can be translated as "gift of the sun". As with all members of the Beryl family, the gem receives its colour from impurities; in Heliodor's case it is from the presence of iron. When impurities in Beryl cause the colourless gem to turn yellow, it is then known as Heliodor; also commonly known as Yellow Beryl.

So as to best display the gem's stunning colours, Lapidarists will normally step cut or emerald cut the gem. Heliodor is normally transparent, but occasionally can be found translucent. When this is the case, the gem is often Cabochon cut and sometimes chatoyancy or asterism can be visible.

It is said that Heliodor can increase self-confidence and self-belief. It's also claimed that meditating with the stone can awaken one's 'inner flame', thus enabling one to find their self worth and their place in the grand scheme of things.

First mined in western Namibia in 1910, the gem has since been discovered in Madagascar, Brazil and Nigeria. The gem is also mined in the Ukraine and some pieces uncovered in this location are of the finest quality ever discovered.

Colour	Vibrant yellow to greenish yellow
Family	Beryl
Hardness	7.5 – 8
Specific Gravity	2.8
Refractive Index	1.57 -1.62
Crystal Group	Hexagonal
Optical Properties	Good clarity
Common Treatments	Occasionally heat-treated
Care	No special care required
Cleaning Advice	Ultrasonic or warm soapy water
Chemical Composition	$Be_3Al_2Si_6O_{18}$

HESSONITE

A stunning, light, peachy orange through to cinnamon red member of the Grossular group of Garnets, Hessonite is a real collector's gemstone that, as with all Garnets, achieves its vivid colours entirely from the work of Mother Nature.

Throughout history the gem has also been refered to as "Gomedhaka" or "Gomethakam" in India and has been believed to prevent laziness, increase one's passion and to change one's fortunes. Astrologers believe that, when worn as a talisman, your life will be both happier and longer. Hessonite was also believed by ancient Hindus to actually be formed from the fingernails of the demon Vala. Hessonite has a slightly lower hardness than most other Garnets and its name is derived from the Greek word

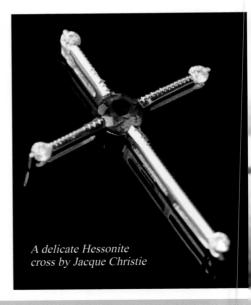

A delicate Hessonite cross by Jacque Christie

'hesson' meaning inferior. However, the gem still registers 7 on the Mohs scale, so is anything but inferior and its magical, almost mystical, colours certainly make it one of my personal favourite members of the Garnet family. One of the main discoveries of Hessonite has been in Sri Lanka (Ceylon) and small amounts have been also found in Brazil and California.

HEXAGON CUT

This cut is becoming increasingly popular for large coloured gemstones, especially when they are used with solitaire rings. Rarely used on gems below three carats, when viewed from above, the hexagon cut is similar in shape to a British fifty pence piece (I know this coin has seven sides and not six, but other than a gazebo try finding another hexagon shape that everyone is familiar with!) It is also worthwhile mentioning that although octagon cuts traditionally have a shape similar to an emerald cut, today some octagon cuts have sides that are equal in length, providing an appearance similar to a hexagon cut, but with two additional sides.

The shape is normally step cut, with one or two steps above the girdle and three or four below. For gems with good clarity, when studying the cut from above, it provides an attractive symmetrical appearance and your eyes are naturally drawn along the lines of the pavilion towards the centralised culet.

HIDDENITE

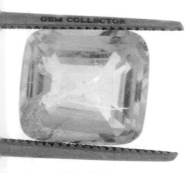

Along with Kunzite and Triphane, Hiddenite is a member of the Spodumene family of gemstones. The easiest way to describe the appearance of this extremely rare gem is to ask you to imagine a very lightly coloured Emerald, with good transparency and clarity. That said, don't expect to find Hiddenite without any internal flaws: the handful of pieces I have collected to-date have all had several large inclusions within them.

A huge 3.77ct Hiddenite from Madagascar.

It is said that the first discovery of Hiddenite was in North Carolina, America back in 1879. These first specimens were given to a geologist named William Earl Hidden who was working in the area at the time and from whom the gem's name is derived. Hidden was actually in the area being employed by Thomas Edison (the inventor of the light bulb and holder of over 1,000 patents in America) to search for Platinum. Whilst he was unsuccessful in his search for the metal, he did end up having a gemstone named after him!

After the discovery of the gem, the village nearest to the initial find was renamed 'Hiddenite' and for a period of around 10 years, the Emerald and Hiddenite Mining Company recovered a reasonable quantity of the gem. Today, the Emerald Hollow Mine located in the town of Hiddenite is the only Emerald mine in the USA that is open to the public for prospecting, so if you ever find yourself in Carolina…! As well this original discovery, Hiddenite has also been found in Madagascar, Brazil and Afghanistan.

In 1882, George Kunz (possible the world's most famous gemologist of all times and the man who discovered Kunzite - a sister gemstone to Hiddenite) wrote in a newspaper about the new discovery stating, 'the gem is always transparent, ranges from colorless (rare) to a light yellow, into a yellowish green, then into a deep yellow emerald green. Sometimes an entire crystal has a uniform green color, but generally one end is yellow and the other green.'

You may be interested to note that Kunz also wrote that the finest crystal found could been cut into a gem of approximately 5.5ct and the wonderful example we have in our collection at Coloured Rocks (the piece in the photo), weighs 6.57ct!

Like Kunzite, Hiddenite has perfect cleavage making it one of the most difficult gems to cut. Due to the combination of scarcity and difficulty in cutting, most Lapadarists will often not risk damaging this rare stone and therefore take the easier option of cabochon cutting this gemstone. The gem benefits from extremely strong pleochroism and slowly rocking a piece backwards and forwards will often yield several colours.

Colour	Colourless
Family	Spodumene
Hardness	6.5 - 7
Specific Gravity	3.18
Refractive Index	1.66 - 1.67
Crystal Group	Monoclinic
Optical Properties	Fluoresent and Pleochroic
Common Treatments	Not normally treated
Care	None
Cleaning Advice	Warm soapy water
Chemical Composition	$LiAlSi_2O_6$

Treat yourself to a rare piece of Hiddenite jewellery.

Indulge in Brilliance

GENUINE TOPAZ
12 BREATHTAKING COLOURS
FINEST CUTTING
PATENTED TECHNOLOGY
NON RADIATED
PRECISION CALIBRATION
EVERLASTING DURABILITY
NON COATED

Patent Number 6872422
Exclusively distributed in Europe by Coloured Rocks

HOPE DIAMOND

The Hope Diamond is steeped in history. Appearing a brilliant blue to the naked eye, under ultraviolet light it looks a fluorescent red. It is currently on display in the Smithsonian Natural History museum in Washington USA and is protected by three inches of bullet-proof glass in the Harry Winston room.

It was originally found in India as a rough crystal weighing a massive 112 carats! The history of the gem commences in 1668 with French traveller Jean Baptiste Tavernier. He was approached by a slave whilst in India, carrying what he believed to be a stunning rough cut triangular Sapphire. But Tavernier was a worldly man and realised that the slave had in his possession the rarest of Blue Diamonds.

As you can imagine, Tavernier bought this stone as quickly as he could and managed to smuggle it to Paris, where he sold it to King Louis XIV. Under royal control, the gem was re-cut by the famous Lapidarist Sieur Pitau into a round shape and became known as the "Blue Diamond of the Crown". Unfortunately, the re-cutting of the gem reduced its size to 67 carats. The king proudly had the Diamond set into a necklace, which he often wore on ceremonial occasions.

In 1791, Louis XVI and Marie Antoinette attempted to flee France. After finally doing so the government seized all of the royal jewellery; this was indeed quite befitting as the unpopular queen was believed to have been involved in the 1785 Diamond necklace scandal. During the French Revolution the entire collection was looted.

Next, the gem was said to have found its way into the possession of George IV of England; it was reported to have been sold after his death to help pay off his enormous debts. In 1839, gem collector Henry Philip Hope, after whom it was later named, acquired it. At this point the gem had been re-cut several times and now weighed 55.2ct. Unfortunately, he died the same year he obtained the gem and after a legal dispute it eventually became the property of his nephew

The Hope Diamond.

The Hope Diamond is on display in the Smithsonian Museum.

Henry Thomas Hope.

In June 1909 'The Times' newspaper wrote an article about the gem, claiming that it was cursed and that many of its previous owners had come to an untimely end.

The Diamond changed hands several times during 1901 to 1909 and was eventually bought by Pierre Cartier in 1910. Mrs Evalyn Walsh McLean, an American gold mining heiress, showed a particular interest in the gem, but was not fond of its setting. Cartier then decided to reset the gem, however Mrs Walsh McLean was still unsure. Cartier then lent her the Diamond for the weekend, with the belief that she would find it difficult to give it back. The strategy worked and she became the owner until her death in 1947.

In 1949 the famous American jeweller Harry Winston purchased the entire jewellery collection of Mrs Walsh McLean from her estate. Also included were the famous 94ct Star of the East, the 15ct Star of the South, the 31ct McLean Diamond (named after her) and a stunning, vibrant 9ct green Diamond. The collection now resides in the Smithsonian Museum.

Jessica Lili Howlite and Pearl Earrings.

Colour	Blue
Family	Does not belong to a family
Hardness	3.5
Specific Gravity	2.6 – 2.9
Refractive Index	1.58 – 1.61
Crystal Group	Trigonal
Optical Properties	Great surface lustre
Common Treatments	Not normally treated
Care	No specific care required
Cleaning Advice	Warm soapy water
Chemical Composition	Fe_2O_3 (iron)

HOWLITE

Howlite is famed for imitating other minerals, such as Turquoise. It is naturally white or grey, but due to the texture of the stone can very easily be dyed a turquoise blue.

It forms in nodules that look like cauliflower heads displaying black veins throughout the gemstone, and although this mineral is not very hard it still has a distinct toughness.

It is said that Howlite can eliminate anger and offensive behaviour. Healers consider it an important gemstone to cleanse auras and purify the blood.

Found in the beautiful tourist destination of Nova Scotia, Canada, this stone is named after its discoverer: Henry How. Due to its softness, the gem is seldom set into jewellery these days.

HUE

Red (R)
Orange Red (oR)
Red Orange or Orange Red (rO / oR)
Reddish Orange (rO)
Orange (O)
Yellowish Orange (yO)
Orangey Yellow (oY)
Yellow (Y)
Greenish Yellow (gY)
Yellow Green or Green Yellow (yG / gY)
Strongly Yellowish Green (styG)
Yellowish Green (yG)
Slightly Yellowish Green (slyG)
Green (G)
Very Slightly Bluish Green (vstbG)
Bluish Green (bG)
Very Strongly Bluish Green (vstbG)
Green Blue or Blue Green (gB /bG)
Very Strongly Greenish Blue (vstgB)
Very Slightly Greenish Blue (vslgB)
Blue (B)
Violetish Blue (vB)
Violet (V)
Bluish Purple (bP)
Purple (P)
Reddish purple (rP)
Red Purple or Purple Red (rP / pR)
Strongly Purplish Red (stpR)
Slightly Purplish Red (slpR)

When valuing a coloured gemstone, most people in the industry will agree that it is the colour of the gem that is its most important evaluation criteria. Colour can be broken down into three components: hue, tone (lightness) and saturation (colourfulness).

'Hue' is used to describe the element of colour through red, green and blue. One way of understanding hues is to imagine that in painting, without the addition of black or white, an artist can create most hues by mixing the three primary colours of red, yellow and blue. Reddish orange and greenish blue are both hues.

There are just thirty one hues that the GIA use to describe nearly all coloured gemstones. Printed pages in books such as this are not always entirely accurate in terms of colour, so rather than show these thirty one shades, I have opted to give you a list of these hues and suggest that as you read them, you allow your mind to visualize each hue. Next to each hue you will see the letters that are used by the GIA as a short code: this may be useful if you ever have your gemstones valued, as you will often see the codes on your valuation certificate. There are two exceptions to this; Pink (Pk) which is a light red and Brown (Brn) which is a dark orange.

HYDROSTATIC SCALE

The Hydrostatic scale is used to measure the specific gravity (also known as relative density) of gemstones. Have you ever wondered why a big looking Amber necklace feels light to wear and how a similar looking necklace with a gem such as Onyx is much heavier? The reason is all to do with the density of the gemstone.

Throughout this book where you see the tables for each gemstone, the specific gravity has been measured using the Hydrostatic Scale (the scale is based on the Archimedes' principle). To do this we compare the weight of the gemstone to an equivalent volume of water.

Zircon measures 4.7 when using a Hydrostatic Scale.

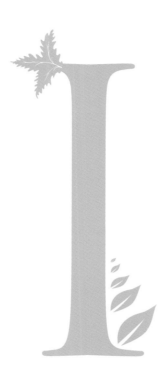

Peridot is an idiochromatic gemstone.

IDIOCHROMATIC

The array of beautiful colours we see in natural gemstones can be created by one of three events:

Firstly, it can be due to the inherent chemical makeup of the crystal; these gems are known as idiochromatic ("idio" meaning inherent). Peridot for example is an idiochromatic gemstone.

Secondly - and most common, gems coloured by the presence of impurities are known as allochromatic ("allo" meaning other). Garnet and Beryl being two examples.

Finally - and to a lesser extent, the colour seen in a few gemstones can be caused by optical properties within the gem and its reflection from, or just under, its surface, examples being Moonstone and Opals. These gems are known as pseudochromatic.

IGNEOUS ROCKS

From the Latin word for fire "ignis", igneous rocks are formed by the solidification of cooled magma (molten rock), with or without crystallisation. This can occur either below the surface as plutonic rocks, or above the surface through volcanoes.

Magma can be derived from the re-melting of existing rocks in the Earth's mantle or crust, and this is one of the reasons why some gemstone varieties keep popping up in areas where you might not expect them. Tourmaline, Quartz and Peridot are just three of the many gems that can be found in igneous rocks.

Quartz can be found in igneous rocks.

ILLUSION SETTING

This is a style of setting gemstones in rings, earrings, pendants and bracelets, whereby the gems are set into a metal or plating - such as Rhodium (a member of the platinum family), where the colour of the metal is similar to the gemstone, thus maximising the aesthetic properties of the gem.

Invented by Oscar Massin (a French jeweller in the late 1860's), illusion settings normally have tiny prongs, which are often pushed up out of the metal to secure the gem, thereby resulting in the setting itself appearing as a continuation of the gem. This style of setting is also known as "Pave Setting" (pronounced "pah –vey").

Here, both the Black and White Diamonds are illusion set.

IMITATION GEMSTONES

One of the oldest forms of deceit and forgery in the world is that of gemstones. Even in 5000BC, early forms of glass were used to imitate gems. Unfortunately, even today it is common to find man-made items trying to imitate the appearance of real gems.

The good news, however, is that they are normally

sold in an ethical manner with the retailer correctly labelling the item as "created", "synthetic" or "lab grown". Do be careful though when buying from catalogues or in-flight magazines: be sure to study the terminology correctly. I recently saw an advert stating, "Genuine lab created Alexandrite" and another offering "the stone is 3.5ct Ceylon Blue Sapphire in Colour". Also be aware of items that have names that sound like gemstones but are not: Moissanite and Cubic Zirconia are two of the main culprits.

IMPERIAL STATE CROWN

The Imperial State Crown was made in 1937 for the coronation of King George VI and is very similar in design to the St Edward's Crown. It is worn at the end of the coronation ceremony when the new king or queen departs from Westminster Abbey and is also worn by the Queen each year at the State Opening of Parliament. Due to the heavy weight of the crown (over 39 ounces) it is reported that the Queen often wears the crown for breakfast on the morning of the opening of parliament, so that she can re-accustomise herself to it.

The current re-casting of the silver crown was produced less than 100 years ago, and many of the gemstones set within it were featured in other royal jewellery throughout the 17th, 18th and 19th century. At the very front of the crown is the famous Black Prince's Ruby, which is in fact not a Ruby at all, but a gorgeous Red Spinel. Legend has it that the gem was given to Edward Prince of Wales by Don Pedro of Castile in 1367, as a sign of recognition for his victory in the Battle of Najera. The Black Prince's Ruby was also reportedly worn by Henry V at the Battle of Agincourt and was set in the crown worn by James II at his coronation in 1685.

In the previous crown the large 104ct Stuart Sapphire was at the front of the crown, however it was moved to the rear of the Imperial State Crown when the Cullinan II Diamond took centre stage: weighing in at 317ct it was the second largest

H.B

known Diamond in the world at that time!

Today in the cross at the top of the crown there is a vivid Blue Sapphire which is believed to have once been set in a ring belonging to Edward the Confessor. He reportedly gave away the ring to a beggar; this was, according to "The Official Guide Book – The Crown Jewels", "returned to him by the influence of St John the Evangelist." As well as the famous historical gemstones in the crown, it also features 2,867 Diamonds, over 270 Pearls (several of which are baroque and were from earrings worn by Queen Elizabeth I), 16 Sapphires and 11 vivid Emeralds (although the cuts are not very good by today's standards).

IMPERIAL TOPAZ

Among the most highly desired of all naturally coloured Topaz, the rich, golden yellow Imperial Topaz is particularly prized. Before heat treating became the norm, Imperial Topaz was one of only a handful of colours to be found in Topaz. Today, when you see a golden yellow Topaz advertised as Imperial Topaz, it is not generally enhanced by treatments. Minas Gerais, in Brazil, is where the most naturally coloured Imperial Topaz comes from.

In the 18th century this gem was hugely popular in Imperial Russia and it is through this association that the gem most likely received its name. That said, if you speak to any mine owner in Brazil, they will tell you that the gem was named in honour of their Emperor Dom Pedro who claimed Brazil's independence from Portugal in 1822.

Imperial Topaz is said to encourage self confidence and to banish bad dreams. Crystal Healers believe that the gem stimulates the appetite and helps in relaxation.

For many years Citrine and Imperial Topaz were not individually identified, therefore many of the legends surrounding Citrine are actually attributable to Imperial Topaz. Because of the richness of its folklore and its natural colours, Imperial Topaz is sold at a premium price.

Colour	Bright yellow to rich golden yellow
Family	Topaz
Hardness	8
Specific Gravity	3.5 – 3.6
Refractive Index	1.6 – 1.63
Crystal Group	Orthorhombic
Optical Properties	Strong pleochroism
Common Treatments	Normally heat-treated
Care	No specific care required
Cleaning Advive	Ultrasonic or warm soapy water
Chemical Composition	$Al_2SiO_4(OH,F)_2$

GEM COLLECTOR

INCLUSIONS

Small foreign bodies and minerals that are trapped inside a gemstone as it forms are known as 'inclusions' or, more poetically, "Mother Nature's fingerprints". As most gems are formed under immense amounts of pressure and extreme stress and heat, the more inclusions you see, the more incredible colossal events the gem has likely witnessed!

Although inclusions are normally regarded as a negative, in stones such as Rutilated Quartz and Amber, their presence adds to the beauty of the gem and is therefore seen as a benefit. Also, as most synthetic and fake gems do not have inclusions, when they are seen in gemstones, at least you know the likelihood is that you are looking at a genuine article from Mother Nature.

Rutile inclusions in Quartz actually add value to the gemstone.

Some gems (such as Bixbite, Rubellite and Emeralds) are more naturally 'included', whereas Aquamarine, Topaz and Amethyst are normally relatively inclusion free.

Inclusions in some gemstones are actually precious metals such as pure gold; in Diamonds they are sometimes small pieces of Peridot locked within the gem.

INDIA

Today, India is by far the largest Diamond cutting country in the world and its jewellery and gemstone history is second-to-none.

Although mining is often restricted by the Indian government, several states have well-established gem mines.

To see the wealth of gemstones unearthed and traded in India, a visit to Jaipur "the Pink City" is a must for all serious gemstone fans. Its local gemstones include Amethyst, Aquamarine, Emerald, Fluorite and Garnet, although gems from other regions of the country are also traded here.

The state of Orissa, found at the same latitude to Mumbai but in the east of the country, produces

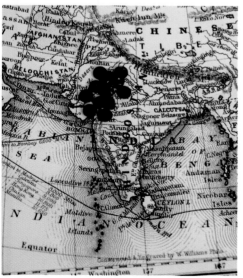

a kaleidoscope of gems including; Aquamarine, Chrysoberyl, Iolite, Garnet, Ruby, Sapphire, Topaz, Tourmaline and Zircon. Although all of these gems are of a high quality, its Garnet is said to be amongst some of the best in the world.

High quality Alexandrite has been discovered in Araku and Narsipatnam and some gem experts believe its exceptional beauty is because it is possibly taken from the same vein as the original Russian location, which lies due north. The state of Andhra Pradesh on the East Coast also produces Alexandrite, alongside Garnet, Ruby, and Tourmaline.

There are also gemstone mining activities along the southern coast of India. Unfortunately several of these mines were destroyed when the Tsunami hit.

We source most of our uncut Emerald in Jaipur, India.

INDICOLITE

The Tourmaline family of gemstones is renowned for its diversity of colour. However, unlike the naming convention of gems such as Sapphire, Zircon and Topaz, where the different colours simply prefixes the gem type (i.e Pink Sapphire, Blue Zircon and Green Topaz), most colours of Tourmaline are identified by non-colour associated names. Rubellite is the red variety of Tourmaline, Schorl the black, Achroite colourless, Dravite greenish brown, Chromdravite green, Paraiba neon blue to green and Indicolite blue, a deep rich almost London Blue Topaz colour.

Indicolite's name originates from the Latin word for a blue coloured plant known as the "Indicum". Although the gem is normally translucent to opaque, transparent pieces can occasionally be found; their rarity and popularity with gem collectors means that they can often demand very high prices.

Crystal Healers believe that Indicolite is useful for creating an air of openness and tolerance. In days gone by, the rich would wear Indicolite (although it was not known as this at the time) to dispel curses and to protect the wearer from danger.

Colour	Blue
Family	Elbaite, Tourmaline
Hardness	7 – 7.5
Specific Gravity	3 3.1
Refractive Index	1.6
Crystal Group	Trigonal
Optical Properties	Highly pleochroic
Common Treatments	Not normally treated
Care	No special care needed
Cleaning Advice	Warm soapy water

This incredibly rare gemstone forms part of the group of Tourmalines known as Elbaite. Similar in colour to that of London Blue Topaz, Indicolite's colour, however, is created purely by Mother Nature.

The gem is beautifully pleochroic (different colours are seen from different angles). Transparent pieces over one carat in size are incredibly rare and normally step cut to maximise the colour of the gem. Larger pieces are often opaque and normally cabochon cut, sometimes revealing chatoyancy (a cat's eye effect).

In Siberia, Russia an even rarer form of Indicolite known as "Siberite" has been discovered. A mesmerising lilac to violet in colour, this gem is also closely related to Paraiba Tourmaline.

In addition to Russia, Indicolite has also been found in Brazil, Mexico and Pakistan.

INVISIBLE SETTING

Look closely at some gemstone rings and you might find that what looks like one big solitaire gemstone, is actually several gems set very close together. When this happens the setting is referred to as an invisible setting.

This technique is most commonly used for Diamond, Ruby and Sapphire pieces of jewellery and sometimes the gems are cut into each other in a "tongue and groove" system. This style is becoming very popular for engagement rings where the centre stone is made up of four independent Diamonds. Even with the increased labour cost involved in faceting four gems rather than one, it is minimal when compared to the cost of using one big one. When the technique is used for lesser-valued gems such as Turquoise and Mother of Pearl, the gems are often glued to the metal to create a mosaic effect.

Please note that invisible setting and illusion setting although similar in sound are very different techniques.

Invisible set engagement rings represent great value for money.

**Kama,
Charms**

colourful memories...

Garnet - an isomorphic gemstone.

Iridescence is a truly beautiful gemstone phenomenon; we see its effects in the orient of Pearls (where it is known as pearlescence), the displays of Fire Agate, certain Obsidians and Iris Agate. It also creates the beautiful colours of Labradorite and its most well-known example is the colour play of Opals (where it is referred to as opalescence).

ISOMORPHIC

Isomorphic crystals are structurally identical. We use this word in jewellery to describe certain gems; for example, all Garnets have the same isomorphic crystal structure, even if their chemical compositions are different.

ITALIAN JEWELLERY

As far back as 400BC, Italian Etruscans were producing elegant necklaces, bracelets and earrings made from gold. Rudimentary Sapphires, Emeralds, Garnets and Ambers were the main focal point of each piece. These gems were surrounded by various mystical and magical beliefs; for example, Romans believed that if a woman wore Sapphires, it enhanced her happiness.

Many in the fashion and jewellery world would argue that Italian jewellers are no longer ranked as highly as they once were (though, of course, we are probably a little biased, being a British jeweller!) However, they are still known for producing quality jewellery chains and the vast majority of lightweight gold chains sold in Europe are still made there today.

Look out for the latest in Italian trends from Viorelli. All designs are highly fashionable and in keeping with Italian jewellery culture, the core collection features lots of Vermeil peices.

Italian style jewellery by Viorelli.

Make
Everyday
A **Glamour**
day

Jacque **Christie**

JACQUE CHRISTIE

Pieces of jewellery from Jacque Christie are said to "begin and end with vibrant colours". In the design process, once shades and tones have been selected, the task of finding Mother Nature's nearest gemstone match begins. Once the gemstone has been cut and polished, the supporting gold work is designed to provide maximum space for the gemstone to sparkle and dazzle.

Only top quality gemstones are selected for the collection, including Ruby, Fuchsia Pink Topaz, Rhodolite Garnet, Emerald, Tanzanite and Pink Sapphire.

The collection is primarily created in solid 9k gold, or palladium making these pieces ideal for daily wear. To ensure complete comfort, every piece is finished by hand. With Jacque Christie's emphasis on making genuine gemstone jewellery affordable, you can make "every day a glamour day".

Multi-coloured design by Jacque Christie.

JADE

Colour	Normally green, but also pastel blue, lavender, white, yellow, black and pink
Family	Jade is effectively a family, with its two siblings being Nephrite and Jadeite
Hardness	6.5 – 7
Specific Gravity	3.25 – 3.35
Refractive Index	1.640 – 1.667
Crystal Group	Monoclinic
Optical Properties	Vitreous lustre
Care	No specific care required
Cleaning Advice	Ultrasonic or warm soapy water
Chemical Composition	$NaAlSi_2O_6$

A stunning ornamental gemstone that is steeped in history and has been set in jewellery for thousands of years. The word 'Jade' is thought to have come from the Spanish phrase 'piedra de ijada' or 'loin stone'. Jade is famously both the name of the gemstone and its colour, and it can be shaped into the most intricate and beautiful designs.

In the 19th century, a French chemist determined that what people referred to as "Jade" was in fact two different gemstones: the first being Nephrite and the second being Jadeite:

Jadeite is usually opaque to translucent, and often has a luscious glass-like quality found in quite a few colour variations. These include delicate pastel blue, lavender, white, yellow, black and pink. The most sought after colour would be a bewitching apple green; this colour is also known as Imperial Jade. The reason it has this enchanting colour, as with many other green gems, is due to the presence of chromium. As it has currently only been found in less than a dozen places in the world, Jadeite is thought to be the rarer of the two.

Nephrite's colours range from green to creamy white to grey. The green of Nephrite is spinach to sage green and is darker than Jadeite. It has a pearly to greasy lustre. During Neolithic times (towards the end of the Stone Age) the main source of Nephrite Jade was China, where it was often used for ceremonial purposes.

As far back as 500AD it is said that Chinese doctors would prescribe finely ground Jade to be mixed into fruit juices to aid the relief of various ailments, such as asthma, heartburn and even diabetes. The drink was said to be a powerful tonic that also soothed and calmed. Doctors believed the finely powdered Jade would pass through the digestive system and the body would absorb all the benefits of the gemstone.

Jade carvings were also created by the Chinese, and are famous around the world. They started carving the gem during the late 1600's and often

White Jade bracelet inspired by Chrisina Aguilera.

sacrificed beautiful Diamonds to make cutting tools, so as to shape and carve their more valuable Jade!

Wearing Jade in bangles and bracelets is said to protect you from sickness. In China, delicately carved bracelets are very popular for this reason. In lovemaking Jade is said to help you connect with your lover on an erotic and spiritual level.

JAIPUR

Sapphire sources in Thailand have dwindled dramatically over the last 20 years or so. Even though it remains a very important country for trading gemstones, Jaipur in India is now taking centre stage for gem cutting and trading. So much so, that when Coloured Rocks decided to open its first gem selection and sorting office, rather than using our existing offices in Bankok, we decided to open a new facility right in the bursting heart of Jaipur.

The old walled city of Jaipur.

The city is also known as the Pink City, as most of the buildings are pink, especially those within the old city. Jaipur is also famous for its coloured treasures: even Prince Charles, Mick Jagger, the Queen of Spain and a host of Hollywood stars have visited in search of their own very special piece of jewellery or in hope of finding a rare gemstone. And when you consider that the city does not yet have an international airport and is almost impossible to drive in, you start to realise the lengths the rich and famous will go to in order to make life colourful!

The city's association with gemstones can be traced back over two hundred and fifty years, and throughout this period it has been the most important city in the world for cutting Emeralds. The picture to the left shows a small team of Lapidarists still using the traditional technique for faceting Emeralds. By slowly moving their bow backwards and forwards, the string which wraps around the central driving mechanism slowly starts rotating the grinding wheel. Using their other hand the Lapidarist facets the gem on the wheel in a technique that hasn't changed for two and a half centuries.

Traditional Emerald cutting using bow and wheel.

If you are into gemstones and ever visit India, then make sure to spend at least four or five days in Jaipur. As well as being able to see the bustling gem trade, you can visit the city's many historical sites and palaces. For me, I find it one of the most beautiful (in its own way) and interesting cities on the planet.

JASPER

Jasper comes in many colours, shapes and sizes and tends to be named by the patterns that appear on its surface. These include: Blood Jasper, Print Jasper, Ribbon Jasper, Orbicular Jasper; one of the most popular and sought after is Landscape Jasper. The latter is said to display pictures or scenery from the area where it was mined; although it is indeed very captivating, this does take a lot of imagination!

Even though Jasper is a variety of Chalcedony, due to its various different names it is often seen as a family in its own right. All types of Jasper are said to help balance the vibrations of the body. There have been many historic fables told or written about shamans and medicine men utilising the gem. Whilst some Crystal Healers believe fully in these stories, others view the gem as simply a work of art performed by Mother Nature.

Throughout Ancient Greek, Egyptian and Roman civilizations, Jasper has been used in mosaic art and ornamental designs. It is also mentioned in the Bible in Ezekiel, Exodus and Revelations. With this historical portfolio it is not surprising that so many healing properties and good luck fables are linked to this interesting gemstone.

As an opaque gemstone with a vitreous to waxy lustre, Jasper is usually cabochon cut. With carat sizes averaging double figures, this large gemstone features more in necklaces, pendants and brooches, rather than in rings and earrings.

Jasper is found in many countries the world over. Madagascar is noted for Orbicular Jasper (also know as Ocean Jasper). Kazakhstan yields red and green varieties, whereas the Urals of Russia

Colour	A multitude of colours
Family	Chalcedony Quartz
Hardness	6.5 – 7
Specific Gravity	2.59 – 2.62
Refractive Index	1.540 - 1.550
Crystal Group	Conchoidal
Optical Properties	Vitreous to Waxy lustre
Common Treatments	Not normally treated
Cleaning Advice	Warm soapy water
Care	No specific care required
Chemical Composition	SiO_2 (Silica Dioxide)

Naturally banded Jasper.

are noted for red, brown and white Ribbon Jasper. Other countries where Jasper has been discovered include Venezuela, Egypt, Germany, Mexico, Paraguay and Australia.

JESSICA LILI

The Jessica Lili Collection combines genuine gemstones with eternally youthful jewellery designs. The company's Creative Directors have a real eye for colour and every piece offers the ultimate in chic, glamour and fashion.

When it comes to big look jewellery, Jessica Lili's fluid lines and sensual gemstones provide the opportunity to wear eye-catching designs, at incredible value for money prices.

Once you have witnessed the Jessica Lili collection with its amazingly priced, genuine gemstone pieces, you will be wondering why anyone would wear costume or imitation jewellery set with glass, plastic or crystals.

JET

How many phrases and descriptive words do we commonly use in conversation without knowing their origin? Have you ever described an item as Jet Black? Did you know that Jet is a gemstone that is as black as any gemstone can be? Along with Amber and Pearl, Jet is a member of a very exclusive club of gems that are created organically and not formed from minerals. It is not considered a mineral, as it is derived from an organic substance - wood!

A creation of decaying wood dating back millions of years held under pressure beneath the Earth's surface has given us this fascinating, unusual and very brittle gemstone. Add salt water into the creation process and the gemstone takes a slightly harder form, but still only achieves a maximum of 4 on the Mohs scale.

Jet can be found in several locations around the world and one of the best sources for Jet is the small town of Whitby on the east coast of England. It became a very fashionable gemstone

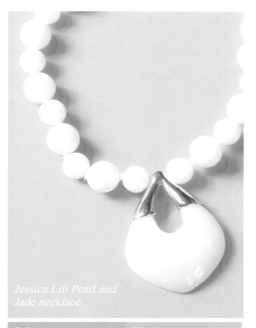

Jessica Lili Pearl and Jade necklace.

Colour	Black
Family	Organic gemstone
Hardness	2 – 4
Specific Gravity	1.3 – 1.35
Refractive Index	1.6
Crystal Group	Conchoidal
Optical Properties	Velvet lustre
Common Treatments	Not normally treated
Care	Be careful as it is a soft gem
Cleaning Advice	Warm soapy water
Chemical Composition	Primarily Carbon

during the reign of Queen Victoria and, because of its sombre colour, formed part of the jewellery she wore with her mourning dress. During the 1920's, Jet was heavily used in long beaded necklaces upon which the wearer would wear multiple strands.

Just like Diamonds, Jet is made from carbon. Furthermore, with a look similar to that of a Black Diamond with high lustre, combined with its unusual source of origin and its unusual electrical properties (Jet has the ability to generate a small electric charge if rubbed) there has recently been an increasing amount of interest in this curious British gemstone.

JEWELLERY

Why do we wear jewellery? Throughout history, jewellery has been worn for a multitude of reasons including: to display wealth or one's status, for functional reasons like pins or clasps, for protection (i.e. amulets, talisman, breastplates and magical wards), artistic display and of course for personal adornment.

Up until the last decade, jewellery was thought to have begun on a practical level, being used as an investment or as a talisman. However, a recent discovery of ancient beads fashioned from Nassarius shells dating back almost 100,000 years have disputed this and are thought to be the oldest known jewellery found to be used purely for decoration.

Another discovery of ancient jewellery was made at the Skhul Caves, on the slopes of Mount Carmel in Israel. Items recovered from here are believed to date back approximately 90,000 years and this is further confirmation that jewellery played an important role in the life of ancient humans. However, it is not known whether the use of jewellery in this instance was to decorate the body or used to demonstrate status.

The first materials used for jewellery consisted of wood, bone, animal teeth and shells. They were primarily used as necklaces or pendants and would be worn by both pre-historic men and women.

A lady can never have too much jewellery...

As time progressed, people of high importance wore jewellery to show their status and wealth. It became commonplace to be buried either wearing or alongside your personal jewellery. The Egyptians believed it would both aid your transit to the next life and be used as a currency.

As beliefs have changed over the last few centuries, it is likely that very few of us will want to be buried with our jewellery, meaning that our precious gold and silver jewellery, set with gorgeous, rare gemstones, can be passed on to future generations.

Who can resist Mother Nature's colours?

Even if our great grandchildren don't appreciate the designs of our time, they will have the option of melting down our jewellery, having it reshaped into the fashion of their time, all the while still carrying around with them a little bit of our heritage! And who knows what the price of gold will be worth to them; maybe the planet's gold supply will be exhausted by then, or the supply of the gemstone that was once found in many places, has completely dried up (it wouldn't be the first time that a gem variety became extinct).

In these early years of the 21st Century, it is fair to say that people are not afraid to wear bold, creative and innovative jewellery. Instead of wearing flamboyant shoes, or an expensive handbag, many people prefer to wear a piece of jewellery as the focal point of an outfit, such as a bright Pink Sapphire cocktail ring or a pair of Tanzanite cufflinks.

The type of jewellery worn can say a lot about that person's personality. Someone wearing a 7 strand necklace, adorned with multi-coloured gemstones will obviously have a lot of confidence to wear such a show stopping piece.

When you wear genuine gemstone jewellery, you not only feel beautiful but also a real connection with nature. After all, every single gemstone is a treasure given to us by Mother Nature. Each piece is rare and individual and deserves showing off. My wife once told me she feels naked if she leaves the house without any real jewellery on and that when she does forget, her outlook for the day never quite seems to be as positive.

Jacque Christie

Make Everyday A Glamour Day

JEWELS OF VALAIS

Jewellery set with Marcasite gemstones was first made popular in Victorian times. The Jewels of Valais collection beautifully combines stunning Swiss Marcasite with Victorian inspired designs. All rings, necklaces and bracelets are crafted with similar techniques to those used in the middle 1800's, with the careful assistance of just a little modern technology.

Those new to this gemstone will be amazed by its almost metallic surface lustre, which closely resembles that of a Champagne or Black Diamond. However, unlike a Diamond, most pieces in the Jewels of Valais collection are shaped by cutting the gem into an inverted cone or pyramid shape. This unusual approach to cutting gemstones maximises its surface sparkle, providing the gem with a life of its own.

Due to the immense amount of craftsmanship that goes into each and every piece, many take several days to craft. Jewels of Valais timelessly captures English designs and sets them with a natural gem from Switzerland.

Jewels of Valais
SWITZERLAND

Kama, Charms

colourful memories...

KAMA CHARMS

Looking to start a charm collection that is designed to last? A collection featuring genuine gemstones and Sterling Silver? Look no further than the stunning collection of charms available from Kama Charms.

Each individual piece is handmade by a small team of passionate silversmiths in Chang Mai, Thailand and the collection is continually growing as new designs and gemstones are added.

If you're looking to build a collection of modern charms, while retaining the characteristics of a style of jewellery that can be traced back to the Egyptian Pharaohs, look no further than Kama Charms. In addition to the necklaces and bracelets available under the Kama Charm brand, Kama charms will also fit on other brand's chains where the diameter is less than 6mm.

KENYA

Famous for Tsavorite Garnet (discovered by Campbell R Bridges in 1970), Kenya is also home to a host of other glorious gems including Amethyst, Aquamarine, Iolite, Ruby and Sapphire.

Ruby has been mined in Kenya for many years and a recent discovery near the town of Baringo in the Rift Valley is now providing the region with Ruby and Pink Sapphires. These are said to be of a higher grade than those being mined in the Tsavo National Park, which are often cut into gem beads or cabochon cut.

Towards the end of 2004, Kenya experienced its second amazing find of Garnet. This time it was a Colour Change Garnet that greatly resembled Alexandrite in that it looks a bluish green in daylight and a reddish pink when viewed under artificial light. This is great news for the country as its famous Tsavorite Garnet is becoming increasingly hard to find, with some reporting the number of Tsavorite mines currently in operation in Kenya down from forty five to just four! That said, at the Lemshuko Mine in the small township of Komolo, near Arusha in Tanzania, mining has recently been up-scaled for Tsavorite.

In an attempt to help better educate these rural gem mining communities, the Association Francaise de Gemmologie (AFG), International Gemstone Association (ICA) and the Swala Gem Traders all made donations in 2007 which provided a new school in Komolo.

In the Taita Hills to the west of the Tsavo National Park, there is currently a flurry of mining activity for Tourmaline, with colours ranging from golden yellow through to vivid greens. This area previously yielded Tsavorite, and there is a pitiable story of an old miner who in his late sixties hired thirty Massi tribesmen from neighbouring Tanzania to dig for the gem. He set up a fenced area around the mine and had several of his dogs guarding its perimeter. Unfortunately, the local lions did not fear the guard dogs and had them all for dinner!

A pair of Jaque Christie earrings featuring Kenyan Colour Change Garnet.

A Jacque Christie ring featuring Kenyan Tsavorite.

KIMBERLITE

The igneous host rock in which many Diamonds, Garnets and Peridots are found is known as Kimberlite. It is named after Kimberley in South Africa where in the late 1800's the mineral was first identified shortly after an 83ct Diamond was found within it.

A Kimberlite Pipe refers to an upside-down, carrot-shaped crack or dyke made of Kimberlite, where magma once raced to the surface from deep within the earth's crust. Whenever a new Kimberlite pipe is discovered, Diamond explorers are sure to follow. Plus, as these structures are derived from possibly 80-90 miles from within the Earth's crust, they provide us with valuable information about the inner Earth, so you might find the odd scientists alongside the gem hunters.

KOH-I-NUR DIAMOND

Meaning in Persian "the mountain of light", the Koh-i-Nur Diamond (also spelt Kohinoor, Koh-e-Noor and Koh-i-Noor) is unquestionably the most famous gemstone of Indian origin. Its 500 year history starts with the gem weighing a massive 739 carats, and some say whoever owns the Koh-i-Nur rules the world!

It was first mentioned in an autobiography by the first Mughal ruler Babur (1526-1530). He had the gemstone beautifully cut, but the reshaping of the gem saw it reduced to 186cts (by anyone's standards that's a low yield). Upon completing the re-cutting Babur said, "Its value was more than enough to feed the whole world for half a day".

In 1849 the Koh-i-Nur became part of the British Crown Jewels when Queen Victoria became Empress of India. After the British flag was raised on the citadel of Lahore, Punjab was formally proclaimed to be part of the British Empire in India. The legal agreement formalising this occupation included the following clause:

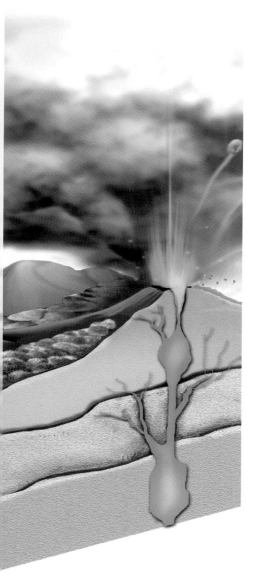

A kimberlite pipe is where magma once raced to the surface of the earth and where Diamonds are often discovered.

"The gem called the Koh-i-Noor which was taken from Shah Shuja-ul-Mulk by Maharajah Ranjit Singh shall be surrendered by the Maharajah of Lahore to the Queen of England".

Two years after arriving in the UK, the gem was shown to the public in an exhibition staged in Hyde Park, 'The Times' newspaper reported:

"The Koh-i-Noor is at present decidedly the lion of the Exhibition. A mysterious interest appears to be attached to it, and now that so many precautions have been resorted to, and so much difficulty attends its inspection, the crowd is enormously enhanced, and the policemen at either end of the covered entrance have much trouble in restraining the struggling and impatient multitude. For some hours yesterday there were never less than a couple of hundred persons waiting their turn of admission, and yet, after all, the Diamond does not satisfy. Either from the imperfect cutting or the difficulty of placing the lights advantageously, or the immovability of the stone itself, which should be made to revolve on its axis, few catch any of the brilliant rays it reflects when viewed at a particular angle."

It wasn't just the press that were unimpressed by this huge Diamond, Queen Victoria's husband Prince Albert felt the gem lacked brilliance and ordered it to be reduced in size until it became more beautiful. The gem was cut and then re-cut and cut some more by Nottingham born Lapidarist and mineralogist James Tennant. The work was carried out under Prince Albert's close attention, and even though he was reported to have paid some £8,000 for the work, which saw the gem reduced from 186ct to 105ct, he was never satisfied with its appearance!

In 1936 the gem was set into the crown of Queen Elizabeth (whom we knew as the Queen Mother); in 2002 it was seen resting on her coffin, as the Queen Mother, at 101 years of age, lay in state. Today, the gem rests in the Tower of London, even though over the past 35 years various leaders from India, Afghanistan and Pakistan have claimed they are the rightful owners of this gemstone, a gem with a long and bloody history

Mukesh developing the Koh-I-Nur Replica Cut.

(BBC news reported that in 1976 the Pakistan Prime Minister, out of the blue, called the British Prime Minister Jim Callaghan and asked for its return).

Like all of the world's famous historic Diamonds, there are many myths and legends surrounding the Koh-i-Nur. Some of these stories say it was originally discovered some 5,000 years ago and is the gem mentioned in the ancient Sanskrit under the name of Syamantaka. What is quite clear is that it originated from the State of Pradesh, India, which until 1730 was said to be the only source of Diamonds in the world.

KOH-I-NUR REPLICA CUT

The famous Koh-I-Nur Diamond has been cut and re-cut so many times throughout history, that it's probably safe to assume that its current shape must therefore be one of the most developed gem cuts ever!

The gem is oval in shape and features a smaller than normal table facet surrounded by kite and triangular shaped facets that almost flow in curve like patterns away from its centre. When studying the cut from the table, through the small window at the top of the gem a flower shaped pavilion can be seen which has eight petal-like shapes connecting to a flower bud like centre.

I love this gem cut so much, that we have invested a lot of time in reproducing the cut and our Lapidaries have made us proud by creating our "Koh-I-Nur Replica Cut".

Now before you go calling up your solicitor concerned about buying a copy of a famous gemstone cut, let me save you the hassle by informing you that the cut is not patented and therefore, as long as it is made clear that it is a replica, then the Queen is not going to get upset. Anyway, as the gem weight needs to be in excess of 5ct to be really effective, then it's unlikely that your Koh-I-Nur replica cut is going to be a Diamond.

KORNERUPINE

Kornerupine was first discovered in 1884 in Greenland, the gem is named after the Danish gemmologist Andreas N. Kornerup.

It is an extremely rare gemstone usually found in a clear brown or yellow crystal form. A good quality Kornerupine, if cabochon cut, can display the "Cat's Eye" effect and sometimes "asterism" (a star effect). It is also sometimes referred to as Prismatine.

One of the rarest colours to find a Kornerupine in is green. What makes these extra special is that they bear a striking resemblance to that of an Emerald; not just in colour, but also in its refractive index. It can be distinguished however by its pleochroic property, which means that it is possible to see different colours when viewed from different angles. Green isn't the only striking colour the gem can be found in, as it can also come in yellows, browns, pinks and even a clear form. A Kornerupine can display colours ranging from a yellowish green colour to a brownish red when turned and looked at through different angles and facets.

This precious stone has long been associated with its supposed ability to have a magical link with breaking one's self doubt and oppressions. It has been said that if you are ever feeling down in the dumps then this is the stone for you. Its capabilities are renowned for lifting spirits and helping you determine where a problem lies and thus transforming your life. Often used in meditation, the gem is said to enlighten and focus one's mind. As with many of the rarer gemstones, Kornerupines prices jumps exponentially for larger pieces. A 2ct specimen is currently typically costing around four to five times more than a one carat.

Kornerupine is usually found in Sri Lanka in deposits known as 'placers'. These form in river bends that retain thick mud and heavy stones, allowing lighter minerals such as Sphene, Iolite, and Garnets etc to flow to another deposit slightly downstream. Deposits of Kornerupine can also be found in Madagascar and Australia.

Colour	Green, greenish brown, brownish red, blue
Family	Does not belong to a family
Hardness	6.5 – 7
Specific Gravity	3.28 – 3.35
Refractive Index	1.66 – 1.68
Crystal Group	Orthorhombic
Optical Properties	Strong pleochroism
Common Treatments	Not normally treated
Care	No special care required
Cleaning Advice	Warm soapy water
Chemical Composition	A complex magnesium aluminum boro-silicate

In Jaipur we take the above rough Kornerupine and turn it into stunning faceted gemstones.

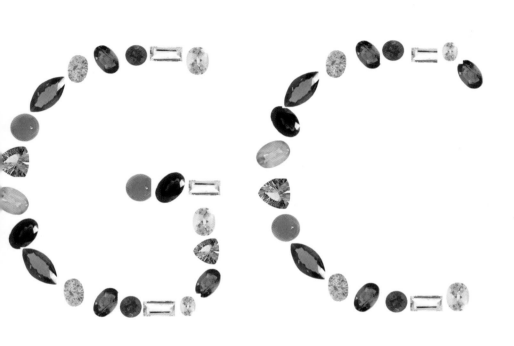

KUNZITE

Colour	Light pink
Family	Spodumene
Hardness	6-7
Specific Gravity	3.17 – 3.23
Refractive Index	1.66 – 1.67
Crystal Group	Monoclinic
Optical Properties	Strong pleochroism
Common Treatments	Not normally treated
Care	Don't expose to extreme sunlight for prolonged periods
Cleaning Advice	Warm soapy water
Chemical Composition	LiAl9SiO$_3$)$_2$

In 1902, the now world famous gemmologist George Frederick Kunz was the first person to give a complete explanation of this gemstone when he discovered it in California.

Its colour of lilac and delicate pink hues is unique in the gem world, and it is thought of as one of the most romantic and feminine of gems. When you look at a Kunzite it can appear pink, violet and sometimes colourless from different angles; this optical effect is known as pleochroism.

It is a member of the Spodumene family and when found in a yellow or greenish blue colour it is known as Hiddenite. While Kunzite is rare, Hiddenite is so scarce it is virtually unobtainable!

One of the most beautiful aspects of Kunzite is its ability to retain light. The effect is known as phosphorescence, which gives the gem the ability to glow in the dark. This luminous appearance is due to the fact that Kunzite is able to absorb energy and slowly releases it in the form of light. The effect is similar to luminous hands on a watch, which help you tell the time when you wake in the middle of the night.

Being such a relatively new discovery, there is little folklore surrounding this gem, other than it is said to amplify love, peace and joy. Kunzite is believed to be an excellent relationship gem, removing obstacles and promoting fidelity. In her book "Healing Crystals" written in 2003, Cassandra Eason suggests, among other things, that Kunzite relieves hormonal problems in pregnancy, the early days of motherhood and lingering post-natal depression. She also suggests that you should "put a Kunzite in a charm bag when travelling by car, both to counter road rage in others and to calm your own tensions in traffic".

Although there are no legends relating to this gem, there is one true story which begins in 1963 when JFK bought his wife Jacqueline Kennedy Onassis a Kunzite ring to celebrate their 10th Christmas together. Regrettably, he was assassinated before he had chance to give it to

Very feminine, very Kunzite.

her. For a very long period after his death, it was almost impossible to separate Jackie Kennedy and her Kunzite.

The gem can be found in Afghanistan, USA, Brazil, Madagascar, Mexico, Myanmar and Sweden and is often found in mines which also herald Beryls and Tourmalines. Kunzite has tiny traces of manganese which creates its famous lilac colour. As this colour can fade, it is not recommended to wear it for prolonged periods in direct sunlight.

KYANITE

Colour	Normally blue, but also green and brown
Family	Does not belong to a family
Hardness	Dual hardness of 4.5 – 7
Specific Gravity	3.56 – 3.68
Refractive Index	1.71 – 1.73
Crystal Group	Triclinic
Optical Properties	Strong pleochroism
Common Treatments	Not normally treated
Care	No special care needed
Cleaning Advice	Warm soapy water
Chemical Composition	Al_2SiO_2

Kyanite, also referred to as Disthene, is best known for its deep rich colours and rarity. The name is derived from the Greek word kyanos, meaning 'blue', and although it is not a birthstone, it is often associated with the zodiac signs of Aries, Taurus & Libra.

Although some in the trade call it a poor man's Sapphire, in my opinion this often just sour grapes as they probably don't have access to faceted gem material. To me, the gem is one of the most misunderstood in the industry and I personally feel that over the next decade the gem will become one of the most sought after gems on the planet.

Its clear, strong blue to bluish-green appearance has placed Kyanite in direct association with loyalty, serenity, calmness, innovation and dreams. It is also said to be effective on the throat and third-eye chakras.

Mainly set in rings, earring and pendants, Kyanite is an ideal gem for self-adornment. This shiny, translucent gemstone is famous for its variations in hardness which is referred to as anisotropism. This rare physical property is also known as polymorphism. Kyanite's hardness varies depending on which axis of the gem you are looking at. In one direction it measures 4.5 – 5 on the Mohs scale and on the other axis it measures 6.5 – 7.

Kyanite is actually made up of many different layers, making it easy to split this gemstone - this is known as perfect cleavage.

The combination of polymorphism and perfect cleavage makes Kyanite a particularly challenging stone to facet for Lapidarists the world over. Because of this, Kyanite for many years was never cut into anything other than cabochons. More recently as Lapadarists have learnt more about this gemstones, some have been brave enough to attempt to facet it.

Occasionally, green Kyanite is found and, understandably, is known as Emerald Kyanite. Ravishing in appearance, it resembles the Zambian Emerald and is valued as a real treasure by gem collectors. In its regular blue form, it has a colour very similar to Sapphire and gems extracted from recent mines in Nepal and Tibet are comparable in appearance to the very finest Kashmir Sapphires.

Even if you don't have a piece of Kyanite yet set in jewellery, you may actually unknowingly have a few small pieces hidden in your car, as none gem-quality Kyanite is often used in the production of Spark Plugs!

This precious stone is also extracted from alluvial deposits in Brazil and the USA.

Kyanite ring from Jacque Christie.

LABRADORESCENCE

When you see a metallic-like shimmer of blues and greens on or near the surface of a gem, you can refer to it as labradorescence. It is only seen in a few varieties of gems and the word comes from Labradorite; a gem which demonstrates the very best example of this wonderful visual effect.

This phenomenon is a type of iridescence caused by repeated, microscopically thin layers at the surface of the gemstone. The finest pieces have very striking looks, which skilled Lapidarists take care to orient to the best advantage when faceting the gemstone. Other gemstones where you will see labradorescence include other members of the Feldspar family such as Moonstone.

A handmade Labraodorite ring by Tookalon.

Labradorescence is an incredibly captivating visual effect, and one of the real treasures gifted from Mother Nature.

LABRADORITE

Colour	Grey to brown, with a rainbow of colours trapped inside
Family	Feldspar
Hardness	6 – 6.5
Specific Gravity	2.7 – 2.71
Refractive Index	1.560 – 1.572
Crystal Group	Triclinic
Optical Properties	Stunning schiller / labradorescence
Common Treatments	n/a
Care	No special care required
Cleaning Advice	Warm soapy water
Chemical Composition	Varies

The Native Americans called this gem 'Firestone' because they loved the way the light captured inside the stone looked as if it was dancing with fire. The gem has a gorgeous iridescence, or play of colours, and is named after the location where it was found on the island of St. Paul, in Labrador, Canada (the same place that the dog bearing the same name was first bred).

Take a quick glance at it in a poorly lit room and you might at first see a dull, uninteresting stone, but turn up the light or take it outside, observe it more closely and the gem's full magic will be displayed. As light dances across its surface it becomes as mystical and as beautiful as the Northern Lights. This effect is known as labradorescence and is truly a one of a kind mineralogical experience that should be viewed first-hand to really appreciate its beauty.

The intense colours seen in this optical effect range from gorgeous blues and violets, to forest greens, golden yellows and sunset oranges. In rare instances it is possible to find examples where all of these colours are displayed simultaneously. This colour effect is caused by the light entering the gem and being refracted like a pinball trapped inside a pinball machine, bouncing off the layers inside the gemstone.

At first sight Labradorite can appear a little boring, with a deep smoky grey to brown exterior. But look past this and slowly rotate the gem. If you don't see a kaleidoscope of colours suddenly appear before your eyes, it's not a great example and not worthy of being set in jewellery!

According to myths and legends, Labradorite is thought to unleash the power of the mind and was even believed to aid in overcoming one's limitations. It is said to protect your aura and to align your personal self with the universe to help you achieve your destiny.

Associated with the third eye (the brow chakra)

Labradorite is a favourite with our designers.

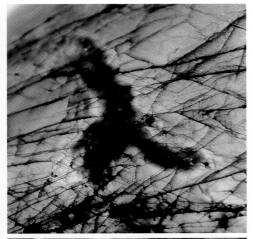

this gem lessens negativity and is used in prayer and meditation. Being a sister to Moonstone, Labradorite grants the inner knowledge of mystery and enhances psychic perception.

As well as in Canada, Labradorite is also found in Madagascar, China, India, Australia, Russia, Mexico, Scandinavia (where it is known as Spectrolite) and the USA.

One of the rarest gems we try and always stock at GemCollector is a gorgeous yellow Labradorite. Unlike the Labradorite coming from Canada, this material is completely transparent and is similar to Red Labradorite (see separate section) in terms of clarity and brilliance. Just like Citrine and Lemon Quartz, when you wear this gem you can't help but smile.

LAPIDARIST

Here I am attempting to improve my lapidary skills

A person who cuts and polishes gemstones is known as a Lapidarist. Lapidary is one of the most skilful jobs in the creation of fine jewellery. I have personally had one of the very best attempt to teach me how to facet gemstones. After days of endless concentration and studying, I decided that it was a skill that could not be taught, unless you had a natural flair for it. I believe it is similar to art or music. Sure, you can go to art classes or take guitar lessons, but unless you already have a modicum of natural ability, you are never going to be top of your class. When it comes to cutting gemstones, I am definitely tone deaf!

There are many tasks involved with cutting a gemstone and even before they begin, the Lapidarist must decide the best orientation of the gem - in other words, at what angle the gem should be cut out of the rough to best show its colour, and to maximise any optical effects. There are five main steps that we go through when we cut gemstones. Each one is vitally important and an error at any stage can either dramatically reduce the final carat weight of the stone or in some instances destroy it completely.

The most underestimated step is the very first one. This is known as the gemstone orientation step. Here very knowledgeable gemstone experts will make the decision of which part of the rough stone will ultimately finish up being the table facet. If a mistake is made at this point, there is every chance that the gemstones brilliance and fire will not be maximised. As you were probably taught if you ever did woodwork or metal work at school, at this stage it is crucial to measure twice and cut once!

Step two is to actually make the first cut, often this is done by the same person who makes the vital decision on orientation, but in other cutting houses this is a separate task. A saw with Diamond tips is used to cut rough material into the required number of pieces.

•The gemstone is then ground on a lap (horizontal wheel) to get an outline shape.

•A paste is used to grind the gem into a pre-formed shape, which is often done in several steps with finer and finer pastes being used at each stage. The paste is often is often made of small, tiny pieces of Diamond.

•After being cut and ground to the right shape, the gem is then polished to a mirror-like finish. To apply the finish, extremely fine grades of Diamond dusts are normally used.

Ancient artefacts show that Lapidary started in approximately 3000BC (Bronze Age) where early techniques of sawing, drilling, faceting and polishing were used to facet gems. However, bruting (a technique using one mineral to shape another by striking it) dates back as far as one million years ago, making Lapidary one of the oldest skills on the planet!

Today, Lapidary has become widely accepted as one of the most challenging forms of art on the planet. Unlike an artist who paints, the Lapidarist's raw materials already possess great value: one mistake could render them worthless. The Lapidarist, alongside trying to create his masterpiece, must also be mindful of carat weight; the finished item will derive

Facets being added on a grinding lap.

Here I am attempting (and failing) to make a round brilliant cut.

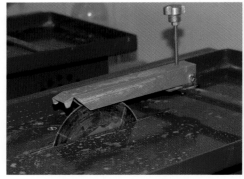

A saw used to perform the first cut on rough stones.

its value not purely from its visual appearance, but also from its size.

To recognise the achievements of this profession, there are now several highly profiled global competitions such as the "Cutting Edge Awards" and in Germany (still one of the largest gem cutting centres in the world) there is the highly acclaimed "German Award for Jewellery and Precious Stones".

LAPIS LAZULI

Colour	Blue
Family	Lazurite
Hardness	5 - 5.6
Specific Gravity	2.4
Refractive Index	1.500 - 1.550
Crystal Group	Cubic
Optical Properties	Veins of different colours
Common Treatments	See details
Care	Keep away from intense heat
Cleaning Advice	Warm soapy water
Chemical Composition	A complex limestone structure

Throughout its long lifetime of use, this beautiful blue opaque gemstone has been considered as a holystone, a friendship stone and a stone of truth, encouraging the wearer to speak their mind and create harmonious relationships.

The name Lapis Lazuli comes from the Latin "Lapis", meaning 'stone' and the Arabic "Azula", meaning 'blue'. Its formation occurred millions of years ago when lime metamorphosed into marble. The gem can often include whitish marble veins and small golden inclusions which are caused by iron.

The value of the stone depends upon the depth and intensity of the colour, which can range from a deep blue to lighter blue shades. Finely and evenly distributed inclusions that shimmer and resemble gold will also add to the price.

Historically, this stone was once ground and used in paint by artists; it provided a bright blue colour that was extremely rare and hence was always used sparingly. If this colour was found in an artwork, it was a sign that the commissioning family had spent a great deal of money on that piece of art. An example is the Titian painting of the 'Greek Myth of Bacchus and Ariadne' where the vivid blue of Ariadne's robe is truly striking.

The gemstone had, however, been popular for many years before the likes of Titian and Michelangelo were painting with it. Archaeologists have uncovered Lapis Lazuli in ancient graves in Egypt, Rome and Greece. There is also evidence of it being traded in the

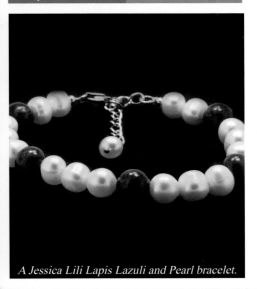

A Jessica Lili Lapis Lazuli and Pearl bracelet.

Middle East as far back as the 4000BC, where it was believed to have been excavated in Afghanistan.

Romans believed that wearing the gem would prevent miscarriages and epilepsy, as well as acting as a powerful aphrodisiac. They also named the gem "Sapphirus", a name that later became used to describe blue Corundum.

When the stone is used for jewellery it is often protected by coating it with a synthetic resin or colourless wax, which is harmless to the stone and simply improves its durability.

A handmade Tookalon Lapis Lazuli ring.

LAPS

For once here is something in the gem world that makes total sense! A "lap" is a horizontal rotating disc that Lapidarists use to facet and polish gemstones. In most cutting houses across Asia, Lapidarists choose to sit on the floor and the "lap" is literally spinning in their lap! Hooray – something easy to remember at last!

But now it gets a little more complex. In nearly every book you read that introduces you to gemstone cutting (including this book), to communicate the process in an easy to understand method you only ever hear of metal wheels and diamond paste. However, the art of Lapidary is more than just developing the skill of knowing how to orientate the first cut and how to angle and arrange the facets, it is also about knowing which tools to use for shaping different types of gemstones.

When it comes to the lap itself, not only is the choice of material significant - plastic, brass, copper, lead and tin all work differently with different gems – but even the finish on the lap (for example, how highly it is polished) makes a difference. Then the polishing compounds and various pastes all have different effects on these different laps. To put this into context, in our cutting house in Jaipur, we estimate that there are over 200 different combinations of laps and pastes used to facet and polish different gems! Even though you can give guidance to your Lapidarist, as this is an art and not a process, in

Colour	Blue
Family	Pectolite
Hardness	4.5 - 5.5
Specific Gravity	2.8
Refractive Index	1.59 - 1.63
Crystal Group	Triclinic
Optical Properties	May Phosphoresce
Common Treatments	None
Care	None
Cleaing Advice	Warm soapy water
Chemical Composition	NaCa2Si3O8(OH)

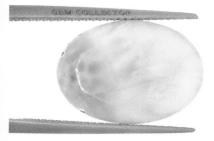

Larimar is only discovered in the Dominican Republic.

the end the choice of tools comes down to the individual's experience and preference.

Here are a few of the most regularly used combinations in our cutting house: Brass laps and Diamond pastes are used to facet Sapphires and Rubies; Copper laps and Diamond powder for Topaz and Quartz; Lead laps used in conjunction with tin oxide or chromium oxide polishing powders are popular for cutting Emeralds (a combination created in Jaipur over 200 years ago); Tin laps are used for polishing a variety of gemstones including Beryls, Garnets and Tourmalines (however, with some gem varieties tin is considered too soft and a tiny amount of antimony is added to harden the lap). Tin laps work with a variety of pastes including tin oxide, alumina powders and Diamond.

LARIMAR

Currently only discovered on the popular holiday designation island of the Dominican Republic, Larimar (also known as Lorimar) is a subtle blue gemstone with an appearance similar to that of Turquoise.

Folklore suggests that the locals used to find 'blue rock' on the beach and after a barren period, they decided to follow a stream up into the mountain and found the original source of the rock. However, no one was able to obtain mining rights and in the early 1900's the stones disappeared in to the history books.

In 1974 a local called Miguel Mendez rediscovered the gem in the province of Barahona. Miguel decided to name his discovery by combining his daughter's name 'Larissa' with the Spanish word for sea, 'mar'. Today the Los Chupaderos Mine is the only source of the gem on the planet. It is located 10km from the city of Barahona and in the rainforest mountainside hundreds of small vertical mining shafts have been created.

The gem is a variety of pectolite and it receives its blue colouring from the presence of cobalt. While other pale colours are also found, it is the original blue Larimar that is most highly prized and which is set into jewellery. As a fairly new gemstone there is little folklore or legend surrounding it; however, the gem is also known by locals as the Atlantis Stone, as it was once claimed by a wise prophet that the Dominican Republic was part of the lost continent of Atlantis.

Next time you visit the Caribbean on holiday, be sure to take time to look in one of their jewellers windows. Not only will you be amazed at how seriously they take the displaying of coloured gemstones compared to many European retailers, you will almost certainly see a small selection of pieces set with their local hero Larimar.

LEMON QUARTZ

The strong citrus tones of this gem type are an unusual quality in the Quartz family. While its sister Citrine enjoys the golden-orange, yellow tones of the sunset, Lemon Quartz has the fresh, vibrant nature of lemon groves in summer. This sensitive tone not only works well in female jewellery but also suits gents cufflinks.

The only difference between Citrine and Lemon Quartz is in the saturation and tone of their colour. Many gem dealers do not even separate the two and use the name Citrine for all yellow Quartz. The gem looks vibrant when set into yellow gold; however, it really steals the show when set into either silver or white gold.

Whilst the Quartz part of its name is derived from the Greek word for ice "krustallos", the Lemon prefix is obviously English. Maybe subconsciously that's one of the reasons that I personally favour the gem marginally over its sister of French derived origin Citrine!

Most of the Citrine we have at Coloured Rocks is cut and polished in our own facility in India. When we study the rough, if it has good clarity so as to maximise the gems incredible brilliance, we will often add a concave cut to the pavilion. However, as my wife is as equally passionate about this gemstone as I am, she will often request that larger pieces are cabochon cut, so that she can set them in her cocktail rings.

Colour	Pale yellow to rich yellow
Family	Quartz
Hardness	6.6 – 7
Specific Gravity	2.6 – 2.65
Refractive Index	1.5
Crystal Group	Trigonal
Optical Properties	Glassy to vitreous lustre
Common Treatments	Some varieties are heat treated
Care	No special care required
Cleaning Advice	Ultrasonic or warm soapy water
Chemical Composition	SiO_2

A large Lemon Quartz ring by Sarah Bennett.

pop
diamonds

LEPIDOLITE

Colour	Pale pink to white
Family	Lepidolite
Hardness	2.8 – 4.0
Specific Gravity	2.8
Refractive Index	1.53 – 1.556
Crystal Group	Monoclinic
Optical Properties	None
Common Treatments	None
Care	Care needed not to knock the stone
Cleaning Advice	Warm soapy water
Chemical Composition	$KLi_2Al(Al,Si)_3O_{10}(F,OH)_2$

Also spelt Lapidolite, this gem is found in a range of hues similar to Amethyst and Rose Quartz. This translucent mineral is considered by many jewellers to be too soft to set in rings and is therefore more often seen in beaded necklaces, bracelets and ornaments.

Its name is said to be derived from the Greek word "lepidos", meaning "scale", due to its scaly appearance.

Lepidolite is never faceted and rarely even cabochon cut. When set in jewellery it is shaped by tumbling and this rough appearance is a stark contrast to its inherent softness.

The gem is surrounded in Crystal Healing myths and is said to bring light and hope to a situation and to promote hope, patience, and self-love.

Lepidolite can help heal depression, lessen anger and release trauma. Smokers and heavy drinkers may also find it helpful as it is supposedly useful for ending addictions.

The gem has been discovered in Argentina, the Czech Republic, Madagascar, Russia, USA and Zimbabwe.

LOCKET

Lockets are normally pendants or charms that have a hinge and open up to reveal something of personal value to their owner.

In the Victorian era, lockets became very popular, and after the invention of photography in the mid 1800's, photos of loved ones were frequently placed inside. Prior to this period, lockets often held hairs of loved ones, ashes from deceased relatives and even powders and poisons!

Often hung from a chain, lockets can come in a variety of shapes, sizes and metals. They are a popular gift for occasions such as weddings, Valentine's Day, christenings and birthdays.

THE LONE STAR CUT

Designed over the Christmas period in 1973 by Lapidarists Dr. Paul W. Worden, Jr. and his brother Gary B. Worden, the Lone Star Cut is normally applied to a round shape gem and when viewed from the table you can clearly see a five pointed star.

Interestingly, the angles of the facets on the pavilion are deliberately designed to allow light to leak out, intensifying the appearance of the star. In Texas, USA the Lone Star Cut is their official state cut!

Our team of Lapidaries at our facility in Jaipur have recently perfected a very similar cut and tell me that it took a long time to master as the angles of the facets on both the pavilion and crown must be accurate within one degree, otherwise the star effect does not appear. "It is without doubt one of the most technically advanced cuts we have decided to work with and all 7 faces on the pavilion must meet at a perfect point for the star to be visible" says one of our most senior Lapidaries, Dali. Although the cut is still performed by hand, we have had to set up a very precise jig to make this cut.

LORIQUE

Ultimate treasures collection by Lorique.

In 2008 the small team of exceptional craftsmen at Lorique made just 2,840 pieces of extremely fine jewellery. The company's commitment to only setting the very finest gemstones, those deserving the title 'ultimate treasures', has been reinforced this year (2009) by limiting the maximum number of coloured gemstone jewellery pieces that can be created to just 2009! From two small workshops, one in Switzerland and one in Asia, each Lorique piece is created without concern for time or expense. For those seeking exclusivity and those who appreciate the finest gifts from Mother Nature, nothing quite compares to owning a Lorique piece of jewellery.

Ultimate treasures collection by Lorique.

The 2009 collection already includes some of the finest Alexandrite ever discovered, incredible museum quality Aquamarine, three large AAA Tanzanite rings which are surrounded by over a carat of VS Diamonds and two 5ct Ceylon Blue Sapphires set in rings made of platinum.

Each item of jewellery from the Lorique Ultimate Treasures collection is engraved with its unique piece number, which records the detail of the piece and provides complete traceability (the first piece produced in January 2009 for example starts with 1/09). Customers who pass on their Lorique jewellery as a gift or as an inheritance piece, are advised to contact Lorique so that the ownership of the piece can be re-registered.

LOUIS DE BERQUEN

Recognised as the inventor of today's method of faceting Diamonds, in 1476 Louis de Berquen of Bruges was the first person to use Diamond dust to facet them. Until this time, as Diamonds are naturally octahedral (an 8-sided shape with triangular planes), they were set into jewellery pretty much in the same shape as they came out of the ground.

By using a spinning metal wheel with Diamond dust suspended in oil, Berquen was able to change the shape of Diamonds and make them even more symmetrical: for the first time in history the gem's amazing brilliance was truly unlocked. His early method was to remove a large amount from one tip to make a table facet and slightly ground the other tip into a tiny culet.

What really places Louis de Berquen in the history books is that he faceted the 'Sancy Diamond', which was originally one of three large rough Diamonds belonging to Charles Le Temeraine, the Duke of Burgundy. Of all the famous Diamonds in Europe, the Sancy has the most interesting history of all.

LOUPE

A loupe is a 10x magnification eye glass used by jewellers. This is the standard magnification that the Gemological Institution of America (GIA) uses to identify the clarity of Diamonds. For example, Internally Flawless (IF) refers to the fact that no inclusions are seen in a Diamond when viewed under a loupe.

Hopefully by now, half way through this book, you are starting to get a little excited by Mother Nature's coloured treasures. If so, in order to fully appreciate gemstones I would recommend that a loupe is one of the next purchases you make.

A traditional jeweller's 10x magnification loupe.

LUSTRE

Lustre (also spelt luster) refers to the surface reflection of light off an object and is a description often used in gemmology to describe the way light interacts with the surface of the gem. Black Diamonds for example, don't display any dispersion or brilliance, but demonstrate as much lustre as a white Diamond.

In fact Black Diamonds and Marcasite often out sparkle and out dazzle colourless Diamonds because their lustre can be greater than the internal brilliance and dispersion of white Diamonds.

Black gems normally have a high lustre.

Opaque gems are normally cabochon cut to maximise their lustre, while gems that are transparent to translucent are often step cut or brilliant cut in order to take advantage of their internal brilliance and their ability to disperse light. That said, step cut and brilliant cut gems still retain the ability to show lustre off their crown and table facets.

The harder the gemstone and the greater its density, the better the lustre tends to be. Diamonds and Zircons, for example, have a gorgeous, sparkling lustre known to gemmologists as an adamantine lustre.

The most common lustre in faceted transparent

Cabochon gems display high lustre.

The table facets on these Diamonds are clearly showing lustre.

gemstones, is similar to that seen in a pane of glass and is known as a "vitreous lustre". Aquamarine, Spinel, Topaz, Emerald and Tourmalines are amongst those that are said to have a vitreous lustre.

Gems with a greasy lustre are those whose surface reflection is similar to that of grease. This is normally caused by a mass of microscopic inclusions within the mineral. Peridot, Alexandrite, Opals and some Garnets are said to have a greasy lustre.

Metallic lustre is similar to that of a polished metal or that of a mirror; Pyrite and Marcasite are classic examples.

Gemstones with a pearly lustre obviously have an appearance similar to that of an organic Pearl. Their appearance is normally due to layers within the gem, from which light reflects in an unorthodox, yet beautiful manner. Opals have a pearly lustre, which is often referred to as Opalescence.

Resinous lustre is similar to the appearance of resin or chewing gum. Amber is one of the most well-known gems that is said to have a resinous lustre. Others include Titanite and Vesuvianite.

Gems with a silky lustre have very fine fibres (just like silk) which are arranged parallel to each other. Malachite and Sillimanite are both said to have silky lustre. A fibrous lustre is similar to a silky lustre, but has a coarser texture; Tiger's Eye has a fibrous lustre.

As the name suggests, gems with a waxy lustre have an appearance similar to that of wax. Jade and Turquoise have a waxy lustre.

To really achieve the most enjoyment possible out of your gem collection, it helps if you can truly understand the difference between lustre, brilliance and fire. Try reading all three of these topics in this book and then take out your gem collection and try and identify all three of these different visual effects. Once you can do this, you will find that your appreciation of your collection will grow immensely.

The triangular facet on this Andesine is demonstrating lustre.

jessica & lili

The Jessica Lili Collection features a selection of genuine Pearl necklaces, starting at just £12!

MABE PEARL

A distinguished Mabe Pearl design by Eleven Seventeen.

A Mabe Pearl is truly without equal. It is an organic gem type and is a half spherical Pearl which has grown on the inside shell of the oyster or Mollusc (as opposed to the round Pearl which grows in the body of the oyster), thus giving the Pearl a flat side, which is perfect for setting into rings, earrings and bracelets.

Mabe Pearls can be found in a range of beautiful colours from light pink to darker blue shades. The outer layer (nacre) of a Mabe Pearl is often a kaleidoscope of colours, which can be truly breathtaking and is normally responsible for their higher price tags.

The Mabe Pearl first saw popularity at the end of the 19th century and there are many Victorian pieces of jewellery that include them in the design.

MADAGASCAR

If you have watched the children's film 'Madagascar', the first thing you should know about this country is that very few of the animals seen in the movie inhabit it in real life.

As the fourth biggest island in the world, situated off the East Coast of Africa, the country is famous for its great vanilla, the huge Baobab trees and a plethora of amazing gems.

Its gemstone treasure chest includes Aquamarines, a rare Blue Garnet, Tourmalines, and Beryls, including Morganite. More recently it has added the discovery of Diamonds to its treasure-trove and with sources of Corundum (Sapphires and Rubies) dwindling in countries such as Thailand and Burma, Madagascar is now one of the world's leading suppliers of these superstar gems too!

With so much potential, The World Bank is funding development projects in cooperation with the Malagasy government in an attempt to retain more of the wealth obtained from gemstones in its own country. Gemmology schools have been set up to teach locals how to cut and polish gemstones, ensuring they are able to export the finished article, rather than the far lesser-valued rough.

In Ilakaka though, the scene very much remains an informal artisanal mining community. The perimeter of the town is surrounded by small-scale mines, which are owned by entrepreneurial individuals or small teams that work with very little technology. Their lifestyle is consistently better than that of subsistence farming: there is always the belief and potential that a substantial reward will be discovered tomorrow! This belief is backed up by the European brick-styled buildings owned by miners who have struck lucky.

Located in the south of the island, Ilakaka was nothing more than a tiny subsistence farming community until gems were rediscovered in 1998 (they were actually discovered some 50

At the Banque Suisse mine, miners share in the profit of any discovered Sapphires.

Sapphire trading in Madagascar.

years prior, but due to the small size of the find and political unrest were never mined). What followed was similar to the famous gold rushes in America. Overnight Ilakaka went from a handful of farmers to tens of thousands of individual first-time miners all seeking their own fortune. Even today, many of them still work with just a shovel, a candle and a bucket. The nearest thing they have to technology is a winch. A relative or friend will lower the miner into the sandstone shaft on a bucket which is attached to an old piece of rope. Once at the bottom of the shaft the miner continues to dig and the potential rough is then winched back to the surface to be taken to the local river to be panned, and hopefully a gem or two will be seen.

I recently met with Jean-Noel Andrianasolo who was at the heart of what has been known as the greatest "gem rush" of the last fifty years. Jean-Noel says, "In 1998 I was working in the capital when I heard rumours of a big find of Sapphires near Ilakaka. So I took the 15 hour drive, set up a tiny home and began digging at the rear of my own backyard. In no time at all I found my first small Sapphire and the further I dug, the more I found. As there was so much potential wealth inside I named the open pit Banque Suisse".

Ilakaka is not the only 'gem boom town' in Madagascar; another is the town of Vatomandry where Rubies of a quality to equal those from Burma are being mined. In 2003, Rubies were also discovered in Andilamena.

The gemstone boom-town of Ilakaka.

MALACHITE

Malachite is a gorgeous green gemstone, named after the Greek word "molochites" for "mallow", a savoury green herb. Its light and dark green bands are very distinctive, making it one of the most easily recognisable of all gemstones.

Malachite was crushed and used as a green pigment in the Bronze Age and its use in jewellery can be traced back as early as 4000BC when it was worn by Egyptians. In the Middle Ages Malachite was worn to protect from black magic and sorcery. It is said that Malachite can be worn to detect impending danger and it is believed to lend extra energy and bring harmony into one's life.

The Russian Tsar was fascinated by the mineral and in 1818 deployed miners to the Ural Mountains in order to extract enough material so as to create the beautiful gemstone pillars of St. Isaac's Cathedral in St. Petersburg, Russia.

The gem is relatively soft, measuring only 3.5 to 4 on the Mohs scale and is therefore often cabochon cut and secured into jewellery using a bezel setting.

Malachite is found in several locations around the world including Australia, Mexico, Namibia and the Ural Mountains of Russia.

Colour	Green
Family	Malachite is a family in its own right
Hardness	3.5 – 4
Specific Gravity	3.6 – 4.0
Refractive Index	1.85
Crystal Group	Monoclinic
Optical Properties	Fibrous Lustre
Common Treatments	None
Cleaning Advice	Warm soapy water
Chemical Composition	$Cu_2CO_3(OH)_2$

MALAIA GARNET

One of the rarest of all Garnets, Malaia Garnet is normally pale orange to pinkish orange in colour. The gem was given its separate name in 1979 when it was identified as a blend between Pyrope and Spessartite Garnet. Prior to this, the gem was thought to be a slightly off-shade of Rhodolite Garnet. Once its different composition had been identified, it was given its name from the Swahili word meaning "outcast".

When you study this gem it almost looks dichroic (two different colours are seen from different angles). However, this cannot be the case as the Garnet family does not feature this characteristic; it is actually due to the fact that it reacts to different light sources (wavelengths) in different ways. This beautiful gem has only currently been discovered in the Umba Valley, which borders Tanzania and Kenya.

Colour	Pale orange to pinkish orange
Family	Garnet
Hardness	7.25
Specific Gravity	3.4 – 4.3
Refractive Index	1.7 – 1.89
Crystal Group	Isometric
Optical Properties	Various
Common Treatments	None

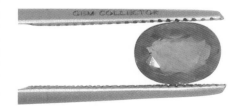

MALAWI

Not to be confused with Mali in north-west Africa, Malawi is a small country in the south of Africa bordering with Tanzania to the north, Mozambique to the south and Zambia to its west. Most Malawians rely on subsistence farming, but this is a difficult task as the country constantly (and frustratingly) battles with extreme weather conditions from drought to heavy rainfall. Many Malawians are currently reducing their reliance on farming and starting to explore for gems.

As with its neighbouring countries, hidden beneath Malawi's soil lies small deposits of Amethyst, Aquamarine, Beryls, Garnets and gem-quality Quartz. In addition to these artisan mines, there are also larger scale Ruby and Sapphire mines at Chimwadzulu Hill in the south of Malawi.

A Malawi mining village.

MALI GARNET

Not to be confused with Malaia Garnet, Mali Garnet is a rare crossbreed of Andradite and Grossular Garnet. It is an even more recent discovery than Malaia Garnet and was first discovered in December 1994 in Mali (still the only known source).

Colour	Light yellow to green
Family	Garnet
Hardness	6.5 – 6.9
Specific Gravity	3.4 – 3.9
Refractive Index	1.75 – 1.89
Crystal Group	Cubic
Optical Properties	Various
Common Treatments	Cannot be heat treated
Care	No special care needed
Cleaning Advice	Ultrasonic or warm soapy water
Chemical Composition	Various

Some in the gem world thought it should be named Grandite, taking the "gr" from Grossular and the "andite" from Andradite, but, let's face it, that's not a pretty name at all for this gem!

Whilst other members of the Grossular family are typically colourless, white, yellow, violet, red or orange, Mali Garnet's appearance is a very striking light, greenish yellow colour and features wonderful dispersion and lots of brilliance.

Mali Garnet has rapidly become a favourite amongst gem collectors and prices of over $500 per carat are not uncommon.

MALLEABLE

Luckily, two of the world's most precious and beautiful metals, gold and silver, are highly malleable (gold is in fact the most malleable metal on the planet). Webster's dictionary describes the word as "capable of being extended or shaped by beating with a hammer or by the pressure of rollers". Because these metals are so malleable, they have allowed jewellers to create gorgeous, intricate designs for thousands of years.

Gold is extremley malleable.

Jewels of Valais
SWITZERLAND

Colour	Golden bronze
Family	Does not belong to a family
Hardness	6 - 6.5
Specific Gravity	4.8 – 4.9
Refractive Index	1.8
Crystal Group	Orthorhombic
Optical Properties	Has Lustre like a Diamond
Common Treatments	Not normally treated
Care	None
Cleaning Advice	Ultrasonic, steam cleaning or warm soapy water
Chemical Composition	FeS_2

The above two pieces from Jewels of Valais feature genuine Swiss Marcasite.

MARCASITE

Marcasite boasts a natural ability to reflect light, and due to its brilliant lustre, jewellery designers often use it as a replacement for Diamond accents. The name is derived from the Arabic word for Pyrite, for which it is often mistaken, so much so that experts within the field of gemmology still discuss the issue at length.

As a pseudomorphic gem, the atoms replace themselves with other minerals so effectively they can change their whole identity (pseudomorph is a Latin word meaning "false shape"). Often the effect with Marcasite is noticeable on the surface of the gemstone as a thin skin of iron, which in turn creates a beautiful iridescent sheen.

It is also interesting that Marcasites with an iridescent oxide coating have been known to shine longer without polishing than non-coated Marcasites. Perhaps the gem is trying to protect itself when it pseudomorphs; in the same way an oyster or mollusc will when alien particles get into the shell - just a thought!

Marcasite was a popular gem in Victorian times and today tends to be associated with antique jewellery. This type of retro antique design is once again becoming fashionable and the demands for such pieces are only set to increase.

The gem is mined in several locations around the globe and a deposit of Marcasite with an intense lustre has been mined in the Swiss Alps since the late 1800's. It has a rating of up to 6.5 on the Mohs scale and is therefore a reliable, durable gemstone that can last when worn on a frequent basis.

When it comes to origin, Switzerland is to Marcasite what Ceylon and Cashmere (Kashmir) are to Sapphire. No other origin yet discovered can match Swiss Marcasite in terms of surface cleanliness and lustre. Whilst Thailand may be the largest producer in the world of Marcasite jewellery, the quality of Marcasite mined within its own borders is nowhere near comparable with those unearthed in Switzerland.

MARCEL TOLKOWSKY

Born into a Belgian family of Diamond cutters in 1899, Marcel Tolkowsky was surrounded by talk of the 'perfect Diamond cut'. He studied mathematics and engineering, and in 1919 wrote a thesis on the ideal proportions for round brilliant cut Diamonds, and for the last 80 years many cutters have followed his exact set of parameters. It is becoming apparent, however, that Tolkowsky detailed a whole range of proportions, not limited to the ones depicted in his original drawing.

By altering the relationship of the crown and pavilion angles, Tolkowsky was one of the first people to realise that there is a compromise to be made between maximising the brilliance and dispersion in a Diamond.

The Tolkowsky story lives on today through Gabriel Tolkowsky, who represents the sixth generation of his family to be in the Diamond cutting business. In 1985 Gabriel invented the "flower cut" and in 1988 he was commissioned by "De Beers" to cut the 273ct Centenary Diamond, which is reported to be the largest flawless Diamond in the world. The delicate task of cutting it took Tolkowsky over three years to complete!

MARILYN MONROE

Part of Marilyn Monroe's charm and appeal was her high glamour. The platinum hair, the beautiful couture dresses and, of course, the exquisite jewellery. Who else could sing "Diamonds are a girl's best friend" with so much passion and truth, but at the same time not be in the least bit offensive? Men and women alike loved her, and still do. She created an image that remains fresh and up-to-date in today's ever changing fashion.

In the film 'Gentlemen Prefer Blondes', Marilyn played a young woman whose love for Diamonds

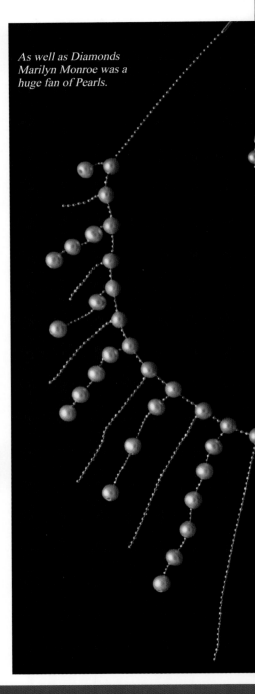

As well as Diamonds Marilyn Monroe was a huge fan of Pearls.

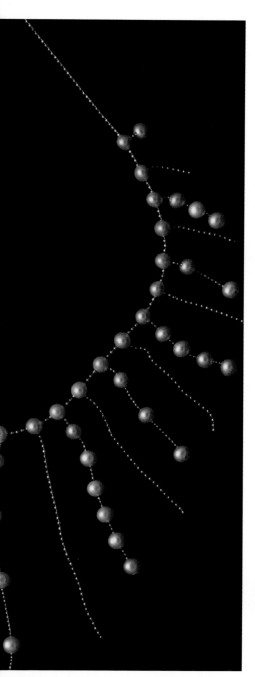

and jewellery ruled her life. It was enchanting to watch her face light up in delight as she tried on the Diamond Tiara of one of the characters in the film. Though that may have just been a script and a film, in real life Marilyn loved and enjoyed wearing jewellery. Iconic pictures of Marilyn include her wearing a Diamond encrusted gold ring and a Diamond bangle. Marilyn loved her Emerald star drop earrings as well as her Diamond pendant necklaces.

Some say that when she died, Marilyn only had a very small private jewellery collection. This may be due to the fact that she gave a huge amount of jewellery to Bebe Goddard, a woman she had met at the age of 13 while living at an orphanage, who later became her foster sister.

MARQUISE CUT

The cut's name originated in the 1700's, when Louis XV of France wanted a Diamond to be faceted similar to the fetching smile of his mistress, the Marquise de Pomadour (a Marquise is the wife or widow of a nobleman).

The marquise cut is an elongated shape that has tapering points at either end (it's not a very elegant analogy, but try picturing a rugby ball). This shape flatters the finger when worn in a ring, as it appears to elongate the finger and is used considerably in designer jewellery. It has the ability to look much bigger in size than an equivalent carat weight in a round cut and typically is brilliant cut with 55 to 58 facets.

A well-proportioned marquise cut gem that is easy on the eye should be twice the length of its widest part, although occasionally in very modern pieces elongated marquise cut gems can work well, especially if they have a vitreous lustre.

MASTER MODEL MAKING

When more than one piece of identical jewellery needs to be made, the first step is to produce a master model. In larger companies this process would start by a jeweller studying a designer's sketch and then creating a master model of the drawing in silver. The replica model would then be presented to the designer for approval and modification, before exact replicas were made. This traditional method of making master models is still used today for designs where the craftsman is encouraged to add their own personal flair to the design.

A more modern way of making master models is for either the designer to make an initial drawing and have it entered into a CAD (computer aided design) software program, or for the designer to create the design for the jewellery personally on a computer. Once the design is finished, often the master model is then created directly from the computer. The best way of understanding the process is to imagine a special laser printer which is not outputting its design on paper, but creating a 3D plastic model of the jewellery.

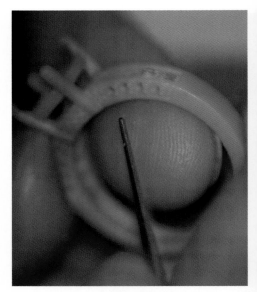

MATTOM

For over 4000 years, warriors, knights and kings have worn coloured gemstones as a sign of prosperity and leadership. Today Mattom take these very same gems and set them into the extremely strong metal, titanium.

Mattom jewellery is not so much designed, but devised. Their contemporary pieces encompass genuine gemstones set in masculine clean lines and finely displayed in titanium. The final twist is delivered in that all gemstones are interchangeable in their unique "gemstone threaded setting". Mattom jewellery is most definitely engineered for men.

Mattom watch with an Aquamarine in the crown.

MAWSITSIT

This gemstone is often found when mining for Imperial Jadeite. It was named after the Burmese town with the same name following its discovery by gemmologist Eduard Gubelin in 1963. Prior to this period as it was often found in the same mines as Jade many people mistook Mawsitsit to be Jade. This gemstone has a similar toughness to the Jade it is often found near to, and is usually

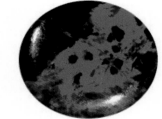

It is easy to imagine how Mawsitsit is often confused with Jade.

dark green to black in colour. It has veins that are beautiful Emerald green to intense neon green.

Mawsitsit is often mistaken for Malachite, but unlike Malachite, Mawsitsit does not have colour banding.

Colour	Transparent
Family	Quartz
Hardness	7
Specific Gravity	2.66
Refractive Index	1.54 - 1.55
Crystal Group	Hexagonal (Trigonal)
Optical Properties	Blue inclusions
Common Treatments	None
Care	None
Cleaning Advice	Ultrasonic or soapy water
Chemical Composition	SiO2

Medusa Quartz, you will either love it or hate it!

MEDUSA QUARTZ

Have you ever seen the HSBC billboard at an airport where they show a picture of an item or an experience and describe how two different people could view the image. One reads "pleasure or pain" while another says "enjoyment or chore". Then we have the Marmite advert "love it or hate it". Well Medusa Quartz is a gemstone that could easily be advertised in the same way.

It has the appearance of moss like patches within the stone intermingled with turquoise coloured, irregular spot-like inclusions caused by the presence of Gilalite. To make matters worse it is often very cloudy and banded. However, it is very rare (some would say that this is a blessing).

For those that love the gem, they will point out to you that it has been mined in the same region in Brazil where Paraiba Tourmaline was first discovered and they will therefore argue that it should be known as Paraiba Quartz. Others that hate it will tell you how sorry they feel for the miners in the region who have searched for years for another Paraiba-like discovery only to unearth Medusa Quartz. So if it's not a pretty mineral, how is it classed as a gemstone I hear you ask. Well, like the Marmite advert says "you either love it or hate it".

First discovered in August 2004, under a loupe you can often find inclusions that look similar to shape to a certain jellyfish known as the "Medusas Rondeau".

I confess to having several pieces in my personal collection, more for intrigue than for its appearance and as we speak we have several pieces available in stock at GemCollector.com. At present we don't intend to set it in our beautiful jewellery designs, but as always will wait to see what feedback we get from customers.

MELÉE

This is a word used in the jewellery trade primarily to describe small accent Diamonds. In India, where the majority of the world's accent Diamonds are now cut, the term is used to describe Diamonds weighing from 0.001ct (1/1000th of a carat) to 0.18ct (just under a 1/5th of a carat).

The majority of all cut Diamonds on the planet are Melée and their route from mine to jewellery is sometimes even more convoluted than that of coloured gemstones. After clearing customs where origin and ethical compliance is checked, the gems are sent to the Lapadarist.

Once faceted, these small diamonds are normally sold in India as small parcels: these can change hand three or four times a day and as they are exchanged, parcels are often merged to form larger parcels. Melée traders sometimes add as little as a quarter of one percent to the price of the parcel, which may seem like an unbelievably small profit margin, but a good trader will do several trades per day.

Once the Diamonds arrive at a jeweller, the first job is to sort them by size. The majority will have been faceted as round cut gemstones and will normally be one of the sizes in the chart on the adjacent page.

The initial sorting is done with a sieve and once all the similar-sized stones are together, the work of the sorter is to then put them into smaller batches of similar colour and clarity. This is a real art and one that you need to specialise in; even those who are professionally trained in sorting larger diamonds and coloured gemstones will struggle to do this task. I once spent four hours in a Diamond sorting room just trying to learn the principles of the grader's work and I lost count of the number of Diamonds that shot out of my tweezers. In fact, the majority of my time was spent on hands and knees trying to search for something less than 1mm in size that was colourless!

The job of setting the Melée Diamonds is also a real art. Depending on the type of setting this can take up to 15 minutes. When you consider, for example, that a piece of jewellery such as a Lorique ring may feature over one hundred accent Diamonds, you begin to appreciate the total amount of work that has gone into the sorting and setting of the Diamonds. And what's more, we haven't yet considered the first step of turning the rough piece of Diamond into a sparkling faceted gem! Even at 1mm in size, these gems are still cut and faceted by hand and will often have 17 facets applied.

Whilst it is true that smaller Diamonds are less expensive than bigger Diamonds, the cost of faceting, sorting and setting smaller pieces can often add up to a price similar to or even greater than that of a single large Diamond of the equivalent combined weight.

Carat	Diameter(mm)
0.005ct	= 1.00 mm - 1.15 mm
0.0075ct	= 1.16 mm - 1.23 mm
0.01ct	= 1.24 mm - 1.40 mm
0.02ct	= 1.56 mm - 1.80 mm
0.025ct	= 1.81 mm - 1.88 mm
0.03ct	= 1.89 mm - 2.10 mm
0.04ct	= 2.10 mm - 2.33 mm
0.05ct	= 2.24 mm - 2.43 mm
0.06ct	= 2.44 mm - 2.50 mm
0.07ct	= 2.51 mm - 2.73 mm
0.08ct	= 2.74 mm - 2.80 mm
0.10ct	= 2.81 mm - 3.10 mm
0.12ct	= 3.11 mm - 3.23 mm
0.15ct	= 3.23 mm - 3.54 mm
0.18ct	= 3.55 mm - 3.83 mm

MERELANI MINT GARNET

Colour	Mint green
Family	Garnet
Hardness	6.5 – 7.0
Specific Gravity	3.4 – 3.7
Refractive Index	1.73 – 1.75
Crystal Group	Isometric
Optical Properties	Various
Common Treatments	Cannot be heat treated
Care	No special care needed
Cleaning Advice	Ultrasonic or warm soapy water
Chemical Composition	Various

Now if you were getting confused remembering the difference between Mali, Malaia and Malaya Garnet, we thought we would add just one more: introducing the very rare and highly sought after Merelani Mint Garnet. The gem is a Grossular Garnet and is very similar to the famous Tsavorite Garnet, but a far lighter shade of green.

It received its name from the area where it was discovered in Tanzania (well, apart from the "Mint" part which, for once, simply describes its colour). The gem is mined in the exact same location as Tanzanite and, although its colour differs, it is equally as beautiful with gorgeous lustre and incredible brilliance; in terms of availability, it is infinitely rarer than its popular housemate Tanzanite! The gem is also known as Mint Garnet or Mint Grossular Garnet.

MEXICO

Mexico is the largest Spanish speaking country in the world, and is located at the southern tip of the North American continent. It is a country known for its deserts, volcanoes, snow-capped mountains, ancient ruins, colonial towns, deserted beaches and glitzy holiday resorts. Its array of gemstones is equally diverse: Agate; Amethyst; Amber; Chalcedony; Danburite; Demantoid Garnet; Haematite; Jasper; Obsidian; Opal; and Rhodonite.

Mexico's flagship gem is Fire Opal, mined in Queretaro which is located about 120 miles north-west of Mexico City. Unfortunately, over the last few years, as the miners search deeper and deeper into the Earth's crust, the average carat weight of each piece mined has radically decreased.

Amber is mined in the state of Chiapas and it is world renowned for its incredible transparency and vivid colours which are almost red. Amethyst and Demantoid Garnet are found in

Two Jacque Christie vibrant Mexican Opal designs.

the state of Guerrero. Unfortunately, many mines were flooded several years ago, and since then mining has been sporadic.

MIKIMOTO (KOKICHI)

Born in 1858 in Toba City, Japan, Mikimoto was the eldest son of a family who ran a noodle restaurant. When he was 29 he began raising oysters and by 1895 he was awarded a patent for his process of culturing Pearls.

For 30 years he worked day and night developing new techniques for culturing Pearls and was admired in the jewellery industry for his relentless efforts to get his technique widely recognised and accepted.

On the 11th of July 1893, Mikimoto and his wife reportedly cultivated five Akoya Pearls; the first ever cultivated Pearls on the planet. "I would like to adorn the necks of all the women of the world with Pearls," said Mikimoto. However, it took him a further twelve years to perfect the technique and to create exquisite, spherical Pearls.

The winner of numerous awards and accolades, Mikimoto died in 1954 at the age of 96; in his honour, there is a huge statue erected on Pearl Island in Japan.

Freshwater cultured Pearls were first developed by Mikimoto.

MILANO CHARMS

If you're the kind of person who likes to stamp their own style on everything, then Milano Charms are created just for you! With Milano Charms, you can change the look of your jewellery, mobile phone, accessories and more by simply clipping on one of our sensational charms.

Crafted in Sterling Silver with Italian-made clasps, each charm is designed to capture the important moments in life. Collections include; Diamond Set Alphabet, Nautical Flags, Technology and Gadgets, Food and Beverages, Fashion Accessories, Famous Landmarks,

Genuine Gemstones, Special Occasions and Handbags and Shoes.

No expense has been spared in creating Milano Charms and they are designed to last many generations. Take the Classic Martini Charm which has a genuine Peridot as its olive, or the Hot Dog Charm studded with Ruby along its line of red sauce, or the Retro Controller with its Garnet fire button, or the Computer Mouse with the Emerald wheel, or the enamelled Perfume Bottle Charm, which actually unscrews to enable a daily amount of perfume to be stored or the Tanzanite studded Locket Charm. All Milano Charms have been designed for those who wish to assemble the definitive charm collection.

MILLENNIUM CUT

Lapidarist Rogerio Graca developed the cut in the late 1990's to celebrate the Millennium. As its name might suggest it has 1,000 facets! The original cut had 376 facets above the girdle and 624 below and was applied to a Garnet. On choosing the gemstone Rogerio says,"Considering the number of facets and the amount of work involved, I had to choose a reasonably valuable gem, available in a large size, to make it worthwhile. My first choice was the Rhodolite garnet, the queen of the Garnets. The reason behind my decision lay not only on its inherent value and availability, but also its beautiful raspberry colour, toughness and affordability. Apart from all these qualities, Garnet is the January birthstone, the first stone of the millennium calendar and also one of the oldest gemstones to be cut and used in jewellery."

It is difficult to comprehend the amount of work needed to make this cut. The initial shaping, the finer cutting and then the various stages of polishing means that some 5,000 to 10,000 minute yet highly accurate separate actions are required.

Many people confuse the Millennium Cut with the Concave Cut, however the latter rarely has 1,000 facets and its uniqueness comes in the fact that the facets are not flat but concave.

MILANO
C H A R M S

MINERALS

Most gems are minerals, with noticeable exceptions being Pearls, Jet and Amber, which are all organically created.

Minerals are a naturally occurring solid substance; they are formed through geological events and each mineral has a characteristic chemical composition, specific physical properties and a well-defined atomic structure.
They are created from a variety of different natural events; some minerals crystallise from molten magma or lava flowing from volcanoes, while others form in gases or crystallise in hydrous solutions. Some minerals re-crystallise under immense pressure and high temperatures as they are pushed lower into the Earth's crust through geological movements.

Minerals can be identified, measured and assessed in a variety of ways: from their relative density to their refractive index, from their crystal structure to their type of lustre. The hardness of a mineral is measured by the Mohs scale, with talc being the softest of all minerals and recording 1 on the scale and Diamond being the hardest measuring 10.

Fascinating mineral patterns by Mother Nature.

MISNOMERS

Nothing winds me up more than reading an advert where the uneducated copywriter (surely they can't do it on purpose) describes a piece of jewellery as 'CZ Diamond' or 'Genuine Lab Created Alexandrite' or 'Real Amethyst Lead Crystal' or 'Ceylon Coloured Sapphire' or 'Glass Fresh Water Pearls' or 'Natural Glass Smokey Quartz' or 'glass gemstone' or 'decorative gold garnet' or 'shiny Amber colour resin necklace' and these are just a few I have noted down this week! Some of the biggest culprits in print are airline magazines and of course many online jewellers are a law unto themselves. Don't get me wrong, I actually love the fact that people use gemstone names as an adjective, but only as long as they make it clear that that is exactly what they are doing. It's not a new problem however, as the Natural Historian Pliny the Elder (born 23AD)

Misnomer	What it normally is!
Alexandrite Garnet	Colour Change Garnet
Almandine ruby	Garnet
Australian Jade	Chrysoprase
Australian Ruby	Garnet
Brazilian Sapphire	Tourmaline
Chatham emerald	Synthetic green material
CZ Diamond	Manmade cheap imitator
Electric Emerald	Green Glass
Esmeralda Emerald	Green Tourmaline
Evening Emerald	Peridot
Fools Gold (at least it's honest!)	Pyrite
German silver	Almost any metal other than silver!
Indian Jade	Aventurine
Japanese Diamond	Danburite
Japanese Opal	Plastic

Misnomer	What it normally is!
Japanese Opal	Plastic
Kandy Spinel	Garnet
Korean Jade	Dyed Serpentine
Lannyte Emerald	Doublet
Mascot Emerald	Doublet
Matara Diamond	Zircon
Mataura Diamond	Zircon
New Jade	Dyed Serpentine
Nevada Black Diamond	Obsidian
Opal Triplet	Thin opal, with glass or Quartz either side
Oriental Emerald	Green Sapphire
Roman pearls	Glass
Siberian Ruby	Spinel
Soude Emerald	Doublet
Swiss Jade	Green Jasper
Water sapphire	Iolite

Hardness	Substance or Mineral
1	Talc
2	Gypsum
2.5 to 3	Pure Gold, Silver, Fingernail
3	Calcite, Copper penny
4	Fluorite
4 to 4.5	Platinum
4 to 5	Iron
5	Apatite
6	Orthoclase
6	Titanium
6.5	Iron pyrite
6 to 7	Glass
7	Quartz
7 to 7.5	Garnet
7 to 8	Hardened steel
8	Topaz
9	Corundum
10	Diamond

commented whilst writing about gemstones, 'there is no more lucrative fraud against society' Here are a couple of tips to avoid being misled by ignorant copywriters or those trying to deceive:

Tip 1
If a piece of jewellery is described as 'Platinum Plated', 'Gold Plated' or 'Rhodium Plated' and does not describe what has been plated, assume that underneath the layer of precious metal (which is probably less than a quarter of a micron thick) is just a regular base metal.

Tip 2
Even if a genuine gemstone name is being used to describe the look of a stone or its colour, if anywhere in the same sentence you find any of the following words: 'crystal', 'lab', 'lab created', 'glass', 'synthetic', 'resin' or even 'coloured', then the article is probably not a real gem.

On the opposite page and to the left are some commonly used phrases found around the globe that could easily be misunderstood.

MOHS SCALE

Created by the German mineralogist Friedrich Mohs in 1832, the Mohs scale is used to measure the hardness of minerals. Mohs based his scale on ten minerals that were available to him at the time. The hardest naturally occurring mineral Diamond is at the top of the scale and therefore is rated 10.

Today, it is possible to measure the scratch hardness of minerals more accurately by using an instrument invented in 1896 called a Sclerometer. However, the Mohs scale is still widely adopted around the globe as an accurate measurement, and is therefore still used to measure the hardness of gemstone.

Whilst many scales and measurements in the world can be quite complex, the Mohs scale is incredibly simple. Imagine you have just discovered a new mineral: if it scratches Apatite (5 on the scale) but does not scratch Orthoclase

(6 on the scale), your new discovery registers a hardness of 5.5 on the Mohs scale.

However, due to the way the scale works, it simply ranks gems in order of their hardness. What it does not do is tell you the difference in hardness, i.e. how much harder a gem that records 8 is compared to one which only reaches 6. For example, Diamonds are presently the hardest known mineral (therefore being 10 on the scale), and are approximately four times harder than Sapphire which registers 9 on the Mohs scale and 30 times harder than Apatite at number 5.

In the chart we have added a few non-gems to help you draw a comparison.

Sapphire is very durable, registering 9 on the mohs scale.

MOISSANITE

Elsewhere in this book we discuss Moissanite as a man-made gemstone. In actual fact the matter is a little more complicated than that.

Moissanite was first created in a laboratory in 1893 by the inventor Eugene Acheson. At the time of patenting his creation he named it Carborundum. 22 years later, French chemist Dr Ferdinand Moissan discovered the exact same silicon carbide composition while studying fragments of meteoric iron at the Diablo Canyon in Arizona; this new discovery was later named Moissanite in his honour. Because the natural pieces are so small it is classed as an element and to-date no piece has been found large enough to facet.

Moissanite first appeared in jewellery in the 1990's and was the creation of a company called C3 Inc of America. They have created a proprietary process for creating this man-made material, which bears a striking resemblance to a Diamond. So much so that when it first appeared, many in the jewellery trade predicted it would dramatically affect the sales of Diamonds and many experts initially struggled to correctly identify the difference between the two.

So, although all Moissanite on the market set in

jewellery is man-made, it shares the same elements as a piece of nature. Essentially, it is the same as a lab-created coloured gemstone. Although it is undeniably beautiful, when purchasing remember that as it is man-made in a laboratory, company owners can produce as much as they want, therefore it cannot be rare. And if it is not rare, then it is not really a gemstone at all.

MOULDS

There are several different ways of crafting jewellery and each one has its own merits. Firstly, handmade jewellery, such as designs made by Tookalon, are all stunningly individual however, as they are entirely made by hand and not produced in moulds or casts, the finish of the Silver work can sometimes appear slightly inconsistent. For those who love the romance of handmade pieces, these minute anomalies are more of a signature of the craftsperson than an unwanted defect. It is also important to note that every piece will be slightly different to the next.

For more precise jewellery or when larger quantities of the same piece are required, most jewellers will create a master model/master mould from the original drawing and then from this master exact replicas can be made.

The master mould can be made in one of two ways: firstly, modern CAD packages can be used to create a 3D drawing of the design and when completed these can be printed using a very special printer which actually prints a physical 3D version of the mould. Although these printers can cost over one hundred thousand dollars they have revolutionised the master model process and without them, my companies for example would find it impossible to make so many new designs each day. The more traditional way of creating the master model/master mould is to actually craft the original piece by hand out of wax or silver. Once it is finished a rubber mould can be made, from which the replicas are produced.

No moulds are necessary when making handmade jewellery for Tookalon.

John Bennett helping the CAD team interpret Sarah Bennett's drawings .

Keeping you in the loupe...

Colour	Dark bottle green
Family	Does not belong to a family, they are from out of space!
Hardness	5.5 – 6.5
Specific Gravity	2.3 – 2.4
Refractive Index	1.47 – 1.51
Crystal Group	Amorphous
Optical Properties	Vitreous lustre
Common Treatments	Not normally treated
Care	No special care required
Cleaning Advice	Ultrasonic or warm soapy water
Chemical Composition	A complex Silica rich composition

MOLDAVITE

A gemstone from out of space!

Moldavite is a rare, dark green translucent gem that was formed when a large rock from outer space (meteorite) struck Earth's surface in the Moldau River valley (hence its name) in the Czech Republic around fourteen million years ago.

It is believed that this huge meteorite did not burn up in space and its hot mass hit the Earth at a speed in excess of 13 miles a second – that's over 45,000 mph!!

First discovered in 1786, this gem has yet to be found in any other location in the world. Part of the mystique and appeal of this gemstone is that some of its components cannot be found anywhere else in the world.

Tests carried out by NASA have found that the pressure of some small bubbles within the gem is the equivalent to the pressure at approximately 13 to 15 miles above the surface of the Earth.

In 1963, Queen Elizabeth II was presented with a Tiara in which the central gem was a natural, un-faceted Moldavite surrounded by Diamonds and Pearls; this was presented to her by the Swiss Government in order to celebrate her 10th year on the throne.

Crystal Healers believe that Moldavite, with its extra terrestrial properties, brings love to all who wear it. The gem is also said to bring clarity and sharpness, and aids vision and telepathic communication.

The gem is said to work on the heart chakra and helps a person to express true love, as well as putting them on the correct path in life.

The gem is also known as Tektite, although this gem has a slightly different composition, and can be found in Australia (where it is known as Australites), Austria, Ivory Coast, Malaysia (known as Malaysianites), Philippines (known as Philippinites), Thailand and the USA.

Moldavite straight from outer space!

MOOKITE

A beautiful member of the Jasper family, Mookite is truly breathtaking. It has many different colours ranging from pale sweetheart pinks to vibrant sunset yellows, often in banded formations across the gemstone. The patterns on Mookite are sometimes described as similar to contemporary oil paintings, and have a warm, earthy flood of colours.

The look of Mookite is unique and is only found in one location in the world: Mooka Creek in Western Australia. Mookite, or Mookaite Jasper as it is sometimes referred to, is actually a ferrous sedimentary rock and is made up of microscopic creatures that have been fossilised and cemented into rock by silica.

Mookite is said to be a motivator and imparts the desire to try new experiences. It is also said to boost the immune system and assists in healing broken hearts.

Colour	Various colours
Family	Jasper, Chalcedony Quartz
Hardness	7.1 – 7.9
Specific Gravity	2.59 – 2.61
Refractive Index	1.53 – 1.55
Crystal Group	Conchoidal
Optical Properties	Beautiful colour bands

Mookite bracelet by Jessica Lili.

MOONSTONE

Moonstones come in a variety of colours, ranging from colourless to white, grey, brown, yellow, orange, green, or even pink. Clarity ranges from transparent to translucent and the traditional place of origin is Sri Lanka, where the Moonstones tend to be almost transparent with a bluish flicker.

This gem owes its name to its mysterious shimmer that bears resemblance in colour to the moon. This silvery to bluish iridescence is caused by the intergrowth of two different types of Feldspar which have different refractive indexes. This always looks different when the stone is moved, and is known in the trade as 'adularescence'.

Surrounded by mystery and magic, this gemstone has featured in different cultures for thousands of years. In India it is regarded as a magical and holy gemstone and is often used as a 'dream stone' bringing the wearer beautiful visions at night. In Arabian cultures Moonstone was oftenworn on female garments as they were

Colour	Colourless to light blue
Family	Feldspar
Hardness	6 – 6.5
Specific Gravity	2.56 – 2.62
Refractive Index	1.518- 1.526
Crystal Group	Monoclinic
Optical Properties	Demonstrates adularescence
Common Treatments	Not normally treated
Cleaning Advice	Ultrasonic or warm soapy water
Chemical Composition	$K(Al,Si)_4O_8$

Colour	Light pink, brownish pink
Family	Beryl
Hardness	7.5 – 8
Specific Gravity	2.71 – 2.9
Refractive Index	1.585 – 1.594
Crystal Group	Conchoidal
Optical Properties	Vitreous lustre
Common Treatments	Often heated
Care	No special care required
Cleaning Advice	Warm soapy water
Chemical Composition	$Be_3Al_2(SiO_3)_6$

viewed as a sign of fertility.

Moonstone was also extremely popular in Roman times, as they thought the gemstone was formed out of moonlight. Romans were setting the gemstone in their jewellery as early as 100AD, and in more recent times the gem was popular in the Art Nouveau period.

Many gemstone collectors find the most pleasing Moonstones have a blue sheen and a colourless body. Due to there being more demand than supply, today good quality blue Moonstones are becoming more and more of a rarity and have therefore risen sharply in price.

The gem is usually set in rings, pendants and earrings, with lesser-graded Moonstone used in beaded necklaces. Its healing ability is said to align your vertebrae, be a good digestive aid and also soothes and balances emotions. Moonstone's mystical powers are said to protect women and babies. It's also associated with the oceans and planting cycles. The gemstone is said to balance yin and yang as well as bringing good fortune to the wearer. Legend says that Moonstone is a highly prized gift for lovers as it arouses tender passion.

Along with Alexandrite and Pearls, Moonstone is one of the birthstones for June.

MORGANITE

Morganite was first discovered alongside other gems, including Tourmaline and Aquamarine, in Pala, California in the early 20th century. News spread quickly about this new and exciting discovery and it became of special interest to George Frederick Kunz, a well-known and respected gemmologist and gem collector from New York. In 1911, Kunz later discovered the gem in Madagascar and suggested naming this pink variety of Beryl "Morganite", after his biggest customer and banker J.P. Morgan. Although this gemstone began its life millions of years ago, it has only been known and recognised in its own right since this time.
Morganite, along with Emerald and Aquamarine, is now one of the most popular gemstones from

the colourful Beryl family (the name Beryl is derived from its chemical make-up beryllium aluminium silicates). Pure Beryl is essentially colourless; however, its structure enables it to integrate foreign elements such as iron, manganese, chrome or vanadium. It all sounds a bit technical, but basically when manganese is found in Beryl, the colourless gemstone turns into the enchanting pink treasure, Morganite.

Its depth of colour determines the quality and value of Morganite. When discovered in its rough form the gem is a pale salmon colour, but when heated its pink hues become more prominent. Sometimes the gem can be confused with Kunzite, however Kunzite is more of a bluish pink, whilst Morganite is more of an orangey, brownish pink.

The rule which says 'the more transparent, the more valuable' only applies to a certain extent. It depends on personal preference; there are plenty of women who prefer a Morganite with small inclusions, as it gives the appearance of fine silk.

The attributes of this gem are said to enable the wearer to focus on the joy in life, alleviate stress and pressure and open the heart chakra, which is not surprising, as even the mere sight of a Morganite cannot fail to cheer you up!

MOSS AGATE

Imagine blue cheese set in stone, and you are picturing the visual appearance of this gem. It has an almost plant-style appearance to it, detailed with colourful speckles due to the presence of chrome or iron.

This opaque gemstone is normally tumbled or cabochon cut and as it will normally have a large carat weight, it is ideal for setting in big-look necklaces and bracelets.

Moss Agate is a member of the Chalcedony group of gems, who in turn belong to the Cryptocrystalline family of Quartz. It is rarely set in jewellery and is popular with both mineral and gem collectors alike.

Colour	Milky white with green specks
Family	Chalcedony Quartz
Hardness	6.5 – 7
Specific Gravity	2.55 – 2.64
Refractive Index	1.53 – 1.54
Crystal Group	Conchoidal

Colour	A kaleidoscope of colours
Family	An organic gemstone
Hardness	3.5 – 4.5
Specific Gravity	2.61 – 2.79
Refractive Index	1.53 – 1.60
Crystal Group	Beautiful iridescence
Optical Properties	Sometimes dyed
Common Treatments	Can be fragile if not set on a solid back
Care	No special care required
Cleaning Advice	Warm soapy water
Chemical Composition	SiO_2

Mother of Pearl and Marcasite combining to create a stunning bracelet by Jewels of Valais.

MOTHER OF PEARL

As an organic gem (meaning a gem that is not a mineral but one which has been created by a living organism), Pearls and Mother of Pearl have been sourced from our oceans for thousands of years.

Mother of Pearl is primarily sourced from the inside of shells and is associated with prosperity and good luck. Because of this it is often offered as a gift for someone who may need good fortune to come his or her way.

Records show that the beautiful iridescent lustre of Mother of Pearl has been enchanting jewellers for over 5000 years! In China, Mother of Pearl has been held in high regard for many thousands of years and decorated objects were often taken to temples as offerings. Because of this, there are numerous references to this gem in Chinese myths and legends. As they believed it helped reduce heart palpitations, dizziness and high blood pressure, in the past the Chinese have also used Mother of Pearl in medicines. It is still used today in a variety of skin creams said to help diffuse small spots and scars.

In the 1500's Mother of Pearl was at a peak in its popularity and over-sourcing meant that supplies in the Persian Gulf were almost exhausted. Consequently, sailors looked further afield for the precious natural gem, and in 1568 the Spanish explorer Alvaro de Mendana discovered the Solomon Islands, which were rich in both gold and Mother of Pearl. He named the islands after King Solomon who, legend has it, owned a secret source of mines that no one knew about; Mendana believed that he had found them within these islands.

Nowadays, Pearls and Mother of Pearl can be cultivated by humans and used for many purposes such as decoration on musical instruments, watch faces and in exotic furniture.

The correct term for Mother of Pearl is in fact Nacre, (from the Arabic word for shell

"Naqqarah") which is the same secretion from a mollusc that forms a Pearl.

The name Mother of Pearl was in fact given to the inner layer of a shell by Queen Elizabeth I. As well as forming Pearls, the nacre is deposited on the inside of the mollusc shell creating a protective coating against parasites.

Mother of Pearl is extremely resilient and tough due to its brickwork-like, layered composition and it is these layers that provide the gem with such glorious iridescence.

The colour of the nacre can be extremely varied, covering almost the whole spectrum from black to white. It is determined by several factors, the most important being: the type of shell, the location in which the shell is found, the food the mollusc eats and any trace metals in the surrounding environment.

Delicate colours of Mother of Pearl in this lovely piece by Annabella.

MOUNTING

Mounting is the component of a piece of jewellery which holds the gemstone. An analogy would be to compare it to the frame around a precious painting. More often than not, the terms mounting and setting are used interchangeably. If applied logically however, just as you mount a horse, you would mount a gem and it would sit in a setting!

A simple yet elegant four prong mounting.

MOZAMBIQUE

When you mention Mozambique in relation to gems the first thing you think of is Mozambique Garnet. Don't be confused by the name however, as not all Mozambique Garnets are mined in this country. The term tends to be used for all red Garnets that are mined in eastern Africa that are a physical combination of Almandine and Pyrope Garnets.

Mozambique is on the East Coast of South Africa: directly opposite is the gem island of Madagascar, and it shares a border with Tanzania.

Most gem mining in the region takes place

A rare 3.17ct Paraiba Tourmaline from Mozambique.

in the Mozambique Orogenic Belt (a range of mountains formed from the movement of tectonic plates). As well as Garnet, artisanal mining activities in the region uncover such gems as Amethyst, Aquamarine, Emerald, Jasper, Morganite, Quartz, Tiger's Eye and Tourmaline and - more importantly - Paraiba Tourmaline.

MOZAMBIQUE GARNET

Technically speaking, Mozambique Garnet is a mixture of Pyrope and Almandine Garnet and is used to describe Garnets that display the natural colours of those originally found in Mozambique. The colour is a warm, deep red and is similar to that of Ruby. Compared to Rhodolite Garnet, it is more of a pure red and its tone is slightly darker. Mozambique Garnet can vary from wonderfully transparent to translucent in clarity. Whilst the gem is normally more affordable than many, transparent samples, which are often on par with Ruby in terms of beauty can regularly command a premium.

Indeed, what an interesting place the gem world is! Mozambique Garnet does not have to come from Mozambique, and Paraiba Tourmaline found in Mozambique is named after the small mining area in Brazil where this new type of Tourmaline was first discovered. The reality is that gems often get their original name from where they were first discovered, then when the same gem is found in other locations around the world, as long as they meet certain criteria (in the case of Paraiba Tourmaline the gem must contain copper) it is accepted that they take on the original name. Just to add to the many complications in the gem world, however, is the case of Ceylon Sapphire: this name refers to more than just its colour and it is incorrect if a jeweller uses the name Ceylon Sapphire unless it originates from Sri Lanka.

Giving someone a piece of jewellery featuring Mozambique Garnet is believed to be the ultimate declaration of love. This gem can be found in Thailand, Tanzania and of course Mozambique.

Colour	Rich deep dark red
Family	Garnet
Hardness	6.5 – 7.5
Specific Gravity	4.1 – 4.3
Refractive Index	1.7 – 1.89
Crystal Group	Isometric
Optical Properties	Various
Common Treatments	Cannot be heat treated
Care	No special care needed
Cleaning Advice	Ultrasonic or warm soapy water
Chemical Composition	Various

MYSTIC QUARTZ

Quartz is well-known to gem fanatics and has as many colours as there are in a rainbow, but Mystic Quartz is somewhat of a newcomer to the gem world.

This fascinating gem is extremely beautiful and is also very durable; meaning it can be fashioned into any piece of jewellery and can appear in large pieces. This superb gemstone has the appearance of oil on water and shimmers with many different colours all at once. These colours are normally derived from a coating applied to the surface of colourless Quartz.

A handmade Mystic Quartz ring from Tookalon.

MYSTIC TOPAZ

Mystic Topaz is the ultimate gemstone cocktail, beautifully combining brilliance with a kaleidoscope of colours. It is also known as Rainbow Topaz, Titanium Topaz, Alaskan Topaz and even Caribbean Topaz. Although the gem features a rainbow of colours, its dominant colours are purple and green.

For all its beauty, it is important to know that the colours in Mystic Topaz are man-made by applying a coating to the outside of the gem. Although the company that created this process claim that it is a permanent treatment, over the past year I have had several customers say that it can be damaged. What I have discovered is that the coating must not be heavily scratched and must be kept away from strong chemicals, which in some circumstances can negatively effect the appearance of the coating. That said, if treated with a little more care than normal, the appearance of the gem should prove to be permanent.

As the real beauty of the gem lies in its magical colours, it is ideally suited to cuts that have a big table facet. Octagon and oval cuts bring this gem to life and if the pavilion is concave cut, the effect becomes even more mesmerising. Topaz is surrounded in a wealth of folklore and legends: many of these are detailed under Topaz later in this book.

Colour	Flashes of green, purple, pink, blue
Family	Topaz
Hardness	8
Specific Gravity	3.5 – 3.6
Refractive Index	1.6 – 1.63
Crystal Group	Orthorhombic
Optical Properties	Strong pleochroism
Common Treatments	Coated
Care	Careful not to scratch
Cleaning Advice	Warm soapy water
Chemical Composition	$Al_2SiO_4(F, OH)_4$

A Pearl and Tourmaline bracelet by Annabella.

NACRE

When a mollusc or an oyster experiences an intrusion from a foreign body such as a piece of shell or a grain of sand, it covers itself in a layer of nacre. As more and more layers are added, a Pearl begins to form. Because the nacre is built up in layers, as light hits the surface of a Pearl, wonderful flashes of a multitude of colours can be seen. This iridescence occurs as the different wavelengths within light strike the layers at differing angles (see also iridescence).

The inner part of a shell, the Mother of Pearl, is also a form of nacre. The better the quality of the nacre, the better its iridescence (also referred to as pearlescence). In addition to Oysters, many other molluscs (a shell fish that has a hinge) have the ability to create nacre and therefore are able to produce Pearls.

NAMIBIA

Located on the West Coast of Africa and with its southern border neighbouring South Africa, Namibia is one of the world's largest providers of Diamonds. But while these mines are very mechanical, many of its coloured gemstone mines are run on an artisanal basis. One noticeable exception is the Demantoid Garnet mine in the Erongo region, which is reportedly discovering between 4000 to 5000 carats per month.

One thing to bear in mind with artisanal gem mining is that mines will open and close as these entrepreneurial explorers chase new finds in different regions. The mines of Neu Schwaben, in the Karibib area of Namibia, yielded a large quantity of blue and green Tourmaline in the 1950's, virtually closed throughout the 90's and today have only a handful of miners working through surface alluvial deposits, hoping that the best finds are yet to come.

In the north of the country, a small quantity of Spessartite Garnet with a vivid orange colour has been found near the Kunene River and is being mined by a handful of people. Namibia annually also uncovers a small quantity of Aquamarine, Helidor and Tiger's Eye.

A Namibian Green Tourmaline.

A Namibian Aquamarine ring from Jacque Christie.

NIGERIA

In 2001, Nigerian miners in the southern state of Oyo discovered something even better than gold: Paraiba Tourmaline! This stunning gemstone is so named as it was first discovered in Paraiba, Brazil. Due to the presence of copper, it displays incredible neon green to swimming pool blue colours. As well as finding this rarest of gems, the region of Oyo also yields stunning Rubellite and amazing Spessartite Garnet.

In the north of Nigeria there are many small mines that unearth Sapphire and Zircon. The Kaduna mines in this region also yield small qualities of Aquamarine, Morganite and the

A 3.4ct Goshenite from Nigeria.

colourless Goshenite.

The historic region of Olode, in the west of Nigeria, produces Aquamarine with stunning clarity, vibrant Amethyst, and a range of Pink, Blue and Green Tourmalines.

Running through the centre of Nigeria is the Jos Plateau, which covers some 4800 square miles at an average altitude of one mile above sea level. This region is home to many valuable gemstones and has been mined by local artisanal miners for many years. Their discoveries include some very large and deep blue Aquamarines, large Bi-Coloured Tourmalines, Beryls, colourless Topaz and Emeralds.

Nasarawa state (which was first populated only in 1838) is also found in the central region of Nigeria, and currently has mining operations that are uncovering such gems as Sapphire, Tourmaline, Amethyst, Lemon Quartz, Garnet, Topaz and Zircon.

The Lemon Quartz in this Tookalon necklace is from Nigeria

ANNABELLA

Colour	Normally black to dark green
Family	Obsidian
Hardness	5.5 - 7
Specific Gravity	2.33 - 2.6
Refractive Index	1.48 - 1.53
Crystal Group	Amorphous
Optical Properties	Vitreous lustre
Cleaning Instructions	Warm soapy water

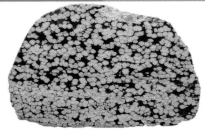

Snowflake Obsidian.

OBSIDIAN

Obsidian (also known as Apache Tears), is a natural amorphous glass. It is in fact the best known glassy rock created from lava which cooled too quickly to crystallise. It is believed to have been first discovered in Ethiopia and was named after the Roman solider who first brought it to Europe.

Tiny air bubbles that have been formed in the layers just before the molten rock is cooled create a golden, and sometimes rainbow-like, vitreous lustre. Snowflake Obsidian, which has been so named due to the white patches (internal bubbles) of potassium Feldspar, has the appearance of snowflakes falling from a black sky. Today, it is seen as one of the main gemstones believed to enhance the sharpness of the brain and vision.

My own personal assistant Barry Wiggins was once told to carry a Snowflake Obsidian in his pocket at all times in order to cure his severe back pains. He was very sceptical about the advice, but several months later in desperation he decided to give it a go. To this day, his Snowflake Obsidian has travelled everywhere with him and his back problems are becoming a distant memory.

In ancient Mexico, Mexicans used the gemstone to make figurines of their god Trecalipoca. Around the same period, it was also used in South America to make mirrors.

Obsidian is usually black, dark green or brown, but can also be found transparent. It is normally mined in the USA, Japan, Mexico, New Zealand and Russia.

An Obsidian tumbled bracelet.

Octagon Cut

An octagon cut and an emerald cut can sometimes be very difficult to tell apart. When viewed from the top, if the octagon cut has slightly truncated corners, it is actually indistinguishable from an emerald cut. The difference only becomes apparent when you look at the side profile and see that the parallel facets are not of an equal distance. Just like the emerald cut, the octagon cut has facets running parallel to its girdle both above and below.

Its culet does not arrive at a single point as in a round brilliant cut; instead its facets on the pavilion join along a ridge, similar to the top of a roof on a house.

Recently, modern-looking octagon cuts with equal length sides (when viewed from the top) have become more fashionable. Although rarely used for Diamonds, they are becoming increasingly popular for coloured gemstones such as Topaz, Amethyst, Citrine and Smokey Quartz.

With a large table facet, the cut is ideal for showing off gems that have great colour and clarity as the eye tends to be drawn into the gem. There is no precise standard for the cut, but nearly all of the gems we have sold feature 41, 49 or 57 facets.

These two pieces have both been octagon cut.

Colour	Normally black, brown, green
Family	Chalcedony Quartz
Hardness	6.5
Specific Gravity	2.59 – 2.61
Refractive Index	1.531 - 1.539
Crystal Group	Trigonal
Optical Properties	Vitreous to waxy lustre
Common Treatments	Dyed
Cleaning Advice	Warm soapy water

ONYX

A member of the Agate group of Chalcedony's, which in turn is a sub species/family of Quartz, Onyx is viewed by many as a jet black, highly fashionable gemstone.

Onyx, meaning 'veined gem', in its natual state Onyx differs from other Agates in that its lines of colour banding (normally black and white) are straighter. When Onyx is pure black it is referred to as "Black Onyx" and owes its distinctive colour to an ancient dyeing process.

In its natural form, this gemstone is available in a variety of colours: white and red bands (Carnelian Onyx), and white and brown bands (Sardonyx).

Roman soldiers wore Sardonyx as talismans, believing that it made the wearer as brave as the heroes they had engraved onto the gem. Onyx is said to eliminate negative thinking and sharpen the wits, instinct, intuition and helps to change one's habits.

Because of its different colour bands, the gem is ideal for making cameos, where the lighter colour tends to be carved, using the darker colour as the background. It is a well-known member of the Chalcedony group of gems, who in turn belong to the Cryptocrystalline family of Quartz. Some also refer to the gem as "Black Magic".

Two Black Onyx designs by Jessica Lili.

Over the past decade the world's leading jewellery designers, such as Cartier, Chopard and Gucci, have all incorporated Onyx into many of their jewellery and watch designs. Sarah Bennett also uses the gemstone to great effect in many of her bold gemstone designs. Sarah believes that the gem's true jet blackness provides it with one of the best eye catching lustres in the gem world. I have to agree (well of course I do because she is my wife), that because Onyx is 100% opaque, it does have one of the best lustres in the gem world, a lustre that in my opinion is only bettered by Swiss Marcasite.

OPAL

Opals are beautiful gems, with the finest specimens containing every colour of the rainbow. The name means 'precious stone', and is thought to have come from the Latin "Opalus" and the Greek "Opallios".

Their unique internal colours are one of the most fascinating visual effects created by nature and is correctly referred to as "play of colour". Opals are doubly attractive as they often also have a beautiful iridescence (known as 'opalescence').

Opals were created from hydrated silicon dioxide, and were formed when water-based solutions containing silica, deposited a gel-like substance in gaps and crevices in rocks. Because of this they often form around areas where there are hot springs or geysers. This process is fairly common and often the resulting stone is a lacklustre 'common Opal' which is 'amorphous', meaning that the atoms are arranged randomly within the stone and there is no crystal structure. Common Opals also come in a variety of different base colours, however these often have little or no play of colour and are therefore considered to have very little value.

Gem-quality Opals do, however, have a crystal structure. They are loved for their kaleidoscope of colours and internal flashes of almost neon coloured lights. There are several varieties of gem-quality Opals and the names used for them by the gemstone industry can be quite confusing to many people. When you hear White Opal, Grey Opal or Black Opal, the name is referring to the background colour of the Opal. See it as a canvas for a painting on which beautiful colours are to be thrown in a random inspiration of modern art.

Opals have been considered both good luck and bad luck throughout history. They were as precious as Diamonds to the ancient Greeks and used in jewellery by the Romans, whereas in Russia the stone was considered by the Tsars to symbolise the evil eye. When Europeans first went to the New World they found the Aztecs

Colour	Milky white, red, brown, blue, dark grey
Family	Opal
Hardness	5.5 – 6.5
Specific Gravity	1.8 – 2.3
Refractive Index	1.39 – 1.46
Crystal Group	Amorphous
Optical Properties	Displays opalescence
Common Treatments	Occasionally layered, see doublet
Care	Wear often and don't be afraid to get them wet
Cleaning Advice	Warm soapy water
Chemical Composition	$SiO_2.nH_2O$

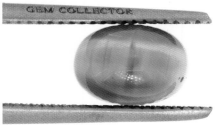

Rare Cat's Eye Opal.

of South America mining the gem, and due to its rareness and beauty they took many back to Europe to be presented to the royal courts.

Even Opals set in jewellery still contain an element of water and this can vary between 3% and 20%. Because of this, Opals are considered to be a fairly soft precious stone, measuring between 5.5 and 6.5 of the Mohs scale.

Common Opals can be found all over the world, whereas gem-quality Opals are mostly mined in Australia; in fact, some reports claim that 97% of the world's gem-quality Opals are sourced from here. Other areas are Mexico, South Africa, Brazil, Honduras, United States, Czech Republic, Guatemala and Romania.

Not all Opals are opaque and there are other body colours available too. Take a look at Fire Opal which, due to its incredible popularity, we have given its own section in this book.

Recently I managed to find a small parcel of Yellow Opal from Tanzania. These gems are totally stunning. Whilst they don't have the transparency of the finest Fire Opals, they do have a body colour which is a beautiful pastel yellow. I have so far only discovered a small amount of this gemstone (less than 100ct), but I have just dispatched one of my buyers to Tanzania to try and find more. Keep a look out on both the Coloured Rocks website and GemCollector.com for more information.

One of the best discoveries recently has been Pink Opals from Peru. Gem hunters the world over are always looking for naturally coloured pink gemstones, as it is one of the most desirable of colours and provides a real feminine touch to jewellery. The Pink Opal which I have recently sourced from South America is stunning. We have had the pieces cabochon cut in our Jaipur cutting house and not only is the colour incredibly attractive, it has a wonderful surface lustre too.

In May of 2009, I secured a parcel of gemstones from a trader who lives in Mali in North Africa. He normally supplies us with Garnet, but had

unearthed an opaque green gem and wondered if we were interested. At first we thought it might be Jade, but as this was so uncharacteristic for the region we sent the samples off to the laboratory to have it checked out. When the results came back, we were amazed that it turned out to be a green Opal! Therefore we decided to call it Mali Opal after its origin. So far we have only secured a small amount of the gem and have had it faceted into both Ovals and Cabochons. Keep your eyes on GemCollector.com and Coloured Rocks to see if we are able to find more!

Opalescence

Similar to iridescence, opalescence is an effect seen in some gemstones, primarily Opals (hence its name) which causes the gem to exhibit a shimmer of different colours when viewed from different angles. Opalescence is caused by the reflection of short wavelength light. It usually occurs in the blue spectrum, and due to this reflection of light a milky blue, pearly appearance occurs.

Opalescence should not be confused with play of colour. The latter is due to the structural pattern of Opals: because the light doesn't have to bend through gaps within the gem's structure, no diffraction takes place.

Australian Opal displaying Opalescence

Opaque

The opposite of transparent, an opaque gem is not able to transmit light, therefore you cannot see through it.

Most opaque gems are cabochon cut. A halfway house between opaque and transparent is translucent. The best way to explain the difference is by comparing transparent gems to glass, translucent ones to stained glass and opaque gems to a wall. If you were to put a large gemstone in front of this text and could still read it, then the gem would be transparent. However, if you could recognise that there was text on the page but couldn't read it, then the gem would be translucent.

Opaque Green Onyx in a handmade ring by Tookalon.

ORGANIC GEMSTONES

Most gems are formed from minerals, however, a handful of gems such as Amber, Jet, Coral and Pearls are derived from animals or plant life.

Each of these is formed from different organic matter: Amber is formed from fossilised tree resin; Coral is formed from the skeletal remains of sea-life; Jet is formed from the remains of wood; Mother of Pearl is derived from shells; and Pearls are formed inside molluscs. For more details, please see their individual entries.

Coral is a hugely popular organic material.

ORIENT

While the term pearlescence is used to described the iridescence in a Pearl, "Orient" is used to describe the depth of lustre, which is created by layers of nacre. It is worth noting that the lustre in a Pearl is more about deflected light (bending of light), than reflected light.

ORIGIN

It is impossible for any gem retailer to 100% guarantee the origin of all the gems that they sell. Some gems, such as Ruby, will differ slightly in colour based on their country of origin: Burmese Rubies tend to be purplish red in colour, while Thai stones tend to be brownish red. This, however, is not always the case.

In certain areas such as Tanzania and Madagascar, it is still often possible to buy direct from the mine owners, but in other parts of the world it is impossible to avoid agents or representatives. As a jeweller's business grows, and the number of gems they require of an identical quality, colour and clarity also increases, it becomes extremely difficult to obtain the required quantities without the help of consolidators.

As it is impossible for gem specialists to identify the origin of all gems from visually

We often test the rough material to confirm the origin.

and technically examining each gemstone, some origins are stated based on the integrity of the gem supplier. However, even with the best due-diligence processes, it is still not possible to 100% guarantee the origin of all gemstones. Therefore origin is, and will always remain in some circumstances, a "best guess".

The location of certain gemstones around the globe has helped scientists and geologists gain a better understanding of how Earth looked billions of years ago. For example, Paraiba Tourmaline has been discovered in both Africa and South America. This has provided additional confirmation of how these two continents were once joined together.

When we buy direct from the mine we can guarantee origin.

ORTHOCLASE

Although Orthoclase is one of the more common minerals found on Earth, gem-quality material is incredibly rare. A transparent to translucent member of the Feldspar family, Orthoclase is a stunning gemstone that is available in several colours. Because the gem has fairly unique planes of fracture which are at right angles to one another, its name is derived from the Greek word for "straight fracture".

Although often found colourless, Orthoclase can also be discovered in a wonderful light green colour which to the naked eye can make it first appear similar to a Green Amethyst. Yellow coloured ortholase similar to Lemon Quartz has been mined in Burma and Madagascar.

Labradorite, with its beautiful labradoresence, is the greyish form of Orthoclase and Oligoclase is a yellow to orange member of the family. If you are struggling to keep up with this, it's a bit like the Beryl family, where the family name "Beryl" is used as a name in its own right for "Yellow Beryl", yet Aquamarine, Emerald and Morganite all have their own names, even though they are all Beryls. Moonstone is sometimes incorrectly labelled as an Orthoclase, however strictly speaking it is formed by a crossbreed of Orthoclase and Albite, albeit (sorry about the pun) the majority is made up of the former.

Colour	Colourless, Yellow, Pink, Orange to Brown.
Family	Feldspar
Hardness	6 - 6.5
Specific Gravity	2.55 - 2.58
Refractive Index	1.51 - 1.54
Crystal Group	Monoclinic
Optical Properties	Translucent - Opaque
Common Treatments	Not normally treated
Cleaning Advice	Warm soapy water
Chemical Composition	K(al,Si)3O8

OVAL CUT

An oval shaped gemstone, or "Oval Cut" as it is normally referred to, can display a brilliance that is similar to that of a round brilliant cut. The standard number of facets on an oval cut gemstone is 56; however, they can often have a varying number of facets on the pavilion.

The modern oval cut was invented by Lazare Kaplan in 1957, whose famous Diamond cutting company started trading in 1919. Incidentally, Lazare Kaplan was a cousin of Marcel Tolkowsky. However, unlike the round brilliant cut - where Tolkowsky set specific measurements for the angles of each facet - the oval cut is left to the discretion and experience of the Lapidarist.

As the table facet is bigger in an oval cut, it is often used to show off gems with good clarity and colour; whereas round brilliant cuts can often hide flaws, the oval cut bares all.

Oval gems are very popular as their length can accentuate long, slender fingers and a well proportion oval cut will have a ratio of approximately 1.5 times the length to the width.

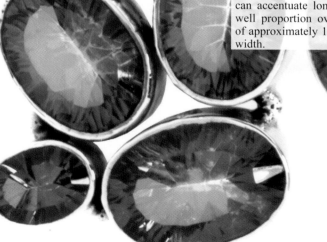

Oval cut Mystic Blue Topaz set in handmade Tookalon earrings.

SPICE
TOPAZ

Indulge in Brilliance

GENUINE TOPAZ
12 BREATHTAKING COLOURS
FINEST CUTTING
PATENTED TECHNOLOGY
NON RADIATED
PRECISION CALIBRATION
EVERLASTING DURABILITY
NON COATED

Patent Number 6872422
Exclusively distributed in Europe by Coloured Rocks

P

Colour	Pinkish orange
Family	Corundum
Hardness	9
Specific Gravity	3.9 – 4.1
Refractive Index	1.76 – 1.77
Crystal Group	Trigonal
Optical Properties	Strong pleochroism
Common Treatments	Normally heat-treated
Cleaning Advice	Warm soapy water
Chemical Composition	Al_2O_3

PADPARADSCHA SAPPHIRE

Padparadscha derives its name from the Sinhalese word "padmaradschen", which is the name of the colour used to describe the Sri Lankan lotus flower. The reality however, is that the Lotus flower is a lot more pinkish than the gemstone. Padparadscha Sapphires are among the rarest gems on the planet. They are strikingly beautiful and almost no other coloured gemstone compares to this unique mix of pink and orange. To be named a Padparadscha, the gem should exhibit both colours.

I am sure if I ever get around to writing a third issue of this book, there will be something more concrete I can offer on the subject of "what really does qualify as a Padparadscha". For now, everyone in the trade seems to have totally different views. I personally follow the thought that if you track the history of the gem's name and if you study some of the first gems originating from Ceylon, then to be a true

345

Padparadscha, a Sapphire should have a degree of both orange and pink present under the same lighting condition. The use of the Padparadscha name when describing an orange Sapphire is a hot topic in the gem industry. Some say it should only be used for Sapphires that are not heat-treated; others say that it should only be used for pinkish orange Sapphires actually mined in Sri Lanka.

Also, the gem world seems to be divided on whether Padparadscha should stand alone as a gem name or whether it is used as a prefix to Sapphire. Other countries that claim to produce Padparadscha Sapphires include Vietnam, Tanzania and Madagascar.

The Sri Lankan Lotus flower from which Padparadscha receives its name.

PAKISTAN

Next door to the gem treasure chest that is Afghanistan, Pakistan's array of coloured gems is also very impressive. Although its mining conditions are difficult and its trade is not as well organised as other gem rich countries, it holds in varying quantities and qualities the following gems in store for us: Ruby, Emerald, Aquamarine, Garnet, Tourmaline, Topaz, Peridot, Spinel, Diopside, Moonstone, Jade, Morganite, Sphene, Lapis Lazuli, Kunzite, Quartz and many other lesser-known varieties.

A Jessica Lili Lapis Lazuli necklace from Pakistan.

Many of these gems are found in the north and north-western areas of Pakistan and in particular the famous mountain ranges of Hindu Kush, Himalaya, and Karakoram. In the picturesque Swat Valley, some of the finest Emeralds in the world are being mined, but the area is very difficult to access. While on the subject of green gemstones, Pakistan also provides us with some of the world's most gorgeous Peridot.

Take the Khyber Pass from Afghanistan into Pakistan and along its routes you will find small tribes mining Lapis Lazuli. These small-scale artisanal mines (informal mining) are owned by individuals or small teams who work with very little technology. This region is renowned as the best place in the world to mine for Lapis Lazuli, both in terms of quality and quantity; however, the terrain makes it very difficult to do so.

Some of the world's finest Peridot originates from Pakistan.

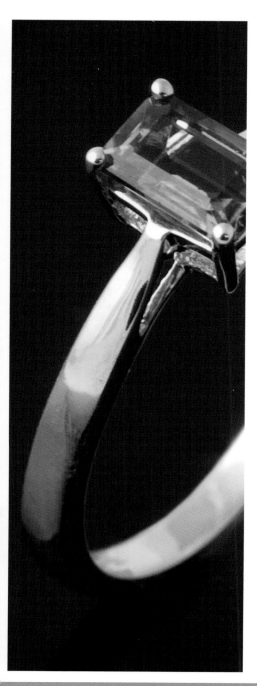

PALLADIUM

Palladium was discovered in 1803 by William Hyde Wollaston, and is named after the asteroid Pallas, discovered two years prior. William Hyde Wollaston was born in Norfolk in 1766: his father was both a priest and an astronomer, hence the likely reason why the metal was named after the asteroid. While studying Medicine at Cambridge University, William became fascinated by chemistry, crystallography and physics. On leaving university he became a chemist; while developing new methods of processing platinum in 1803, he discovered palladium and a year later found rhodium.

Palladium is mined in South Africa, USA and Canada, although it is said that today over 50% of the world supply is found in Russia. It is a member of the platinum metal group and is a relatively soft, silver metal that resembles the looks of platinum.

Palladium is very dense and has the lowest melting point of the platinum group of metals. The principal use of palladium in jewellery is its use as an alloy in the production of white gold.

At the time of writing this second edition, the Assay office in the UK (which is responsible for the hallmarking of precious metals) have announced that due to the increase of Palladium being used in jewellery, it will soon start hallmarking the metal. Although there may still be changes to the forthcoming legislation, it is believed that the fineness levels will be set at 50%, 95% and 99.9%. As it is totally tarnish resistant and very striking in look, it is believed that the metal will become extremely popular, especially when you consider that it is a member of the Platinum family, but with a price that is currently closer to that of 9k gold! When the amendment is made to the Hallmarking Act of 1973, it will initially be an optional hallmark, but it is believed that in January 2010 it will become a legal requirement to hallmark all articles weighing over 1gram.

An email I received from the Assay Office just days before this book went to press stated, "In addition to the compulsory hallmark, there will be an 'optional' mark for Palladium. This is an image of Pallas Athene who was the Greek Goddess of wisdom, war and crafts, after whom the asteroid Pallas was named".

PARAIBA TOURMALINE

This is one of the most sought after gemstones on the planet.

The stunning Paraiba Tourmaline ranges from neon, swimming pool blue to an electric greenish blue. Its name is derived from the Paraiba State in Brazil, where it was first discovered.

What makes this gem so different to other Tourmalines is the presence of copper and, to a lesser extent, manganese. The copper within the gem is what makes it appear to glow and this almost neon effect is truly a delight to see.

Due to its range of intense colours, which are similar to that of a peacock, this most spectacular gem is known in the gem trade as the "Peacock Gem".

Crystal Healers have already embraced this new gemstone and believe its powers are the greatest of all Tourmalines. Many state that the different hues have different abilities: these include promoting general wellbeing, increasing self-motivation and intensifying the desire to help and support others.

The Paraiba story would make a great film and would provide an even better sequel. Its original discovery was back in 1989, due to the work of Heitor Barbosa. This lone gem hunter was convinced that under a tiny little hill measuring no more than 400 by 200 metres and standing only 60 metres high lay a new gemstone waiting to be discovered. He told his close friends that he was not digging just to extract a quantity of gems which had already been discovered in this famous gem area of Brazil, but was going to make a new discovery.

Colour	Neon swimming pool blue to greeny blue
Family	Tourmaline is the family name
Hardness	7 – 7.5
Specific Gravity	3.02 – 3.1
Refractive Index	1.62 – 1.64
Crystal Group	Trigonal
Optical Properties	Strong pleochroism
Common Treatments	Occasionally heat-treated
Care	No specific care required
Cleaning Advice	Warm soapy water
Chemical Composition	A complex ferromagnesian silicate

He first cut ground in 1981 and worked relentlessly for many years without success. Then, in the autumn of 1989, while he was at home recovering from an illness, a tiny amount of a new Tourmaline was discovered by his assistants. For several years after, the small hill (later renamed Paraiba Hill) was trawled in an attempt to find more Paraiba, but it was mainly unsuccessful.

The sequel took place in Nigeria in 2001, when a discovery of Tourmaline was found to exhibit the same optical beauty of Paraiba and after scientific examination was found to contain copper. Bingo! The plot then gathered pace and the gem industry ferociously debated whether the gem should be called Paraiba Tourmaline, or whether a new name should be given as it was found in a completely different continent. In the end, it was decided that because it is of the same chemical composition and therefore very difficult for gem experts to distinguish between the two, it would be simpler to allow it to take on the Paraiba title. The film thus came to an end, and as the camera drew back, we realise that these two films, both shot on location, on different continents, have been delicately scripted to succinctly confirm the theory of continental drift.

Tomas Rae and Paraiba Tourmaline, a perfect partnership.

PAVE SETTING

The term pave (pronounced "pah–vay") setting is used to describe gems that are set very close together and are only separated by tiny prongs or metal beads. Because of the look that this style creates, it is named after the word "pavement".

The setting is constructed by leaving small holes in the metal that the gems are going to be set into. Once the gems have been selected, they are placed into the holes and a small amount of the surrounding metal is forced over the girdle of each stone.

The Diamonds on the shoulders on this Tomas Rae ring are pave set.

It is hard to explain how this is done without the aid of a video, but the best way to visualise this technique is to imagine that the jeweller uses a tool that pushes the metal over the girdle of the gem similar to how butter curls as a spoon or knife is pushed along its surface.

If the colour of the metal being used is similar to that of the gem, then the setting is referred to as an "Illusion Setting".

PAVILION

The pavilion of a gem refers to the portion below the girdle (its widest point). I often describe the crown (the portion of the gem above the girdle) as the lens of the gem and the pavilion as the mirrors. The pavilion on a round brilliant cut gem has 24 facets or 25 if there is a culet added.

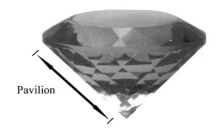

Pavilion

The depth of the pavilion varies depending on the gem type being used. In theory, the higher the refractive index of a gem, the less steep the sides of the pavilion need to be in order for the light to bounce off it and be reflected to the pavilion facet opposite. That said, with most coloured gemstones the pavilion is cut shallower than its optimum; this is because when cutting the gem, there is often more focus placed on showing its best colours, rather than optimising its brilliance.

PEAR CUT

Also known as the "Drop Cut" or the "Tear Drop Cut", the "Pear Cut" is typically based on the brilliant cut and, as its name suggests, is pointed at one end and rounded at the other. The cut can look beautiful if it is proportioned correctly and the most aesthetically pleasing examples have a length that is one and a half times their width. However, some people prefer a slightly thinner style. When used with Diamonds the dispersion and brilliance is very similar to that of the round brilliant cut and often the point of the pear cut can light up like a torch.

Pear cut Topaz in a Tookalon ring.

One thing to be aware of in the pear cut, as with the oval cut (and especially in Diamonds), is what is known as the "bow tie" effect. If the angles of the facets on the pavilion have not been cut correctly, when viewing the gem from the table you can sometimes see a darker shape that looks like a bow tie. Although some people

have commented that they actually like this effect, the reality is that the pavilion facets are not refracting light at the appropriate angles.

PEARL

It is amazing to think how nature can turn an unwanted grain of sand into one of the most gorgeous gems in the world. Learning and understanding the growth and development of a Pearl is the first step towards truly appreciating how unusual and precious this gem really is.

A Pearl is one of just a handful of organic gems (the other well-known ones being Coral, Amber and Jet). Rather than being a mineral, Pearls actually grow inside a mollusc (a term used for all shells that open and close on a hinge, such as oysters, clams, and mussels).

If a foreign object, such as a grain of sand, enters a mollusc it becomes an irritant to the creature inside, so in order to protect itself it releases a silky substance, known as nacre, to cover the uninvited guest. Over time the mollusc will continue to release nacre over the foreign body and when the mollusc is opened three to five years after the initial intrusion, the uninvited foreigner has been turned into a glorious Pearl.

It may be a very beautiful thought to think natural Pearls form in the sea and are discovered when divers find them at the bottom of the ocean, but at what expense are we retrieving this treasure? Diving for Pearls is destructive for the Coral and the sealife alike, therefore it has been prohibited in many seas for this reason. Cultured Pearls on the other hand, refer to Pearls that are grown in environmentally-friendly Pearl farms. Simply put, a cultured Pearl is one that is grown under supervision and not one that is taken from natural surroundings.

Many people today prefer to know that their Pearls are cultured so as to avoid the possibility that they may have been taken from the likes of a protected Coral Reef: the good news is that around 99% of today's Pearls are indeed cultured.

Most natural Pearls one sees today are found

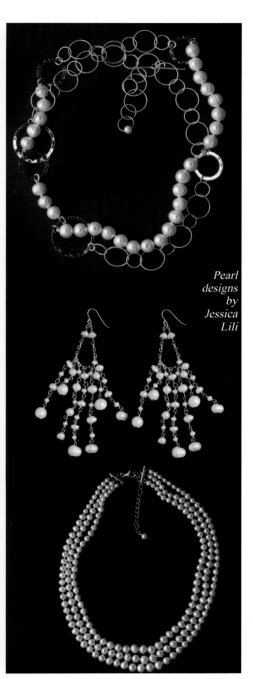

Pearl designs by Jessica Lili

in estate jewellery collections or museums, so when buying new Pearls, it is not really a case of natural Pearls versus cultured Pearls, but Pearls versus synthetic.

If you own Pearls and are not sure if they are genuine or not, a great way to test them is to rub them on your teeth; you want the Pearl to feel slightly grainy rather than smooth. If it's smooth you know it is not a real one, as companies who produce synthetic Pearls have yet to master the grainy effect of natural nacre.

Round, flawless, and orient are words you'll hear relating to Pearls and these are qualities used to determine their value. The word round seems a bit of an obvious one to describe a Pearl but it is in fact the most important. It's a common mistake to think Pearls have been faceted in some way to give them their perfect spherical shape, when in fact the shape of a Pearl is all down to the work done by the mollusc.

Because no two Pearls are identical in shape or size, it takes a quality jeweller hours and hours to select matching Pearls when stringing them together for necklaces and bracelets.

The finest Pearls do not have any flaws, bumps or marks in the nacre and they should have an even and clean surface. The final consideration when valuing Pearls is their orient. This is the word used to describe the lustre of a Pearl (also referred to as pearlescence). The orient is a soft iridescence caused by the refraction of light off the layers of nacre.

Pearls are one of the oldest and most precious gems discovered in the world and are believed to have been traded more than 5000 years ago.

There are many myths and legends surrounding Pearls, and one of the most common sayings is, "Pearls bring tears". This originates from ancient times when people thought that Pearls were the tears of angels or of the moon. Despite the widespread use of this phrase, most cultures actually believe the opposite to be true.

The Greeks have always regarded Pearls highly

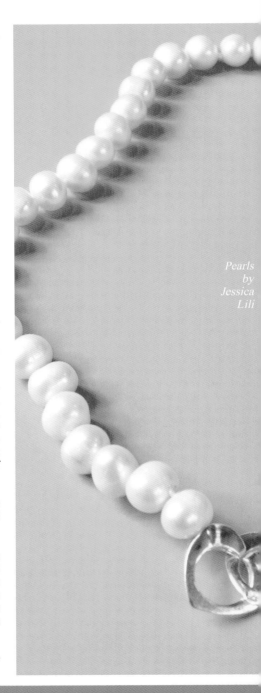

Pearls by Jessica Lili

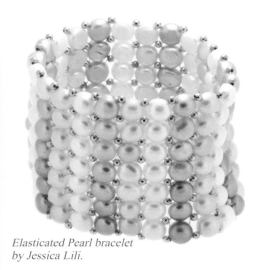

Elasticated Pearl bracelet by Jessica Lili.

for their beauty and association with love and marriage. They thought Pearls would promote marital bliss and prevent the bride from crying on the wedding day, which is where the tradition of giving Peals to a bride came from.

In Ancient Rome, Pearls were recognised as a definitive sign of wealth and social status and it was believed that they would promote a long and healthy life. During battle in the Crusades, knights would wear them as a talisman, believing they would help protect the wearer. During the Renaissance period, Pearls were regarded so highly that some countries passed laws allowing only the nobility to wear them.

When cared for properly, Pearls will last a lifetime. It is recommended to wear them often as the body's natural oils help maintain the Pearl's orient, but it is also advisable to keep them away from household chemicals, as well as perfume, make-up and hair spray. Along with Moonstone and Alexandrite, Pearl is also a birthstone of June.

See also Baroque Pearls, Mabe Pearls and Mother of Pearl.

PENDANTS

Pendants are famous for their stylish look and their power of defining love and romance. A pendant can come in many shapes, sizes and forms, but will almost always be worn alone as a striking piece hung delicately on a chain or a lace. In addition to wearing them just for their sheer beauty, pendants are sometimes worn for reasons of healing, protection, self-affirmation (i.e. a name or initials) or even to proudly show off an award.

A pendant differs from a necklace, as it allows more movement and flexibility and, as it is not fixed to a chain, has the ability to change and create new looks. If one wears a large Pink Topaz suspended from a tiny trace chain for a formal event, it can easily look very different when hung from a thick black lace and matched with a pair of jeans!

PERIDOT

Colour	Green with golden flashes
Family	Olivine
Hardness	6.5
Specific Gravity	3.34
Refractive Index	1.635 – 1.690
Crystal Group	Orthorhombic
Optical Properties	Strong brilliance and pleochroism
Common Treatments	Sometimes heat-treated
Care	No special care required
Cleaning Information	Warm soapy water
Chemical Composition	$(MgFe)_2SiO_4$

Aptly the birthstone of August with sparkling, summery golden greens, Peridot is a sophisticated gem that has rightfully regained its position as one of the most popular gemstones around the world.

This gem is one of only a few available in just one colour. Its greens range from bottle green to an almost yellowish, olive oil colour. Its appearance often has an oily, greasy look and for that reason some say its name is derived from the French word for "unclear", "peritot", although others believe its name is derived from the Arabic word for a gem, "faridat". The gem is pleochroic, meaning that it is possible to see different shades from different angles. It is also an idiochromatic gem, which means that its colour is derived from the basic chemical composition of the gem (in Peridot's case, iron) and not from impurities within the gem, which is how most gems receive their distinctive colours.

Like its colour rival Emerald, Peridot often has inclusions which can be caused by the presence of small particles of Silica; occasionally you will find needle-like inclusions which are commonly referred to as Ludwig needles.

Cutting the gemstone can be quite tricky as it has high birefringence (meaning that the gem significantly bends light as it enters) making the angle of the facets on the pavilion crucial. It is also a brittle gemstone with strong cleavage; both of these qualities mean that the Lapidarist must be sure to take extra care while faceting this gem.

Peridot has been mined as a gemstone for over 4000 years and is mentioned in the Bible - although you may not recognise the name as it is referred to by its original title, Chrysolite (see Exodus 28:20, Song of Solomon 5:14, Ezekiel 28:13, Revelations 21:20). The name Chrysolite was taken from the Ancient Greek word "chrysolithos" meaning "golden stone", as it often has flashes of gold seen within it. The gem is the only famous member of the

Olivine mineral family, which is a species of magnesium rich silicate minerals.

Some of the first Peridots were mined by Egyptians on an island located in the Red Sea. Today this island is known as St John's Island, but historically it was named Zagbargad after the Arabic word for Peridot and also Topazios, which was the Ancient Greek word for the gem. But before you go getting confused and start to research the relationship between Peridot and Topaz, there isn't one; today the name is used to describe a totally different gem family!

3000 years ago, these early miners on Topazios Island did not work in the daytime as they believed the gem was invisible in daylight. As it could absorb the sun's rays it had the ability to glow in the dark, therefore making it easier to discover.

Half way around the globe from Topazios is the small Hawaiian island of Oahu; here very small grains of Peridot colour the beaches green! Islanders here believe that the gems are the tears of the goddess Pele. As these grains are too small, there is no mining on the island, although mining has taken place in Hawaii for thousands of years. Even so, although the gem is today still sold to tourists as indigenous, most of it is actually sourced from Arizona!

Peridot is found in the San Carlos Apache Reservation in Arizona, where the U.S Bureau of Mining claim that approximately 80% of the world's supply is currently being sourced. Luckily for the Apaches, many decades ago they were given sole rights to all mineral deposits in the region. Most of the mines are run by families and, similar to mining communities in Africa, every day they take their haul to local gem traders in Tupperware boxes, carrier bags, fruit bowls and buckets! There is very little sophisticated about family-run artisanal gem mining.

Although mining for the gem over the centuries has also taken place in China, Australia, Brazil, Norway and Burma, the most recent discovery was in Pakistan in 1994. Located some 15,000 feet above sea level in the ice-capped mountains

Radiant Peridot designs by Annabella.

of the western Himalayas lies the remote, and often inaccessible, Peridot mines. From the nearest town, you would first ride 10 hours on horseback, and then set off on a two to three day hike (or climb!), before you reach the first mines. What's more, because of snow, the miners (some two thousand of them) can only make the trip in July, August and September. However, it all seems worthwhile as the quality of the Peridot is amongst the finest in the world.

In October 2003, possibly the most incredible gem find of all time happened, when a NASA spacecraft identified the gem on Mars!

Throughout history it has been mistaken and confused with other gemstones, including Emerald - which is surprising due to the yellow green colour of the stone. It has also been mistaken for Apatite, Green Garnets, Green Tourmaline, Moldavites and Green Zircon.

Having long been associated with luck, many cultures have celebrated this unusual and magical stone in their myths and legends due to its apparent power to ward off evil spirits! Historically, if the stone was then set in gold or any precious metal its capacity to bring the bearer luck and good fortune was intensified even more. In days gone by, goblets and sword handles of the rich and powerful land owners and aristocracy were encrusted with Peridots. It was thought that what you then drank from the goblet would become a potion to stimulate greatness - the same theory applied to the swords, as it was thought it would bring power on the battlefield and strength to the bearer's legions.

This precious gemstone can often be seen in Egyptian jewellery from as early as 2000BC. Historians have said that they suspect that many of the Emeralds worn by Cleopatra were actually Peridot. The Romans were also big fans of this gem and named it the "evening Emerald", due to its seeming ability to almost glow in the dark.

Today the stone is cherished by people more for its beauty than its powers, but the history of this stone still remains a great part of its mystery and fascination for all who wear it. In addition to

Peridot set into a figural Kama Charm.

Colours of Nature by Eleven Seventeen.

Mattom - interchangeable gem cufflinks.

White Opal mined in Peru.

Colour	Colourless, Grey, Yellow, Yellow Gray to White
Family	Petalite
Hardness	6 - 6.5
Specific Gravity	2.45
Refractive Index	1.5 - 1.51
Crystal Group	Monoclinic
Optical Properties	Vitreous Lustre
Common Treatments	None
Care	Careful not to bash!
Cleaning Information	Warm soapy water
Chemical Composition	LiAlSi4O10

being the birthstone for August, it is associated with the star sign of Capricorn and used to celebrate the 16th wedding anniversary.

PERU

The third largest country in South America, Peru is known for its headwaters to the Amazon, the Andes Mountain and luscious rainforest. Peru also makes a small, but important, contribution to the Opal world, thus preventing Australia from completely dominating the market.

Blue Opals, Pink Opals and Green Opals are all mined in the province of Arequipa in southern Peru. While yields of Pink Opals have been on the rise for several years now, Blue Opals have become increasingly harder to find.

In addition to Opal, the country also mines a small quantity of Marcasite, Rhodonite and Diopside.

PETALITE

Also known as Castorite, Petalite is a rare colourless gem that is a real favourite with collectors around the planet. As its unusual perfect cleavage can at times appear leaf like in pattern Petalite's name is derived from the Greek word for a leaf "petalon".

The gem was first discovered in Brazil in 1800 by Brazilian Gemmologist J Andradae Silva.

The gemstone is extremely difficult to cut and until recently Lapidarists would only attempt to make Cabochon cuts. Although the gem has a hardness of 6 to 6.5 on the Mohs scale, it is quite brittle, so it's important when set into jewellery, especially in rings, just to take a little more care when wearing this gem.

In addition to the colourless variety, which has incredible brilliance, the gem is also available in pastel shades of yellow and grey. However it is the colourless variety that is most popular.

Petalite has also been discovered in the UK, Italy, the USA and Afghanistan.

PEZZOTTAITE

Colour	Pink - Red
Family	Pezzottaite
Hardness	8
Specific Gravity	3.1
Refractive Index	1.60 - 1.61
Crystal Group	Trigonal
Optical Properties	Transparent - Translucent
Common Treatments	Not normally treated
Care	None
Cleaning Advice	Warm soapy water
Chemical Composition	Cs(Be2Li)Al2Si6O18

Under this heading of Pezzottaite, I would like to try and put something in to plain English, something that had me confused for over 18 months. What is the difference between Red Beryl, Bixbite and Pezzottaite?

Firstly, let's remember that Beryl is the family name (more correctly the species name) for such gemstones as Emerald, Aquamarine, Morganite, Yellow Beryl etc. Remember that Beryl in its purist form is colourless (known as Goshenite) and only through the presence of impurities do the various members of the species gain their colour. These types of gemstones, which receive their colour from impurities, are known as allochromatic gems.

In the GIA gem reference guide issued in 1998 (issued well before I became a gem collector but given to be by my good friend and gem mentor Manuj), they stated "Red Beryl – rare variety with darker and more saturated colour than in Morganite; proposed variety name Bixbite never gained wide acceptance".
So firstly we know that Bixbite is a trade name for Red Beryl. Its raspberry pink colour is simply breathtaking and, like its sister Emerald, it is often heavily included.

Pezzottaite is easily misidentified as Bixbite.

What many were labelling as Bixbite or Red Beryl for many years, later turned out to be a totally different gemstone which today we know as Pezzottaite. This was not through ignorance or for fraudulent reasons, it was simply because the two gemstone were very similar in appearance, composition and structure. In 2002 a new deposit of Bixbite was thought to have been discovered in Madagascar. However, after scientific research was carried out on the mineral, it was discovered to be a new gemstone and it was named Pezzottaite the year after in recognition of the work carried out in Madagascar by Dr Federico Pezzotta.

Bixbite and Pezzottaite have a slightly different chemical composition and not to bore you but the obvious difference is Beryl is "Be3Al2Si6O18" as opposed to Pezzottaite being "Cs[Be2Li] Al2Si6O18"! As you can see Pezzottaite contains lithium, which is not found in Beryls, and it also has a slightly different crystal structure.

PHOSPHORESCENCE

This is a term used by many experts to describe gems that appear to glow in the dark. The effect is similar to the luminous hands on a watch that help you tell the time when you wake in the middle of the night.

Phosphorescence is a process in which the energy absorbed by certain gems from ultra violet light is slowly released in the form of light from within the gem. For example, Kunzite, Diamond and Tourmaline are sometimes phosphorescent. Kunzite is possibly the best gem in which to observe phosphorescence and most high-quality Kunzite will appear to glow for several minutes after the ultra violet light source is removed. A famous example of a phosphorescent gem is the infamous Hope Diamond: it is said that after shining an ultraviolet light on it, it will glow red-orange for about five minutes when the light source has been removed.

PHOSPHOSIDERITE

With a colour similar to that of the stunning purple Thai Orchid, Phosphosiderite's name is derived from its make up of phosphorous and iron oxide.

Until recently, as this gem is very soft, it has not been set in jewellery. However by stabilising it through the use of treatment, its hardness can be increased making it more durable. As the gem's wonderful opaque purple lustre makes a perfect companion to Amethyst, the designers at Annabella are currently experimenting with setting Cabochon cut stabilised Phosphosiderite alongside Amethyst in a collection of earrings and pendants.

Phosphosiderite can be found in Cornwall England, Columbia, Chile, Canada, Brazil and several other mining locations around the world.

Kunzite is highly Phosphorescent.

Colour	Pink - Purple
Family	Phosphosiderite
Hardness	3.5 - 4
Specific Gravity	2.76
Refractive Index	1.69 - 1.73
Crystal Group	Monoclinic
Optical Properties	Vitreous to resinous
Common Treatments	Not normally treated
Care	Careful not to scratch
Cleaning Advice	Warm soapy water
Chemical Composition	FePO4(H2O)

Turquoise Bracelets
From £15

Turquoise Necklaces
From £29

jessica
lili

Colour	Pink
Family	Corundum
Hardness	9
Specific Gravity	3.9 – 4.1
Refractive Index	1.76 – 1.77
Crystal Group	Trigonal
Optical Properties	Strong pleochroism
Common Treatments	Normally heat-treated
Care	None
Cleaning Advice	Ultrasonic or warm soapy water
Composition	Al_2O_3

Colour	Pink to reddish pink
Family	Tourmaline
Hardness	7 - 7.5
Specific Gravity	3.02 - 3.1
Refractive Index	1.62 - 1.64
Crystal Group	Trigonal
Optical Properties	Strong pleochroism
Common Treatments	Occasionally heat-treated
Care	No specific care required
Cleaning Advice	Ultrasonic or warm soapy water
Chemical Composition	A complex ferromagnesian silicate

PINK SAPPHIRE

Pink Sapphires have recently become incredibly popular and in some instances have demanded a higher price per carat than Ruby!

Although the lighter pinks are incredibly beautiful, the price of more vivid pinks, especially if the clarity is good, can be thousands of pounds per carat.

While Diamonds have dominated engagement rings for the last fifty years, I believe that over the next decade, Pink Sapphires (as long as supply keeps up with demand) could be the number one choice.

PINK TOURMALINE

The name Tourmaline comes from the Sinhalese word "turamali" which means "mixed precious stones". In the gem trade (due to its almost electrifying colour) the pink variety of Tourmaline is often known as "Shocking Pink Tourmaline".

This gem is often confused with other gems. Indeed, the Russian Crown Jewels were thought to contain beautiful large Rubies but they turned out to be dark Pink Tourmalines. Its sensual colour occurs because it is rich in lithium.

The Empress Dowager Tz'u, the last empress of China, loved Pink Tourmaline so much she went to rest eternally on a pillow carved from Pink Tourmaline.

When women wear Pink Tourmaline, it is said to empower; it also said to help in reaching one's full potential.

PIN SETTING

A pin setting is used primarily for Pearls where they are set on a ring. In this instance, the surrounding precious metal is sculpted into a dish shape to support the gem, which is then partially drilled and bonded onto a metal pin. A similar style of setting is used for briolette cut gems suspended from earrings. Here though, the gem sits in a piece of metal similar in shape to an upturned ice cream cone and the pin is once again inserted into the gem.

Pique Diamond

A term used to describe cloudy Diamonds that are full of inclusions - normally visible to the naked eye. Pique Diamonds (sometimes abbreviated to PK) are often used by jewellers as accent stones.

The CIBJO (Confédération Internationale de la Bijouterie, Joaillerie et Orfèvrerie) - or in English often referred to as the World Jewellery Confederation - actually use PK1, PK2 and PK3 to replace the GIA ratings of I1, I2 and I3. However, many people see them as a lower rating and a continuation of the GIA scale.

The pique measurement actually predates the GIA and can be found in many old writings. PK1 is said to clearly show inclusion under 10x magnification (a standard gem loupe). PK2 is used to describe Diamonds with inclusions visible to the naked eye, and a Diamond described as PK3 has many large inclusions that noticeably diminish the gem's brilliance.

Platinum

Platinum is a heavy, malleable precious metal, resistant to corrosion; in addition to its use in exclusive jewellery, it is also used in laboratory equipment and dentistry.

In the 18th century, the rarity of platinum was brought to the attention of King Louis XV of France, who declared that it was the only metal fit for a king. In the 19th century, due to its rarity, difficulty to work with and sheer expense, it was used in a very limited manner in the jewellery industry. This changed in the 20th century when the metal became popular for expensive Diamond engagement rings.

Platinum is a third heavier than 18k gold and is the most expensive metal used in making

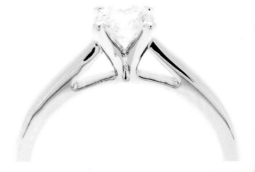

jewellery (other than the rhodium used in plating). At the time of going to press, pure platinum is twice the price of pure gold. Since 1975, it has been a legal requirement in the UK to hallmark platinum jewellery. The current standards of fineness are 850 (85% pure), 900, 950 and 999, with 950 (95% pure) being the most common.

To help comprehend the rarity of platinum, it was once suggested that if all the platinum in the world was poured into an Olympic swimming pool it would not even cover your ankles! It is also said that all of the gold in the world would only fill approximately three or four pools.

So when you see two identical band rings, one made of 950 platinum and one made from 18k gold and wonder why one is four times the price of the other, remember there are three factors: the price of the raw material is double; more weight is used because it's a third heavier; and the purity is higher.

PLAY OF COLOUR

This is a term that is used to describe the wonderful "play of colours" seen inside Precious Opals. The visual effect is similar to viewing a child's rotating kaleidoscope. It is truly one of the most striking visual effects seen in minerals and the very finest examples sell at prices in excess of equivalent sized Diamonds. If the Opal does not display "play of colour", it is known as a Common Opal and has little value.

Australian Opal is famous for its play of colour.

So what causes an Opal's "play of colour"? Firstly, its structure is one of silica, water and air. The silica is made up of small, round spherical pieces, far bigger than those of atoms found in a crystal; this is best understood by imagining apples stacked in an orderly pattern on a fruit vendor's cart. The play of colour is seen if the spheres are between 0.2 and 0.5 microns in size, similar to the iridescence seen on the back of a CD, which is caused by similar size differences in the grooves of the track. As light falls on to the spheres, different wavelengths are refracted at different angles from different portions of each sphere, producing an array of beautiful colours.

PLEOCHROISM

Derived from the Greek word "pleion", "more", and "chros", "colour", pleochroism is an optical effect where different colours can be seen in a gemstone when observed from different angles. Depending on the colours and the attractiveness of the pleochroism, gems are cut either to maximise or hide the effect.

As light is made up of different colours, all with different wavelengths, in certain crystal structures different colours of light are absorbed along different axes. All gems that show pleochroism are doubly refractive, meaning they split rays of light within the gemstone. For example, if in one direction all wavelengths except for yellow and blue are absorbed, then the gem will appear green (a mixture of the two colours) from that angle, whereas from a different direction if all wavelengths but yellow are absorbed, then it will appear yellow. As the two rays have a distinctive mix of colours, by rotating the gem different colours are seen. Some pleochroic gems such as Sapphire, Ruby and Emerald split the light into almost identical colours and the effect is normally not noticeable.

The level pleochroism is also affected by how a gem's crystals are arranged. Gems with a single optic axis (tetragonal, trigonal and hexagonal minerals), such as Morganite show two colours or shades and are sometimes referred to as dichroic (meaning two colours). Gems with two optic axes (monoclinic, triclinic and orthorhombic minerals), such as Tanzanite and Tourmaline show three colours. The effect of which is named trichroic (meaning three colours). It is worth noting that there are never more than three colours caused by pleochroism.

Due to their crystal structure, isometric gems including Diamond, Spinel and Garnet do not demonstrate any pleochroism. When we hold gemstone courses at the Rocks Academy, the lack of pleochroism in Diamonds often surprises many people. Its important to remember that the multiple colours seen in Diamonds as you rotate them is not due to pleochroism, but is the effect of dispersion.

Iolite, Morganite and Tanzanite are highly pleochroic.

PLINY THE ELDER

Gaius Plinius Secundus was born 23AD in Northern Italy, at Novum Comum (later simply renamed Como), which is located 28 miles north of Milan; today he is known as Pliny the Elder.

Born to a wealthy family, he was the son of a Roman equestrian. His father took him to Rome in 35AD where he was educated, served in the military and later studied botany. His scientific curiosity was overwhelming and his writings documented many subjects throughout his life. During his time in the Roman navy he must have travelled considerably as he documents gold mining in Britain, as well as the continents of Africa and Asia.

Pliny the Elder wrote many books, and as a keen student of philosophy and rhetoric he began practising as an advocate. His book "Natural History" (Naturalis Historia) is a phenomenal work which covers subjects such as astronomy, zoology, botany, medical drugs and mineralogy. The book is an encyclopaedia of ancient knowledge which originally filled 37 volumes, and has been used for centuries by countless scholars.

Pliny documented many minerals used by the Romans for personal adornment and for ornamental use too. He lists Rock Crystal, Amber, Diamonds, Emeralds, Beryls and Sapphires among many other gemstones.

Although born to a wealthy family, as part of the equestrian rank they tended to frown upon lavishness and luxury; in his Natural History he states, "Next among items of luxury comes Amber, although as yet it is exclusively an adornment for women. Not even luxury has been able to invent a reason for its use." That said, he correctly identified Amber as the fossilised resin of pine trees. Another of Pliny's obsessions was with fraud and forgery, where he stated that "other gems can be made from other stones, indeed there is no more lucrative fraud against society".

Pliny opens his writings on gemstones with, "The

only topic that remains that I set out to cover is that of precious stones. Therein Nature reaches its utmost concentration and in no department does she arouse more wonder. So much store do men set by the variety, colour, texture and elegance of gems that they consider it criminal to tamper with precious stones by engraving them as signets. Some they consider beyond price on any human scale of valuation. Consequently, for very many people a single precious stone can provide a matchless and perfect view of Nature".

It is astonishing that even in the first century AD, Pliny accurately detailed the crystal structure of a Diamond and discussed how non gem-quality could be used for industry. When referring to Emerald he recorded that, "no colour is more delightful in appearance. For although we enjoy looking at plants and leaves, we regard Emeralds with all the more pleasure because compared with them there is nothing that is more intensely green". Although not a believer in myths, Pliny did go on to say, "And after straining our eyes by looking at another object, we can restore our vision to normal by gazing at an Emerald". He also correctly identified Emeralds as part of the Beryl family.

The Natural History also reveals to us the personality and character of Pliny the Elder which complements what has been learnt from the letters of his nephew, Pliny the Younger. Pliny the Younger reveals how Pliny the Elder's scientific curiosity led to his death at Pompeii. On August 24, 79AD he was in charge of a Roman fleet at Misenum. Having witnessed the eruption of Vesuvius, he had a desire to observe the phenomenon directly, and also to rescue some of his friends from the Bay of Naples. Having lingered too long studying and observing the volcanic eruption he was engulfed by ash and poisonous gases and was found dead on the 26th August after the plume had dispersed. The account of Pliny the Elder's last hours were documented by Pliny the Younger and were sent in a letter to Tacitus 27 years after the event.

Interestingly, Pliny is still remembered in volcanology where the term Plinian refers to a very violent eruption of a volcano.

POLYMORPHIC

Although this word has many different meanings throughout science, in gemmology it is used to describe gemstones whose crystal structures have different hardness in different directions. Kyanite is very polymorphic; its hardness varies depending on which axis of the gem you are looking at. In one direction it measures 4.5 – 5 on the Mohs scale and on the other axis it measures 6.5 – 7.

Also known as anisotropism, this effect is one of the best ways for those that evaluate gems to correctly identify Kyanite. Although its polymorphic structure may aid gemmologists in identifying Kyanite, it causes Lapidarists a real headache when cutting the gem. If the orientation is not perfect, then the polymorphic structure causes the gem to literally fall apart! So much so, that until recently the gemstone was only ever cabochon cut. If you do manage to purchase a faceted piece, don't worry about this, as once cut the gem is durable.

Kyanite is highly Polymorphic.

POP DIAMONDS

For girls who want to wear colourful, stylish diamond jewellery, designed for special occasions and big nights out, Pop Diamonds offer an exciting new approach to fashionable jewellery. Each piece featured within its Sparkling Rocks and Clubbing Collections is set with a genuine conflict free Diamond.

Each item is fashioned in Platinum over Sterling Silver and features genuine diamonds, which are often accompanied by other coloured Diamonds or other sparkling precious gemstones.

The Pop Diamond Clubbing Collection features funky, black designs with vivid green, orange, pinks and red gemstones, which are sure to make your friends envious.

By selling direct to the public, Pop Diamonds are designed to be the most affordable Diamond collection available, yet without compromise of design, precious metals or quality.

A Multi Sapphire and Diamond ring from Pop Diamonds.

pop
diamonds

PRASEOLITE

Here is a confusing one. Praseolite is the name given to a leek green Iolite, whereas Prasiolite is the name given to a Green Amethyst (see opposite page).

What makes matters even more confusing is that (upon visual inspection) this very rare form of Iolite and the heat-treated green Amethyst are extremely difficult to distinguish. Although this is literally the only gem to make it into this book that I have never personally physically examined, I felt it necessary to make an exception as you often see people using the name to incorrectly describe Green Amethyst.

PRASIOLITE (GREEN AMETHYST)

Prasiolite, also known as Vermarine or Green Amethyst is quite simply Green Quartz. Although the gem can be formed naturally, it is often produced by carefully heating Amethyst or Citrine, a technique mastered at the Montezuma mines in Brazil.

When natural, this beautiful, vibrant grass-green gemstone is an extremely rare member of the Quartz family. To find a large example of this gem is even rarer, as the crystal structure is different from other Quartzes and so does not produce a very even colour, even in a single stone.

Green Amethyst is reputed to have many miraculous powers attributed to it. It is said to bring good fortune and luck and was symbolic of someone with high ranking. Many other myths and legends can be transferred or borrowed from Amethyst.

Praisiolite, Vermarine, Green Amethyst (or whatever you prefer to call it) is often confused with other gemstones such as Peridot, Green Tourmaline and Green Beryl.

Colour	Green
Family	Quartz
Hardness	7
Specific Gravity	2.65
Refractive Index	1.54-1.55
Crystal Group	Trigonal
Optical Properties	Normally good clarity
Common Treatments	Heat treatment to enhance colour
Care	Can fade with prolonged exposure to sun
Cleaning Advice	Ultrasonic or warm soapy water
Chemical Composition	SiO_2 (Silicon Dioxide)

PRECIOUS GEMSTONES

During the 19th century, there were only four gemstones (Diamond, Ruby, Sapphire and Emerald) that were classified as precious; all other gems were referred to as semi-precious.

This phrase is very misleading because many gems such as Tanzanite and Alexandrite often demand higher prices than the big four, and in certain sizes and qualities are infinitely rarer.

Today, it is more common to refer to all gems as precious, because after all, to be named a gem, the mineral must be rare!

PREHNITE

Prehnite is an attractive, transparent stone, usually greenish in colour although sometimes found in yellow, grey or whitish tones. It creates attractive jewellery and can be faceted or cabochon cut and is occasionally found to display chatoyancy.

The gem often falls between transparent and translucent and its appearance often reminds me of Moonstone. Its surface can often have a good lustre and it looks beautiful when cabochon cut and set into gold rings and pendants.

Crystal collectors believe that Prehnite enhances dreaming and improves memory; it is also said to focus inner knowledge to prepare for situations. The stone is sometimes used to make predictions and allegedly the most accurate predictions are those made for one's personal, spiritual growth.

It was first discovered in South Africa by an early Dutch governor of the Cape of Good Hope Colony called Colonel Hendrik Von Prehn, and in keeping with traditional gem naming convention, it was named after him.

Since its discovery in South Africa it has been found in Germany, Austria, Switzerland, Scotland, Namibia, Canada, China, Australia, France, the USA, India and even Antarctica.

Colour	Light green, yellow
Family	Does not belong to a family
Hardness	6 - 6.5
Specific Gravity	2.9 - 3
Refractive Index	1.61 - 1.64
Crystal Group	Orthorhombic
Optical Properties	Vitreous lustre
Common Treatments	Not normally treated
Care	No special care required
Cleaning Advice	Warm soapy water
Chemical Composition	$Ca_2Al(AlSi_3O_{10})(OH)_2$

PRINCESS CUT

This is a relatively new cut, which has quickly risen to become the second most popular cut for solitaire Diamonds, beaten only by the round brilliant cut. It is very popular for use in engagement rings.

Rarely used for coloured gemstones, the princess cut is not as standardised as other cuts and so there are often differences in opinion as to what constitutes as a princess cut.
It was first introduced in 1960 to offer Lapidarists the ability to maximise yields when faced with cutting a flattish piece of Diamond rough. The cut often yields as much as 62%! Although there is less lustre from the facets on the crown than a round brilliant cut, it is excellent at displaying brilliance and dispersion.

So what is a princess cut? The term is normally used to describe shapes that are square, without truncated corners. Whereas a round brilliant cut could be described as a cone when viewed from the side, the princess cut is more like an upside down pyramid.

The crown is constructed with triangular facets and is not as tall as other cuts; often only 15% of the gem's overall depth is in the crown (be careful of princess cuts that have less than 10% of total height in the crown as they will display very little life). Just like the crown, the pavilion's facets are also triangular. As the cut sometimes has 76 facets, it is often referred to as a "Square Modified Brilliant".

Finally, if your fiancé's name is Sarah, then this cut would make an ideal engagement ring, as the name Sarah means 'Princess'.

PROMISE RING

A promise ring is often given to one's girlfriend as a way of demonstrating the seriousness of and commitment to a relationship.

Some people give a promise ring as a precursor to an engagement ring, and it is sometimes

Two princess cut engagement rings.

Ruby is a romantic promise ring.

Orange Moonstone is pseudochromatic.

engraved with such messages as "I love you", or "My Valentine" etc. Others give promise rings if they are too young to get married. They are also known to have been given when two people meet later in life and, although they know they want to stay together, feel the time has passed for marriage.

Although there is no set finger on which to wear a Promise Ring, many people place them on the wedding finger.

PSEUDOCHROMATIC

The array of beautiful colours we see in natural gemstones can be created by one of three events:

Firstly, they can be due to the inherent chemical make-up of the crystal; these gems are known as idiochromatic.

Secondly, gems coloured by the presence of impurities are known as allochromatic.

Finally, when a gem's colour is caused by optical properties within the gem and its reflection from, or just under its surface, this is known as a pseudochromatic gem.

PURPLE AND VIOLET GEMS AND ASSOCIATIONS

Believed to be a very powerful colour by religious leaders, purple or violet can take the attributes of red and blue to create a magical colour with special properties. Linked with sensitivity and creativity, it has always been popular with creative artists who like the sensual properties of red, combined with the refined calmness of blue. However, it can also display a level of insecurity and lack of self-assurance, so needs to be worn with confidence.

There is much confusion about when to use the word purple to describe a gem's colour and when to use violet. Firstly, the word violet is derived from that of a flower and purple from a creature of the sea. Still confused? Violet is also the last colour seen in a rainbow and has the shortest wavelength (380 to 420 nanometers) beyond which are invisible ultraviolet wavelengths. More confused? Normally, the two colour descriptions are interchangeable, but many in the gem industry tend to use violet when the colour has more blue tones and purple when the colour has more red tones.

Historically, when the colour was worn by a man, it symbolised sober judgment and gravity; when worn by a woman it demonstrated that she was fond of religion. In ancient times the colour was associated with Thursdays and the planet Jupiter.

When it comes to the colour purple one gem dominates: Amethyst. This official birthstone of February can often demonstrate some of the clearest, most vivid of all colours naturally found in gems. Because the colour has such strong links with religion, for centuries, many religious leaders including the pope have worn Amethyst rings.

PYROPE GARNET

Pyrope from the Latin "pyropos", meaning "fire", is normally red in colour. Its tones usually vary from deep red to almost black, although when found in a violet-red shade it is better known as Rhodolite Garnet (taken from the Greek meaning for a rose).

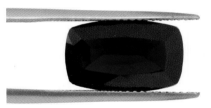

The deep red of Pyrope Garnet can be seen here.

In 1990, a Blue Garnet was discovered in Madagascar and this has been identified as a cross between a Pyrope and a Spessartine Garnet. This new find is important for two reasons: firstly, it is amongst the first Blue Garnets to be discovered (it used to be said that Garnets come in all colours except blue); and secondly because it is a colour change gemstone.

One Pyrope, found in Arizona, is not mined by humans, but is said to be brought to the Earth's surface by ants! If you ever come across the term "ant hill Garnet", you now know the origin.

Colour	Red to black red
Family	Garnet
Hardness	7.25
Specific Gravity	3.51 – 3.6
Refractive Index	1.7 – 1.73
Crystal Group	Isometric
Optical Properties	Various
Common Treatments	Cannot be heat-treated
Care	No special care needed
Chemical Composition	Various

Colour	A kaleidoscope of choice
Family	Quartz
Hardness	6.6 – 7
Specific Gravity	2.6 – 2.65
Refractive Index	1.544 - 1.553
Crystal Group	Trigonal
Optical Properties	Glassy to vitreous lustre
Common Treatments	Some varieties are heat-treated
Care	No special care required
Cleaning Advice	Ultrasonic or warm soapy water
Chemical Composition	SiO_2

QUARTZ

The Quartz family is one of the largest in the gemstone world. Throughout history Quartz was often used as a stand-in for more expensive and luxurious gemstones. This led to it once being known as the common chameleon of gemstones.

Although Quartz is found in abundance around the world, and also most likely in your back garden, finding gem-quality Quartz is like finding a needle in a haystack.

The fine crystal qualities of Quartz have been admired since ancient times, with its name deriving from the ancient Greek "krustallos", meaning 'ice'. It is believed that the Greeks and the Romans thought that Quartz was in fact ice that had been made by the gods because it couldn't melt.

The two main varieties of Quartz are

Cryptocrystalline Quartz and Crystalline Quartz.

Cryptocrystalline Quartz simply means the crystals within the gem are so small they are practically microscopic. Varieties within this type of Quartz include: Onyx, Chalcedony (a translucent waxy gem formed not of one single crystal, but a number of finely grained microcrystals), Agate (often featuring multiple bands of colours) and Jasper (an impure, opaque variety of red, green, black, or mottled Quartz). The remarkable attribute of Crystalline Quartz is the sheer variety of forms it is found in, available in a myriad of colours ranging from Rose Quartz to Rock Crystal and Milky Quartz to dark Smokey Quartz. See also Amethyst, Citrine and Ametrine.

I'm often asked questions about the value of certain members of the Quartz family, especially Smokey, Amethyst and Citrine. In today's market the prices for many Quartz based gems does seem to be on a permanent rollercoaster! The best advice I can give is the same advice I give for most gems: the price per carat will normally depend on how vivid the colour is; how good the clarity is; and, probably most important, how well the gem has been cut.

QUENCHED CRACKLE

Many people in the gem trade will not agree with what we have done with this gem, but it's incredibly attractive and, to be quite honest, a bit of fun! One of the reasons some don't like it is because the technique has been used for over a thousand years to make Ruby and Emerald imitations. However, that's not what we are doing here: we are using it as a technique to make some very attractive looking Quartz for our fashionable jewellery and clearly stating what it is - Quenched Crackle Quartz! But what does it mean? Well, we take colourless Quartz, normally from Brazil, facet it and then rapidly heat it up so that it cracks (that's the crackle). Into the cracks we pour various coloured dyes (that's the quench) and then we cool down the gem trapping the dye inside.

Two large Quartz rings from the Sarah Bennett collection.

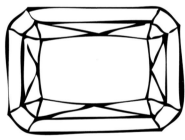

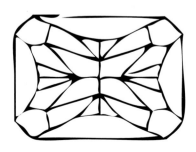

RADIANT CUT

Henry Grossbard introduced the first "Radiant Cut" in 1977. His aim was to capture the brilliance and lustre of the round brilliant cut, whilst combining the elegance of the emerald cut.

The radiant cut received a patent; however, as its popularity soared, so did the copy-cats and within five years, the princess cut was born.

The main difference between the radiant cut and the princess cut is that the princess has pointed corners and is always square, whereas the radiant cut has truncated corners and can be either square or rectangle in shape.

Just like the emerald cut, the radiant cut has truncated corners, but rather than long, parallel facets, the radiant cut has triangular and kite shape facets similar to the round brilliant cut. The original radiant cut had 70 facets: a table, 25 on the crown, 8 on the girdle and 36 on the pavilion.

RARITY

All gems have to be rare, beautiful and durable to be classified as a gem. As old mines become extinct and new mines are found, it is almost impossible to devise a rarity scale. Also, rarity can vary for the same gem, depending on its quality. For example Diamonds are not hugely rare per se - but a 1ct flawless, colourless Diamond is extremely rare. In fact, it is often said that only one white Diamond in a million faceted Diamonds is over 1ct in weight!

Based on the annual amount of carats faceted, Tanzanite is said to be a 1,000 times rarer than Diamond and the likes of Taaffeite and Benitoite are closer to a million times rarer than Diamonds!

Quartz the crystal is certainly not rare, as a large proportion of the Earth's crust consists of it. However, gem-quality Quartz of a level that you would be happy to have set in a piece of jewellery is rare.

Alexandrite is one of the rarest gemstones on the planet.

RED GEMS AND ASSOCIATIONS

Viewing the warm colour red is said to increase the pulse and respiration. The colour is associated with love, desire and passion. It is said to represent masculinity if worn by a male, as well as demonstrating command, nobility and lordship. When worn by a female it has an alluring and seductive nature, and historically was said to show pride and obstinacy. Associated with the planet Mars and Tuesdays, in antiquity the colour was used to cover those who had bravely died in battle. It was often worn in battle to strike fear directly into the hearts of the opposing army.

For those wanting a red gemstone, there is surprisingly little choice. The best known and historically most sought after is the Ruby. Although it is often the most expensive of red gemstones, Rubies are normally heavily included. If you are after a very transparent red gemstone then there are currently some beautifully clear Spinels on the market.

One of the reddest gems must be the Songea Ruby.

ANNABELLA

RED LABRADORITE

In the gem world, there is a real debate at present regarding what the difference is between Red Labradorite and Red Andesine. What some gemmologists are suggesting is that the difference between the two depends on the percentage of Sodium and Calcium within the gem: if it's high in Sodium then it's Andesine; and if it's high in Calcium then it's Red Labradorite. Don't worry if this is getting a little confusing, as it's also confusing the industry!

Colour	Red
Family	Feldspar
Hardness	6 - 6.5
Specific Gravity	2.7 - 2.71
Refractive Index	1.56 - 1.57
Crystal Group	Triclinic
Common Treatments	Heated
Care	None
Cleaning Instructions	Warm soapy water

Red Labradorite is a stunning member of the Feldspar family and is a very close relation to Sunstone. Just like Paraiba Tourmaline, it receives much of its internal brilliance from the presence of copper.

The gem is incredibly rare and I have seen some gem traders trying to sell Red Labradorite for over $1000 per carat, placing it amongst the most expensive red gemstones on the planet. Its colour is a delicious cherry red and what I say to all gem fans, is that once you own one piece, you will certainly be hunting for more.

The gem has been discovered in very tiny quantities in Tibet, India, Bolivia and Inner Mongolia (where it is often heat treated with diffusion to increase its colour). See also Andesine.

A glamorous Red Labradoite ring.

REFRACTIVE INDEX

The returning of white light to the eye after entering the gem is known as refraction.

The refractive index of a gem measures the amount of refraction, and has a direct connection to the speed of light travelling through the gem. The higher the refractive index, the greater the amount of brilliance and often will result in greater dispersion.

Transparent and translucent gems are normally faceted primarily to display their refraction, whereas opaque gems are normally cabochon cut, to show their surface lustre.

Citrine has a high refractive index.

Amethyst has a high refractive index.

A Mattom retro watch.

A refractometer is used to measure the level of refraction and its results are one of the more accurate methods for gemmologists to identify different gems.

Completely transparent glass has a refractive index of 1.5. This means that the light travels at 1/1.5 or 0.67 times the speed in air. The higher the refractive index of a gem, the greater its brilliance will be.

RETRO JEWELLERY

The retro style was alluring, sophisticated and elegant and covered the years 1935 – 1950. The era of retro jewellery followed on from the Art Deco movement, encompassing its style but also adding its own unique individuality. Bold, heavy lines, strong shapes and large gemstones are usually included in the designs from this era.

Gold, as it is today, was very fashionable and used extensively in jewellery of this period. Incidentally, silver was scarce at this time due to the war.

During this time different coloured golds were combined in pieces: especially yellow gold and rose gold. Green gold was also sometimes added and this created a remarkable effect, very rarely seen in Europe today. In France, it was said goldsmiths would work with over 25 different shades of coloured gold.

Coloured gemstones dipped in popularity towards the end of this era, as an exeptional amount of money was spent marketing Diamonds. Some people suggested that more was spent each week on Diamonds than the entire amount ever spent across all coloured gemstones!

RINGS

The wearing of rings can be traced back tens of thousands of years, where grasses and woods were worn for both personal adornment and as a talisman. Around 4,900 years ago, there is evidence that ancient Egyptians exchanged bands in an early form of the wedding ceremony and it is believed that these bands were associated with never ending and immortal love. It is also said that these ancient Egyptians also wore the band on the 4th finger, as they believed it contained a special vein that connected the finger directly to the heart.

Whilst the Egyptian tradition of giving a ring was based on demonstrating love and affection, Roman men gave their brides a ring to show ownership!

In Medieval times, while the rich were wearing rings made of Silver and Gold, the poor were able to obtain bands made from iron and cooper. See also Wedding Rings, Engagement Rings, Eternity Bands, Cluster Rings and Solitaires

Hand made Tookalon rings are often inspired by past civilisations.

RING SIZES

Just as it is important to wear the right dress size or shoe size, it is also important to select the right ring size. Just like the dress size you will need changes as you lose or put on weight, so too does a ring.

In fact, just a weight change of three or four pounds, or a big change in weather conditions, can make the size of your ring vary by a whole size! Why is this so? Well the difference between a size J and a K, or an L and an M, or an N and an O, is less than half of one millimetre in diameter! That's a tiny amount.

Around the globe there are five or six different standards in ring sizes. Whilst the British system, known as the WheatSheaf and also used in Australia and Ireland, uses letters, in the USA and Canada they use a numbering system.

At Coloured Rocks in order to standardise our sizing internationally, we changed our strategy in May 2009. We opted to standardise on the American sizing as it is easier to understand for both the consumer and our manufacturing partners. In fact almost all jewellery

Every new customer at Coloured Rocks receives a free kit for measuring their finger.

Easily resizable to any size.

Resizable one or two sizes.

Difficult to resize.

manufacturers around the world who produce rings from rubber or cast moulds only have these moulds made in USA sizes.

I once asked the Managing Director of one of the world's largest jewellery factories what they did if a UK retailer asked for an English size, he told me that it was common practice to ship the nearest US equivalent. After all, with the British standard only being less than half of one millimetre difference between sizes, it didn't make sense for them to stock eight different sizes in each ring.

After a huge research campaign carried out over a period of six months, we discovered that 73% of people surveyed said their existing rings were either too tight or too loose! Therefore by adopting the American standard, we were able to address many of these issues and to ensure the sizes that we ship are exactly as described.

All of the rings we sell at Coloured Rocks can be resized up or down by at least one American size or two UK letter sizes.

If a ring does not have gems set on the shoulder and as long as the gems are not channel set, then they normally can be resized considerably more. If you are unsure of your ring size, then there is no need to worry. Simply order the ring which you think is going to best fit and it can always be returned for a replacement or resized later.

U.S	Diameter (mm)	Wheat Sheaf	UK - suitable
5	15.7	J 1/2	J or K
6	16.5	L 1/2	L or M
7	17.3	N 1/2	N or O
8	18.1	P 1/2	P or Q
9	18.9	R 1/2	R or S
10	19.9	T 1/2	T or U
11	20.7	V 1/2	V or W
12	21.5	X 1/2	X or Y
13	22.3	Z+	Z+

SARAH BENNETT
GEMSTONE
JEWELLERY

*Rhodium plating under white
Diamonds is known as illusion setting.*

RHODIUM

A precious white metal from the platinum family, rhodium (at the time of writing this guide) costs eight times more than pure gold (23 times more than 9k gold) and four times more than its relative platinum!

A very hard and scratch-resistant metal, it is sometimes used to plate silver, where it also prevents it from tarnishing. As it is whiter in appearance than white gold and platinum, it is often used as a coating and is sometimes referred to as rhodium flashing. It is often electroplated on the shoulders or prongs of yellow gold rings, in order to create an illusion setting for Diamonds.

Englishman William Hyde Wollaston discovered rhodium in 1804. While studying Medicine at Cambridge University, William became fascinated by chemistry, crystallography and physics. On leaving university he became a chemist; while developing new methods of processing platinum in 1803 he discovered palladium, and a year later he found rhodium.

RHODOCHROSITE

Colour	Pink through to reddish brown
Family	Does not belong to a family
Hardness	3.5 – 4.5
Specific Gravity	3.4 – 3.7
Refractive Index	1.6 – 1.8
Crystal Group	Trigonal
Optical Properties	Vitreous lustre
Common Treatments	Not normally treated
Care	Not to be worn next to other pieces of jewellery
Cleaning Advice	Warm soapy water
Chemical Composition	$MnCO_3$

Rhodochrosite is for the heart: it is believed to cultivate love and compassion, and considered to promote intuition and aid in creative pursuits. This crystal is typically rose red in colour, but can also be found in beautiful shades of pink to pale brown. The gem's name is derived from combining the Greek words for rose "rhodon" and "chroma" meaning colour.

As the gem is relatively soft and has perfect cleavage, it is very difficult to cut and is rarely found faceted. That said, Lapidarists who have taken the time to study this gemstone are able to create cabochon cuts and the result is a truly sumptuous, pinkish red treasure that is ideal for gem collectors or for setting into pendants.

In 2002, Colorado officially named Rhodochrosite as its state mineral; although found worldwide, some of the best specimens ever were found at the Sweet Home mine near Alma, Colorado.

RHODOLITE GARNET

A blend of two parts Pyrope to one part Almandine, this rare Garnet is found in many wonderful shades of pink, red and occasionally lavender.

Named after the Greek "rhod" and "lithos", which together translate as "rose stone", this name was first used to describe a pink coloured Garnet from North Carolina, USA.

Rhodolite Garnet tends to be lighter in colour than most other red Garnets and has even been confused with Ruby due to their similarity in colour. Rhodolite is highly refractive which leads to its stunning brilliance.

As the gem is a fairly new member of the Garnet family, it does not have a lot of legends and folklore attached to it in its own right. That said, due to its similarity in colour to several other members of its family, it is believed that Indian tribes used the gem to enhance the potency of fire and placed it next to those who were sick in order to aid recovery.

Colour	Rose pink to deep pink
Family	Garnet
Hardness	7 – 7.5
Specific Gravity	3.4 – 4.3
Refractive Index	1.7 – 1.76
Crystal Group	Cubic
Optical Properties	Various
Common Treatments	Cannot be heat-treated
Care	No special care needed
Cleaning Advice	Ultrasonic or warm soapy water
Chemical Composition	Various

RHODONITE

Just like Bette Davis, Rhodonite is the official gem of Massachusetts. Its name is derived from the Greek word "Rhodon" meaning rose. It was discovered in the 17th century and for several years it was considered the national stone of Russia.

Its uses vary from cameos to beautiful jewellery. Its pink body colour has a vitreous lustre and the gem is distinguished by black veins called dendrites, which form patterns across the main body. Very rarely, transparent Rhodonite is found which is exceedingly fragile and greatly prized by collectors.

As the stone is usually opaque, it is commonly cut as cabochons or into beads. It has also been claimed to have specific therapeutic qualities, promoting relaxation and the soothing of the

Colour	Pink through reddish brown
Family	Does not belong to a family
Hardness	5 – 6
Specific Gravity	3.37 – 3.81
Refractive Index	1.7
Crystal Group	Prismatic
Optical Properties	Vitreous lustre
Common Treatments	Not normally treated
Cleaning Advice	Ultrasonic, steam cleaning or warm soapy water.
Care	No special care requirement
Chemical Composition	Variable composition

nervous system. It is said to aid self-worth and imbue confidence in romantic matters.

As well as being discovered in Massachusetts and Russia, the gem has also been found in Sweden and Australia.

I recently acquired a small parcel of Rhodonite from a very good friend of mine. He informed me that when he received the rough material he tried to have it faceted in Bangkok, but unfortunately because the gemstone was very brittle, too many pieces were damaged. He then sent it to a cutting house in China and then tried one of our cutting houses in Jaipur. Unfortunately, time after time the Lapidarists were damaging too many stones. Then, as a last resort, he sent the rough material to Brazil, where an expert in cutting Kyanite (this gem is extremely difficult to cut as it is polymorphic – meaning that it has different hardness across its different axis) and at last was able to cabochon cut the gemstone with an acceptable amount of breakages. The big trick for the Lapidarist was knowing at which angle to make the all important first cut.

Don't worry about the gem once it has been faceted though. Although this glorious pink gemstone is brittle and difficult to cut, once the cut has been achieved its hardness of 6 to 6.5 on the mohs makes it durable.

Colour	White or colourless
Family	Quartz
Hardness	7
Specific Gravity	2.65
Refractive Index	1.544-1.553
Crystal Group	Trigonal
Optical Properties	none
Common Treatments	none
Care	none
Cleaning Advice	Ultrasonic, steam cleaning or warm soapy water.
Chemical Composition	SiO_2

ROCK CRYSTAL

Quartz is one of the most abundant minerals on Earth and can be found in large crystals, sometimes measuring many feet in length. Most Quartz however, cannot be regarded as a gem as it is neither rare nor beautiful.

The term Rock Crystal is often used to describe colourless Quartz, which for many centuries has been used to create such items as crystal balls.

Ancient Romans believed that Rock Crystal was formed by gods who were able to permanently freeze ice. It is often formed in igneous and metamorphic rocks; however smaller, finer quality Rock Crystals are discovered in geodes and pegmatites.

Rock Crystal should not be confused with "lead crystal glass". Rock Crystal is made by Mother Nature, whereas lead crystal glass is man made. With lead crystal, lead oxide is added to the molten glass, which dramatically increases the refractive index of the glass, giving it greater sparkle. For example, Swarovski - the famous producers of jewellery and sculpture - is believed to add approximately 32% lead in their manufacturing process, in order to produce items that demonstrate maximum brilliance.

Although natural Rock Crystals can be found worldwide, some of the better quality samples those regarded as gem-quality, are located in the UK, Switzerland, Madagascar and Brazil.

ROCKS

To understand what rocks are, we first need to be aware that a mineral is an inorganic compound that features an orderly internal structure and is of a constant crystal form and chemical composition.

All rocks fall into one of three categories: igneous rocks are formed from molten magma or lava from volcanoes; sedimentary rocks are those which are formed as a result of sedimentary deposits being compacted under pressure over a sustained period of time; and metamorphic rocks are those that change their structure (hence "morph") through pressure or heat - or in most cases a combination of both.

When the Earth was originally formed, 100% of its surface was igneous rock. Over billions of years, due to the movement of tectonic plates, changes in the environment and weathering, much of the world's surface has been replaced with sedimentary and metamorphic rock. Today, less than a third of the Earth's surface remains as igneous rock.

To avoid confusion, it is important to understand that there is a big difference between where gems are formed and where they are later found. For example, many gems are discovered

sedimentary alluvial deposits; however, virtually no gems are actually formed in sedimentary rocks.

Igneous rocks yield such gemstones as Apatite, Beryl, Topaz and Tourmaline; Sapphires, Emeralds, Spinel and many Garnets are created via metamorphism.

ROCKS ADVISOR

As you flick through the pages of this book, I would hope that you start to feel a real sense of connection with the treasures we are provided with by Mother Nature. If you would like to make money out of your newfound passion by selling Gemstone Jewelllery, then our Rocks Advisor program might be ideal for you. Let me first explain why I introduced the scheme...

Throughout history gemstones gifted to us from Mother Nature, have been surrounded in a mass of folklore, myth and legends, there are hundreds of references to coloured gems in the bible, there is virtually a gemstone story for every famous king and queen of Europe and Shakespeare regularly used gemstones to describe colours. But today, why is it that something so undeniably beautiful, so pure and natural and something so well documented for over 2000 years, is so hard to find? The answer is actually simple. Since the late 1800's, the availability of one type of gemstone, has steadily grown. With supplies increasing and availability rarely a problem, in 1940 a massive advertising campaign stated "Diamonds are a Girl's Best Friend". Prior to this, coloured gemstones were previously far more popular than Diamonds. However, as many coloured gemstones are rarer and their availability often sporadic, they have never been seriously marketed or advertised by large corporations and the knowledge of their mystical powers has relied solely on stories being passed on from generation to generation.

One of the beautiful things about coloured gemstones, with their history dating back thousands of years, is that there is always something new to learn and discuss, making it easy for Rocks Advisors to earn money. When

someone pays you a compliment as they see the flash of coloured light illuminating your finger, or from a stunning pendant or earrings, you will find yourself automatically launching into a conversation about your particular gemstone. As you show others your jewellery, talk about where the gemstone originated, what the cut is, what the setting is, before you realise it you will have just earned yourself commission and the satisfaction of knowing you have just introduced someone to something quite magical.

For more information take a look at

www.rocksadvisor.com.

ROMAN JEWELLERY

The Roman Empire was unquestionably one of the largest and strongest empires history has ever seen. It grew from the ancient city of Rome, to the Roman Kingdom, to the Roman Republic and finally, before its collapse, into the great Roman Empire. The Roman Empire at its strongest encapsulated much of the globe and ruled many nations.

Finding evidence of Roman jewellery is obviously harder than looking at a more recent period such as Victorian, Edwardian, or Georgian, as most of the evidence we have is archaeological. Archaeologists have had to piece together traces and fragments of information to build up a picture of what it was like to live thousands of years ago.

After the start of what is now recognised as 'The Roman Empire', in the year 27BC, there was little change or innovation in the design and creation of jewellery. Pre-existing designs and shapes continued to be used and only small and insignificant changes were made. Throughout the many years of the Empire, different styles and fashions came and went. Much of the inspiration for Roman jewellery was borrowed from other cultures and lands. We find that a lot of early Roman jewellery took its inspiration from Greek and Etruscan jewellery. The 'Etruscan' culture was built up of people that lived in Etruria in Italy, a non-Italian group of people, whose culture was primarily based upon the Greeks.

An increasingly popular piece of jewellery throughout the duration of the Empire was the ring. In the 1st and 2nd centuries AD, rings were so popular they were often worn on all 8 fingers and on both thumbs! Unlike today though, the rings were usually worn in front of the knuckle, and were therefore a lot smaller.

During the Roman Empire, women of the ruling class were extremely privileged and wore lots of jewellery. The displaying of their jewellery, as it still can be today, was often a sign of status and

Garnet was often used for jewellery in the Roman era.

Peridot was often mistaken for Emerald by early Romans.

Early Roman seamen used to take Aquamarine on their ventures for protection.

great wealth.

Whilst women wore a great deal of jewellery, Roman men often wore a single ring, made from either gold or stone. These rings were called 'signet' rings and had a design on them, personalised to the owner. As each ring was unique they were used to stamp a wax seal onto important documents. Some Romans even had their own faces engraved onto their rings.

The Roman Empire was rapidly expanding, and after 300BC, it was aided further by an increase in gold supplies. It is believed that the supply reached ten tonnes annually by 100AD; a level which was not achieved again for over a thousand years. During this period, gold coins became a popular choice for making jewellery and each coin was said to be worth the equivalent of the combined annual salary of four soldiers.

The Ancient Romans had access to a wide variety of natural resources and gemstones from across Europe and further afield. Sapphire, Emerald, Garnet, Topaz, Aquamarine, Cornelian and Amber were all introduced into jewellery. Uncut Diamonds were also occasionally used.

One piece of jewellery that people often associate with the Romans is the brooch. As well as being worn for purely decorative reasons, they would often be used to fasten cloaks. Special brooches would be designed to celebrate festivals, of which there would be around 160 a year! The 'fibula', a type of safety pin, was another piece commonly used to fasten cloaks. As Roman clothing was commonly pinned together rather than sewn, the fibula was the focus of the garment, and was therefore often extremely ornate.

Britain also played a small part in Roman jewellery making. High quality Jet, from the town of Whitby, in Yorkshire, was made into jewellery and then shipped off to Rome.

Sarah Bennett often uses metal textures inspired by Roman Jewellery.

ROSE GOLD

Pure Gold as it comes out of the ground is yellow in colour. When 9k Gold and 18k Gold is used in jewellery, it is alloyed with other metals to make it stronger and more affordable. It is therefore possible to change the appearance of the gold by using different types of alloys. Whilst Silver or Palladium is used to change gold into White Gold, copper is normally used as an alloy to create Rose Gold (also known as Pink Gold or Red Gold). Many people believe that Rose Gold is old Gold and whilst it is true that copper has been used as an alloy for many years, possibly longer than using Silver, the colour of a gold piece of jewellery has little to do with age, other than the styles of certain era.

Today Rose Gold is becoming increasingly popular as designers make light Pink Gold by annealing gold with a mixture of both silver and copper. This light pink colour can look stunning when used with gemstones such as Morganite, Pink Spinel and Pink Sapphires.

Rose Gold and Amethyst always make a graceful combination.

ROSE QUARTZ

The colour of Rose Quartz ranges from a very tender pale pink to a delicate powder pink and can be transparent through to translucent. This gem has adorned ornaments and jewellery since ancient times. Truly transparent Rose Quartz is extremely rare, and is usually so pale that it does not show much colour at all, with the exception of when it is available in larger sizes. Translucent Rose Quartz, however, is a lot more readily obtainable and unless its colour is especially vibrant, tends to be used for beaded jewellery and carvings.

Rose Quartz is similar to other forms of the Quartz family in that it is prone to inclusions and when of a rutile nature can create asterism. However, while most asterisms appear when light hits the gemstone, light needs to be shone through the gem in order for the asterism to be visible.

Known as the gemstone of true love, it is said that Rose Quartz allows you to get to know your true self and to love that true self in all its beauty. As Whitney Houston once sang "learning to love yourself is the greatest love of all"; if you are struggling with self-esteem then maybe this gem is for you.

Colour	Pale pink to powder pink
Family	Quartz
Hardness	6.6 – 7
Specific Gravity	2.6 – 2.65
Refractive Index	1.540 - 1.550
Crystal Group	Trigonal
Optical Properties	Glassy to vitreous lustre
Common Treatments	Some varieties are heat-treated
Care	No special care
Cleaning Advice	Ultrasonic or warm soapy water
Composition	SiO_2

ROYAL JEWELLERY

Throughout history, Royal Families across the world have had a huge influence on both fashion and the creation of jewellery. Although Elizabeth II no longer holds as much influence as Queen Victoria did in jewellery, there is still much adoration of the outfits she wears.

It is not just the Queen who is admired and whose style is coveted, but also the Princesses. Young girls dream of being a Princess, and most would give anything to have a slice of a royal lifestyle. It is for this reason that Royalty has had such a influence upon the jewellery world. Members of the Royal family have been the celebrities of yesteryear, having had all the influence and notoriety that Hollywood A-listers enjoy today.

Most women have their own personal collection of jewellery, but one lady's is famous the world over. This collection, of course, is the British Crown Jewels. Having been treasured and collected by Kings and Queens for 800 years, today they are priceless. The Crown Jewels are much more than mere gold, Diamonds and other precious gemstones; they represent hundreds of years of British history.

The current Crown Jewels are not the first. King John lost the original jewels dating back to the Anglo-Saxon period in Britain in 1216. It is said that he lost them in quicksand! Replacements were made, but in 1330 they were stolen from Westminster Abbey. Just days later they were recovered after being discovered for sale in a jeweller's shop window in central London. Oliver Cromwell sold or melted down the majority of the Jewels in 1649, stating that they were a symbol, as he described it, of the 'detestable rule of kings'. It wasn't until the restoration of the monarchy in 1661 with Charles II that they were fully replaced.

The ultimate jewels in the collection are the Cullinan Diamonds, commonly known as the 'Stars of Africa'. The Cullinan, discovered in South Africa in 1905, was the largest Diamond ever found. Weighing in at 3,106ct, in its rough state it was more than three times the size of its

nearest competitor. The gem was purchased at a price close to a million dollars and was given as a present to King Edward VII on his 66th birthday. The stone was later cut into nine large gems and dozens of smaller ones by the famous Asscher Brothers, who were at the time believed to be amongst the best Lapidarists in the world. The Cullinan I is set in the royal Scepter and weighs a massive 530ct. Until 1985, when the Golden Jubilee Diamond was discovered weighing 545.67ct, it was the largest faceted Diamond in the world. The Cullinan II at 317ct is set into the Imperial Crown.

Also in the crown above the Cullinan II is 'The Black Prince's Ruby' which is one of the oldest stones in the Crown Jewels collection. Its British Royal possession can be dated back to 1367 when it was received as a gift by Edward of Woodstock, who was known as 'The Black Prince' - hence the stone's name. The interesting thing about this stone is that it is not a Ruby at all but a Spinel, a gemstone historically mistaken for a Ruby.

During WWII the Jewels were taken and hidden in a secret location to protect them; to this day no one knows where they were hidden. Today the Crown Jewels are kept under strict guard at 'Jewel House', in the Tower of London.

One piece of jewellery associated with Royalty that has had a big impact on the jewellery world is Diana Spencer's engagement ring to Prince Charles. Diana Francis Spencer became officially engaged to the heir to the throne on February 24th, 1981. Her engagement ring was an 18-carat Sapphire surrounded by 14 individual Diamonds. Ever since Prince Charles asked for Diana's hand in marriage, Sapphire engagement rings have become synonymous with elegance, royalty and romance. Shortly after the proposal, Cartier brought out a whole line of Sapphire and Diamond rings. Princess Anne also had a Sapphire engagement ring. Sarah Ferguson, when she became engaged to Prince Andrew wore a Ruby ring. After this event Ruby engagement rings soared in popularity, people again wanting a slice of the royal lifestyle for themselves.

Tomas Rae.

1ct Diamond Ring
set in 18k White Gold
£1068

RUBELLITE TOURMALINE

When Tourmaline appears to look like a Ruby it is renamed Rubellite. However, just like the debate about when a dark Pink Sapphire becomes a Ruby, Tourmaline is only renamed Rubellite if its deep red colours are seen in both daylight and artificial light. If its hues are not profound under both lighting conditions, it is renamed Pink Tourmaline.

Rubellite's name is derived from the Latin word "rubellus" which literally translates to "coming from red".

Inclusions in Rubellite are fairly common, as the chemical structures responsible for its wonderful colour also create "jardin" (the French word for garden, and is used to describe Mother Nature's inclusions).

The gem is a real treasure. It is far rarer than its closest rival Ruby and many people find it infinitely more attractive. However, as often happens in the gem world, it does not command such a high price as its competitor, due to it being less well-known.

Colour	Red
Family	Tourmaline
Hardness	7 – 7.5
Specific Gravity	3.02 – 3.1
Refractive Index	1.610 – 1.640
Crystal Group	Trigonal
Optical Properties	Strong pleochroism
Common Treatments	Occasionally heat-treated
Care	No specific care required
Cleaning Advice	Warm soapy water
Chemical Composition	A complex ferromagnesian silicate

RUBY

The gem of love, Ruby is the red member of the Corundum family and is often given as a gift to show the strength of one's relationship. Its rich, vivid red colours are due to the presence of chromium and its almost identical twin sister, the Sapphire, is similar in all but colour.

Until the early 1800's, its association with Sapphire lay undiscovered; prior to this period many other gemstones, including Spinel and Garnets, were often misidentified as Ruby.

Most Rubies show purplish red to orangey red hues; however, the overall colour (colour being a combination of hue, shade and saturation) can provide gem dealers with an indication of the stone's original geographic origin. Burmese

Colour	Red
Family	Corundum
Hardness	9
Specific Gravity	3.9 – 4.1
Refractive Index	1.757 - 1.779
Crystal Group	Trigonal
Optical Properties	Vitreous lustre
Common Treatments	Heat-treated, glass filled, diffusion
Care	No specific care required
Cleaning Advice	Ultrasonic or warm soapy water
Chemical Composition	Al_2O_3

A lavish 3ct Ruby ring by Jacque Christie.

A Ruby entwined ring hand-made by Tookalon.

Rubies tending to be purplish red in colour, while Thai stones tend to be brownish red.

Ruby shows pleochroism, which means that the colour varies when viewing the gemstone in different directions and many can appear incredibly bright when exposed to the sun (see fluorescence). Inclusions in Rubies are called "silk", and if sufficiently abundant and precisely arranged this can lead to wonderful asterism; with the correct cutting, Star Rubies can often be created.

Ruby has been a popular gemstone for centuries and has been set in many famous historic pieces of jewellery. Ruby mining can be traced back over 2500 years ago in Sri Lanka. The famous mines in Mogok, Burma were first explored as early as the 6th century AD. Historically, the gem has had many different names around the globe, which highlights how popular it has been with many different civilisations. In Sanskrit, the Ruby was known as "ratnaraj" which stood for "the king of precious gems", and later "ratnanayaka"; "leader of all precious stones". The gem was referred to in the Bible as a Carbuncle, although today research has shown that this name was also used for several other red gemstones. Its more recent name, Ruby, is derived from the Latin word "rubers" simply meaning "red".

As can be imagined, the gem is surrounded by a great deal of folklore and legends. In the ancient world people believed that Rubies could help them predict the future and they have been worn as talismans to protect from illness or misfortune ever since. It has also been said that the wearer of a Ruby would enjoy romance, friendship, energy, courage and peace.

Pliny the Elder, influenced by the writings of the ancient Greek philosopher Theophrastus (371 – 287BC), wrote "In each variety of Ruby there are so called "male" and "female" stones, of which the former are the more brilliant, while the latter have a weaker lustre". Considering Pliny's work took place almost 2000 years ago, this remains one of the few theories relating to gemstones that he misinterpreted!

In Burma and Thailand one legend tells of the ancient Burmese dragon who laid three magical eggs. From the first egg came forth Pyusawti, king of Burma, from the second emerged the Chinese Emperor and the third egg provided all of the vivid Rubies in Burma, many of which local gem traders will tell you are yet to be discovered.

Shortly after Marco Polo documented his travels (in which he recited how Ruby was used by people of the Kahn to protect themselves in battle), Sir John Mandeville wrote a book of his own global experiences (compiled circa 1365). Mandeville believed that "once a man had touched the four corners of his land with his Ruby, then his house, vineyard and orchard would be protected from lightning, tempests and poor harvest".

Heart cut Rubies, a true symbol of love.

For many centuries, Ruby has been thought to remove sadness, prevent nightmares and protect against many illnesses. With its likeness in colour to blood, it has often been said to help stem haemorrhages and cure inflammatory diseases.

It is said that over 95% of Rubies on the market today have been heat-treated, therefore whenever buying a Ruby it is best to assume that the gem's colour has been enhanced. Large, natural Rubies of good colour and clarity are so valuable that they often demand a higher price per carat than even the most flawless Diamonds. For example, in 1988 Sotheby's auctioned a 15.97ct Ruby which sold for more than 3.6 million dollars under the hammer!

Some of the finest Rubies are from Burma, where their colour is said to be comparable to that of "pigeon blood". Other sources include Thailand, Vietnam, Sri Lanka, Kenya, Madagascar, Tanzania, Cambodia, Afghanistan, and India.

Ruby is the birthstone for July and is also the anniversary gemstone for both the 15th and 40th year of marriage. As it has a hardness of 9 on the Mohs scale, it is a tough and durable gemstone, and when set in precious metal should continue to shine for thousands of years to come. Besides being used in jewellery, Rubies are also used extensively in laser technology.

Two gents pieces of Ruby jewellery from Mattom .

RUSSIA

Famous for Alexandrite, Russia also yields two other highly prized green gemstones: Emerald and Demantoid Garnet.

In addition to its world-renowned gems, Russia is also the home of the historical jewellery brand "Fabergé".

Alexandrite, one of the rarest gemstones in the world, was first discovered in the Ural Mountains in 1834. Due to its discovery on the birthday of Tsar Alexander II, it was later given his name.

Also in the Ural Mountains, and the nearby region of Siberia, high clarity Topaz, Emeralds and Demantoid Garnets can be found. However, due to adverse weather conditions, mining can only take place for a few months every year. Although it is believed that the area has sizeable gem deposits, compared to other mining regions around the globe, very little has yet been discovered.

When found in Russia, Chrome Diopside is renamed Russian Diopside.

Colour	Normally colourless
Family	Quartz
Hardness	6.6 – 7
Specific Gravity	2.6 – 2.65
Refractive Index	1.5
Crystal Group	Trigonal
Common Treatments	Some varieties are heat-treated
Cleaning Advice	Ultrasonic or warm soapy water
Composition	SiO_2

RUTILATED QUARTZ

Rutilated Quartz is almost the complete opposite to most varieties of gemstones as its value dramatically increases when more inclusions are present!

Rutilated Quartz is effectively transparent Rock Crystal with golden needles of rutile inclusions set in patterns within the crystal. Each pattern is individually unique to each and every gemstone and its inclusions are sometimes referred to as Venus hair.

Crystal Healers believe that Rutilated Quartz assists with mental focus, rectifies many food disorders, boosts the immune system and helps to remove fatigue.

The gem is associated with the solar plexus chakra, and is often used to form a link between the root and crown chakras.

RUTILE

Rutiles can often be found trapped inside gemstones, where they appear as microscopic inclusions. Rutile is primarily made of titanium dioxide and can be responsible for causing amazing optical effects such as cat's eye or asterisms.

Gems such as Tourmaline, Ruby and Sapphire often have rutile inclusions and Rutile Quartz is famed for its beautiful needle-like inclusions.

As it can sometimes be seen as a red inclusion within certain gemstones, its name is derived from the Latin word for red, "rutilus", which is also responsible for the name given to red Corundum (Ruby).

A huge rutilated Quartz featuring golden inclusions.

RUTILE TOPAZ

You may have read about Rutilated Quartz in the first edition of this book; you may have even acquired a piece. Now I would like to introduce you to Rutile Topaz.

Firstly, in all of my travels I have only ever been offered two parcels of this gemstone. On both occasions, once a price had been agreed and I started to select from the parcels, I only selected about 5% of the pieces to purchase. Unlike Rutilated Quartz, Rutile Topaz only tends to have a very small amount of rutile inclusions in each gem, and to truly appreciate the wonderful appearance of these inclusions, you need quite a high concentration of them to make the gem attractive. I only select pieces where the inclusions are parallel to the table, as when this occurs their image can often be reflected off the facets on the pavilion and you get to see a wonderful mirror image.

The golden threads within the crystal white Topaz are truly stunning, but as I have only ever purchased around 30 pieces to-date, I doubt that we will ever be likely to set them in jewellery. This gemstone really is one for the collectors. If you are looking to add Rulite Topaz to your collection, but aren't really worried about the

Colour	Colourless
Family	Topaz
Hardness	8
Specific Gravity	3.5 - 3.6
Refractive Index	1.60 - 1.62
Crystal Group	Orthorhombic
Optical Properties	Rutile
Common Treatments	Not normally treated
Care	No special care required
Cleaning Advice	Ultrasonic or warm soapy water
Chemical Composition	$Al_2SiO_4(OH,F)_2$

Incredibly rare Rutile Topaz.

quality, then shop around, if you are looking for top quality pieces then check GemCollector.com to see if we have any in stock.

Please note that although we refer to this gem as Rutile Topaz, the GIA (who have tested this material) believe that the inclusions don't stem from rutile but are "open channels colored by limonite". The material I have sourced is mined in Brazil and I have recently heard that it can also be found in Burma.

TOOKALON

Combining classic artisanship, genuine gemstones
and individualistic designs, each piece of Tookalon
jewellery is made entirely by hand.

SANCY DIAMOND

One of the most historically fascinating Diamonds ever found has to be the Sancy Diamond. The history of this gem started over 600 years ago, when it was reputed to have been discovered in the fabled mines of Golconda, India.

The Sancy Diamond was once the largest Diamond ever discovered, but since Diamonds were discovered in South Africa in the late 1800's, its size is no longer quite as significant. The gem's outline shape is comparable to a cross between a shield and a pear cut stone. What makes it so unusual is that its profile is the same shape either side of the girdle.

The Sancy was believed to impart invincibility to anyone who wore it. The Diamond has been worn by several members of France's royalty. Elizabeth I pursued the Diamond for decades. The gem has also funded many battles; after being stolen from the Louvre it was sold to help pay for

Napoleon's war efforts. There is so much history and fascination surrounding this Diamond that we would highly recommend Susan Ronald's book "The Sancy Blood Diamond".

SAPPHIRE

Sapphires are known and revered the world over for their beauty and mystery. In many ancient cultures this gem has been admired not only for its elegance but also for the magic and good luck often associated with it. In western civilisations the Sapphire has long been the traditional stone of choice to set alongside Diamonds for a man wanting to express his love and commitment to someone special.

For over a thousand years, Sapphires have enjoyed a close association with royalty. The unquestionably exquisite and perfectly turned out Mrs. Simpson received many gems from Edward VIII. Her collection included incredible Emeralds, vivid Rubies and large, flawless Diamonds; however she always maintained that her favourite gemstone was Sapphire. Indeed, she was so proud of one bracelet, designed by Van Cleef and Arpels, that apparently she asked her tailor to shorten the sleeves of all her dresses and blouses so that everyone could see her Sapphires. In the 1980's, resurgence in the popularity of Sapphire rings occurred shortly after Prince Charles purchased a stunning Ceylon Blue Sapphire ring as Princess Diana's engagement ring.

Sapphires come in a range of colours, from summer sky blues to jet black, colourless and all colours in between. Sapphire is a member of the Corundum family; pure Corundum, known as White Sapphire, is colourless. The wide array of differing hues seen in Sapphires is due to the presence of different impurities found in their crystal structure. Blue Sapphires are formed due to the presence of titanium. Chromium trapped inside Corundum allows us to enjoy Pink Sapphire and in larger quantities gives us the Ruby (when Corundum is red it is renamed Ruby instead of Sapphire). When admiring a Sapphire, turning it back and forth will allow the light to

Colour	Almost every colour other than red
Family	Corundum
Hardness	9
Specific Gravity	3.9 – 4.1
Refractive Index	1.757 – 1.779
Crystal Group	Trigonal
Optical Properties	Strong pleochroism
Common Treatments	Around 95% of Sapphires are heat-treated or diffused
Cleaning Advice	Ultrasonic, steam cleaning or warm soapy water
Care	No special care required
Chemical Composition	Al_2O_3

Hot Pink Sapphire by Tomas Rae

travel through the gem and display even more colours; this beautiful array of colours emitted as the gem is moved is known as pleochroism.

In addition to being surrounded by many myths and legends, this gemstone also enjoys one of the richest histories. In antiquity Persians believed that Blue Sapphires were actually chips from a huge pedestal that supported the earth, the reflections of which coloured the sky. In the Middle Ages it was thought to be an antidote against poisons and to possess a magical power to influence the spirits.

It is also mentioned numerous times in the Bible: "Under his feet was something like a pavement made of Sapphire, clear as the sky itself" (Exodus 24:10). "In the second row a Turquoise, a Sapphire and an Emerald" (Exodus 28:18). "Sapphires come from its rocks, and in its dust contains nuggets of gold" (Job 28:6). "His body is like polished ivory decorated with Sapphires" (Song of Solomon 5:14). "O afflicted city, lashed by storms and not comforted, I will build you with stones of Turquoise, your foundations with Sapphires" (Isaiah 54:11). "You were in Eden, the garden of God; every precious stone adorned you: Ruby, Topaz and Emerald, Chrysolite, Onyx and Jasper, Sapphire, Turquoise and Beryl. Your settings and mountings were made of gold; on the day you were created they were prepared" (Ezekiel 28:13). "The foundations of the city walls were decorated with every kind of precious stone. The first foundation was Jasper, the second Sapphire, the third Chalcedony, the fourth Emerald" (Revelation 21:19).

Sapphire and its sister, Ruby, share a common attribute. Although Ruby has been unearthed in several countries, there is one country where its source is most highly prized: Burma. Likewise, though Sapphires are unearthed in countries as far afield as Madagascar, Australia, Thailand and China, the most highly regarded Sapphires come from a country known as "gem island": Sri Lanka. These Sapphires, especially when blue, are known as Ceylon Sapphires (Sri Lanka was previously known as Ceylon) and command incredibly high prices per carat, particularly when they have not been heat-treated. The only region to take the limelight away from Ceylon was Kashmir in India, where in the early 1900's a deposit was discovered that yielded superb violet-blue Sapphires that were described as velvet in appearance. The Songea region of Tanzania has provided one of the more recent discoveries of a kaleidoscope of stunning Sapphires. This gem is the birthstone of September and is associated with the Zodiac sign of Taurus. It is also the gift for the 5th, 45th and 70th anniversaries. Its hard crystal structure measures 9 on the Mohs scale, making it incredibly durable. When set in a ring or pendant, and given proper care, it should continue to shine for thousands of years to come.

The most famous of all Sapphire: Celyon Blue.

SARAH BENNETT
COLLECTION

The Sarah Bennett Collection of jewellery is focused on uniquely cut, large, colourful gemstones, set into modern, elaborate designs. Firstly, by working hand in hand with the gemstone cutter, each piece is elegantly shaped to bring genuine gemstones to life. From the uniquely developed "Spiral Cut" to the "Inverted Brilliant Cut", The Sarah Bennett Collection applies a very modern approach to cutting genuine gemstones. Only after the gem has been boldly and elegantly faceted is the supporting jewellery designed. Here the attitude is simple, creating elaborate designs that will get the wearer noticed and, above all, avoid subtlety.

Most of the collection is crafted in Jaipur India, where the gemstone cutting houses are regarded as some of the finest in the world. The jewellery supporting each gem is created by a perfect marriage of hand craftsmanship and the latest in modern technology. This approach is evident in the intense amount of small detail that goes into each piece. Some Sterling Silver rings, earrings and pendants in the collection feature 18k gold prongs, where all four have different designs carved into them. It is unusual to discover this fusion of Sterling Silver and 18k gold in most designers' work, as accurately executing the assembly of these two different precious metals is an incredibly specialised skill.

SARAH BENNETT
GEMSTONE
JEWELLERY

SARDONYX

Throughout the ages there have been many myths, legends and folklore surrounding the spiritual qualities of Sardonyx (also known as Banded Agate). Romans soldiering into war would wear the stone, engraved with a picture of Mars (god of war), believing it would bring them courage in times of doubt.

The name Sardonyx itself is an amalgamation of its composition, the two minerals 'Sard' and 'Onyx'. During the Renaissance in Europe it was believed that this stone gave speakers eloquence when talking. In Ancient Greece people used to carve them into the shape of scarab beetles, a mythological creature that was believed to eat people! The gem also has many links with royalty and it is said that Queen Elizabeth I gave the Earl of Essex a large Sardonyx gold ring as a present.

Sardonyx is the reddish brown coloured member of the Agate family and it normally has varying coloured layers and a vitreous to waxy lustre. The main use of Sardonyx throughout the ages has been to make carved cameos (a carving made out of a gemstone).

Today Sardonyx is mined in various locations around the world, however in years gone by it was considerably rarer and more valuable. There was even a time when it was worth more than gold! Most of the world's supply is mined in the Sardonyx Mountains in India and it is generally agreed that this is where the highest quality Sardonyx comes from. The gem is also found in Russia, Australia, Brazil and Madagascar.

Colour	Reddish brown with white or cream bands
Family	Agate, Chalcedony Quartz
Hardness	6.5
Specific Gravity	2.59 – 2.61
Refractive Index	1.54
Crystal Group	Trigonal
Optical Properties	Vitreous to waxy lustre
Common Treatments	Not normally treated
Care	No specific care needed
Cleaning Advice	Ultrasonic, steam cleaning or warm soapy water
Chemical Composition	SiO_2

SATURATION

As discussed elsewhere in this book, colours are made up of three elements: hue, saturation and tone. 'Saturation', also referred to as colour purity, describes the pureness of the hue: its vividness and intensity. If a gemstone was pure grey or pure brown, it would be described as having zero colour saturation. When greys or browns are seen in a coloured gemstone, they

A highly saturated Amethyst by Sarah Bennett.

A London Blue Topaz showing great saturation.

tend to dilute the beauty of the colour. At the other end of the scale, if the colour has very little grey or brown in it, it is described as a vivid colour (it is worth noting that no colour produced by Mother Nature has 100% saturation). The GIA describes six levels of saturation; Greyish Brown, slightly Greyish Brown, very slightly Greyish Brown, moderately strong colour, strong colour and vivid colour.

As a general rule of thumb, the higher the saturation in a gemstone, the more valuable it becomes. Sometimes the saturation is even more important than the hue itself. For example a violetish Blue Sapphire with a vivid saturation, would most likely cost more than a pure Blue Sapphire which had a greyish brown saturation.

SAUTOIR

Derived from the French word "to chain", "sautoir" is the name given to a long necklace. Although popular during the Edwardian Era, the sautoir became a "must-have" item of jewellery alongside the cocktail ring in the Art Deco Era.

SCAPOLITE

This family of gemstones is identified primarily by its unusual crystal structure which is known as tetragonal dipyramidal (the only two other minerals on Earth that share this structure are the even lesser-known Powellite and Scheelite). Its structure provides a prismatic shape and its name is derived from the Greek word "scapo" meaning 'rod' or 'shaft'. Normally found in colours similar to Rose-de-France Amethyst or Lemon Quartz, Scapolite is a gemstone that is highly prized by both gem collectors and jewellery connoisseurs. When the gem's appearance is similar to Amethyst it is thought to help the wearer make important decisions, whereas the more lemony, citrus colours are said to provide relief from aches and pains.

Historically the gem was known as Chrysolite, which was a name given to many greenish yellow gems including Peridot (see also the Breastplate of Aaron). During the last century,

Colour	Yellow, pink, purple, blue, grey and white
Family	Scapolite
Hardness	5.5 - 6
Specific Gravity	2.5 – 2.7
Refractive Index	1.54 – 1.60
Crystal Group	Tetragonal Dipyramidal
Optical Properties	Will often fluoresce yellow to orange under UV light
Common Treatments	none
Care	Care should be taken due to its relatively low hardness
Cleaning Advice	Warm soapy water
Chemical Composition	$Na_4(Al, Si)_{12}O_24Cl$ to $Ca_4(Si, Al)_{12}O_{24}(CO_3, SO_4)$

the gem has also been known as Wernerite, Mizzonite, Dipyre and Marialite. Today its new name Scapolite is widely recognised throughout the gem industry.

Some believe Scapolite was first discovered in Burma, but others maintain it was originally found on Egypt's St. John's Island (once known as Topazios and today renamed Zeberget) in the Red Sea. The confusion surrounding its discovery is likely to be due to its previous identification as Chrysolite.

In addition to purple and yellow The gem can be discovered in various attractive colours including, pinkish purple, blue, grey and colourless. In its transparent form it is often brilliant cut and when discovered translucent it is normally cabochon cut, which occasionally enables the gem to display chatoyancy (a cat's eye optical effect). The finest samples on the market today are from the Umba River area of Tanzania; other locations for the gem include Australia, Madagascar and the USA.

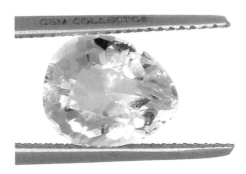

A dazzling 3.3ct Scapolite from Madagascar.

SCHILLER

Originating from the German word for "play of different colours", Schiller is commonly used as an alternative word for fire or dispersion. The more correct use of this term however, is in describing iridescent-type lustre in gems such as Labradorite, where layers of inclusions provide a bronze-like lustre. Other gems that exhibit schiller include Spectrolite and Sunstone.

Delightful schiller seen in this Labradorite.

SCINTILLATION

Very similar to lustre and brilliance, scintillation is used to describe the optical effect seen in gems such as Diamonds, where an area of light on a polished facet seems to flash on and off as either the gem or the light source moves. I often referr to scintillation as the lighthouse effect. The GIA (Gemological Institution of America), who invented the four 'C's as a way of measuring the quality of Diamonds, use scintillation as one of the seven criteria for assessing the quality of a gem cut.

Table View

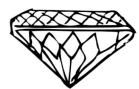

Side View

Pavillion View

SCINTILLATOR BRILLIANT CUT

In a world where everything is done in a rush, where time is money, where value seems to dominate over quality, you will be pleased to know that there are still a few Lapidarists around that view their craft more as a hobby and challenge, than a financially rewarding job. Just like great painters, those who view Lapidary as an art, have the wonderful ability to create masterpieces that are truly spectacular.

Take the classic brilliant round cut, it has become our staple diet in the gem world ever since Tolkowsky developed it in 1919. But when time and profit is put to one side for a moment, then imagine what happens when a gem cutter enlarges the table facet and adds around 80 small triangular and kite shaped facets to the crown? Then by turning the gem over, makes time to patiently do the same to the pavilion. The result is a gemstone that offers incredible scintillation (the effect seen when you slowly rock a gem backwards and forwards and the entire facet on a crown flashes on and off like a lighthouse) and yet still retains its internal brilliance.

This cut is only suitable for gems with great clarity, as its larger table facet hides nothing; it's also a great cut to use if you want to show off strong vivid colours within a gem. Due to the complex arrangement of facets, don't expect to see it on gems weighing less than two carats and do expect to pay a little more than a standard round brilliant cut gem.

SCRIBBLING RING

Exchanged by lovers in the 16th century, "Scribbling Rings" were set with a Diamond faceted not with a table facet, but with a sharp point, which was then used to engrave messages of love on glass.

Queen Elizabeth I and Mary Queen of Scots were two of the most famous scribblers: Sir Walter Raleigh was said to have scribbled upon his queen's window: "Fain would I rise but that I fear to fall." Elizabeth's reply was: "If thy heart fail thee, do not rise at all."

Today, after a long absence, scribbling rings are returning to fashion; however, this time it is coloured gemstones that are being used. Those buying these pieces are usually unaware of the history behind the cut of the gem and are likely to wear the piece as a fashion statement, rather than a writing tool!

Having said they were popular in the 16th century a Scribbling Ring was recently discovered in Leicestershire, England, which experts have dated back to the early medieval period, possibly the 11th century. A report in "The Times" newspaper on 21st of August 2008 states that a Mr Stevens, who was using a metal detector, found the Black Diamond ring in a local field and experts believe it once belonged to either the Church or royalty.

An elaborate 4ct White Topaz scribbling ring.

SEMI PRECIOUS

In the 1700's and 1800's the phrase 'precious gems' was applied to the three most desirable gems of the period: Ruby, Sapphire and Emerald.

In the early 1900's Diamond also earned the title 'precious gemstone', whilst all other gemstones became known as 'semi-precious'. Today the term 'semi-precious' is frowned upon within the industry, as many gemstones such as Paraiba Tourmaline, Alexandrite, Sphelerite, and several others, often fetch substantially higher prices per carat than those previously belonging to the exclusive 'precious gemstone' club.

Andesine is most definitely not semi precious.

The International Colored Gemstone Association (ICA) goes as far as to say, 'The problem with semi-precious, and the reason why the jewelry industry has banned its use, is that it is quite misleading. Rubies, emeralds, and sapphires can sell for less than $100 per carat and a fine Paraiba tourmaline, for example, can sell for $20,000 per carat. That seems pretty precious, doesn't it?' Incidentally the French word for gemstones is "pierres précieuse."

Nobody could describe Tanzanite as semi precious.

SETTING

A setting is the mount in which gems are set into rings, earrings, pendants and bracelets. There are many different styles of settings used in modern jewellery making; the more common ones being illusion setting, prong setting (also known as a claw setting), pave setting, channel setting, tension setting, milgrain setting, bezel setting and invisible setting.

It is important to consider the setting when buying jewellery set with gemstones. Always remember that gold and silver are relatively soft metals and therefore only a small amount of pressure applied to a prong setting in the wrong direction can easily alter its shape. Simply by catching a prong on a fibre as you remove a jumper could bend a prong and therefore I recommend that prong set pieces are quickly checked prior to putting them on, to ensure that the gem is not loose.

One well-known setting for rings is the Tiffany setting (named after the famous jewellers who first made it popular), this is a 4 or 6 prong setting that elevates a solitaire gem above the band of gold or platinum. If a gem is completely enclosed, as in a bezel setting, it is referred to as a closed setting; the term open setting would apply to prong set gems

Bezel set heart cut Abalone.

A semi bezel setting.

Colour	Green, Yellow, White, Brown
Family	Serpentine
Hardness	2.5 - 4.1
Specific Gravity	2.57
Refractive Index	1.56 - 1.57
Crystal Group	Monoclinic
Optical Properties	Translucent to opaque
Common Treatments	Dying
Cleaning Advice	Warm soapy water

SERPENTINE

Although we tend to refer to Serpentine as a gem type, it is in fact a gem family featuring several different minerals including Antigorite, Chrysotile and Lizardite (named after the Lizard Peninsula in Cornwall where it was first discovered). As Serpentine is relatively soft (2.5 to 4.1 on the Mohs scale), gem-quality material is normally kept for gem collectors rather than being set into jewellery. Unfortunately for those of us that live in the UK, all gem-quality Serpentine is Antigorite, rather than the Lizardite which is found in plentiful supply in the South West of the country!

In some countries, Serpentine is dyed and sold as "Korean Jade" or "New Jade". In times gone by in New Zealand, the Maori people use to carve ornaments out of the mineral, as the gem is relatively soft and easy to work with.

Similar to the likes of Chalcedony and Agate, Serpentine is a microcrystalline gem and therefore is normally opaque to translucent in appearance. Colours range from whiteish grey, to yellowish green, to very dark brown, almost black.

The Serpentine we currently have in our vault is from Afghanistan, but it can also be discovered in Cornwall, England, Ireland, California, Canada and Norway.

SHANK

When you hear the word shank in relation to a ring, it is usually referring to the piece of metal that runs around the ring from one shoulder to the other. It is important that the shank is well finished and slightly rounded at the edges, so that it is comfortable to wear.

If 18k gold or higher is used, it is important that the shank is sufficiently deep; otherwise the gold's relative softness could result in the ring bending and losing its shape. Unfortunately, with gold being such an expensive metal, this is not always the case. With stronger metals such as titanium, it is less critical to have a deep shank.

SHAPES

Although the whole industry blurs the boundaries between shapes and cuts, I have always been taught that in the strictest sense, the cut of the gem refers to either the quality of the faceting or the shape and arrangements of the facets. Whilst the shape refers to the outline shape of the gem when viewed from the top. The shapes below are the main recognized shapes, onto which Lapidarists will apply facets and at which point we can start discussing cuts.

To the right are 42 of the most commonly used shapes for gemstones. These shapes represent the view from the table.

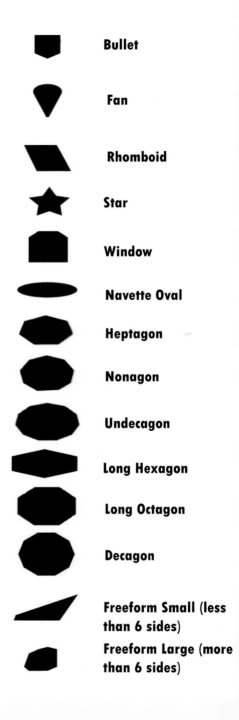

Bullet

Fan

Rhomboid

Star

Window

Navette Oval

Heptagon

Nonagon

Undecagon

Long Hexagon

Long Octagon

Decagon

Freeform Small (less than 6 sides)

Freeform Large (more than 6 sides)

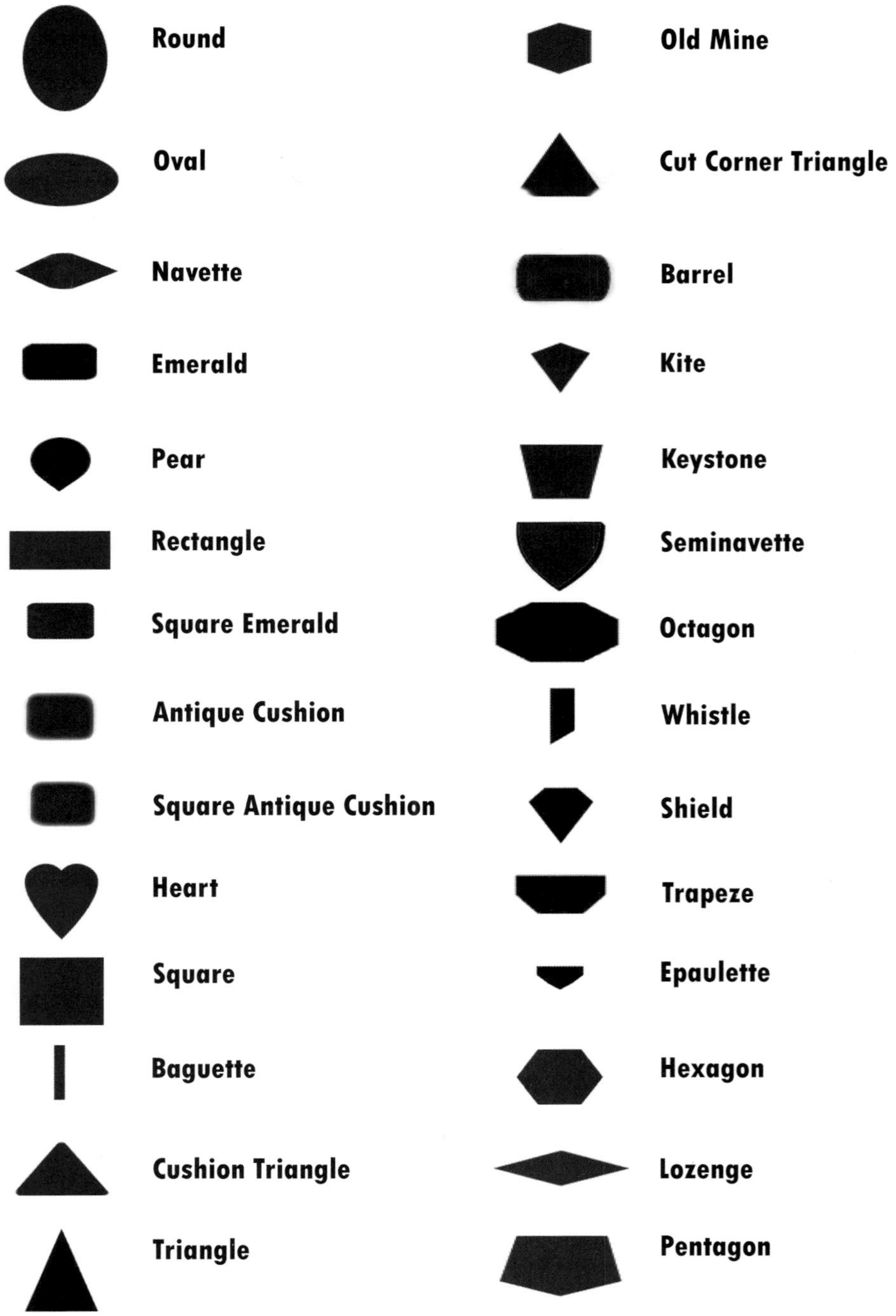

Round

Oval

Navette

Emerald

Pear

Rectangle

Square Emerald

Antique Cushion

Square Antique Cushion

Heart

Square

Baguette

Cushion Triangle

Triangle

Old Mine

Cut Corner Triangle

Barrel

Kite

Keystone

Seminavette

Octagon

Whistle

Shield

Trapeze

Epaulette

Hexagon

Lozenge

Pentagon

Jacque Christie

Make**Everyday**A**Glamour**Day

SHEEN

An optical phenomenon exhibited in certain gemstones caused by alternating layers of different materials within the gem. As light hits these different elements with their different refractive indexes, it creates a beautiful optical effect. Sheen is best seen in gems such as Moonstone.

Sheen is different to lustre and brilliance. The former is the return of light from the surface of the gem, while the latter is the return of light from within the gem.

Beautiful sheen optical effect can be seen in Moonstone.

SHIVA EYE

Also known as Shiva Shell or sometimes Pacific Cat's Eye, Shiva Eye is a stunning natural gem whose pattern is completely made by Mother Nature.

Discovered on the seabed in the shallow tropical waters of Thailand and Indonesia, the gem is actually the protective door found at the opening of the Turban Snail's shell, which towards the end of the snail's natural life, detaches and sinks to the seabed. Although each spiral is similar in pattern, as with all organic gemstones, each one will vary slightly.

Across the gem-rich countries of India, Tibet and Sri Lanka, many Hindus worship the god Shiva. Many pictures of Shiva show a third eye in the middle of the god's forehead and it is from this that the gem's name is derived.

As with many shells the Shiva Eye is made of calcium carbonate. Although its body colour is always whitish, its beautiful swirl can vary in colour, depending on the snail's diet!

SHOULDER

On most gem set rings, the shoulder is the part of the shank on either side of the gems. It effectively forms part of the shank and is often set with small accent stones. If the lead stone is large the shoulders can sometimes be split.

Split shoulders in a futuristic design by Sarah Bennett.

Today seals are used more in business than they are in quality jewellery.

SIGNET RING

Throughout history and until only 100 years ago, seals were used to provide authenticity to all sorts of transactions. From land deals to purchasing bales of hay, from property deals to barrels of wine, and even royal commitments to invitations, everything was authenticated with a seal. Even today some business transactions rely on a company seal, which is believed to be more authentic than a signature and in some countries the signet ring is still used for this purpose.

Even thousands of years ago (in the Bronze Age), Jews used seals and each of the twelve tribes of Israel had their own seal carved for them. A craftsman given the responsibility of creating these seals was regarded as a highly important person, who was not only the artist but also effectively acted as the librarian for each seal he created. Anyone who lost their personal seal ring was regarded as lowlife and it was said that they had lost not only their signet, but their personality too.

Many of the crowns of early signet rings were set with Peridot, Sardonyx and Jasper; these gemstones were not only highly valued, beautiful and strong, they were also not too difficult to carve.

Today signet rings are worn more as a fashion piece of jewellery and few remember the hugely significant part they have played in history.

SILLIMANITE

Sillimanite (also known as Fibrolite) is found in various colours including green, yellow, brown, blue, white and even black. It is a 'polymorph' with two other minerals, Kyanite and Andalusite, which simply means that it shares the same chemistry but has a different crystal structure.

Like Kyanite, this precious stone has a brittleness and directional cleavage that makes it difficult to facet. The scarcity of Sillimanite, combined with the difficulty in cutting it, adds incredible value

Colour	Black, colourless, green, yellow, blue
Hardness	6 – 7
Specific Gravity	3.24
Refractive Index	1.65 – 1.67
Crystal Group	Orthorhombic
Optical Properties	Transparent to opaque
Common Treatments	Not normally treated
Cleaning Advice	Warn soapy water
Composition	Al_2SiO_5

to this gem once it has been successfully faceted.

The gem is a complete Jekyll and Hyde; it can be discovered as a truly transparent gem, or completely opaque with a waxy lustre. The gem's name was given in memory of geologist Bejamin Silliman.

It appears in deposits in several countries including Tanzania, South Africa, Korea, India, Madagascar, England and the USA. The rare transparent variety is mined in the Mogok Valley, Burma, where the deposit has also yielded some extremely rare violet-blue gems.

SILVER

With big look jewellery now highly fashionable, Silver is often used by jewellers who prefer precious metal in their designs rather than simply using a coated base metal. Whilst less expensive than Gold, Silver is still a very costly alternative to base metals, so designs tend to incorporate hollow silver tubes and pressed pieces over casted components. As this precious metal is extremely pliable, beautiful intricate designs can be created. It also benefits from a wonderful lustre, a lustre which is so strong that it is used as a component in mirrors where a superior level of reflectivity is required!

Silver designs by Viorelli now available in the UK.

What you may not know is that Silver is sometimes used as an alloy in gold to turn it white. In 9k White Gold, it is possible for the Silver content to be of a higher level than the Gold (9k Gold has a minimum fineness of 37.5%, with 62.5% being made up of different alloys).

Another interesting fact about Silver is that for over 2700 years it has been used as a currency in many countries. So much so that the word for money and silver is the same in at least 14 languages. The French word 'Argent' for example means both money and Silver. As Silver is the best conductor of electricity - even better than copper - the biggest use of Silver today is in industry, with only 19% of all production being in jewellery and 6% being made into Silverware.

That said, coins and medals still account for over 4% of the annual usage of Silver.

In the UK it is a legal requirement to hallmark all Silver items over 7.78 grams. There are four levels of fineness: 80% (hallmarked 800), 92.5% (hallmarked 925 and commonly known as Sterling Silver, 95.8% (hallmarked 958 and known as Britannia Silver) and 99.9%.

According to the 2007 British Geological Survey, Peru is the world's top producer of Silver, closely followed by Mexico. The next eight largest suppliers in descending order are; China, Chile, Australia, Poland, Russia, United States, Canada and Kazakhstan.

Colour	Green, Brown, Yellow
Family	Sinhalite
Hardness	6.5 - 7
Specific Gravity	3.48
Refractive Index	1.66 - 1.7
Crystal Group	Orthorhombic
Optical Properties	Highly Pleochroic
Common Treatments	None
Care	None
Cleaning Advice	Warm soapy water
Chemical Composition	$MgAlBO_4$

SINHALITE

If you are looking for something a little different, a gemstone that has real earthy colours that often looks like a crossbreed of Peridot and Smokey Quartz, a gemstone that's highly pleochroic and one that, as yet, I believe has not reached its full recognition in the gem world, then you might want to add Sinhalite to your collection.

The gem was first discovered in the Ratnapura District of Sri Lanka (previously known as Ceylon) and was at first thought to be an "off colour Peridot". In 1952 the gem was studied by two mineralogists, Claringbull and Hey, and found to be a new mineral, which was to be named after the Sanskrit word for Ceylon.

Sinhalite is an incredibly rare, collector's gemstone and in addition to the small deposit discovered in the gravel pits of Ratnapura, a handful of specimens have also been discovered in New jersey, USA and in Tanzania. This is a very rare gemstone and a must for all serious collectors.

SLEEPER

Most sleepers are made of hollow gold tubes and they are similarly shaped to a small hooped earring. They are often worn in bed so as to stop a pierced ear from closing up, hence the name.

SMOKEY QUARTZ

Also known as Cairngorm Quartz after the Cairngorm Mountains of Scotland where it was once mined, Smokey Quartz is the national gemstone of Scotland

It is believed that Smokey Quartz helps to build a strong relationship and instill peace and harmony. It is thought to transform negative energy and is reported to be effective at dealing with anger.

Most Smokey Quartz coming out of the ground is not very consistent in colour and is therefore often heat-treated. In addition to Scotland, the gem has been discovered in Brazil, Germany, Australia, India, Madagascar and the USA.

Colour	Pale brown to deep brown
Family	Quartz
Hardness	6.6 – 7
Specific Gravity	2.6 – 2.65
Refractive Index	1.540 - 1.550
Crystal Group	Trigonal
Optical Properties	Glassy to vitreous lustre
Common Treatments	Some varieties are heat-treated
Care	No special care required
Chemical Composition	SiO_2

SODALITE

You may think that you have yet to see a Sodalite, however if you have a piece of jewellery, an ornament or gemstone globe made of Lapis Lazuli much of its deep rich blue colour is most likely to be attributed to the mineral Sodalite.

As well as being a vivid opaque blue gemstone, Sodalite is also the name given to the family of gemstones which includes Hackmanite and Lazurite.

Although the gemstone was initially discovered and documented in Greenland in 1806, it took a further century for a sufficient quantity to be unearthed in Ontario Canada before it started to become faceted and set in jewellery.

The gem receives its name from the presence of sodium. It is sometimes also referred to as Princess Blue after Princess Patricia of Connaught fell so much in love with the gemstone whilst staying in Canada, that on her return to the UK she had whole areas of various rooms in Marlborough House decorated with Sodalite. Today gem-quality Sodalite has been found in Australia, Brazil, Colombia.

Colour	Blue
Family	Feldspathoid
Hardness	5 - 6
Specific Gravity	2.25
Refractive Index	1.48
Crystal Group	Cubic
Optical Properties	Opaque
Care	None
Cleaning Advice	Warm soapy water
Chemical Composition	Na8Al6Si6O34Cl2

Crystal Healers believe that the gem can prove useful if you are in a state of mental confusion and that it is good for relieving stress. Sodalite is associated with the Chakras (especially the third eye) and is said to calm emotions and instil an inner peace.

SOUTH AFRICA

It seems hard to believe that the initial discovery of Diamonds in South Africa was made in December 1866 by fifteen year old Erasmus Jacobs, who was out playing on his family's farm, 550 miles north-east of Capetown. The discovery was the catalyst for the "Great South African Diamond Rush", which turned a tiny little village known as Kimberley into a town of 50,000 people within a period of less than five years. Over the next ten years, South Africa became responsible for 95% of the world's Diamond supply. What was once regarded as the rarest gem on the planet was suddenly more widely available.

Although Diamonds were first discovered in India some 3000 to 4000 years ago, more Diamonds have been extracted from South Africa in 20 years than the entire amount ever recovered from Indian deposits!

The knowledge gained in South Africa led gem hunters to realise that Diamonds were likely to be discovered wherever distinct volcanic pipes could be found, leading them to explore other countries for the gemstone. These volcanic pipes are now known worldwide as Kimberlite pipes, after the small village in South Africa.

For twenty years after the initial discovery, there was continual, fierce rivalry for the control of the mines. In 1888, two of the largest mining companies owned by a Mr Rhodes and a Mr Barnato joined together and formed the De Beers Consolidated Mines Ltd, who remain the largest supplier of Diamonds in the world until this day.

Outside of Diamond mining, South Africa is

one of the world's largest producers of Tiger's Eye. Other than these two gemstones, very little else is mined in commercial quantities, other than a handful of small mines producing a limited amount of Emerald and Amethyst.

SPESSARTINE GARNET

This family of Garnets is orange to reddish orange in colour and can be found in China, America, Nigeria, Namibia and Madagascar.

Mandarin Garnet (also known as Tangerine Garnet), as its name suggests, is a stunning orange gem and is one of the most valuable members of the Spessartine family. It was only discovered last decade, and as well as its fascinating colour it also benefits from amazing brilliance.

Its colours are more like imagining a sunset over a desert or picturing the skin of a peach, rather than the bright orange of the Easyjet logo and are as fascinating to study as a Padparadscha Sapphire.

Colour	Orange to reddish orange
Family	Garnet
Hardness	6.5 – 7.5
Specific Gravity	4.1 – 4.2
Refractive Index	1.79 – 1.89
Crystal Group	Cubic
Optical Properties	Various
Common Treatments	Cannot be heat-treated
Care	No special care needed
Cleaning Advice	Ultrasonic or warm soapy water
Chemical Composition	Various

SPHALERITE

The most amazing thing about collecting coloured gemstones is that Mother Nature never fails to shock you. Until February this year, all I knew about Sphalerite was that the Smithsonian Museum of Natural History and the Liverpool World Museum had samples of this mineral; I had never contemplated setting the mineral in jewellery and had therefore not included it in the first edition of this book.

Then over dinner one day, a very good friend of mine told me he had recently seen a specimen that was bright orange and that it had an amazing amount of dispersion. The next day I spent several hours on the internet researching the gem type and was amazed at what I found. My friend's observation of a strong amount of fire was very accurate indeed: the gem has a dispersion that is over three times that of a Diamond (technically

Colour	Orange, Green or Brown
Family	Sphalerite
Hardness	3.5 - 4
Specific Gravity	4.05
Refractive Index	2.36 - 2.5
Crystal Group	Cubic
Optical Properties	Incredible dispersion
Common Treatments	None known
Care	Careful not to scratch
Cleaning Advice	Warm soapy water
Chemical Composition	$(Zn,Fe)S$

speaking it has a B-G interval of 0.156)!

Sphalerite consists mainly of Zinc and Iron. Normally the Iron content dominates and the mineral looks similar to the dull pieces seen in the museums. Most Sphalerite is opaque and black and is sometimes referred to as Marmatite (was this the origin of our Marmite spread or was it a French stew?). Isn't the gem world so exciting, when the graphite in your pencil has the exact same chemical composition as a Diamond (see allotropic) and dull old Marmatite is the same mineral as the most incredibly dazzling and monumentally rare Sphalerite! To my knowledge only a handful of yellow, orange and red specimens have been found so far and nearly all are below 1ct.

Only two mines have ever been reported to discover gem quality pieces; the Chivera mine, in Sonora Mexico and the Las Manforas Mine in the Picos de Europa Montains (the first national park in Spain) located on the North Coast of Spain near Santander. Its name is derived from the Greek word for 'treacherous rock', as non-gem quality specimens can easily be confused with other minerals. The gem is also known as Blende which is the German word for 'blind' (most likely so for the same reason as the Greek meaning).

Colour	Greenish yellow, brown, grey
Family	Does not belong to a family
Hardness	5.5
Specific Gravity	3.4 – 3.5
Refractive Index	1.88 – 2.05
Crystal Group	Monoclinic
Optical Properties	Greater dispersion than Diamond
Common Treatments	Not normally treated
Care	None
Cleaning Advice	Warm soapy water
Chemical Composition	$CaTiSiO_5$

SPHENE

Sphene is one of the newest gemstones to be discovered, taking its name from the Greek word for "wedge" - due to its typical wedge-shaped crystal structure. It is sometimes known as "Titanite", due to its titanium content. Its colour is generally green, yellow or darkish grey, yet in some forms it can also be brown and even black.

Registering 5.5 on the Mohs scale, the softness of the stone makes it difficult to facet; but because it is so beautiful, many Lapidarists are often tempted to give it a go. The gem is transparent to translucent in appearance and can often feature the most amazing adamantine lustre. Sphene also has fire (dispersion) greater than that of even Diamonds and is therefore ideal when set in earrings or pendants that are designed to be fluid. Its double refraction enables the light that travels through the gem to be split into two directions, creating an exceptional array of colours. Strongly coloured Sphenes are also heavily pleochroic. The gemstone is mined in Pakistan, Mount Vesuvius, Italy, Russia, Canada and the USA.

SPICE TOPAZ

Spice Topaz uses a revolutionary patented technique to add spectacular colours to genuine Topaz. With 12 colours to choose from and with a continual research program to develop more, Spice Topaz offers a range of coloured gemstones unlike any seen before. Choose from Summer Blue, Aqua, Liberty Blue, True Blue, Neon Paraiba, Padparadscha Sunset, Pristine, Deep Sage, Fern Green, Diva Green, Peru and Dusky Black.

Using exactly the same colouring agents that Mother Nature uses to add colour to allochromatic gems, Spice Topaz uses its revolutionary and entirely safe process to penetrate colour deep inside the gem. Since the importing of Topaz with radiation treatment was banned in the USA, some American jewellers now only offer Spice Topaz (alongside very rare untreated pieces) and the owner of one store recently told me that the only difficulty consumers now face is which of the 12 brilliant colours to choose.

The technical stuff: why did two scientists spend years developing and patenting Spice Topaz? Well to understand this you need to understand the limitations of other techniques used to add colour to Topaz. Mystic coating can be damaged if not properly looked after. Radiation treatment of Topaz has had a rocky road in the USA over its potential health hazards. Regular diffusion does not penetrate deep into the gem and can therefore be negatively affected by small chips and scratches, plus it is not very effective when used with Topaz. However Spice Topaz diffuses colour deep into the gemstone and is 100% stable and totally permanent.

Exclusively available in the UK through Coloured Rocks. USA: Patent number: 6872422

Colour	12 Different Colours
Family	Topaz
Hardness	8
Specific Gravity	3.5 - 3.6
Refractive Index	1.607 - 1.627
Crystal Group	Orthorhombic
Common Treatments	Patented diffusion
Care	None
Cleaning Advice	Ultrasonic or warm soapy water
Chemical Composition	AlSiO4(OH,F)2

Imperial Topaz   Dusky Black   Diva Green

Dark Cyan   Aqua Blue   Deep Sage

Paraiba Blue   Padparadscha   Liberty Blue

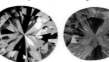

Peru   True Blue   Fern Green

SPICE
TOPAZ

Indulge in Brilliance

GENUINE TOPAZ
12 BREATHTAKING COLOURS
FINEST CUTTING
PATENTED TECHNOLOGY
NON RADIATED
PRECISION CALIBRATION
EVERLASTING DURABILITY
NON COATED

Patent Number 6872422

Exclusively distributed in Europe by Coloured Rocks

SPINEL

Colour	Red, pink, purple, blue
Family	Is a family in its own right
Hardness	8
Specific Gravity	3.6
Refractive Index	1.712 - 1.717
Crystal Group	Cubic
Optical Properties	Normally better natural clarity than Rubies
Common Treatments	Not normally treated
Care	No specific care required
Cleaning Advice	Ultrasonic, steam cleaning, warm soapy water
Chemical Composition	$MgAl_2O_4$

We all hate doing nasty jobs and often procrastinate when we have to deliver bad news, but who can imagine how difficult it must have been telling the Queen of England that her beloved Ruby in the crown jewels was not a Ruby at all, but a lesser known gem; a Spinel!

Spinel is a robust and strong gem for gents to wear. The "Black Prince's Ruby", which was set into Henry V's helmet, saved his life when his helmet was struck by an axe in the battle of Agincourt in 1415. This only goes to show how certain gemstones are far stronger than the precious metals into which they are set. For hundreds of years Spinels have been mistaken for Rubies. The "Black Prince's Ruby", which is now set in the British Imperial State Crown, was thought by Henry V to be a Ruby (hence its name); but it is actually a 170ct Spinel. The "Kuwait Ruby", another piece in the British crown jewels, is also a Spinel; weighing a massive 352ct.

It is easy to understand why Spinels were mistaken for Rubies for so long. In fact, until the late 19th century, there was no distinction between Ruby and red Spinel, as they look almost identical and are often found in the same localities. They also share the same desirable visual properties, as well as similar chemical structure, and both even obtain their red colour from chromium. This is how red Spinel obtained its title as "The Master of Disguise".

Nowadays, distinctions can be made through comparing the hardness of the two gemstones: Ruby registers 9 on the Mohs scale, while Spinel registers 8. Ruby also has a slightly higher refractive index. Most Spinels also have the ability to glow in natural daylight (fluorescence) but with a more pinkish hue than Rubies.

Red Spinel is actually rarer than Ruby, but unlike the latter can be found in large sizes. These big red stones were often referred to in ancient texts as Balas Rubies, which referred to Badakshan in Northern Afghanistan - still an active gem-

producing region. According to historical records, Badakshan produced the biggest and most spectacular "Rubies". Some of these gems were owned by the Mongol conqueror, Henry VIII of England, and Peter the Great of Russia.

Spinel's name is believed to have derived from the Latin word "spina" meaning "thorn" and refers to the fact that its crystals are often shaped like the thorns of a rose bush. Along the same theme, its vivid colours are often very similar to those seen in an English rose garden. Pure Spinel is white and, as with many gem families, its impurities provide us with an array of different colours. The main colouring agents in Spinel are iron, chromium, vanadium and cobalt. Not only can this precious gem be found in beautiful rich Ruby reds; a very small amount has been found in electrifying blues. You can also find a range of pastel colours of purples and pinks. One of the most spectacular gemstone colours, vivid hot pink with a hint of orange, can be found in Spinels mined in Burma.

Though most Spinels on the market don't have prefixes, several trade names do exist. Flame Spinel (also known as Rubicelle) as the name suggests is a vivacious orange to orangey red gem. Ceylonite (also known as Pleonaste) is an opaque dark green Spinel, and Gahnite (also known as Zinc Spinel) is a blue to bluish green Spinel.

Because this crystal is a newly recognised gemstone there is little folklore and legend surrounding its powers, although it has been associated with sorcerers and alchemists alike. There is reference to its use as a talisman to protect the wearer from fire, and as Spinel contains the magnetic mineral Magnetite, many believe it was used to help ancient mariners with navigation.

In 2005, whilst conducting a scientific study at the University of Chicago, Denton Ebel (Assistant Curator of Meteorites at the American Museum of Natural History), along with Lawrence Grossman (a Professor in Geophysical Sciences), discovered that the environment in which certain Spinels were formed proved that

Kama Charms often feature Spinel.

it was the impact of an asteroid some 65 million years ago that ended the dinosaur era.

Now treasured in its own right, Spinel is a favourite of many gem dealers and gem collectors. It has fantastic brilliance with a vitreous lustre, and as it is very durable and tough, it makes it an ideal gem to set into jewellery. It is mined in Burma, Sri Lanka, India, Tanzania, Madagascar, Australia, Italy, Sweden, Turkey, United States and Russia.

Spinel Kama Charms.

SPODUMENE

What an unfortunate name for a gemstone family that heralds such beautiful gems as Kunzite and Hiddenite Its name is derived from "spondumenos" which is Greek for "burnt to ashes" and came about due to the similarity that some Spodumene specimens have with the greyish appearance of ash. All members of the Spodumene family are highly plechroic.

Even though Spodumene is rarely set in jewellery itself, its three descendants Kunzite, Green Hiddenite and (the more recently discovered) transparent yellow Triphane are amongst some of the most desirable gems on the planet. This last gem, Triphane, should not be confused with the sleeping agent tripophane, which is found in its most concentrated form in turkeys - hence the real reason you fall asleep after Xmas dinner.

Hiddenite may not be as well known as Kunzite, but it is highly collectable!

SQUARE CUT

The most famous of all square cuts and extremely popular when applied to a Diamond is the princess cut. This cut typically has 76 facets and is based on the same principles as the round brilliant cut.

When a Diamond is square cut, it can offer real value for money, as less of the gem is lost while being shaped. When a square cut is not based on the brilliant cut (its facets are not triangular or kite shaped), it is then quite simply referred to as a "Square Cut". These standard square cuts have facets running parallel to the girdle and their number normally varies from 13 to 25.

A square cut Fern Green Spice Topaz.

Turquoise is often stabilised.

Square cuts are becoming increasingly popular for coloured gems such as Topaz and Smokey Quartz. With a large table facet, this cut is ideal for showing off gems that have great colour and clarity as the eye tends to be drawn into the gem.

STABILISED GEMS

A stabilised gem is one that has been impregnated with another material in order to improve its durability and sometimes improve its appearance. Turquoise, for example, is often stabilised.

STAR FACET

A Star Facet is a triangular-like facet on the crown of a brilliant cut gemstone, located next to the table.

STAR SAPPHIRE

A Star Sapphire is a Sapphire that has a pattern within the stone that emits a star-like effect known as asterism.

A skilled cutter will be able to determine from the rough if a Sapphire is likely to possess the star effect, which is not visible to the naked eye before cutting. The value of the gem will always depend upon how close the star is to the centre of the gem, its clarity, and the depth of colour of the Sapphire. Most stars witnessed on the surface of Sapphires have four prongs; however, in the rarest of cases a six-prong star can be seen, making the gemstone a truly collectible item.

You will find that a Star Sapphire is always cabochon cut, with its dome allowing the asterism to shine through; if it were cut in any other shape the star would be lost.

A 6 ray Star Sapphire from Thailand.

STAR OF INDIA

The Star of India is said to be the largest and most famous Sapphire in the world! It was discovered in Ceylon in the early 1700's and is believed to have formed over a billion years ago. Its home is now in the New York Museum of Natural History: it was presented to them by the financier J.P Morgan in 1900. In appearance the Star of India looks quite milky. It receives its star effect (also known as aterism) from the presence of tiny rutile inclusions which all run parallel to one another within the gemstone. The gem weighs a huge 563cts and is similar in size to a ping pong ball.

Like many of the world's famous Diamonds, this Sapphire is surrounded by scandal. In 1964 the Star of India was the object of a famous burglary when it was stolen by Jack Murphy (also known as 'Murph the Surf'). Although he was arrested within a few days, the Sapphire wasn't recovered for several months and was allegedly discovered in a locker in a Miami bus station.

STAR OF THE SOUTH

This famous Diamond was discovered in 1853 by a young girl who was a slave working at the Bagagem Diamond Mine in Brazil. At the time it was a custom that anyone finding a Diamond of great significance would be granted freedom and on unearthing a huge Diamond which weighed over 250cts in its rough state, the girl was apparently not only set free but also given a pension for life. The owner of the mine had little idea of its true value and it is reported that he sold the gem for around £3,000, only for the new owner to sell it for 10 times more just a few months later!

Also known as Estreal do Sul, the Star of the South is today a 128.48ct beautifully cushion cut, VS2 clarity Diamond that is light pink in colour. The Diamond has enjoyed a very eventful and well documented history over the past 100 years and in 2002 Cartier purchased it from Rustomjee Jamsetjee of Mumbai. Not long after their purchase, the Diamond became subject to a legal case as it was claimed to be listed as an heirloom of the wealthy Gaekwad family.

I find the cut of this gem as impressive as the gem itself. Therefore we have recently had two of our head Lapidaries develop our "Replica Star

Top view

Side view

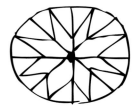

Pavillion view

of the South Cut". This wonderful oval cut is a direct replica of the arrangement and shape of the facets and we have closely adhered to the angles of the facets both on the crown and the pavilion.

ST. EDWARD'S CROWN

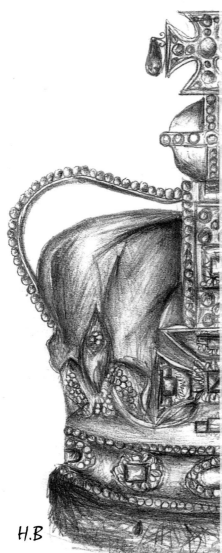

Although throughout history there have been two crowns known as 'St Edward's Crown', the one currently on exhibition in the Tower of London dates back to 1661 and was produced the year after the restoration of the monarchy.

The crown is used at the coronation ceremony and is placed on the head of the incoming monarch by the Archbishop of Canterbury. However, due to its incredible weight of 2.23kg, both King George VI and Elizabeth II replaced it with the lighter weight and more comfortable Imperial State Crown before leaving the Abbey at the end of the coronation.

Made of solid gold, such was the cost of precious gemstones at the time that the crown only featured hired gems, rented from jewellers several weeks before the coronation and given back afterwards.

From the coronation of Anne 1702 until the early 19th century, the crown was not actually worn by the incoming king or queens (not surprising as it was so heavy), but was carried separately to the ceremony as a symbolic object. In 1902, Edward VII decided that he would wear the crown for his coronation and commissioned its restoration. However, on the day of his coronation Edward was suffering with appendicitis and was unable to wear the hefty crown!

Prior to the coronation of George V in 1911, Garrard the Crown Jewellers were employed for the first time in the crown's history to permanently set over 400 genuine gemstones. According to "The Official Guide Book – The Crown Jewels", Garrards were responsible for 'removing the antique enamelled mounts, all the pastes (stones) and resetting them with semi precious stones'. These included Amethysts, Sapphires, Tourmalines, Topaz and Citrines.

H.B

STEP CUT

It's best to imagine brilliant cuts and step cuts as two different families, in which most styles of cuts fall into. Whereas brilliant cuts tend to have triangular and kite-shaped facets, step cuts tend to have rectangular facets. The emerald cut, for example, falls into the step cut family.

Step cuts have facets that run parallel to the table, tend to have two or more steps cut onto the crown angling towards the table, and normally have more steps faceted below the girdle on the pavilion. With a larger gem, more steps will often be used. If you are unsure of what type of cut you are looking at, if the table facet looks square, rectangular, hexagonal or octagonal, then the chances are that it is a step cut gem

A step cut Swiss Blue Topaz.

STERLING SILVER

Like 9K gold and 18K gold, the British Assay Office have a certain standard which must be reached in order for Sterling Silver to be named as such: more than 92.5% of the metal must be pure silver. In America, Sterling Silver only needs to be 92.1% pure to achieve its status. The reason Sterling Silver is made into an alloy is that, on its own, silver is a fairly soft metal and therefore copper is normally added to the blend to make it stronger.

The term "Sterling Silver," emerged in the 13th century and it is no coincidence that the British currency is also called Sterling. Interestingly, in French, the word "argent" also means both silver and money. Another silver standard is Britannia. This is purer than Sterling and to achieve its official hallmark at least 95.84% of the alloy needs to be silver. However, as it is softer than Sterling Silver it is not used as often in jewellery.

In the UK it is a legal requirement for retailers to ensure that all silver items that weigh in excess of 7.78 grams have an official hallmark. Be careful though, as most manufacturers will stamp 925 on the silver jewellery they produce and this should not to be confused with the official hallmark applied by the Assay Office.

A wonderful handmade Sterling Silver bracelet by Tookalon.

More recently the Assay Office have added a new hallmark standard for silver known as 800 or "Continental Silver". To receive this hallmark the silver content must be in excess of 80% of the alloy. This exciting development means that by adding a higher percentage of other metals to the mix, just like gold, we can now create slightly different colours of silver. This new standard is also more tarnish resistant than Sterling Silver

STRAWBERRY QUARTZ

Found in only a few locations, Strawberry Quartz receives its unique colouring through Hematite and Lepidocrocite inclusions. Many people have wrongly mistaken Strawberry Quartz for Quenched Crackle Quartz, but under closer examination, it becomes apparent that Strawberry Quartz is completely natural. Also, it's worth pointing out that the name has been incorrectly used by several jewellers who are selling glass and passing it off as a gemstone!

A stunning Sterling Silver bangle by Tookalon

Depending on the location where each gemstone has so far been found, the gemstone has different visual qualities. Those sold so far at Coloured Rocks have all been from Madagascar and are 100% natural, without treatment, without enhancement and without heating! They are truly a miracle produced by Mother Nature.

This find that we have is from a big open pit mine. We have sourced a lot of material from this mine: most of it is opaque and only has black spots; less than 4% of the material appears transparent and has the strawberry coloured spots. The only problem is, we have to continually cut away at the less attractive material to reach the fascinating gem quality Strawberry Quartz.

For a gemstone whose availability is so scant, because of its unusual appearance, it has already received a lot interest from crystal healers and astrologists. Strawberry Quartz is said to 'stimulate the energy of the heart filling one with the feeling of love'.

SUGILITE

Colour	Purple
Family	Sugilite
Hardness	5.5 - 6.5
Specific Gravity	2.74
Refractive Index	1.6 - 1.61
Crystal Group	Hexagonal
Optical Properties	Opaque
Common Treatments	Often Stabilised
Care	None
Cleaning Advice	Warm soapy water
Chemical Composition	Complex

Sometimes referred to as "Royal Lavulite" or "Royal Azel", Sugilite appears in a small range of colours from a stunning light lavender through to a rich purple. It is opaque with a waxy lustre and its appearance always reminds me of the small round violet sweets I was given as a child. The gem received its name from a Dr Ken-ichi Sugi, a Japanese scientist who first documented the gemstone in the 1940's.

Sugilite occasionally features red, brown or yellow spots, when these are present the gem is often called Wild Horse Sugilite. Similar to the process used to stabilise Turquoise, the gem is often treated to make it more suitable for setting in jewellery.

Some crystal healers believe that Sugilite helps in strengthening the heart, as well as reducing levels of stress, whilst others suggest that it balances your mind, body and spirit. I was recently told that a friend's mother uses Sugilite to stop her from developing a negative outlook on life and for over four years she has been more at ease and better equipped to deal with the troubles she watches on the evening news.

In addition to its discovery in Japan, the gem has also been discovered in Quebec, Canada, Tuscany, Italy and New South Wales, Australia. The largest discovery to date has been in the Northern Cape Province of South Africa.

SUNSTONE

This gemstone has a gorgeous glittering appearance (known as aventurescence) and is also called Oligoclase, Aventurine Feldspar and Heliote. Sunstone has many sought after attributes, but its aventuresence is the most striking. This is usually caused by either Haematite or Goethite inclusions; but in the Sunstone from Oregon in the USA, this phenomenon owes its appearance to copper inclusions. Although its colour is normally a reddish brown, it has also been discovered in green, grey, and yellow.

viorelli

The gem has been set in jewellery for thousands of years and is steeped in history and folklore. The Vikings were said to have used the gem as a navigational aid, whilst early American settlers ground the gem and used it in medicine.

Sunstone is a member of the Feldspar family and is closely related to Labradorite. As it is normally opaque or translucent the gem is often cabochon cut; on rare occasions it can be found transparent.

The gem registers 6 to 6.5 on the Mohs scale and can be found in Norway, Canada, India and the USA.

Colour	Clear, yellow, red and green
Family	Feldspar
Hardness	6 – 7
Specific Gravity	2.64 – 2.66
Refractive Index	1.525 – 1.58
Crystal Group	Triclinic
Optical Properties	Slight birefringence
Common Treatments	None
Care	No special care required
Chemical Composition	$(Ca,Na)(Al,Si)_2Si_2O_8$

SWITZERLAND

Without doubt when it comes to watch-manufacturing, Switzerland is the undisputed world champion. Even though many well-known brand names are moving their watch production to Asia, the very patriotic Swiss are still making their watches in their wonderfully landscaped and land-locked country.

In a world that is changing so rapidly, there is still something magical about owning a Swiss watch. Although very few people can afford a true Swiss watch, in second place come watches bearing the engraving or label "Swiss Movement". When you see this on a watch it does not necessarily mean the watch is made in Switzerland, but refers to the provenance of the mechanism within the watch.

Just like the French who protect the use of the name "Champagne", the Swiss have fought hard recently to ban companies from abbreviating "Swiss Movement" to "Swiss Movt", in an attempt to protect the authenticity of the genuine Swiss watch makers.

When it comes to mining, Switzerland has several gold deposits, glorious Marcasite and small deposits of gem-quality Quartz, Prehnite, Unakite, Idocrase and Haematite.

With the exception of its gold and Marcasite mining activities, it is important to stress that Switzerland's other gems are not really mined in commercial quantities.

High in the Alps in the Canton of Valais, very near the Italian border, some of the most fantastic Marcasite in the world is being mined. Its colours range from creamy to glorious, metallic golden tones with a pale rose tint. The mine has been in operation for over 100 years and, as with most things in Switzerland, runs like clockwork!

In my humble opinion, no other Marcasite on the planet has the same quality of lustre and surface integrity to that which is mined in the Swiss canton of Valais. My view is not clouded by the fact that I spend a fair amount of time in Switzerland overseeing our Lorique watch making, it's simply because the gem is truly amazing.

One gem that is not mined in Switzerland is Swiss Blue Topaz. This trade name is generically applied to Blue Topaz that are of strong clarity and medium dark in colour. Lighter Blue Topaz is referred to as Sky Blue Topaz and dark Blue Topaz is often named London Blue.

SYMMETRY

A gemstone that is well cut is said to have good symmetry. The accuracy with which a gem is fashioned has a major part to play in how much brilliance and dispersion the gem will display.

Of the 4 C's (clarity, colour, cut and carat weight), the symmetry of the cut can often have the most profound effect on the value of the gem.

As the cut of a gem is normally applied by hand, it is the only one of the 4 C's that is not taken care of by Mother Nature. Therefore as there is room for human error, spending a minute or two to observe the quality of the cutting (particularly the symmetry) before purchasing is highly recommended. As the biggest element of my job is buying loose gems for the company, I have to take studying symmetery very seriously!

Colour	Pink to red, violet to purple
Family	Taaffeite
Hardness	8-8.5
Specific Gravity	3.6
Refractive Index	1.71 - 1.72
Crystal Group	Hexagonal
Optical Properties	Vitreous Lustre
Common Treatments	None
Care	None
Cleaning Advice	Warm soapy water
Chemical Composition	MgBeAl4O8

TAAFFEITE

An incredibly rare gem, Taaffeite is a stunning mauve to purple gemstone of which only a handful of pieces have ever been faceted. It is named after the Irish gemologist Edward Taaffe who identified the gem in 1945. At first, as he sorted through a box of faceted gems that he had bought from Dublin jeweller Robert Dobbie, he assumed the gem was a Spinel, but on closer inspection he noticed that it was birefringent, a characteristic not seen in Spinels.

If industry gossip is correct and less than 4,000cts have ever been faceted, then that's only 60cts per annum. With annual global production of gem quality Diamonds currently running at over 60 million carats per year, that makes Taaffeite a million times rarer than Diamonds!

The gem was first discovered in Ratnapura, Ceylon (now known as Sri Lanka) and a handful of gem quality pieces have now been found in Tanzania, as well as some tiny pieces weighing less than .005ct being discovered in China.

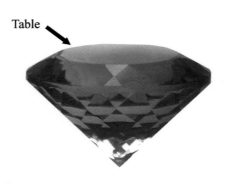

Table

TABLE

The table is the single top facet of a gem (when viewed from the side) and is sometimes referred to as the window of the gem. Round brilliant cut gems have smaller tables than emerald cut gems of the same carat weight.

TALISMAN

A term used to name gems, charms and jewellery worn to bring good luck or to ward off evil. Throughout the last 3000 years, different talismans (also known as amulets) have been worn by different religions and cultures for the effect they have on one's wellbeing. Shah Jahan, the famous builder of the Taj Mahal, was so fanatical about gemstones and their ability to bring good fortune and wealth that he asked a Glyptographer to inscribe his favourite Emeralds with the Persian inscription "he who possesses this charm shall enjoy the special protection of god".

TANZANIA

Tanzania is on the East Coast of Africa, with its shores facing the Indian Ocean. It is home to some of the oldest known civilisations unearthed by archaeologists and is located in what some people call the "Cradle of Mankind". It boasts one of the largest and most varied collection of wild animal populations in the world, including lions, monkeys, wildebeest, antelope, cheetah, gazelle, crocodile and flamingo to name a few.

Approximately 120 different tribal groups are found here: one of the more well-known tribes is the Maasai, who fiercely guard their culture and traditions in the northern areas. The Maasai live in small, round, temporary mud huts, farming the land and herding animals. In direct contrast, the towns and cities of Tanzania bustle with day-to-day trading and economic activities, and

Tanzanite is without doubt the most famous discovery in Tanzania to-date.

*Songea Ruby from Tanzania
is amongst the finest Ruby on the planet.*

*Tsavorite was
first discovered
in Tanzania.*

boast many historical areas and cultural sites of interest to tourists.

Tanzania is home of the world-famous gemstone Tanzanite. It was discovered in 1967 near the northern city of Arusha, nestled in the Meralani foothills of Mount Kilimanjaro. This extinct volcano stands 19,340 feet tall and is the highest point on the continent.

A lesser-known gemstone mine in Tanzania is the Williamson Diamond Mine which is famous for being the first significant Diamond mine on the continent outside of South Africa. It was established in 1940 by Dr. John Williamson and has been in production ever since.

The country produces a host of other gemstones too; indeed, it was Tanzania, not Kenya, where Campbell R Bridges (the Scottish gemmologist) first discovered Tsavorite Garnet. However, in 1967 the Tanzanian government nationalised the mine and Campbell left the country. He was later able to trace the same belt of gems to neighbouring Kenya where he rediscovered the gem in 1970.

Close to the border with Mozambique are the mines of Songea. These mines are producing some of the most gorgeous Fancy Sapphires in the world, with great clarity and amazing depths of colour. Their Rubies have breathtaking transparency and some say that once you have owned a piece of Corundum from Songea, you will never want one from anywhere else.

Rubies and Sapphires are also found in the Umba region, along with Rhodolite Garnet and Tourmaline; however, sources have told us that these mines are starting to become depleted. Likewise, in the north the Alexandrite and Emerald mines of Mayara are also starting to run out. Recently, though, Iolite has been found in the region. One thing you might find in common between many gemstones discovered in Tanzania, is that they generally seem to have above average clarity. I have yet to find a scientific reason for this, but if I look at all of the gems in my personal collection, a disproportional percentage originate from Tanzania.

TANZANITE

Tanzanite is truly spectacular! This precious gemstone is only found in one location in the world: Tanzania, Africa. Claimed to be a 1000 times rarer than Diamonds, Tanzanite is the blue variety of Zoisite.

Even though Zoisite occurs widely, the geological conditions that are required to enable the gem to turn into its trademark blue is so rare that it has been described as 'more astounding than the stone itself'.

Tanzanite is extremely popular due to its trichroic nature, which means that three different colours can be seen when looking at the gem from different angles. In Tanzanite's case these colours are: blue, pinkish violet and yellow.

As with many gemstones, the darker, more vivid its colour the more valuable it is; and dark blue Tanzanite is currently amongst the most desired, and therefore most expensive, gemstones in the world. So enchanted is anyone who sees this gemstone that today it is often talked about with the same reverence as Diamonds.

On discovering this beautiful gem in 1967, word of the unearthing reached the celebrated New York Jewellers, Tiffany's. At that time Henry B Platt (the great grandson of Louis C Tiffany) was working with Tiffany's president, Walter Hoving. He was completely awestruck by the beauty of the gemstone, a gem which he later named Tanzanite, after the country where it was discovered, and this amazing gemstone was launched at Tiffany's in 1969.

Hailed the "gemstone of the 20th century", it has been recommended to wear Tanzanite as an anti-depressant, due to the nurturing, emotionally supportive and cheering energies it is said to bestow.

The huge demand for this gemstone led to the Gemological Institution of America adding the gem to the official birthstone list in 2002, for the month of December.

Colour	Blue and sometimes green
Family	Zoisite
Hardness	6.5 - 7
Specific Gravity	3.3 - 3.35
Refractive Index	1.68 - 1.72
Crystal Group	Orthorhombic
Optical Properties	Strong pleochroism
Common Treatments	Nearly always heat treated
Care	None
Cleaning Advice	Warm soapy water
Chemical Composition	Ca2Al3Si3O12OH

Two vivid blue Tanzanite pieces set in 18k gold by Tomas Rae.

Tapered baguettes have been used here to draw the eye to the central stone.

TAPERED CUT

Also known as "Tapered Baguettes", these cuts work extremely well on the shoulders of rings, where their shape naturally draws the eye towards the centre gemstone.

A tapered cut gem is oblong or baguette in shape and when viewed from the top, its two shortest sides are of different lengths. There are no set ratios for how much the gem should taper, however it is normal to find the shorter of the two lengths to be approximately 40 to 60% of the other. Tapered cuts are traditionally step cut with facets running parallel to the girdle.

TARNISHING

Certain metals will tarnish over a period of time due to their reaction to with elements present in the environment such as Sulphur. Silver in particular tends to tarnish quite quickly and what started off as a very shiny bright metal, with incredible surface lustre, can in certain environments quite quickly become yellowish to almost black in appearance.

Many people incorrectly believe it has something to do with the purity of the Silver. This is not the case (nor could it be, as the purity of Silver on larger pieces of jewellery is independently hallmarked by the Assay Office) and in fact pure Silver will actually tarnish quicker than the approved 80% and 92.5% standards.

If your Silver Ring comes in contact with items such as petrol, wool, rubber, hairspray and certain paints then it may start to tarnish. Even everyday foods like eggs and onion can act as a catalyst to your Silver beginning to tarnish. You may also find that on holiday your Silver tarnishes quicker, as the process speeds up in high humidity.

So that's all the bad news; the good news is that tarnished metals are easily cleaned, especially if dealt with promptly. Once you find your Silver jewellery beginning to tarnish, simply wash it using a detergent that does not contain

Even when tarnished this badly, with the correct treatment, most jewellery can be returned to pristine condition.

any phosphate-based chemicals. If the tarnish has gone from a light yellow colour to a more darkish brown or even black, then you will need to purchase a specialised polish to remove the tarnish. Today there are many of these available over the internet. In the most severe of cases, you may need to take your jewellery to a jeweller, who will dip your jewellery in a chemical solution. To help keep Silver jewellery in a pristine condition for longer, it is often plated with Rhodium or Palladium whilst being manufactured. Depending on the quality of the manufacturer and the depth of the plating, this process can often delay the tarnishing process by many years; however, if not properly applied to the jewellery in an even manner, it can eventually lead to jewellery developing patches of tarnish.

TAYLOR - BURTON DIAMOND

The Welsh actor Richard Burton is probably just as renowned for his love life as for his prolific film career. At one point he was one of the highest paid actors in the world. Richard Burton met Elizabeth Taylor on set of the notorious film "Cleopatra". Talk of their adulterous affair was rife. Elizabeth loved the publicity for her hair, jewels and clothes but didn't particularly like it when it turned into gossip about her private life.

Many agree Richard's life changed when he met Elizabeth. She loved the jet-set life and Richard developed a taste for the beautiful things the world had to offer. Take for example the ravishing 33ct Asscher cut Diamond he gave Elizabeth Taylor in 1968.

In 1972, for Elizabeth's 40th birthday, Richard gave her a pear shaped Diamond known as the Taj-Mahal. It has Arabic inscriptions on either side and is set into a stunning necklace, accompanied with Rubies and accent Diamonds. Richard is famously quoted for saying "I would have liked to buy Elizabeth the Taj-Mahal, but it would cost too much to transport". He went on to say "The Diamond has so many carats, it's almost a turnip". Burton was also famously

Elizabeth Taylor has a love affair with Pearls!

quoted as saying, "Diamonds are an investment. When no one wants to see me on screen we can sell them on".

Possibly the most famous Diamond that Richard gave to Elizabeth would have to be the 69ct pear shape Diamond, which was renamed the Taylor–Burton Diamond. It was originally cut from a rough stone weighing 240ct found in 1966. The Diamond attracted a huge amount of publicity and was first worn by Elizabeth in public at Princess Grace's 40th birthday party in Monaco. After Elizabeth and Richard divorced, the Diamond was sold in 1979 for around five million dollars.

Elizabeth is probably just as famous for her jewellery as she is for her films, she has even written a book called 'My love affair with Jewellery'. She has an exquisite collection of Pearls (both natural and cultured), Diamonds, Rubies, Sapphires and Emeralds. In the past, Elizabeth has said of her jewellery that she doesn't own the pieces, but that she is merely looking after them so that when she is gone, they will be passed on for other people in the world to enjoy.

TENNIS BRACLET

Used to describe a bracelet that has a line of gemstones closely set together. The name became a popular way of describing this style of bracelet when in 1987 the tennis player Chris Evert, famously dropped her Diamond bracelet during the US Open Tennis Tournament and the match was halted whilst she searched for it!

TENSION SET

A tension set gem or gems (as the name suggests) is one that is secured in the jewellery by tension. Quite often channel settings with a very small rim can mimic a tension setting, but are in fact secured by the channel. Diamonds, Rubies and Sapphires are the most common gems used in tension settings as they are very strong. This style can only be used for single gems or where all are faceted to precise dimensions.

Tennis bracelets don't necessarily have to be Diamonds.

A 3ct tension set Amethyst in a contemporary design by Jessica Lili.

THAILAND

It is said that 90% of the world's Rubies and Sapphires pass through Thailand to be cut, polished and treated on their route to being set into jewellery.

Historically, Thailand was a hub of mining activity for Corundum (the family name given to Ruby and Sapphire), but today many of these mines are sadly depleted and Thailand's activities are now more focused on the trading of, cutting and enhancement of gems. Whilst I personally find that I can source a wider range of gemstones in India, especially in Jaipur, and that with a lower average income in the country Lapidary costs are lower, Thailand still plays a huge part in the gem world.

There are three prime areas for gem mining in Thailand:

Chanthaburi: three hours to the east of Bangkok and not far from the Cambodian border. It is known for its Ruby (known as Siam Ruby in the trade), Yellow Sapphire and the only mine in the world so far that produces Black Star Sapphire.

Kanchanaburi: famous not only for its deep Blue Sapphires but also for the infamous bridge over the River Kwai.

Phrae province: 340 miles north of Bangkok is where you will find the Phrae Sapphire mines and the ancient town of Chiang Mai (although it does not look so ancient anymore with its five lane highway!)

Although the above are the three main mining areas, if you are ever visiting Bangkok on holiday, be sure to check out the multitude of gem shops on the famous Silom Road. Be careful if you are buying however, because even though 99% of Thai people are friendly and honest, the odd few do prey on tourists and one of their favourite scams involves gems. If you stick to the larger stores and don't buy them in the street or from a location recommended by a Tuk-Tuk driver you should be ok.

Our famous 'Hedgehog Rings' are produced in Thailand.

TIARA

A tiara is a piece of jewellery that is worn on the head and is very popular with royalty and the very well-off. A tiara is often worn at weddings by both the bride and the bridesmaids.

It is said that upon receiving an Emerald necklace from Queen Elizabeth, Princess Diana had it converted to a gorgeous tiara. The Queen also gave Diana a Sterling Silver tiara complete with dangling Pearls and Diamonds, which is known as the "Cambridge Love Knot".

The single largest collection of tiaras in the world is believed to be that of Queen Elizabeth II. Many of her pieces are said to be priceless and she is often seen wearing them on official occasions.

TIFFANY SETTING

Introduced by Charles L Tiffany in 1886, the Tiffany setting is widely used in solitaire rings today, especially when the gemstone is a Diamond, Sapphire or Tanzanite.

The setting features a simple band of gold or silver and the gemstone is secured by six prongs set high above the band.

TIGER'S EYE

Tiger's Eye is believed to be a protective stone endowing courage and willpower. It is used to promote creativity, focusing of the mind, and cultivate clear thinking.

This gemstone displays chatoyancy (a small ray of light on the surface) and when cut to a cabochon it resembles the eye of a tiger. The golden yellow colour of the stone is produced by the presence of brown iron.

A striking Tiger's Eye bracelet by Jessica Lili.

When the gem is bluish in colour it is renamed Hawk's Eye Quartz and when a greenish grey, it is renamed Ox Eye Quartz or sometimes Bull's Eye Quartz.

This member of the Quartz family, with its brown and golden stripes, has been fascinating man for thousands of years. Romans would wear Tiger's Eye as a talisman in battle and it was often set into swords and helmets.

Since antiquity, Tiger's Eye has been worn as an amulet to bring about good luck and to protect against witchcraft. The gem is said to help put you on the right path of life, as well as helping you understand your own faults.

Crystal Healers believe that the gem can help those who suffer from hypochondria and asthma.

It is primarily mined in South Africa, though Tiger's Eye is also found in Western Australia, Burma, India and California.

Colour	Brown with golden stripes
Family	Quartz
Hardness	7
Specific Gravity	2.46 – 2.71
Refractive Index	1.54 – 1.55
Crystal Group	Trigonal
Optical Properties	Patterned like a Tiger's back
Common Treatments	Not normally treated
Cleaning Advice	Ultrasonic or warm soapy water
Care	No specific care required

TITANIUM

The first discovery of the metal titanium was in 1791 in Cornwall by an amateur geologist named William Gregor. At the time of the discovery William was actually a vicar of the parish church.

In the 1950's the Soviet Union pioneered the use of titanium in building structures for submarines. Due to the strength and lightness of the metal, it has been used since that time in high-speed military jets and is a major metal in spacecrafts and missiles.

The famous T-1 fountain pen by Parker used titanium for its tips, but they stopped the process in 1972 due to the increased cost of the metal. The pen has become so famous that it is now a collector's piece.

Because it is light, strong, lustrous and corrosion resistant, the metal is becoming very popular in jewellery, especially in ranges for men. In America, it is becoming very popular as a wedding band for both the husband and wife. Take a look at the Mattom Range of Titanium Gent's Jewellery.

TOOKALON

Originating from Greek "The Beautiful", Tookalon jewellery is made exclusively by hand. Using techniques that are centuries old, each piece is skillfully handcrafted by extremely experienced and talented jewellers.

From small silver sheets and silver wires, all pieces are crafted without the aid of modern technology. Each craftsman has just four main tools: his saw, his hammer, his blow torch and his experience.

Tookalon's commitment to combining classic artisanship, genuine gemstones and individualistic designs, results in every single piece being unique.

A handmade Tookalon Smokey Quartz pendant.

TOMAS RAE

This exciting new jewellery brand delights its owners by setting diamonds and coloured gemstones in refreshing designs made exclusively for the European market.

Within days of its launch in Spring 2009, Tomas Rae jeweller was featured on popular TV shows and female fashion magazines in the UK.

From the striking crisp clean lines of its Diamond Princess Cut Engagement rings to the multi-coloured petals found in its Rainbow Sapphire Evening Pendant; from the fluid movement of its Chandelier Ruby Earrings to the deep rich blues in its Palladium Tanzanite Tennis Bracelet, Tomas Rae designs have the ability to arouse a feeling of luxury and a pride of ownership.

What's more, just as with Lorique, I personally take responsibility for all of the coloured gemstones that are used in Tomas Rae designs. I personally guarantee that very single gem is of an incredibly high standard and is what I regard as best in class.

Tomas Rae, for very special pieces of jewellery, made of the finest materials, at a price that always represents great value for money.

Tomas Rae.

.59 Marquise Cut Tanzanite
.19ct SI/J Diamond
Set in 18k White Gold

TONE

Scale	Code	Description
0	c	Colorless or White
1	ex1	Extremely light
2	vl	Very light
3	l	Light
4	ml	Medium light
5	m	Medium
6	md	Medium dark
7	d	Dark
8	vd	Very dark
9	exd	Extremely dark
10	bl	Black

As discussed elsewhere in this book, colours are made up of three elements: hue, saturation and tone. 'Tone' is used to describe the depth of color, ranging from colourless to black, i.e. the lightness or darkness of the stone. When describing the tone of a gemstone we will often use words such as 'very light', 'medium-light', 'medium', 'medium-dark', and 'very dark'.

Tone is effectively describing the intensity of the colour. Take Blue Topaz as an example: Sky Blue Topaz is a light blue tone and London Blue Topaz is a medium dark tone. Think of Blue Sapphire: which varies from very pale blue, to vivid Ceylon Blue Sapphire, through to Midnight Blue Sapphire, where the blue is only just detectable even with strong lighting. If you were to have a coloured gemstone valued by the GIA, you would find that they would grade the tone with a numerical value: 1 being "extremely light" through to 9 being "extremely dark".

A medium to medium dark Tanzanite.

TOPAZ

Colour	A rainbow of different colours
Hardness	8
Specific Gravity	3.5 – 3.6
Refractive Index	1.607 – 1.627
Crystal Group	Orthorhombic
Optical Properties	Strong pleochroism
Common Treatments	Normally heat-treated
Cleaning Advice	Warm soapy water
Chemical Composition	$Al_2SiO_4(OH,F)_2$

Along with Citrine, Topaz is the birthstone for November. It is also a suggested wedding gift for both the 4th and 23rd anniversary. That said, its gorgeous brilliance and crystal clarity makes it a wonderful gift for all occasions.

It is unclear how the gem was first named. What we do know is that the small island in the Red Sea which is today known as Zabargad, was once named "Topazios". Pliny the Elder, author of the Natural History in the first century AD, links the gem to the island and states that the island's name was derived from the Greek word "topazos", "to seek". Although the island was the source of Peridot for Cleopatra, Topaz was not mined there at that time. That said, throughout history the two gemstones have been repeatedly confused with one another, both of which can be found with vibrant golden greenish hues. Others believe that the gem's name originates from the Sanskrit word "tapaz", which means fire.

Topaz set into the crown of a Mattom watch.

A Mattom money clip featuring a Swiss Blue Topaz.

Tomas Rae Swiss Blue Topaz encircled by Diamonds.

A cushion cut Sky Blue Topaz set in Sterling Silver.

There is possibly more folklore and legend surrounding Topaz than any other gem. It has been known as a powerful magnetic stone throughout the ages that attracts love and fortune. It has been mentioned in the Bible and is one of the gemstones adorning the twelve holy gates of Jerusalem.

Having been discovered over 2500 years ago, Topaz gems are also called apocalyptic stones. They are known to protect against enemies and are used as a symbol of splendour and love. It is even suggested that if you wear Blue Topaz along with Moonstone it may help encourage the right mindset and willpower for weight loss.

It is said that Topaz holds the distinction of being the gemstone with the widest range of curative properties. The Greeks felt that it gave them strength, as well as supposedly relieving insomnia, and restoring sanity; it was even said to be able to detect poisons. Furthermore, they thought it had supernatural powers and could even make its owner invisible!

The Egyptians believed the stone received its colour from the golden glow of the Sun God - Ra. This made Topaz a talisman of power that protected its owners from harm.

In the 1100's a large Golden Topaz was said to have been donated to a monastery by Lady Hildegarde (wife of Theodoric, Count of Holland), which was so luminous that it was used at night to light the inside of the chapel. Its glow was so bright that the congregation were able to read their prayers without the use of lamps. In Europe during the Renaissance (1300 – 1600) Topaz was believed to break evil spells and dispel anger. In India it was worn as a pendant, just above the heart to ensure long life, beauty and intelligence.

Topaz is its own species and comes in a wide variety of colours. It can be found in yellow, brownish yellow, brown, green, blue, light blue, red, pink and colourless. The Portuguese call the colourless type "pingos D'agoa" which means "Drops of Water". How wonderful to imagine you can capture a drop of water in a piece of jewellery! Most colours of Topaz on the market today, with the exception of colourless, light blue and yellow, derive their colour from either irradiation or heat treatment (if you heat yellow Topaz from the Ouro Preto region of Brazil, it is possible to turn it pinkish). The irradiation process used to turn colourless Topaz blue replicates the natural irradiation process found in the state of Minas Gerias in Brazil, where Mother Nature naturally used irradiation to turn Topaz blue (natural Blue Topaz has also been found in Russia). Today Topaz is sometimes coated, resulting in glorious multi-coloured Mystic Topaz.

When we refer to the term "Precious Topaz", we are talking about stones of a golden yellow to a peachy orange colour. Prior to the 1950's, these hues accounted for virtually all Topaz which had been discovered thus far. Throughout history this gem was available in multiple shades of oranges, yellows and golden browns, hence prior to the last century it was often mistaken for certain gems of similar shades, such as Citrine and Smokey Quartz. The confusion was heightened by the Brazilian word "Topazio", which means yellow gem.

Topaz is a fantastic gem to use in jewellery, not only for its stunning colours but also because of its durability. Reaching 8 on the Mohs hardness scale only Diamonds, Sapphire and Ruby are harder. It is a pleochroic gemstone, which means that different colours can be seen from different angles as you move the gem in the light. For example, a Red Topaz may show dark reds, yellows and pinkish reds. Although Topaz is very strong, it does have perfect cleavage, which - although reliable once faceted and set into jewellery - often creates challenges for Lapidarists when cutting the gem.

Topaz is found in several mining locations around the world, with the most important areas being Minas Gerais, Brazil, the Ural Mountains of Russia, Madagascar and Nigeria. Samples of the gem have also been discovered at various locations in the UK: St Michael's Mount in Cornwall; the isle of Lundy near Devon;

A gorgeous Tomas Rae bracelet featuring very tough Tanzanite.

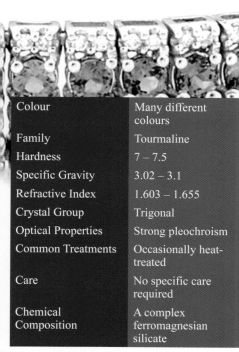

Colour	Many different colours
Family	Tourmaline
Hardness	7 – 7.5
Specific Gravity	3.02 – 3.1
Refractive Index	1.603 – 1.655
Crystal Group	Trigonal
Optical Properties	Strong pleochroism
Common Treatments	Occasionally heat-treated
Care	No specific care required
Chemical Composition	A complex ferromagnesian silicate

Northern Ireland; and Cairngorm Mountains in Scotland.

TOUGHNESS

A term often used when discussing the durability of gemstones is 'toughness'. Not to be confused with hardness (which relates to the surface ability of the gem to withstand scratches - see Mohs scale), the toughness of a gem has more to do with its ability to withstand hard impact and its resistance to fracturing. The toughness of a gem is just as important as its hardness and knowledgeable Lapidarists will always consider the gem's toughness when deciding what type of cut to apply. The less tough a gem, the more likely it is to have truncated corners and to be step cut rather than brilliant cut. Jewellers also have to be aware of which gemstones need to be better protected when setting them in jewellery.

To understand toughness better, think about Diamonds: they are the hardest mineral known to man, yet they are not the toughest, meaning they are just as prone to chipping and fracturing as several other gemstones.

TOURMALINE

Tourmaline has been fascinating its owners for thousands of years, although it was not identified as a gem variety in its own right until 1703, when a parcel of mixed gems was sent from Ceylon to Holland. The package was simply labelled "turmali", which translates from Sinhalese to "mixed precious stones". The legend goes that children playing on Dutch streets with the stones found that they attracted dirt particles as they were heated by the sun. On showing the strange effect to their parents, they passed the stones to a local gemmologist who realised they were a unique mineral group, and he later named them after the label on the original package.

This unique ability to attract particles is

known as pyroelectricity. When Tourmalines are heated or rubbed they create an electrical charge, and for this reason non gem-quality specimens are used in electrical devices.

Early observers of the gemstone believed that its wide variety of colours was thanks to the gem being formed whilst passing over a rainbow and absorbing all of its magical shades. This exquisite gemstone naturally occurs in a myriad of stunning colours and its crystal structure makes it look like it is almost pre-faceted by Mother Nature. Tourmaline is rarely found colourless. As with other gemstone families, the presence of different chemicals during the time the gem was crystallising has provided Tourmaline with an array of spectacular colours.

A Jessica Lili bracelet demonstrating the wonderful colours of Tourmaline.

When a deep, vivid green, they are often rich in chromium and are sometimes named Chrome Tourmaline. Iron-rich Tourmalines are normally black to deep brown and magnesium-rich varieties can occur in a yellowish brown colour. Lithium-rich Tourmalines come in a rainbow of colours.

Members of the Tourmaline family are not from the same crystal structure and their chemical compositions also vary. What they do have in common is that they all occur in nature as long, thin, straight gems and usually have a triangular cross-section.

Red Tourmaline is renamed Rubellite.

Tourmaline is pleochroic, which means you can see different colours when viewed from different angles. As well as being pleochroic, the crystals may grow to be green at one end and pink at the other: this variety is called Bi-Coloured Tourmaline. When found with green on the outside and pink inside, they are known as Watermelon Tourmaline.

Throughout history, Tourmaline was often mixed up with other beautiful gemstones. Green Tourmaline was said to be confused with Emerald. The folklore and legend surrounding Tourmaline has only begun to emerge in the last few hundred years. Black Tourmaline (known as Schorl) has been associated with grieving. Tourmaline is considered a good luck gem and

Because of Tourmaline's crystal structure you will often see elongated cuts.

Paraiba Tourmaline has taken the gem world by storm over the last decade.

is sometimes referred to as the "stone of wisdom". It is also said to be "resistant to all vagaries of fate" – in other words it protects the person wearing it from ill fortune. It is the gemstone of friendship, relationships and love, and is said to help strengthen and intensify these. Believed to possess healing warmth, if you hold the gemstone it has been said it can balance your "prana," the energy of your soul. Wear the gemstone as a talisman and it will bring to you good friends and good lovers. It is also said that Tourmalines encourage artistic intuition. In fact, Tourmaline is known to have many faces and expresses every mood!

Tourmalines are found in various parts of the world; however, most on the market today are from Brazil. That said, there is a Tourmaline mine in Maine, California that has been in operation since 1822.

TRANSPARENCY

Technically known as diaphaneity, transparency refers to the way light interacts with the surface of a gemstone. There are three different levels of transparency for all objects: they are described as transparent, translucent or opaque.

Transparent objects, including gemstones, are those that allow light to enter and exit in a relatively undisturbed manner.

Translucent objects are those that allow light to enter, but disturb and distort it. To explain the difference between transparent and translucent, imagine holding an object in front of this text. If you can see through it and still read it, then it is transparent. If you can still make out that there is something behind the object, but cannot read it then it is a translucent object. If the light cannot penetrate the object, then it is said to be opaque. If you were to hold a large Agate in front of this text, you would see nothing at all; Agate is therefore opaque.

It is worth noting that some gemstones that are normally transparent, become translucent if heavily included.

Mystic Topaz is coloured via a special coating.

Turquoise is often stabilised to improve appearance and durability.

Drusy Quartz is normally treated to produce a kaleidoscope of colours.

TREATMENTS

Treatments in the gem industry are common practice and are used to enhance the natural beauty of a gemstone. Treatments are an accepted enhancement as long as they are permanent and stable.

The most common form of gemstone treatment is heat treatment. Prior to being faceted, around 90% of all Corundum (Ruby and Sapphire) is heat-treated and when purchasing these gems, unless stated otherwise you should always expect them to be treated. Heat treatment is primarily used to enhance colour, and without heating some gem types would not exist. For instance, if we didn't heat green-brown Zoisite we would not have Tanzanite! Heat treatment is considered totally acceptable, after all it is only carrying on what Mother Nature started.

Another treatment used, especially in Emeralds, is oiling; this is where colourless oil is used to penetrate voids and fissures. This does not harm the gem, although a treated Emerald will most likely have to be re-treated every ten years or so for it to continue looking ravishing.

Both of the treatments above are so widely used in the gem industry that it is common practice for them not to be disclosed. Therefore, when buying most gemstone varieties, it is best to assume that they have some form of treatment.

There are other types of treatments that are used within the gem industry: while several have been used for centuries, new technologies and treatments are continually being developed. Although it is globally accepted that it is not necessary to disclose heat treatment, or oiling or waxing of Emeralds, all other treatments such as dyeing gems (with the exception of Onyx which is always dyed) and coating gems should always be disclosed.

One of the newest and most exciting advancements in treatments is "Spice Topaz". This revolutionary development offers new colours in Topaz that are both completely safe and completely permanent.

460ct Rose Quartz
Bracelet
£13

jessica
lili

TRILLIANT CUT

This cut was introduced by the Asscher brothers in Amsterdam and was later trademarked by the Henry Meyer Diamond Company of New York in 1962. Today, now that this trademark has elapsed, the term "Trilliant Cut" is used to refer to all triangular shaped gems. It typically features 15 - 25 facets on the crown, but only 13 -19 on the pavilion; however, these numbers can vary and it is not uncommon to see trilliant cut Diamonds with 50 facets.

The cut is based upon the brilliant cut, the points of the triangle are cut short (truncated) and the facets can vary in shape and style. Just like other brilliant cut gems, the trilliant cut provides lots of sparkle and brilliance.

There are two slightly different forms of trilliant cut. When used on a large solitaire, the three sides of the triangle, when looking down on the table, are slightly curved, whereas when accent stones are trilliant cut, they tend to have straight edges.

A trilliant cut vivid blue Spice Topaz.

TROY OUNCE

This is a measurement used today primarily for weighing precious metals such as gold and silver.

One Troy ounce equals 31.1034768 grams. A normal ounce equals 1/16th of a pound in weight, but the Troy ounce is only 1/12th of a pound. The measurement became standardised in 1758 as a weight measurement of distilled water! Whenever you see the price of gold or silver being mentioned on the news or in newspapers, it is usually the price of a Troy ounce that is being detailed.

An impression of traditional gold weighing scales.

TSAVORITE GARNET

Tsavorite has a beautiful, vivid green colour and is a bright, lively gem with a high refractive index. It belongs to the Grossular group within

Colour	Vivid green to rich green
Family	Garnet
Hardness	6.5 – 7.0
Specific Gravity	3.4 – 3.7
Refractive Index	1.73 – 1.74
Crystal Group	Isometric
Optical Properties	Various
Common Treatments	Cannot be heat-treated
Care	No special care needed
Chemical Composition	Various

the Garnet family and has to be seen to truly appreciate how radiant it is.

Tsavorite is considered amongst the most desirable of all Garnets and until its discovery in the 1968, no other gemstone except Emerald could offer such a rich green colour.

The first deposit was discovered in Tanzania by Scottish gemmologist Campbell R Bridges, who later traced the gem to the Tsavo National Park in Kenya, from where its name is derived.

Just as they had done with Tanzanite, in 1974 the famous jewellery company Tiffany & Co. started heavily promoting the gemstone in the USA. In fact, it was the company's president Henry Platt, who (together with Campbell R Bridges) decided to give this green Grossularite its own name.

Tsavorite is said to comfort and warm the heart and also stimulates the immune system. It has also been said that Tsavorite can be used as a gentle pain reliever and can sometimes treat problems with eyesight.

Sources of the gem are becoming rapidly depleted in Kenya, with some reports stating that during the last decade, yields are down by 80%. However, there is some good news for the many fans of this gemstone: a new deposit was discovered in Madagascar in 1991, and although small in terms of the carat weight found, the quality of Tsavorite from this mine is equally as impressive as that from Kenya.

1.1ct of Tsavorite Garnet in a pendant from Jacque Christie.

TUMBLED GEMSTONES

When gemstones are found in alluvial deposits, they have already been pre-faceted by Mother Nature as they tumble along the stream or river bed. The less dense the gem, the further it travels and the more it is tumbled.

Gems worn by ancient Egyptians and Greeks were only faceted by nature. Today, when jewellery is designed to have a similar historical

look, the gems used are either tumbled by Mother Nature, or they are tumbled in a mechanical "Rock Tumbler". These man-made machines, which look like a quarter-sized washing machine, effectively carry on the work of Mother Nature. Inside, silicon grit is used, which is harder than sand found in a river bed, making the process quicker than the natural one. If the final gem requires polishing, then very fine silicon is added to the tumbler after the gem has finished taking its shape.

A tumbled Quartz bracelet by Jessica Lili

TURQUOISE

The gemstone Turquoise has been highly prized since Egyptian times and its name means "Turkish Stone" as it was imported to Europe via Turkey. The colour of this historic gemstone ranges from a greenish blue to a beautiful, striking sky blue and is one of several instances where the name of a colour is derived from the name of a gemstone.

It is interesting to note that in order for it to be deemed Turquoise it has to be of the highest quality. When Turquoise is mined it can often have traces of chrome or iron set deep within it and it is these elements which give the gemstone its unique colour.

If Turquoise has definite visible patterns viewable to the naked eye these are known as "Turquoise Matrix". The patterns are caused by differing elements running through veins and, more often than not, are brown, grey or even black depending on the area the gem was mined. As the gem is opaque, it is rarely faceted and is usually cabochon cut or made into beads.

Turquoise is said to have been mined more than 6000 years ago in Sinai. In Persian times people would adorn themselves with Turquoise, usually around the neck or on the wrist, as it was believed the stone would prevent fatalities.

It has long been thought to be a holystone bringing the wearer good fortune and a prosperous life: even today Turquoise is thought to clear the mind and cheer people up. Its colourful blues denote a sense of wellbeing and spiritual harmony. Turquoise often gets given

Colour	Light blue to bluish green
Family	Turquoise
Hardness	5 - 6
Specific Gravity	2.6 - 2.8
Refractive Index	1.6
Crystal Group	Triclinic
Optical Properties	Vitreous to waxy lustre
Common Treatments	Waxing or dying
Care	Avoid contact with chemicals
Chemical Composition	Various

a gift to a loved one or dear friend and as it is one of the birthstones for December, it makes an ideal Christmas present!

Because Turquoise is porous, when wearing a piece it is important to avoid contact with any chemical liquids. Therefore, it is strongly recommended that any item of Turquoise should only be put on after showering or applying make-up. It should ideally also be kept away from heat and intense light.

Deposits are found in a number of places around the globe; these include America, Mexico, Iran, Israel, China and Afghanistan.

Indulge in Brilliance

GENUINE TOPAZ
12 BREATHTAKING COLOURS
FINEST CUTTING
PATENTED TECHNOLOGY
NON RADIATED
PRECISION CALIBRATION
EVERLASTING DURABILITY
NON COATED

Patent Number 6872422
Exclusively distributed in Europe by Coloured Rocks

Colour	Brownish pinkish orange
Family	This cross breed does not belong to a family
Hardness	6 – 7
Specific Gravity	3.3 – 3.6
Refractive Index	1.71 – 1.79
Crystal Group	Monoclinic
Optical Properties	Vitreous lustre
Common Treatments	Not normally treated
Care	No specific care required
Cleaning Advice	Ultrasonic or warm soapy water
Chemical Composition	Various

UNAKITE

Due to its stunning blend of 'moss' green, unusual pink and earthy orange, Unakite boasts a unique and striking mixture of colour, pattern and 'mottled' appearance. Its unusual colour scheme, unique appearance and solid structure all combine to make it a good stone for distinctive jewellery.

As with all gems and minerals, there are numerous beliefs regarding the spiritual and healing qualities of Unakite. Most of all it is believed to bring unity and balance to all areas of the owner's life. It is also thought to help release elements in one's life that inhibit and stunt emotional growth. Some also believe that it stimulates self-awareness, and allows the owner to be aware of causes and symptoms of illness, which goes deeper than just the physical.

At this point we must stress that healing properties are mainly mythical; although Crystal

Healers suggest using the gemstone to ensure a safe pregnancy and birth, we would recommend seeing a consultant!

Unakite is also called 'Epidotized Granite' or 'Grandodiorite'; and is usually made up by a combination of three minerals: Pink Feldspar, Green Epidote and Quartz. But not all Unakite contain Quartz; specimens that don't are called 'Episodite'.

Although the first find was in America, sources tell us that rare examples have also been found in Brazil, China, Sierra Leone, South Africa and Switzerland.

UNITED STATES

Although its population is the largest consumer of coloured gemstones in the world and even though some sixty different gems lie beneath its soils, only a very small percentage of the world's gems are actually mined in the USA. In fact nearly all of its mines are very small scale and since the turn of the century it is reported that its annual output has dropped by around 30%. There are several American companies which own large scale gemstone mining operations in different countries. However, when it comes to the American's home soil, most mining is run by family owned businesses and gem clubs.

Of its 50 states only five have any serious mining activities worth mentioning:

The San Carlos Apache reservation in Arizona is one of the world's largest Peridot mining areas. The region also yields a smaller amount of Malachite and Turquoise.

In California, most of its famous gem mines are now closed, but they once produced reasonable quantities of Quartz and Tourmaline. Small companies are still able to obtain "fee-to-dig" licences in areas where commercial mines once stood. California is also where Morganite was first discovered. In Montana, where there were once fourteen separate Sapphire mining companies, today there are only around half a dozen. Oregon was once a state active in mining

Opals, Agate and Jasper; today most of its mining activities focus on Oregon Sunstone. The state gem of Utah is Topaz, although historically, Utah produced gem-quality Snowflake and Mahogany Obsidian and some stunning Red Beryl.

Amethyst from Uruguay, along with those discovered in Africa demonstrate deep vivid colours.

URUGUAY

Sharing its borders with Brazil to the north and Argentina to the west, Uruguay is a small country with a population of just 3.3 million. Most of its gem mining activities take part in Artigas, which is the most northern region of the country.

There are currently around 25 to 35 small scale mines in operation and most search for two members of the Quartz family: Amethyst and Agate.

The Amethyst is of a very high quality with a deep violet colour, and although very little is found in terms of carat weight, it is generally more highly prized than those of neighbouring Brazil and Bolivia.

UVAROVITE GARNET

This gemstone family was first documented by Count Uvarov (the president of the St. Petersburg Academy for mineral collectors), whom it is named after.

This rare group of Garnets is special as they are restricted to just one colour: a beautiful rich green, which is derived from Chromium. Uvarovite Garnets are only found in a few countries, including the famous gem region in the Russian Ural Mountains, Canada and South Africa.

Unfortunately, their crystal structure is such that they do not grow very big, therefore they are very rarely faceted into gemstones for use in jewellery (we have yet to set any at Coloured Rocks).

Colour	Green
Family	Garnet
Hardness	7
Specific Gravity	3.4 – 3.8
Refractive Index	1.87
Crystal Group	Cubic
Optical Properties	Vitreous lustre
Common Treatments	Not treated
Care	No specific care required
Chemical Composition	$Ca_3Cr_2SiO_4$

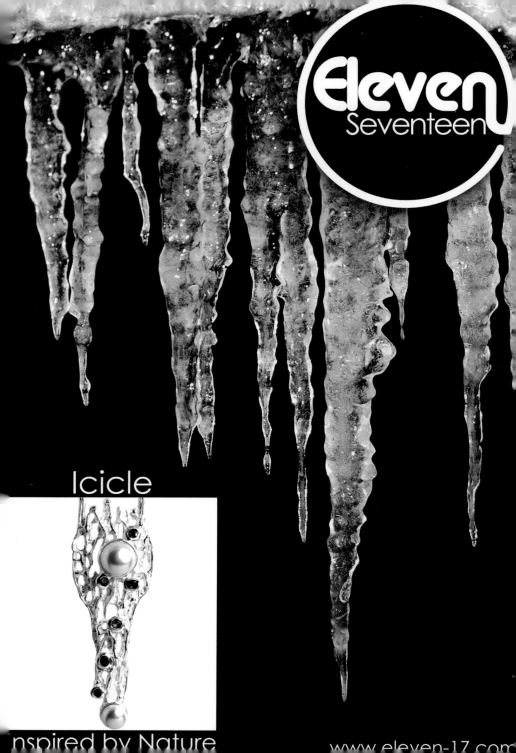

Eleven
Seventeen

Icicle

Inspired by Nature

www.eleven-17.com

VALENTINE HEART CUT

Slightly rounder than a traditional heart cut, with a height that is approximately 20% more than its width, the Valentine Cut is a very romantic cut that was designed for use with Diamonds but works brilliantly with coloured gemstones.

The cut can be applied to either a heart or pear shaped gem and the table of the gem appears to look like a shield. The romantic in me believes that if you give someone a piece of jewellery with a Valentine Heart Cut gem, you tell the recipient that the gem has been cut to shield and protect their heart.

All of the facets on the crown and pavilion are triangular in shape and when our team produce the cut we tend to leave a higher proportion of the total gem in the crown than is normal with heart and pear cuts as we have found that, with the Valentine Heart Cut, this brings out the best in a gem's brilliance and dispersion.

VALUATIONS

It is important to know the value of your more expensive items of jewellery or loose gems, especially when it comes to insurance. Jewellery appraisals or valuations are normally carried out by a jeweller (somebody who makes jewellery) or a qualified valuer. However, the matter is always subjective, i.e. it is the opinion of the person valuing the jewellery. To complicate matters, there are also various types of valuation and to make matters even worse, you are going to need to gauge whether you believe your valuation is truly independent, as some jewellers don't like valuing competitors pieces (I don't blame them - I personally find it a massive conflict when I am asked to value my competitor's work and do everything possible to avoid it).

For insurance purposes, you may need to receive a valuation based on replacing the item if it was stolen. For standard pieces of jewellery without gemstones this is never too much of an issue and most jewellers can offer this type of valuation. However, if your jewellery has a rare gemstone then the matter does become more complicated. In this case (especially if you are totally in love with the piece), you need to insist that the valuer gives a price that he would charge you to make an exact replica.

If they couldn't make it themselves or source the gemstone, find another jeweller who can; the last thing you want is a valuation that does not cover you for a replacement.

The next type of valuation is for resale. This will always be lower than an insurance valuation, as effectively you are asking the valuer for a price that you could sell the piece for, given a reasonable period of time.

Another type of valuation is for probate or dividing up of estates. These types of valuations often tend to be at an even lower price, as they assess the price that could be achieved in a quick sale.

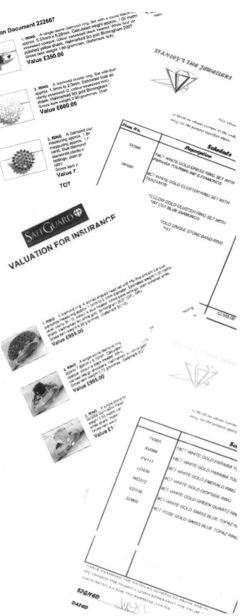

Many of our customers are so happy with the valuations they receive, that they send me copies. Please do send me yours.

A huge Amethyst set in vermeil by Sarah Bennett.

Viorelli - specialists in vermeil jewellery.

VERMEIL

Invented in France in the 18th century, Vermeil is the name given to Gold-plated Silver, where the coating is in excess of 1.5 micron thick. Early French jewellers used mercury in the process, and unfortunately over a period of time many of them became blind. Eventually the French Government banned the process and for a long time very little Vermeil jewellery was produced.

Today, using electrolysis, Vermeil is being produced safely and has become incredibly popular especially with Italian design houses. Depending on how the jewellery is cared for and what chemicals and elements it comes in contact with, Vermeil should retain its golden look for several years. However, over time, as with all plating, eventually the coating will begin to wear and the Silver underneath will be seen. Therefore with items that are worn on a daily basis, such as watches, a thicker coating is often applied. If the Gold plating is not at least 1.5 micron thick, then it should not be referred to as Vermeil and instead should be called Gilded Silver.

In the White House in Washington DC, there is a room known as the Vermeil Room which features a wide range of Vermeil artefacts and cutlery. The collection includes pieces by English silversmith Paul Storr, created around 1810 and also by French silversmith Jean-Baptiste-Claude Odiot of the same period. There is a rumour that President George Bush added to the collection whilst in office, after purchasing pieces in Mexico, but it is said that he could not recall the silversmith's name as he had had a few too many tequilas.

VESUVIANITE (IDOCRASE)

With beautiful green hues, Vesuvianite was originally discovered at Mount Vesuvius in Italy and is named after its origin. In the gem world, it is also known by its pseudonym, Idocrase, which is derived from Greek: "idea" meaning "likeness" and "krasis" meaning "mixture". This name relates to the fact that the gem sometimes has a visual resemblance to Peridot, Tourmaline and several green Garnets.

Whilst Vesuvianite is a gemstone in its own right, it also has two other members in its family. Californite (guess in which American state this was discovered!) which is similar in appearance to Jade; and Blue Cyprine which is primarily mined in Norway.

Although Vesuvianite is generally green, brown, blue and yellow, in very rare instances purple specimens are found. The gem is transparent to translucent in appearance and in order to best display its glorious hues it is normally step cut.

A 2.3ct rich coloured Vesuvianite.

In addition to Mount Vesuvius, California and Norway, the gem has also been discovered in Québec, Canada, The Ural Mountains in Russia, and in Switzerland.

Pliny the Elder (see page xx) is not the only link in this book to Mount Vesuvius in Italy; the famous volcano is also the origin of a gemstone known as Vesuvianite. The more modern name for gem quality Vesuvianite is Idocrase, which derives its name from the Greeks words meaning "mixed form", referring to its unusual crystal structure.

A 1.7ct Emerald cut Vesuvianite.

As with many gemstones that are discovered on or near to volcanos, Vesuvianite is a metamorphic gemstone. Its wonderful greenish blue colour, which is easily distinguishable from almost any other gemstone, receives its appealing hue from the presence of copper.

Around the globe there have been other discoveries of Vesuvianite and they have all been given different names. Californite, as its name suggests, is from California and is green in colour (and is also known as Vesuvinaite Jade).

VICTORIAN AGE

In the year 1837 change was in the air. An 18 year old girl was about to ascend to the throne in what would prove to be the longest reign in

Many of the designs in the Jewels of Valais Collection are Victorian inspired.

British history: the country would never be the same again.

Britain was about to see the start of what was to be called 'The Industrial Revolution'. When Victoria began her reign in 1837, the British economy was based around agriculture and rural businesses. The Industrial Revolution saw the creation of the steam engine, enabling major changes in agriculture, manufacturing and transportation. Consequently, Britain saw an enormous growth in the middle classes, giving way for people to run successful businesses, making them rich along the way.

As people now found themselves with this new 'disposable income', there emerged a big growth in the market for jewellery. Men would lavish their wives with expensive necklaces, brooches, rings and bracelets.

During the Victorian age many styles came in and out of fashion. As Queen Victoria's reign was a long one, the era is often talked about as three different periods. They are the Romantic (early), the Grand (middle) and the Aesthetic (late). The changes between the styles are not clear-cut and many styles existed together as tastes and fashions changed.

The Romantic period of the Victorian age reflected a time of wellbeing for Queen Victoria and her jewellery displayed this with brightly coloured Pearls, Turquoise beads and Pink Coral. This jewellery utilised light through subtle designs with elaborate, detailed, sophisticated engravings.

During the middle of the Victorian era (the Grand period) these subtle designs developed into heavier, bolder designs, changing into the style that most of us would associate with the era.

One of Queen Victoria's first loves was Scotland, and so in 1848 she purchased the 'Balmoral Estate' a place now famous as the royal retreat. From around this time, Scottish influence was apparent in jewellery on the market. One popular design was the foot of a game bird, called a 'grouse', set in silver or gold. One of the most popular pieces of jewellery in the Victorian age was the brooch. As well as being worn on the chest (as it is today), they were also worn on the shoulder, the waist and even in the hair. Many of the brooches were not made of silver or gold, but instead used less precious metals. The design of the piece and its gemstones were at the time regarded as far more significant than the choice of metal.

During her reign Queen Victoria became an important influence upon the design and ultimate creation of jewellery. The jewels she wore became a blueprint upon which the rest of society based their designs.

The inspiration from nature continued from the preceding Georgian era, with pieces being designed in the shape of bunches of grapes, bouquets of flowers and clusters of berries.

It was also during Victoria's reign that gold was first discovered in Australia and California, guaranteeing an easier and more reliable supply route of precious metal for use in British jewellery.

Jewels of Valais earrings similar to those worn in Victorian times.

VIORELLI

Viorelli is a small yet exciting Italian jewellery brand whose expertise is in Vermeil and Sterling Silver fashionable jewellery. If you're looking for stylish, chunky Sterling Silver necklaces and bracelets, and if you're a big fan of the Vicenza three tone metal look, then Viorelli is definitely for you. Now that the brand is part of the Coloured Rocks family, expect to see the introduction of coloured gemstones into many of its designs.

Look out for the 'Toccato dai diamante' collection launching in the summer of 2009, which includes a small diamond incorporated on the inside of Viorelli rings within the collection, as well as 'piccole Viorelli etichette' (small tags) on necklaces and bracelets that incorporate a small diamond in the Viorelli logo.

Very Vicenza, Very Vermeil, Very Viorelli!

VITREOUS LUSTRE

This term is used to describe a gem that has a lustre similar to that of glass. Topaz and gems from the Quartz family such as Amethyst and Citrine are often said to have a vitreous lustre.

A striking Tookalon hand made bracelet featuring vitreous Lemon Quartz.

WATCHES

*1ct of Diamonds featured in a
Coloured Rocks masterpiece.*

Man has been measuring time for thousands of years. Around 3500 BC, Egyptians created very basic sundials, which divided the day into two parts, using the sun to create shadows on a simple device. Though the Greeks substantially improved these early mechanisms, little advancement was made regarding the mechanics of clocks during the Middle Ages.

From the 15th Century onwards, the growth in sailing and navigating increased the need to tell the time more accurately. Early in this century, the first pocket watch was made by a German locksmith called Peter Henlein. Although they had a tendency to slow down (due to the gradual winding down of the mainspring), they were instantly very popular with the wealthy, as their small size made them easily portable.

Unlike modern watches, these pocket watches only had an hour hand; there was no minute hand. As there was no glass protection, these pocket watches often had a metal case to protect the hour hand. Though the minute hand was found on a pocket watch from approximately 1670 onwards, there was no glass face until the next century. In 1884 the town of Greenwich in England became internationally recognised as the base time for the entire world, a standard that is still used today (GMT – Greenwich Mean Time).

Pocket watches were common right up until the beginning of the 20th century. After this period, scientists and engineers improved their skills of miniaturising things, thus allowing the wristwatch to be invented. In 1905 in Switzerland, Hans Wilsdorf formed a small company known as the Rolex Watch Company. In 1918 in Japan a company was formed that eventually became Citizen Watches. In 1923, John Harwood designed the first self-winding wristwatch for mass production and a year later in Tokyo, Seiko was set up.

During the 1960's, people were very proud to own an electronic quartz watch: the first prototype was designed in 1962 in Switzerland, and came into production in 1969. It is rather exciting to learn how Mother Nature constantly proves essential in improving our lives. In an electronic quartz watch, Quartz Crystal is used as an oscillator in an electronic circuit, which is then used within the electronic mechanics of a watch. It is very technical indeed, but basically the Quartz Crystal vibrates with such regularity it makes it very reliable for telling the time accurately. Also, though most quartz movements are electronic, they are designed in such a way to drive mechanical hands on the clock face, which even in the computer age, tends to be the preferred method of telling the time.

What many people may not realise, however, is that Quartz was not the first gem to be used in watch movements. Back in 1704, long before the quartz movement watches, brothers Peter and Jacob Debaufre used Rubies and then Sapphires to regulate the movement in their watches! These gems were shaped into small round balls and their extreme hardness (remember they

Colourful watches by Jessica Lili.

register 9 on the Mohs scale), combined with their low and predictable friction made them the perfect central component in a watch, from which everything else then rotated. In the early 1900's, as man learnt to recreate these gems in laboratories, they were eventually replaced by their lower costing, synthetic look-a-likes.

Today, there is a whole host of different watches available to us. Analogue watches have a numbered dial on the clock face, and typically have an hour hand and a minute hand. More often than not there is also a second hand. If the watch uses a quartz movement, this second hand will 'tick' on every second. Where the watch uses a mechanical movement, the hand will move in a 'sweeping' fashion around the clock face. Many jewellery and watch designers have great fun in designing the different hands of a watch: for example, making the minute and hour hand in the shape of a stem, and the second hand in the shape of a flower.

Also available to us today are digital watches. However, as these require less craftsmanship when making them, collectors have little demand for them. There is also less variety in quality, and usually it is more difficult for a designer to apply a personal touch.

Watches do not have to be worn as functional objects, forgotten on our left or right wrist. A careful selection of colour and design and your watch becomes a piece of jewellery valued as much as a favourite ring or necklace. Of course, as with all jewellery, once you have more than one watch to choose from, you are left with the difficult decision of which watch to wear with which outfit.

All of the watches across the Coloured Rocks brands are crafted to the highest standards. Whilst many of them are made in Hong Kong, they often feature either Japanese or Swiss Movement. Watches made by Lorique are actually crafted in Switzerland and are amongst some of the finest watches available on the market today. With prices from £19 to £2999, Coloured Rocks offers a wide selection of watches, all of which feature gems and a minimum of a one year warranty.

WEDDING RINGS

Today the wedding ring is usually given as part of the wedding ceremony to act as a symbol of the binding commitment a husband and wife make to each other.

Some of the oldest records of wedding rings date back to Egypt some 4900 years ago and the circle of metal was said to represent eternal love. However, it was only traditionally worn by the wife.

In Roman times the wedding band was made out of iron and was said to represent strength. Today in many countries the majority of married men also wear a wedding band to demonstrate their fidelity and commitment.

Whilst in the UK and America we always wear wedding rings on our left hand, in many countries around the world such as Argentina, Germany, Norway, Russia and Poland the ring is worn on the right hand.

In some European countries, the engagement ring is used as the wedding ring. Its upgraded status to wedding ring is signified by the changing of the hand on which it is worn and often by engraving a message on the inside of the shank.

A modern gents wedding band featuring 3 Blue Diamonds, set in 10 grams of white gold.

A contemporary wedding band designed by Jacque Christie.

WHITE GEMS AND ASSOCIATIONS

Imagine the intense brightness of the sun shining on a pool of ice; a cold, crisp, frosty day when your windows frost with a beautiful pattern. Then think of a beautiful white Zircon and its fascinating play of prismatic colour.

The level of transparency in colourless gemstones has a direct bearing on how beautiful they look. The more transparent a gem is, the more flashes of dispersion (also known as fire) can be seen. Colourless Diamonds, Zircon, Goshenite and Danburite are incredibly alluring and when given plenty of light will explode with a massive array of colour flowing throughout. In the same category, there are not only transparent,

SARAH BENNETT
GEMSTONE
JEWELLERY

colourless gemstones, but also several white gems. Who could resist the milky white nature of Opal, a gem that with only the slightest movement of the hand flashes a rainbow of electrifying colours? Or the rather heavenly iridescence seen on the surface of a Pearl?

For women, the colour is associated with contemplation and purity, whilst for men it is linked with friendship, religion and integrity.

Unlike today, in ancient times, the colour white was associated with mourning and sorrow. Greek widows wore the colour from head to toe on the passing of their husbands.

White gems have also been linked with the Moon and it is loosely through this association that the Pearl became the birthstone for June along with Alexandrite and Moonstone.

WHITE GOLD

Following the same rules as yellow gold, white gold is hallmarked based on its level of gold purity. Its white colour is obtained from other elements that are added to the alloy; these are normally silver, platinum and palladium.

It is important to ensure when buying white gold, that if nickel is included, its quantity is kept to a minimum amount to ensure that the piece of jewellery is "nickel safe". The official measurement for safe nickel exposure is that it should not exceed 0.05 mg/cm per week (0.02 mg/cm for piercings); this means that the metal should not release more than the stated amount of nickel.

Although this all sounds very complicated, as long as you are buying white gold from a reliable source, it should always conform to the legal requirements.

WITTELSBACH DIAMOND

The Blue Wittelsbach Diamond was not featured in the first edition of this book, as I

White Gold is becoming increasingly popular for Engagement Rings.

felt it did not have as rich a history as the likes of The Hope Diamond or The Koh-I-Nur etc. However, on the 10th December 2008, The Blue Wittelsbach Diamond rightfully earned its place in history, becoming the most expensive gemstone ever sold at auction, when purchased by Laurence Graff for £16.4 million ($24 million) at an auction held by Christie's.

The Wittelsbach Diamond is greyish blue in colour, weighs an impressive 35.56ct, measures almost an inch in diameter, is VS2 in clarity and is wonderfully cushion cut featuring 82 facets.

The history of the gemstone is a little hazy. It is almost definitely of Indian origin and several experts believe it to have once been part of the French Blue Diamond from which the famous Hope Diamond was once cut.

Although the gem's history is not as certain as other famous gemstones, it is believed to have been passed as a gift from one royal family to another.

The Diamond was apparently lost at the end of the First World War and documentation of its history is said to have been destroyed during the Spanish Civil War (1936-39).

In 1931 Christie's attempted to auction the diamond but it did not meet the reserve price. In 1960 the owners of the gem asked the legendary Lapidarist Joseph Komkommer to re-cut the gemstone to make it more symmetrical, but realising its historical importance he refused to do so.

At one time the gem was the central gem in the Bavarian crown; in fact some suggest that several of its flaws on its crown facets were inflicted as it was removed. In 2006 a major embarrassment was caused to the Bavarian authorities when it was discovered that the central gem was now blue glass, in place of the real diamond.

Days prior to the 2008 auction, Bavaria's Prime Minister told British newspapers that he was going to attempt to buy the gem in the auction to restore Bavarian pride, but was in the end outbid!

YELLOW GEMS AND ASSOCIATIONS

Yellow is the colour of happiness and cheerfulness. It is also a colour associated with making changes. It is a great colour for people always on the go and living life to the full.

In antiquity, when a lady wore yellow it indicated that she was a generous person and when worn by a man it was said to denote secrecy. The colour has also been associated with the sun, which then led to an association with Sunday. Likewise, historically it had an association with a lion and later the zodiac sign of Leo. George Kunz's book "The Curious Lore of Precious Stones" states that "of the seven ages of man, yellow typified adolescence".

Citrine, one of November's official birthstones, is one of the most vivid of all yellow gems. Its name is derived from the French word for lemon and it can be found in shades from sunflower yellow to orangish yellow. Another well-known yellow gemstone is Amber; although this is usually more of an orangish yellow, occasionally it can be a vivid yellow.

YELLOW SAPPHIRE

Yellow Sapphires come in a wide variety of tones and saturations; from vivid sunflower yellows, to the glowing orange and golden colours of a summer sunset. The most in-demand Yellow Sapphires currently seem to be the vibrant canary yellows, especially those that have good clarity and strong brilliance.

A round brilliant cut Yellow Sapphire can almost be indistinguishable from a Yellow Diamond, and is strikingly similar in the way it behaves in direct sunlight. Yellow Sapphire can be found naturally in Australia, Burma, Cambodia, Thailand and the USA. Some of the very finest specimens are currently being discovered in Songea, Tanzania.

YIELD

After a gemstone has been cut and polished, the final carat weight that remains is expressed as a percentage of the weight of the original uncut rough gem. The less wastage, the higher the yield is said to be. Lapidarists take different approaches to different gemstones. For example, large opaque gemstones are often cut to maximise carat weight, whereas gems that have strong brilliance and dispersion should be cut to maximise the gem's beauty.

Unfortunately, today, we all too often see gems that are cut so as to reach certain rounded carat weights, rather than to truly unveil the beauty of the gem. When buying gems such as Tanzanite and Paraiba, be sure to check the quality of the cutting, especially if its weight is marginally over a rounded carat weight.

Tomas Rae.

The famous Zambian Victorian Falls.

ZAMBIA

When you think of the gemstone industry of Zambia, the first gem that springs to mind is the Emerald. This is not surprising as, in monetary terms, Emerald contributes around 80% of Zambia's gemstone exports. Zambia's second largest gemstone export is Amethyst (Zambia is currently the largest exporter of Amethyst in Africa). The World Bank believes that this Third World Country should be able to export as much as £400 million worth of gems per year, up from current levels of around £10 million.

Emerald mining primarily takes place in the north of the country in an area named Kafubu. Mining is undertaken by both artisanal mining communities and larger companies who use more modern, mechanical mining techniques. Government figures suggest that around two million carats a year are produced, but little of this is gem-quality.

On the country's East Coast, near the border of Malawi, mines in the Lundazi area specialise in extracting another gem from the Beryl family, Aquamarine. On a smaller scale, yellow and golden Tourmalines are also found along with a small quantity of Spessartite Garnet.

The Mkushi region in central Zambia is better known for its gold prospecting activities of the late 1800's and for its commercial farming. It is also home to small-scale mining activities that produce both Bi-Coloured Tourmaline and another Tourmaline family member, Rubellite.

Quality Aquamarine discovered in Zambia.

ZEESHAN KHAN

"So, who is Zeeshan Khan?", I hear you ask. Well he is one of my gem hunters and he has gone to inordinate lengths and put himself at high risks lately in order to search for some of the rarest gems on the planet. Before you read Zeeshan's notes from his latest buying expedition, I must point out that he went on this adventure against my wishes and in my opinion he is not only one of the best gem hunters on the planet, but also the craziest!

Let's hear from Zeeshan about his latest trip:
'My most recent adventure took me to the Northern area of Pakistan and the tribal belt between Pakistan and Afghanistan and also between Pakistan and Iran. In the regions of the Baltistan and Kohistan Valleys, some of the world's most prized and rare gems await discovery. Sourcing gemstones from these areas is not just any other job. During my recent trips, I found that people in these mining communities use the most unconventional means to mine minerals. Since the law and order situation in these areas is not normal these days, I had to use my father's connection to get in touch with some influential local tribal chiefs to provide me not only with local guides but also security.

From Islamabad, capital of Pakistan, I drove to Peshawar, the Provincial capital of the north

Above and left a few of Zeeshan's finds; Sphene, Axinite, Hickmanite, Bastnasite and Peridot.

west frontier of Pakistan. I was here in search of some of the finest Sphene yet unearthed (Mr Bennett does not let me say anything is the very best). There are three different mines in the region where you can source fine Sphene (1) Warsik: This mine produces dark brownish colour Sphene. Warsik is a place between Peshawar and Mohmand agency. Basically it is a disputed territory, as the government call it part of Peshawar and tribes call it their part. Let me tell you though, that there is no Pakistani law applicable in the tribal areas. Funnily enough I felt safer on the tribal side of the agency where I had tribal protection rather than the provincially administrated side where the law rules. (2) Another place where I source Sphene for Mr Bennett is Badrakhshan, which is part of Afghanistan. The color of Sphene from this mine tends to be more yellowish. (3) The third mine, which produces Sphene is from Skardu in the northern territory. This mine produces greener color Sphene. Next to this Sphene mine, about a half day walk, there is a mine which produces Zoisite. I sourced most of my Sphene from Warsik, as they are much better in colour. Unfortunately local people use local blasting methods, which results in a lot of wastage of the material.

After my two day stay and sourcing of Sphene I went to Khyber agency, which is again the tribal area, and it produces one of the rarest gems, called Bestnasite. Badshah Khan (no relative) told me there has been no mining for the last couple of years now due to constant fighting between Taliban and the Pakistani Forces, but through some sources we found out there is a guy called Noroz Khan, who has got some rough Bastnasite available. But now the hardest part was to find Mr Noroz Khan, as lot of people have left their homes recently and have moved to safer places. I told Badshah Khan that I will give him an extra tip, if he can find Noroz. After four hours of hard work we finally found Mr Noroz Khan, he was living in a temporary camp site. Luckily he had managed to retain 26 grams of Bastnasite rough. After spending one full day in Khyber agency, I was disappointed to have only got 26 grams of Bestnasite rough, but I guess it's still better than none. From here I went to the Kohistan valley to source quality Peridot. The mine which produces Peridot is 17,000 feet high and takes 10 hours by pony. I had heard that people dig under their shacks to mine Peridot in the region, but until I arrived I hadn't believed the stories. But it was true, I was so surprised at how shallow the material is available.

Hickmanite also comes from near the Kohistan Valley on the Khunjrab Pass, which is very near to the Pakistani and Chinese border. The Peridot miners here face terrible weather conditions for most of the year and the mine only opens for a few months each summer. But through some sources I could find some of last year's stock of Hickmanite at the Peshawar gem Mandi (Mandi is the name for Market in Urdu). From here I had to say goodbye to my guide Badshah Khan as I was now planning to go to Balochistan to hopefully get my hands on some Axanite.

Balochistan is the biggest province of Pakistan bordering Afghanistan and Iran. There I got some very small parcels of Axanite and Enstatite. On my next trip to Pakistan, I am planning to go to Sawat Valley, which produces some of the rarest and best Emeralds as well as absolutely natural pink and yellow Topaz.'

A top quality Kunzite, found in a new deposit by Zeeshan on one of his adventures.

ZINCITE

Similar to Sphalerite in appearance, Zincite is a stunning bright orange gemstone that has a real fiery character. Gem-quality material is incredibly rare and to-date has only been discovered in New Jersey, America. The Sterling Hill and Franklin Mines which produce the rough minerals are also famous for yielding other gem minerals such as Hemimophite and Willemite.

Very few transparent pieces have ever been discovered and very, very few are over one carat in weight. Also, as the gem is high in metal content (Zinc) it is very dense, meaning that even a one carat piece looks smaller than many other gemstones of an equivalent weight.

The gem is also relatively soft and when acquired it is best set in pendants and earrings.

Colour	Orange, Yellow to Brown
Family	Zincite
Hardness	4
Specific Gravity	5.4 - 5.7
Refractive Index	2.01 -2.02
Crystal Group	Hexagonal
Optical Properties	Translucent
Common Treatments	None known
Care	Careful not to scratch
Cleaning Advice	Warm soapy water
Chemical Composition	$(ZnMn2)O4$

The vivid orange colours seen in Zincite make it a real favourite with collectors.

Its incredible rarity makes it highly sought by serious gem collectors. Buyer beware: as this is a very expensive gemstone, if you see it being sold cheaply it is most likely synthetic Zincite which is easily replicated in a laboratory, of which unfortunately there is a lot on the market.

ZINNIA CUT

As discussed several times in this book, Lapidary is more than a skill, it's a real art. Gabi Tolkowsky, a member of probably the world's most famous family of Lapidaries was hired by De Beers to create a group of original flower cuts during the late 1980's and 90's.

Of the collection he created, my favourite by far is the Zinnia Cut (also the name of a flower). With 25 facets on the crown and 48 facets on the pavilion, the arrangement of the facets really brings a Diamond to life. Because of its shape, the cut also retains more weight than the traditional brilliant cut.

ZIRCON

Zircon occurs in a wide spectrum of colours including yellow-golden, red, brown, blue and green. For many years, the most popular was the colourless variety which looks more like a Diamond than any other natural stone due to its luminosity and dispersion. Some gem collectors believe that Zircon is the most brilliant natural gem that exists and it has been set into jewellery since antiquity. Historically the gem was known as Hyacinth, after Pliny the Elder described the gem's colour as similar to that of the flower. Its modern name Zircon is said to have been derived from either the Persian language, simply meaning "golden coloured" or from the Arabic word for red, "zarkun". As one of the oldest gems to be set into jewellery, it may not be surprising that it has been known by many different names in the past. With its Diamond-like appearance, for a period it was known by many in the trade as the Matara Diamond. This name was soon abandoned, however, as it was often fraudulently sold as a real Diamond. Blue

Colour	Colourless, blue, yellow, orange, brown
Family	Zircon
Hardness	7.5
Specific Gravity	4.6 – 4.7
Refractive Index	1.77 – 1.98
Crystal Group	Tetragonal
Optical Properties	Birefringence and adamantine lustre
Common Treatments	Often heat-treated
Care	Can fade if exposed to prolonged extreme light
Cleaning Advice	Warm soapy water
Chemical Composition	$ZrSiO_4$

Zircons have previously been referred to as Starlight and many on the market achieve their colour through heat treatment. Yellow Zircon, straw-like in colour, was known as Jargon, and Red Zircon was known as Jacinth (this is how it is recorded in the Bible). Today, life is a little simpler and we tend to describe different coloured Zircons by simply prefixing them with their hue (e.g. Blue Zircon, Yellow Zircon etc).

One of the reasons the gem has such amazing brilliance is that it is doubly refractive (also known as birefringence). As light enters the gem, it splits in two and effectively the facets on the pavilion act like a wall of mirrors, sending its double rays in different directions. When you combine this with the fact that it has an adamantine lustre, you begin to realise why it is often confused with Diamonds.

Zircon is said to be the oldest gem on earth and is far older than even the most ancient Diamond! In 1984, Dr Simon Wilde (a university professor) discovered a sparkling Zircon while searching for gold in the Jack Hills of Western Australia. Four years later Wilde met up with another professor, John Valley, and together they performed a series of scientific tests on the Zircon and were able to ascertain that it was an incredible 4.27 billion years old! Later they tested other Zircons from Wilde's collection; using a £1.5 million spectrometer, they were amazed to find one specimen that was formed 4.4 billion years ago. This result contradicted other scientists' research, who previously did not believe that Earth was first formed from a dense body of gas and dust 4.4 billion years ago. Thus, after Valley and Wilde's Zircon discovery, scientists now believe the earth was formed around 4.5 million years ago, making Zircon the oldest gemstone on the planet.

By studying the construction of the gem, scientists have been able to gain a far better understanding of how the Earth was actually created. It indicates that in its early stages, Earth was far cooler than it was initially believed to be, lacking the meteorite onslaught geologists had previously imagined (how clever to be able to tell all that from a gemstone).

"Circles of life" by Jacque Christie, set with sparkling Zircon.

Dazzling Zircon, a real match for Diamond!

Blue Zircon often demonstrates incredible fire.

Moldavite surrounded by dazzling Zircons in a design by Jacque Christie.

Sign	Dates	Gem
Capricorn	Dec 21 – Jan 19	Ruby
Aquarius	Jan 20 – Feb 18	Garnet
Pisces	Feb 19 – Mar 20	Amethyst
Aries	Mar 21 – Apr 20	Diamond & Bloodstone
Taurus	Arp 21 – May 20	Sapphire
Gemini	May 21 – Jun 20	Agate
Cancer	Jun 21 – Jul 20	Emerald
Leo	Jul 21 – Aug 21	Onyx
Virgo	Aug 22 – Sep 22	Carnelian
Libra	Sep 23 – Oct 22	Peridot & Opal
Scorpio	Oct 23 – Nov 22	Aquamarine
Sagittarius	Nov 23 – Dec 20	Topaz

In the Middle Ages, Zircon was believed to induce sleep, and encourage honour and wisdom. It was said to bring prosperity to its owner and thought to drive away plagues and evil spirits. It was also believed to increase ingenuity, glory and wealth and would prevent travel-sickness. During the Black Death it was also worn as a protective talisman.

Purely because of its similarity in name to Cubic Zirconia, today this most glorious and ancient, genuine gemstone often wrongly gets confused with the man-made Diamond look-a-like. With a hardness of 7.5 on the Mohs Scale, Zircon perfectly fits the description of a top quality gem: it is rare, extremely beautiful and very durable. The gem is often rich in the metal "zirconium", which is a metal now famous for its use in nuclear reactors and its name suggests it is derived from the gemstone. Zircon is currently mined in such countries as Cambodia, Australia, India and Brazil.

One last thought on Zircon; next time you are wearing a piece of Zircon and its stunning sparkle or dispersion catches someone's eye, be sure to pass on the news that you are in possession of a piece of history. Right there on your finger is a crystal that possibly started its journey at the same time as Earth first started to spin.

ZODIAC GEMSTONES

Also known as Astral Stones, each sign of the zodiac is associated with different gemstones. Unlike birthstones however, there are various different beliefs about which gemstones relates to which sign.

Ancient astrologers are said to have turned to the heavens to search for answers about why certain gemstones held magical powers when worn under the correct constellation. Their theory, as with talismans and amulets, is based on the harmony that exists between all things. Some believe that the power of wearing the correct Zodiac gem is due to it actually receiving vibrations from the constellation and this is said to strengthen the planetary or zodiacal influence.

Though there are many different sources and

different lists, the table to the left shows the more common associations.

ZOISITE

First discovered at the beginning of the 19th century in Austria, Zoisite is named after the Slovenian scientist Ziga Zois, who first identified the mineral. Today Zoisite is considered a gem family rather than an individual gem type. It has three members; Anyolite which is a green opaque mineral, Thulite which is a pink opaque mineral and the superstar of the family, the world famous Tanzanite.

Tanzanite is a member of the Zoisite family.

ZONING (COLOUR BANDING)

This term is not to be confused with bi-coloured gemstones such as Ametrine or Bi-Coloured Tourmalines, which is where the Lapidarist deliberately facets the gem to best demonstrate its variation in colour. Zoning, or colour banding, which appears in gems such as Citrine, Smokey Quartz, Amethyst, Sapphire and Ruby, is more often regarded as unevenness in colour.

When zoning occurs in a gemstone, the Lapidarist will tend to orient the gemstone so that the bands run parallel with the table facet. Then, when the gemstone is viewed from the table or the facets on the crown, the colour will appear uniformed.

Normally, the darker band will be placed in the culet, as it reflects its colour throughout the gem. In fact, a technique known as foiling was once used by fraudulent jewellers to increase the apparent colour of a gemstone: a tiny piece of tinted foil was placed under the culet to exaggerate the colour throughout the whole gem.

Once a zoned gemstone has been faceted, the gem is often concealed in a bezel or channel setting so that the banding is not visible from the facets below the girdle.

On the flipside, if you have a gemstone that is

A collection of Sapphires showing colour zoning.

normally susceptible to banding and it is set in an open gallery or a Tiffany setting, and when you view it from a side profile no banding is visible, then you know you have a fine specimen of that gem variety.

ZULTANITE (DIASPORE)

Although Zultanite is a very new name in the gem world, under its previous name "Diaspore" it has been available since the early 1800's.

In the book "The Curious Lore of Precious Stone", written by George Kunz, it is linked with the Christian name Dorothy. Diaspore (Zultanite) is believed to help improve ambition, intellect and is said to help one develop psychic powers.

The gemstone is extremely attractive and similar to Alexandrite, in that it has the ability to show different colours under different lighting conditions. The gem is mined in one location in the world: Anatolia, Turkey, and it is indeed a true Turkish delight (sorry, I couldn't resist that one!) although supply is said to be very limited.

Some in the gem trade say it has the colour change of an Alexandrite, a single location similar to Tanzanite (although i personally disagree with this as you can get wonderful Diaspore elsewhere) and benefits from the fact that, like Garnet, it is never heat-treated.

Like the Peridot from the mines of Pakistan, Zultanite is mined at altitude; although Peridot is mined is at 14,000 feet, whereas Zultanite is at 4,000! The mine is located seven miles from the nearest village, Selimiye. The owners of the mine describe the gem as follows:

"Depending on the light source, Zultanite can shift from a kiwi green to a Rhodolite purplish-pink. This same gem can also exhibit a khaki-green to cognac-pink, or pinkish-champagne to ginger colour. You can easily see the kiwi green when the gemstone is viewed outdoors in daylight, except under direct sunlight."

Colour	Generally pale greeny yellow
Family	Diaspore
Hardness	6.50 – 7.00
Specific Gravity	3.30 – 3.39
Refractive Index	1.70 – 1.75
Crystal Group	Orthorhombic
Optical Properties	Colour change
Common Treatments	None
Care	No special care required
Cleaning Advice	Warm soapy water
Chemical Composition	AlO(OH)

A 2.2ct Zultanite discovered in Turkey.

TOOKALON

Combining classic artisanship, genuine gemstones and individualistic designs, each piece of Tookalon jewellery is made entirely by hand.

NUMBERS

4 C's

The 4 C's are used within the gem industry to classify the quality of Diamonds and to a less formal extent coloured gemstones.

The four C's are;

Cut
Colour
Clarity
Carat weight

Nature dictates colour, clarity and carat weight, however the cut is directly influenced by man and in some instances it is the most important. All have been discussed in greater detail throughout this book.

12 APOSTLES

Christianity and the Bible have many connections with gemstones and George Kunz's book "The Curious Lore of Precious Stones" says that each of the 12 apostles were associated with a gemstone:

Simon / Peter	Jasper
Andrew	Ruby
James / John	Emerald
Philip	Carnelian
Bartholomew	Peridot
Thomas	Aquamarine
Matthew	Topaz
James	Sardonyx
Thaddeus	Chrysoprase
Simon	Zircon
Matthias	Amethyst
Paul	Sapphire

Simon / Peter was associated with the vividly coloured Jasper.

12 TRIBES OF ISRAEL

In Exodus 28:17-21, specific gemstones were associated with the twelve tribes of Israel. Throughout the past 2000 years, historians have compiled various different lists of which gemstone is linked with which name. The list varies, depending on how the old gemstone names are interpreted. Paul E. Desautels, author of "The Gem Kingdom" and curator of minerals at the US National Museum of Natural History offers the following list, which uses modern gemstone names for each of the twelve tribes:

Reuben	Carnelian
Simeon	Peridot
Levi	Emerald
Judah	Garnet
Issacher	Lapis Lazuli
Zebulun	Rock Crystal
Joseph	Zircon
Benjamin	Agate
Dan	Amethyst
Naphtali	Citrine
Gad	Onyx
Assher	Jasper

Carnelian is said to be connected with Reuben.

IMPORTANT METAL NUMBERS

Below are numbers that you may see hallmarked on your jewellery. Please note that as this book went to print, the hallmarking of Palladium had not actually commenced in the UK, however the standards shown are those that are soon to be adopted.

375 – 9k gold (37.5% pure)
500 – Palladium (50% pure)
585 – 14k gold (58.5% pure)
750 – 18k Gold (75% pure)
800 – Silver (80% pure)
850 – Platinum (85% pure)
900 – Platinum (90% pure)
916 – 22K Gold (91.6% pure)
925 – Sterling Silver 92.5% pure)
950 – Palladium (95% pure)
950 – Platinum (95% pure)
958 – Britannia Silver
999 – Pure Silver, palladium, Gold or Platinum

A pair of Diamond earrings with the hallmark applied to the post.

IMPORTANT WEB ADDRESSES

annabella.co.uk
colouredrocks.com
jacquechristie.com
jessicalili.com
jewelsofvalais.com
kamacharms.com
lorique.com
mattom.co.uk
milanocharms.com
tomasrae.com
tookalon.com
viorelli.com
gemcollector.com
rocks.tv

THE QUICK GUIDE

SHAPES & CUTS

Briolette Cut

Baguette Cut

Barrel Cut

Buff top Cut

Cabochon Cut

Checkerboard Cut

Cushion Cut

Emerald Cut

Flower Cut

Heart Cut

Hexagon Cut

Inverted Brilliant Cut

Marquise Cut

Octagon Cut

Oval Cut

Pear Cut

Princess Cut

Round Brilliant Cut

Single Cut

Square Cut

Swirl Cut

Tapered Cut (shoulders)

Trilliant Cut

Cupio Cut

SETTINGS

Bar Setting

Bezel Setting

Channel Setting

Illusion Setting

Invisible Setting

Pave Setting

Pin Setting

Prong (Claw) Setting

Semi-Bezel Setting

Tension Setting

Tiffany Setting

V Prong Setting

GEM FINDER

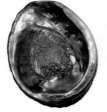
Abalone Shell P23

Alexandrite P27

Amazonite P33

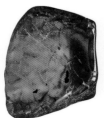
Amber P30

Amethyst P38

Ametrine P41

Andalusite P43

Andradite P47

Apatite P51

Aquamarine P52

Aventurine P62

Azurite P65

Beryl P72

Bixbite P77

Black Opal P337

Bloodstone P80

Please note: For a full list of gemstones please refer to the gemstone contents page 16 & 17

Blue Agate P25   Blue Topaz P85   Blue Tourmaline P85   Carnelian P102

Chrysoberyl P120   Chrysoprase P122   Citrine P124   Coral P147

Danburite P167   Demantoid P168   Diamond P171   Diopside P177

Elbaite P189   Emerald P191   Epidote P196   Fluroite P208

Garnet P212

Green Sapphire P406

GR Tourmaline P459

Haematite P238

Heliodor P243

Hessonite P244

Howlite P249

Imperial Topaz P254

Indicolite P256

Iolite P259

Jade P264

Jasper P266

Kornerupine P280

Kunzite P282

Kyanite P283

Labradorite P286

Lapis Lazuli P289

Malachite P303

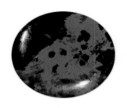

Mawsitsit P310

Moldavite P323

Mookite P324

Moonstone P324

Morganite P325

Moss Agate P326

Mozamb.. Garnet P329

Obsidian P335

Onyx P337

Opal P338

Pearl P351

Peridot P354

Pink Tourmaline P361

Praseolite P370

Prehnite P371

Pyrite P209

Quartz P375

Rhodochrosite P385

Rhodonite P386

Rock Crystal P397

Rose Quartz P394

Ruby P398

Rutile P402

Sapphire P406

Tanzanite P446

Tigers Eye P351

Topaz P456

Tourmaline P459

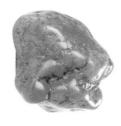

Turquoise P468

Zircon P499

BIRTHSTONES

January - Garnet

February - Amethyst

March - Aquamarine

April - Diamond

May - Emerald

June - Pearl, Alexandrite & Moonstone

July - Ruby

August - Peridot

September - Sapphire

October - Opal & Tourmaline

November - Citrine & Topaz

December - Tanzanite, Zircon & Turquoise

ZODIAC GEMS

Capricorn - Ruby

Aquarius - Garnet

Pisces - Ameythst

Aries - Diamond

Taurus - Sapphire

Gemini - Agate

Cancer - Emerald

Leo - Onyx

Virgo - Carnelian

Libra - Peridot

Scorpio - Aquamarine

Sagittarius - Topaz

BIBLIOGRAPHY

Finlay, Victoria. Jewels A Secret History. Random House inc. New York 2006

Schuman, Walter. Gemstones of the World. N.A.G Press Munich 1995

Oldershaw, Cally. Collins Gem, Gemstones. Cambridge Publishing Management Ltd Cambridge 2006

Voillot, Patrick. Diamonds and Precious Stones. Thames and Hudson Ltd London 1998

Newman, Harold. An Illustrated Dictionary of Jewelry. Thames and Hudson Ltd London 1987

Kunz, George Frederick. The Magic of Jewels and Charms. Dover Publications Inc. New York 1997

Oldershaw, Cally. Philips Guide to Gems. Philips London 2003

Newman, Renee GG. Gemstone Buying Guide How to evaluate, identify, select & care for colored gems. International Jewelry Publications 2007.

Costelloe, Marina. The Complete Guide to Crystal Astrology. Earthdance GmbH 2007.

Dickinson, Jean Y. The Book of Diamonds General Publishing Company Toronto 2001.

Crowe, Judith. The Jeweler's Directory of Gemstones. Firefly Books New York 2006.

Evans, Joan. A History of Jewellery 100 – 1870. Dover Publications Inc 1970.

Patch, Susanne Steinham. Blue Mystery, The story of the Hope Diamond. Harry N. Abrams Inc 1999.

Jarvis, Charles. Jewellery Manufacture and Repair. N.A.G Press London 2001.

Fowler, Marian. Hope, Adventures of a Diamond. Simon and Schuster UK Ltd London 2003.

Newman, Renee GG. Gem and Jewelry Pocket Guide. International Jewelry Publications. Los Angeles 2003.

Pellant, Chris. Dorling Kindersley Handbook Rocks and Minerals. Dorling Kindersley London 1992.

Matlins, Antoinette P.G. Colored Gemstones. Gemstone Press, Vermont 2007.

Matlins, Antoinette, P.G and A.C Bonanno, F.G.A., P.G., A.S.A. Jewelry and Gems The buying guide. Gemstone Press, Vermont 2005.

Post, Jeffrey. E. National Gem Collection. Harry N. Abrams Inc. New York 1997.

Kunz, George Frederick. The Curious Lore of Precious Stones. Bell Publishing New York 1989.

Kurin, Richard. Hope Diamond The legendary history of a cursed gem. HarperCollins Publishers Inc. New York 2006.

Ward, Fred. Opals. Gem Book Publishers Bethesda 2000.

Hubbard-Brown, Janet. A History Mystery The Curse of the Hope Diamond. Avon Camelot 1991.

Healy, John F. Pliny the Elder Natural History: A Selection. Penguin Classics London 2004.

Walters, Raymond J. L. The Power of Gemstones. Carlton Books Ltd 1996.

Symes, Dr. R.F. Eyewitness Rocks and Minerals. Dorling Kindersley Ltd. New York 2004.

Snowman, Kenneth A. The Master Jewelers. Thames and Hudson London 1990.

Bennett, David and Mascetti, Daniela. Understanding Jewellery. Antique Collectors Club, Suffolk 2003.

Kunz, George Frederick & Stevenson, Charles Hugh. The Book of the Pearl: Its History, Art, Science and Industry. Dover Publications, New York 2001.

Wallis, Keith. Gemstones: Understanding, Identifying, Buying. Antique Collector's Club Ltd, London 2006.

Thomas, Arthur. Gemstones: Properties, Identification and Use. New Holland Publishers Ltd, London, 2007.

Hall, Judy. The Crystal Bible: A Definitive Guide to Crystals. Godsfield Press Ltd, London 2003.

Eleven Seventeen

English Rose

Inspired by Nature

www.eleven-17.com

MILANO
C H A R M S

viorelli

Jewels of Valais
S W I T Z E R L A N D

Tomas Rae.

SARAH BENNETT
GEMSTONE
JEWELLERY

L O R I Q U E

MATTOM

Jacque Christie

TOOKALON

14 JEWELLERY
COLLECTIONS
ONE SHOPPING DESTINATION
WWW.COLOUREDROCKS.COM

Kama, Charms

colourful memories...

INDEX

COLOURED ROCKS
WWW.COLOUREDROCKS.COM

Rocks.TV is a cross between eBay, Sotheby's and a quality jewellery store. Just like eBay all items are sold in online auctions; similar to Sotheby's there is a live auctioneer. All items of jewellery are designed and created by Coloured Rocks.

GLAMOUR UNDER THE HAMMER

From 2ct Diamond rings, to Pearl necklaces, every item goes under the auctioneers hammer in a live TV studio and the auction is broadcast live on the internet. Each auction lasts for approximately five minutes, giving online bidders the chance to watch and then bid on many different styles of jewellery every evening.

It's interactive, it's fun and highly addictive.

WWW.ROCKS.TV